The Definitive SCUNTHORPE UNITED F.C.

A statistical history to 1996

Statistics by Michael Norton
Production by Tony Brown

Volume 7 in a series of club histories
The Association of Football Statisticians

First published in Great Britain by Tony Brown, on behalf of the
Association of Football Statisticians, 22 Bretons, Basildon, Essex
SS15 5BY.

Photographs by courtesy of the Scunthorpe Evening Telegraph
and from the author's collection. In the event of a lack of
acknowledgement to the copyright owner, please notify the
publisher so that this can be rectified in any future edition.

Other volumes in this series are:

Volume 1: Rochdale
Volume 2: Northampton Town
Volume 3: Chesterfield
Volume 4: Portsmouth
Volume 5: Barnsley
Volume 6: Queen's Park Rangers

and clubs under consideration for future volumes include
Aldershot, Hartlepool United, Torquay United, Barrow
and Luton Town

ISBN 1 899468 07 2

SCUNTHORPE UNITED F.C.

Contents

FOREWORDS .... by Kevin Keegan

I remember my time at the Old Show ground with much affection. Manager Ron Ashman and players such as George Kerr, Terry Heath and Billy Punton had a big influence on my career. Although I have played all over the world, you never forget your first club and your first games, my debut coming against Peterborough in September 1968, a game we lost 3-2.

I had three great seasons at Scunthorpe, playing well over 100 games, and managed to score goals in each of those seasons. My first goal came at Bradford Park Avenue's ground in February, a delightful ground that no longer exists of course.

Two more matches stand out in my mind. Firstly; the 6-1 F.A. Cup defeat by Arsenal in 1968, who were in a different class from us. At the end of that game I along with a few others actually spent time cleaning the terraces of rubbish! The other game was our great win at Sheffield Wednesday in the fourth round of the FA Cup in 1970, when we won 2-1 in front of some 38,000. Of course, Sheffield Wednesday were in the First Division at the time.

Today I still look for Scunny's results along with my home town team Doncaster Rovers. It doesn't seem like it was almost 30 years ago when I pulled on my Scunthorpe shirt for the first time!

Kevin Keegan, with Ron Ashman (left) and Jack Brownsword (right)

...... Jack Brownsword

I came to Scunthorpe United in 1947 having left Hull City at the end of the 1946/47 season. I was still working down Bentley Colliery and had played for Hull City as a part time player. I continued to work down the mine after joining Scunthorpe United, who were at that time members of the Midland League.

After three years, Scunthorpe were admitted to the Third Division (North). At 27 years of age, I had no thoughts of playing in League football. Leslie Jones was appointed manager, and asked me to sign forms as a full time professional; £9 a week in the playing season, and £6 a week in summer. I later turned down transfers to Derby County and Manchester City and remained a full time player until I was forty four. I then decided to take the vacant position of trainer coach, leaving in 1972 after 25 years service. I am pleased to be the one that brought Kevin Keegan to the club.

Scunthorpe United have many loyal supporters who are desperate for success! Let's hope that this year will be the one.

N. J. Brownsword

Jack holds the record number of League appearances for the club, 597. He was also the club's penalty taker, scoring more than 40 in League games, a total probably only bettered by Ray Stewart of West Ham United.

..... and Barrie Thomas

I don't mind admitting that there were a few tears in my eyes as I walked around the Old Show Ground before the last game in 1988. My old injuries have caught up with me, so I don't get to the new ground as often as I would like, but my daughter is a Scunthorpe lass and I keep a close eye on the club's progress

I have many happy memories of my two spells at the club. Players such as Archie Gibson, (one of the finest half backs in the Country at the time), Johnny Kaye and Brian Godfrey meant we had an outstanding side that really took some beating. We were fourth in the second division in 1961/62, and I managed 31 goals in 24 games before my move to Newcastle United.

I didn't have much say in my transfer; players

were told what to do in those days. I learned later that Don Revie would also have liked to sign me. I moved for a record fee of £45,000 at the time, which like Alan Shearer finds today, adds a weight to the shoulders. I left a great side at Scunthorpe to one that was struggling.. Jackie Milburn was very kind to me; I'd been billed as the "new Jackie", and he helped relieve some of the strain. I was a member of the World Cup squad in the summer of 1962, though didn't make the trip to Chile. I enjoyed my time in the North East; the fans are fanatical in their support, but I always felt the Scunthorpe fans were just as good.

I returned to Scunthorpe in November 1964, largely due to the influence of Jack Wharton, a father figure at the club. The fans were again very good to me despite time away and the injuries I had picked up along the way.

As the PFA delegate at Scunthorpe, I was closely involved in the negotiations at the time the restraint on player's wages was lifted. I have some concerns as to how clubs like Scunthorpe will survive in the modern era of £15 million transfer fees. I hope the fans will keep supporting them, and I send everyone at the club my very best wishes.

Barrie's career with Leicester, Mansfield, Scunthorpe, Newcastle and Barnsley had many outstanding moments ..... such as his league debut for Leicester against Sheffield United on Christmas Day, 1954; the day shortly after when he scored a hat-trick against Bolton Wanderers with his boyhood hero, Nat Lofthouse, leading the Wanderer's attack; the time, during his Scunthorpe days when he scored four goals against Rotherham and followed up with four more against Leeds United in the next match; and Easter Monday, 1967 when he netted his 200th goal in League football against Halifax Town in a 4-1 Barnsley victory. His fine career was tragically cut short through injury.

AUTHOR'S NOTE

It is hoped that this publication will go a long way towards answering those inevitable questions that crop up from time to time whenever something out of the ordinary happens. I also personally hope that it will prove interesting, not just as a statistical history, but as a memory jerker of those long-forgotten games and a provider of information for the younger supporters who wish to gain some knowledge of the club's past. It is about time the facts and figures from United's career in the Football League were collated in one reference book. I hope the effort was worthwhile!

Michael Norton
September 1996

PRODUCER'S NOTE

Though Scunthope's League career only dates back to 1950, I am pleased to be able to include many details of the club's record before then. I'm most grateful to Michael for not only providing the information but also doing most of the typing on his computer! My thanks to the usual helpers without whom production of the book would have been much more difficult; Leigh Edwards and Michael Joyce (despite the arrival of young Master Thomas!) for player details, and Brian Tabner for the Football League attendances. Special thanks from me to the ex-players for writing the forewords, especially Kevin Keegan, who took time out on a day Newcastle were engaged in a European game to help. Finally, thanks to the Sports Editor at the Scunthorpe Evening Telegraph, Bob Steels, for his help and support. Bob's 1990 "Pictorial History" published by Archive Publications is now difficult to find, but is well worth searching out for its illustrations and narrative history of the club.

Scunthorpe's contribution to Football League records is admittedly small! Jack Brownsword's penalty count (mentioned earlier) is notable, as is their home run in the F.A. Cup. Scunthorpe did not loose a home game after November 20th 1976 until beaten by Birmingham City on December 14th 1994. It's a pity such a record didn't give them confidence to proceed further in the competition than they did! I'm indebted to Martin Thorpe of the Guardian for pointing out that Scunthorpe were the first club to finish 93rd in the League, and the first to be knocked out of the F.A. Cup on penalties!

Finally, I can't resist the temptation to ask one of the famous pub quiz questions: name the three England captains who played for Scunthorpe at some time in their career. Needless to say, the answer can be found somewhere in this book!

Tony Brown
September 1996

A Midland League line up of 1920/21. Whitham, Broadhead, Meredith, Brandon, Ackroyd, Bates, Gibson, Lloyd, Richards, Betts, Maycock, Moran (trainer).

SCUNTHORPE UNITED - A SHORT HISTORY

Scunthorpe United may never have been one of the country's top clubs, nor have they achieved any major success, but they have been a solid, reliable member of the Football League since 1950.

The 'old timers' amongst the club's current supporters, however, will probably say that better times were had in the Midland League when the club twice won the Championship and enjoyed several seasons of F. A. Cup glory.

But, where did it all start? Lengthy research some years ago established that football was played in Scunthorpe as far back as 1881 when there existed a team known as Scunthorpe Town. There is no link between that team and the Scunthorpe United of today because financial difficulties caused Scunthorpe Town to fold in 1897. At that stage another team, called Brumby Hall, came to prominence as the leading local side and they played their games on the field which staged the annual Scunthorpe Show which, not unsurprisingly, was to be known as the Old Show Ground. Two years later Brumby Hall joined forces with another team (or teams, the reporting of those days was not so precise!) and the merged teams called themselves Scunthorpe United. It is in 1899 therefore that the origin of the present day club is set although the true Scunthorpe United as we know it today did not emerge until eleven years later. Then, in 1910, a proposed merger with rivals Lindsey United was agreed, the idea being to create a bigger, stronger club capable of progressing from local league level to more serious competition. Scunthorpe United had previously made unsuccessful applications to join the Midland League in 1907 and 1908 and had entered the English Cup for the first ever time in 1909.

The resulting merger, the new club being called Scunthorpe and Lindsey United, created a team which dominated the local league and cup competitions during 1910/11 and 1911/12 earning themselves the nickname of the "Nuts". (Some reports at the time spelled this as "Knuts"!). The nickname was prompted after yet another trophy presentation when the speaker was quoted as saying that "the team were indeed tough nuts to crack". This dominance, coupled with crowds of over 1,000, brought further recognition when the team was admitted to the Midland League in 1912. The first season at higher level proved hard but nonetheless encouraging and over the next three years the club justified their place.

After the First World War caused a break in activities the club returned to Midland League duty for 1919/20 and ended the season in third spot, their best placing so far. This was followed by a fourth place in 1920/21 and the club submitted their first application to join the Football League but were well short of the number of votes required.

Maybe it was just as well, because the 1924/25 season saw the club hit by financial problems. Attendances dropped and a fire badly damaged the West Stand. Things were so bad that the club tendered their resignation from the Midland League and arranged to have the Old Show Ground put up for sale. However, a last-minute plea for aid was answered by Barnsley Brewery Company who stepped in with a loan to safeguard the club's immediate future. The club's fortunes changed rapidly and the 1926/27 season saw them win the Midland League Championship. The title was clinched with a 10-0 slamming of Sutton Junction with former England international

Ernie Sims scoring six times. The team finished 11 points clear of nearest challengers Boston United and Gainsborough Trinity.

The club couldn't repeat that success in the immediately ensuing seasons but were still a force to be reckoned with. One milestone was reached during 1929/30 in the F.A. Cup. The team had made it to the First Round Proper for the first ever time and were paired with Football League side Hartlepools United. Home advantage for this tough tie helped Scunthorpe squeeze through by 1-0 to create further club history. Rotherham United were next in line at the Old Show Ground and a record attendance of 8,030 saw an exciting 3-3 draw. The replay was just as thrilling but Scunthorpe were on the wrong end of the 5-4 scoreline.

For much of the thirties their final league placings varied, but this was no disgrace as the standard of Midland League football was ever improving. The team continued to find fame in the F.A. Cup, however, regularly appearing in the First Round Proper and producing epic displays against Football League sides which earned three appearances in the Second Round.

After twelve years of trying for a second Championship success they eventually found the right formula again in 1938/39. A free-scoring forward line proved to be the important factor with centre-forward Harry Johnson bagging 51 of the side's 133 league goals. The club was confirmed as Champions when beating Frickley Colliery by 4-2 on April 24. But not even a second title success could persuade Football League clubs to look favourably on another application for membership.

The club were prevented from building on their successful season by the outbreak of the Second War although they did win a curtailed version of the competition during 1939/40. Upon resumption of football for the 1945/46 season the club continued to feature amongst the leading sides and each summer submitted an application for Football League membership but made little headway until reaching a turning point in 1949. Tired of continual rejection the club tried a new approach by persuading clubs to vote for an increase in the number of teams from 88 to 92. The proposal was agreed and the door was opened for two clubs to be admitted to each of Division Three's Northern and Southern sections for the 1950/51 season. All that remained was for the Old Show Ground club to gain favour as one of the chosen few.

The Football League AGM in the summer of 1950 proved a tense, and perhaps controversial, occasion. In the ballot for the two Northern Section places Shrewsbury Town topped the voting with Workington and Wigan tied for second place with Scunthorpe close behind. So Shrewsbury were duly elected but it was decided that a second ballot to fill the remaining place would be contested between the next three clubs, not just Workington and Wigan. This time Wigan and Scunthorpe had equal votes with Workington third. League officials then decided on a straight vote between the two tied participants and this time Scunthorpe came out in ahead! A new chapter in the club's history was to begin, but one wonders what might the situation have been today for the respective clubs if that second ballot had only been contested by Wigan and Workington. Would Scunthorpe have ever gained Football League membership?

Having achieved their goal the club steadily acclimatised themselves into life at this higher level and showed their potential when finishing third in successive seasons, 1953/54 and 1954/55. This was the prelude to winning the Third North Championship in 1957/58. That season also saw the club's finest achievement in the F.A. Cup when they visited Newcastle United for a Fourth Round tie and won 3-1. This performance earned them the Sunday Pictorial Giant Killers Cup.

They then spent six seasons in Division Two coming close to achieving the ultimate goal of a place in the First Division when finishing 4th in 1961/62 after at one stage jostling for the leadership. Had it not been for the sale of 31-goal leading scorer Barrie Thomas to Newcastle in the January of that season the club may have gained promotion. It was a decision that still rankles among the old supporters today, however the team had slipped to eighth place at the time of the transfer and only two teams were promoted in those days.

Unfortunately the club did not trouble the leaders again and relegation came in 1964. Although they came close to regaining a Second Division place when finishing fourth in 1966 relegation was suffered again in 1968 taking them into Division Four. By now the club had discovered, and sold, a young goalkeeper by the name of Ray Clemence who played just 48 games before being bought by Liverpool in the summer of 1967. Then the 1968/69 season saw the emergence of Kevin Keegan who eventually followed Clemence's footsteps in 1971.

After eight years of mediocrity the 1971/72 season brought a modicum of success with promotion to Division Three. But it was almost thrown away, the team just clinging on to fourth place after topping the table through February and March. Sadly the team was never strong enough to hold its own in higher company and came straight back down a year later. It was then all downhill for another eight years as the club suffered its worst period during its Football League history so far, never finishing above halfway in the table and having to apply for re-election in 1975. It was a struggle for survival as attendances plummeted.

The eighties proved better, potentially at least if not always in actuality. After finishing next to bottom in 1981/82 there was an amazing transformation the following season as the team won promotion, albeit by the narrowest of margins. A last gasp victory at Chester on the final Saturday was enough to take the fourth promotion place from Bury who lost at home against Champions Wimbledon. Once again though, the team were not equipped to compete at the higher level and summer 1984 saw the club back in the lowest section where they have remained ever since. Generally speaking, though, things have improved with the move to a new ground in 1988, four qualifications for the League play-offs (including a trip to Wembley in 1992), and several excellent performances against big clubs in the two main cup competitions. But, at the end of the day, the club is still stuck in the basement and if survival as a professional outfit is to be ensured, as part of whatever form the F.A. Premiership and Football League is to take shape in the future, then promotion is a necessity - and quickly!

SCUNTHORPE UNITED RECORDS PAGE

PLAYERS:

Most Appearances	Jack Brownsword, 663 (597 League, 56 FA Cup, 10 FL Cup)
	Paul Longden, 463 (368+29+31+35 other)
Most Goals	Steve Cammack, 121 (110+6+3+2)
	Andy Flounders, 100 (87+3+6+4)
Most League Goals in a Season	Barrie Thomas, 31, 1961/62
Most International Appearances	No Scunthorpe player has played for his country whilst at the club.

THE CLUB:

Honours	Midland League Champions 1926/27, 1938/39
	Third Division North Champions, 1957/58
Best League performance	4th in Division Two, 1961/62
Best F.A. Cup performance	5th round 1957/58, 1969/70
Most League points	83, Division 4, 1982/83 (three points for a win)
	66, Division 3 (North), 1957/58 (two points for a win)
Most League goals	88, Division 3(N), 1957/58
Most League wins in a season	29, Division 3(N), 1957/58
Best League win	8-1 v. Luton Town, 24/4/1965
Best League away win	5-0 v. Bradford Park Avenue, 4/4/1970
Best F.A. Cup win	9-0 v. Boston United, 21/11/1953 (rounds proper)
	11-3 v. Lysaghts Sports 29/10/1938 (qualifying rounds)
Best League Cup win	4-1 v. Chelsea, 27/9/88 and Rotherham Utd., 15/8/95
Best League run undefeated	15, from 30/11/1957 and 13/11/1971
Undefeated League games, home	21, from 30/9/1950
Undefeated League games, away	10, from 14/5/1982
Best run of League wins	6, from 24/8/54, 6/11/65 and 18/10/69
Best run of home League wins	7, from 8/3/85 and 21/3/87
Longest run of League draws	6, from 2/1/1984

Midland League Champions 1926/27

1933/34. Back: H Allcock (secretary), N Davidson, J Staniland, unknown, G. Young, E Pattison, W Nicholson, L Benkley, F Hill. Front: S Allen, W Sumpter, R Fenwick, J Barry, H Mills, W Reed, unknown (trainer).

The first team to appear in the Football League. Back: J Barker, J Brownsword, W Allen, G Thompson, R Taylor, J McCormick. Front: H Mosby, J Payne, E Gorin, M Rees, W Boyes.

Third Division (North) Champions 1957/58. Back: J Hubbard, F Marshall, K Hardwick, J Haigh, B Horstead, J Brownsword. Front: J Marriott, E Davis, R Waldock, L Sharpe, M Jones

INTRODUCTION TO THE STATISTICS PAGES

The season by season grids show the results of games in the Football League, the F.A. Cup, the Football League Cup, and other first team competitions. Home games are identified by the opponents name in upper case, away games by the use of lower case. Scunthorpe's score is always given first. Attendances for League games are taken from the official Football League records. Since Scunthorpe are a relative newcomer to the Football League, the book also includes results from their early years in regional football and the Midland League.

Substitutes when used have the numbers 12, 13 and 14. 12 is used if only one substitute appeared (no matter what number was on the player's shirt). 14 is used for the second substitute until 1994/95 unless he was a goalkeeper. In 1995/96, 13 is used for the second substitute, 14 for the third. The players who were substituted are underlined.

A full player list is provided for every player who made a Football League appearance. Date and place of birth are shown, where known, and the year of death. Players with the same name are given a (1) or (2) after their name to avoid confusion. The next two columns, "seasons played", act as an index to the season by season grids. The years shown are the "first year" of the season; for example, 1971 is season 1971/72. The two columns show the season in which the player made his League debut; and the final season that he played. However, if he only played in one season, the second column is blank. An entry of "1995" in the second column does not imply that the player has left the club, but means that he appeared in this "final season" of the book.

Note that some players also made F.A. Cup appearances before 1951. If a player also made a Football League appearance his F.A. Cup appearances and goals from these seasons are included in the list.

Previous and next clubs show where he was transferred from, and the club he moved to. Non league club information is included when known. The appearance columns have separate totals for the League, F.A. Cup, Football League Cup and miscellaneous tournaments. In Scunthorpe's case, the latter category includes the League play-offs and the Associate Members' Cup (played under a variety of sponsors' names). "Goals scored" are also shown under the four headings.

If a player has had more than one spell at the club, a consolidated set of appearance and goals are shown on the first line. Subsequent lines show the seasons involved in his return, and his new pair of previous and next clubs.

A full record of meetings against all other League clubs is included. Some clubs have played in the League under different names, but the totals are consolidated under the present day name in this table. Other pages show the club's line-ups for F.A. Cup matches in non Football League seasons and the list of managers.

SCUNTHORPE AND LINDSEY UNITED: THE EARLY YEARS TO 1911/12

Key to Competitions:

LL = Lindsey League; LS = Lincolnshire Shield; HC = Hull Charity Cup; GL = Gainsborough & District League; FC = Frodingham Charity Cup; HN = Horncastle Cup; SN = Scunthorpe Nursing Cup; GR = Grimsby Charity Cup; LJC = Lincs Junior Cup; MC = Moreing Cup; IC = Ironstone Cup; GC = Grimsby Charity Cup. AC = Amateur Cup;   BC = Bellamy Cup.

Note: It was not always reported which competition the fixtures were in and it is possible that many of those unmarked are Lindsey League games although some could be friendlies.   Also, not all results were recorded.

SCUNTHORPE UNITED

1902-03

Sep	27	North Lindsey Utd	1-2	LL
Oct	11	GRIMSBY UNITED	3-2	
	25	Frodingham United	2-4	LL
Nov	1	GRIMSBY TRADESMEN	1-4	
	8	NORTH LINDSEY UTD	2-2	LS
	15	North Lindsey Utd	0-2	LS replay
	29	BARTON ST. CHADS	1-0	HC Rnd 1
Dec	6	NORTH LINDSEY BEES	11-1	LL
	13	FRODINGHAM UNITED	2-4	
Jan	10	Crowle	10-1	
	17	FRODINGHAM ROVERS	4-1	
	24	North Lindsey Utd	?	HC Rnd 2
	31	Broughton	3-3	
Feb	21	NORTH LINDSEY UTD	4-1	LL
	28	NORTH LINDSEY BEES	9-1	LL
Apr	19	ATTERCLIFFE	0-3	Friendly

1903-04

Sep	5	ASHBY RISING STARS	8-0	LL
	12	Ashby Town	5-1	
	19	BROUGHTON	4-1	
	26	FRODINGHAM ROVERS	2-2	
Oct	10	Frodingham United	0-10	
	24	Broughton	1-2	LL
Jan	9	Frodingham United	0-3	GL
	16	FRODINGHAM UNITED	2-5	HC
	30	FRODINGHAM UNITED	0-7	LL
Feb	13	NORTH LINDSEY UTD	1-2	GL
	20	NORTH LINDSEY BEES	7-1	GL
Mar	12	ASHBY TOWN	4-0	FC

1904-05

Results not properly documented but it is recorded that Scunthorpe United were Lindsey League Champions and winners of the Winterton Charity Cup and the Frodingham Charity Cup.

NORTH LINDSEY UNITED

1902-03

Sep	27	SCUNTHORPE UTD	2-1	LL
Nov	1	NORTH LINDSEY BEES	4-1	
	8	Scunthorpe United	2-2	LS
	15	SCUNTHORPE UNITED	2-0	LS rep
	29	FRODINGHAM UNITED	0-3	LS
Jan	3	Frodingham United	0-1	
	10	NORTH LINDSEY BEES	2-1	
	17	Crowle Parish Institute	3-3	
	24	SCUNTHORPE UNITED	1-0	HC
	31	FRODINGHAM ROVERS	6-0	
Feb	7	GRIMSBY ST. JOHNS	1-6	GR
	21	Scunthorpe United	1-4	LL
	28	Frodingham Rovers	3-3	
Mar	21	GRIMSBY ST. JOHNS	1-3	HC Final

1903-04

Sep	12	Ashby Rising Stars *	5-1	LL
	26	BARNETBY	15-0	
Oct	10	Broughton	1-0	GL
Nov	21	Broughton	3-4	
Jan	9	ASHBY RISING STARS	2-0	LL
	23	Frodingham United	6-1	GL
	30	Ashby Town	3-1	
Feb	6	NORTH LINDSEY BEES	7-1	GL
	13	Scunthorpe United	2-1	GL
	20	FRODINGHAM UNITED	2-1	LL
	27	Winterton Rovers	13-1	FC
Mar	12	FRODINGHAM ROVERS	3-0	HC

* Abandoned due to crowd disturbances.

1904-05

Oct	1	Broughton	2-1	
	8	Ashby Town	2-1	
Nov	19	BROUGHTON	3-0	
Dec	24	Winterton	2-0	
	31	FRODINGHAM	2-1	GL
Mar	4	Broughton	6-1	

It is not recorded what competition the above fixtures were in, except for Dec 31.

SCUNTHORPE UNITED

1905-06

Sep	23	FRODINGHAM UNITED	3-1	
Nov	25	BROUGHTON	3-2	
Dec	2	Broughton	4-0	
	16	Broughton	1-1	GL
	23	GRIMSBY ROVERS	0-2	HC

No results recorded for rest of season.

1906-07

Oct	13	ASHBY RISING STARS	2-2	GL
Nov	3	GRIMSBY ROVERS	1-1	HN
Jan	5	ASHBY RISING STARS	8-0	
	12	Frodingham United	1-1	FC
	19	GRIMSBY ST. JOHNS	0-0	HC
	26	GRIMSBY HAYCROFT ROV.	1-0	HN
Feb	2	Frodingham United	2-4	
	9	Grimsby St. Johns	3-2	HC s/f
	16	Frodingham United	2-4	SN s/f
Mar	2	FRODINGHAM UNITED	1-3	GL
	9	North Lindsey United	2-1	LL
	16	NORTH LINDSEY UTD	0-1	LL
	23	GRIMSBY ROVERS	3-4	HC Final
Apr	13	Barton Town	0-3	LL
	20	Broughton	2-0	LL

1907-08

Sep	21	GRIMSBY HAYCROFT R.	1-6	
	28	Frodingham & Brumby Utd	1-1	LL
Oct	5	Ashby Rising Stars	4-0	
	12	FRODINGHAM & BRUMBY	2-1	HN
	19	FRODINGHAM & BRUMBY	2-0	
	26	GAINSBOROUGH AMATEURS	10-1	
Nov	2	Kirton	6-1	
	9	North Lindsey United	0-1	
	16	SCUNTHORPE ALL SAINTS	4-2	LJC
	23	SCUNTHORPE WMC	4-3	FC
Dec	7	Barton	4-1	GL
	?	Frodingham & Brumby Utd	won	HC
	11	SCUNTHORPE ALL SAINTS	4-2	FC
	18	Frodingham & Brumby Utd	1-2	HC
Feb	8	Lincoln St. Catherines	3-1	LJC (aet)
	15	GRIMSBY ROVERS	2-0	
	22	Frodingham & Brumby Utd	2-2	FC *
	29	SPALDING	2-2	LJC
Mar	14	North Lindsey Utd	1-0	
	21	Broughton Rangers	2-1	LL
	28	Frodingham & Brumby Utd	1-2	FC
Apr	17	CLEETHORPES	2-0	LJC Final
	18	Frodingham & Brumby Utd	0-0	GL
	25	GAINSBORO' TRINITY INST.	1-2	MC

* Abandoned after 75 minutes.

NORTH LINDSEY UNITED

1905-06

Oct	14	BARNETBY	23-1	
Dec	16	GRIMSBY HAYCROFT ROVS	1-2	HC

No results recorded for rest of season.

1906-07

Jan	5	Broughton	1-2	GL
	12	Scunthorpe All Saints	1-2	
	19	FRODINGHAM UTD	2-4	GL
	26	FRODINGHAM UTD	1-0	LL
Feb	2	Gainsborough Trinty Institute	0-7	LS
	9	SCUNTHORPE ALL SAINTS	1-5	FC
Mar	2	Barton	*	
	9	Scunthorpe United	1-2	LL
	16	SCUNTHORPE UNITED	1-0	LL

No results recorded for first part of season.
* North Lindsey United failed to turn up !
Game awarded to Barton.

1907-08

Sep	21	Frodingham & Brumby Utd	0-0	GL
	28	SCUNTHORPE ALL SAINTS	2-2	LL
Oct	5	Barton Town	0-0	
	26	Gainsborough Trinity & Inst.	1-3	LJC
Nov	2	ASHBY RISING STARS	3-1	
	9	SCUNTHORPE UNITED	1-0	
	16	ASHBY RISING STARS	2-1	
	23	GAINSBOROUGH WMCI	6-1	
Dec	14	ASHBY RISING STARS *	1-2	
Jan	4	Frodingham & Brumby Utd	0-1	LL
	18	Broughton Rangers	3-2	LL
Feb	1	Frodingham & Brumby Utd	0-2	HC
	15	Scawby Swifts	1-0	Friendly
	29	Frodingham & Brumby Utd	4-1	LL
Mar	14	Scunthorpe United	0-1	
	21	Frodingham & Brumby Utd	1-4	

* Abandoned after 75 minutes
due to bad light

Not all results were recorded;
this applies to both clubs.

SCUNTHORPE UNITED

1908-09

Sep	12	GRIMSBY ROVERS	3-1	
	19	LINCOLN CITY	0-2	Lincs Cup
	?	GRIMSBY RANGERS	2-0	
	26	Grantham	0-2	
Oct	3	WORKSOP	4-0	
	10	BROUGHTON RANGERS	4-0	
	17	North Lindsey United	2-1	
	24	GRIMSBY HAYCROFT ROV.	2-2	SN
	31	FRODINGHAM & BRUMBY U	3-1	LL
Nov	7	Hull City Reserves	0-1	Friendly
	14	GRIMSBY VICTORIA	2-0	
	21	GAINSBORO' TRINITY RES.	1-1	Friendly
	28	GRIMSBY HAYCROFT ROVS	2-0	
Dec	5	NORTH LINDSEY UTD	1-1	
	12	GRIMSBY VICTORIA	4-1	HC
	19	Frodingham & Brumby Utd	1-3	
	25	LINDSEY WMC	7-1	
Jan	2	GRIMSBY RANGERS	1-1	
	9	North Lindsey Utd	2-1	GL
	16	Ashby Rising Stars	3-0	
	23	Grimsby Rovers	1-2	HN
	?	ASHBY RISING STARS	7-0	GL
	30	FROD. & BRUMBY UNITED	3-1	
Feb	6	GRIMSBY ROVERS	1-3	IC
	13	Frodingham & Brumby Utd	2-2	
	20	NORTH LINDSEY UTD	4-0	
	27	Gainsboro' Trinity Reserves	3-4	
Mar	13	CLEETHORPES	5-3	SN
	20	Frodingham & Brumby Utd	3-0	
	27	ASHBY RISING STARS	0-1	FC
Apr	3	Scawby Swifts	4-1	
	17	NORTH LINDSEY UTD	3-3	
	24	NORTH LINDSEY UTD	1-2	
	29	Frodingham & Brumby Utd	1-2	LL

1909-10

Sep	4	GRIMSBY ROVERS	3-2	
	11	HULL DAY STREET O.B.	1-1	
	18	WITHERNSEA	8-0	FAC Prelim
	25	FRODINGHAM & BRUMBY U.	2-0	LJC Rnd 1
Oct	2	York City	0-4	FAC Q1
	9	GRIMSBY TOWN RES	1-1	Friendly
	23	Broughton Rangers	3-1	LJC Rnd 2
	30	NORTH LINDSEY MIDGETS	7-0	LL
Nov	6	NORTH LINDSEY UTD	1-1	LL
	13	GRIMSBY HUMBER ROVERS	1-2	LJC Rnd 3
	20	HULL CITY RES.	0-8	Friendly
	27	NORTH LINDSEY UTD	5-1	HC
Dec	4	FRODINGHAM & BRUMBY U.	2-2	LL
	11	GRIMSBY HUMBER ROVERS	2-3	IC
	18	North Lindsey United	3-3	LL
	25	GAINSBORO' TRINITY RES.	2-3	Friendly
	27	GRIMSBY RANGERS	1-2	SN
Jan	8	BRIGG BRITANNIA	6-1	LL
	15	Brigg Britannia	1-3	
Feb	5	FRODINGHAM & BRUMBY U.	2-5	LL
	12	Scunthorpe Midgets	1-2	LL
Mar	5	ASHBY RISING STARS	2-3	LL
	12	Frodingham & Brumby Utd	1-1	HC
	19	BROUGHTON RANGERS	4-0	LL
	25	Broughton Rangers	2-5	
	27	FRODINGHAM & BRUMBY U.	0-2	HC
Apr	4	NORTH LINDSEY UTD	3-3	

NORTH LINDSEY UNITED

1908-09

Sep	12	Frodingham & Brumby Utd	1-1	
Oct	3	NORTH LINDSEY MIDGETS	6-0	GL
	10	FROD. & BRUMBY UTD	3-1	
	17	SCUNTHORPE UNITED	1-2	
	24	BROUGHTON RANGERS	6-2	LJC
	31	Broughton Rangers	3-3	GL
Nov	7	GRIMSBY RANGERS	1-2	SN
	14	FRODINGHAM & BRUMBY U	2-1	LJC
	21	Scawby Swifts	2-1	LL
Dec	5	Scunthorpe United	1-1	
	12	Immingham	6-0	IC
	19	ASHBY RISING STARS	1-0	
	25	Lincoln South End	0-3	
Jan	2	Frodingham & Brumby Utd	1-1	FC
	9	SCUNTHORPE UNITED	1-2	
	23	FRODINGHAM & BRUMBY U	1-3	
Feb	6	FRODINGHAM & BRUMBY U	0-1	FC
	13	GRIMSBY ROVERS	3-1	IC
	20	Scunthorpe United	0-4	
	27	ASHBY RISING STARS	2-1	GL
Mar	13	GRIMSBY ROVERS	1-1	
	20	Ashby Rising Stars	0-2	
	27	Frodingham & Brumby Utd	0-0	
Apr	3	Grimsby Rovers	1-7	IC
	17	Scunthorpe United	3-3	HC
	?	Scunthorpe United	2-1	

Not all results were reported.

1909-10

Sep	4	Frodingham & Brumby Utd	3-2	
	11	ASHBY RISING STARS	3-5	
	18	SCUNTHORPE MIDGETS	1-2	
	25	BROUGHTON RANGERS	6-1	LJC Rnd 1
Oct	2	Grimsby Rangers	2-5	
	9	FRODINGHAM & BRUMBY U.	1-3	
	23	NORTH LINDSEY MIDGETS	2-2	
	30	Broughton Rangers	0-2	
Nov	6	Scunthorpe United	1-1	LL
	27	Scunthorpe United	1-5	HC
Dec	4	Broughton Rangers	1-1	
	11	Frodingham & Brumby Utd	2-2	
	18	SCUNTHORPE UNITED	3-3	
Jan	1	Grimsby Haycroft Rovers	1-3	GC
	8	BROUGHTON RANGERS	3-1	FC
	15	Grimsby Rovers	1-7	SN
Feb	12	Frodingham & Brumby Utd	1-10	FC
Mar	5	BRIGG BRITANNIA	9-0	LL
	12	Ashby Rising Stars	0-2	
Apr	4	Scunthorpe United	3-3	
	16	GRIMSBY RANGERS	0-1	IC

North Lindsey United merged with Scunthorpe United, the new club being named Scunthorpe and Lindsey United

1910-11

Sep	3	HULL CITY JUNIORS	3-2	Friendly
	10	GRIMSBY ROVERS	2-3	Friendly
	17	Denaby	0-6	FAC Prelim
	24	ASHBY RISING STARS	6-2	
Oct	1	SCUNTHORPE MIDGETS	4-2	LJC Rnd 1
	8	FROD & BRUMBY UTD	2-1	HN
	15	GRIMSBY ROVERS	2-2	IC
	22	Brigg Britannia	6-2	LJC Rnd 2
	29	Grimsby Rovers	1-5	HC
Nov	5	Grimsby Rovers	0-2	IC
	12	Barton United	4-1	
	19	ASHBY RISING STARS	6-0	LL
	26	Scunthorpe Midgets *	0-2	
Dec	3	BARTON TERRIERS	9-0	LJC Rnd 3
	10	CLEETHORPES	0-0	SN
	17	LINCOLN LIBERAL CLUB	3-1	LJC Rnd 4
	24	Ashby Rising Stars	1-2	LL
	26	SCUNTHORPE MIDGETS	5-2	Friendly
Jan	7	CLEETHORPES	1-1	SN replay
	28	FROD & BRUMBY UTD	2-0	LL
Feb	11	Scunthorpe Midgets	2-2	LL
	18	NORTH LINDSEY MIDGETS	1-1	FC
	25	CLEETHORPES	1-0	Friendly
Apr	1	SCUNTHORPE TERRIERS	7-2	FC
	8	Grimsby Rovers (1)	1-2	LJC Final
	15	NORTH LINDSEY MIDGETS	2-0	LL
	18	Cleethorpes	1-1	SN rep 2
	25	Frod & Brumby Utd. (2)	2-1	FC Final
	?	GRIMSBY HUMBER ROVERS	3-0	SN s/f
	29	GRIMSBY RANGERS	4-3(e)	SN Final
May	3	Cleethorpes (3)	(3)	

* Abandoned after 79 minutes.
(1) Played at Blundell Park, Cleethorpes.
(2) Played at Brumby Hall, Scunthorpe.
(3) Not played, United defaulted.

1911-12

Sep	9	GRIMSBY ROVERS	3-1	
	16	York City	2-1	FAC Prelim
	23	BENTLEY	3-3	Friendly
	30	Mexborough	2-3	FAC Q1
Oct	7	NETHEREDGE (SHEFFIELD)	0-1	AC
	14	Grimsby St. Johns	2-0	SN
	21	WINTERTON	8-0	LL
	28	ASHBY RISING STARS	2-1	IC
Nov	4	GRIMSBY ST. JOHNS	3-1	GC
	11	FRODINGHAM & BRUMBY U	2-2	LJC Rnd 3
	18	Frodingham & Brumby Utd	1-0	LJC replay
	25	Ashby Rising Stars	0-0	LL
Dec	2	YORKSHIRE DRAGOONS	6-2	Friendly
	9	Grimsby St. Johns	1-0	SN
	16	ASHBY RISING STARS	4-2	LJC Rnd 4
	25	FRODINGHAM & BRUMBY U	2-2	LL
	31	Broughton Rangers	4-2	LL
Jan	6	Frodingham & Brumby Utd	0-0	LL
	13	BROUGHTON RANGERS	1-0	LL
	27	SPALDING	2-0	LJC Rnd 5
Feb	3	ASHBY RISING STARS	4-0	LL
	10	BROUGHTON RANGERS	10-2	FC
	17	FROD & BRUMBY UTD	4-0	SN s/f
	24	Lincoln South End	1-5	LJC Rnd 6
Mar	2	GRIMSBY HAYCROFT ROV.	5-1	Friendly
	9	GRIMSBY ROVERS	2-3	HC
	16	Grimsby St. Johns	4-1	IC
	23	NORTH LINDSEY JUNIORS	7-0	LL
	30	Grimsby Rovers	1-1	BC
Apr	6	CLEETHORPES	4-0	GC
	8	GRIMSBY ROVERS	2-0	BC replay
	8	Winterton	6-2	LL
	13	FRODINGHAM & BRUMBY U	1-0	FC Final
	15	NORTH LINDSEY JUNIORS	0-0	LL
	17	GRIMSBY HAYCROFT ROV.	4-0	BC
	20	GRIMSBY HAYCROFT ROV.	4-0	IC
	27	CLEETHORPES	2-0	SN Final
	29	Cleethorpes	0-3	BC Final

SCUNTHORPE IN THE MIDLAND LEAGUE

	P	W	D	L	F	A	Pts.	
1912/13	38	13	8	17	55	78	34	15th
1913/14	34	16	4	14	55	55	36	7th
1914/15	38	13	9	16	70	79	35	13th
1919/20	34	18	7	9	71	39	43	3rd
1920/21	38	18	9	11	64	43	45	4th
1921/22	42	22	8	12	87	60	52	4th
1922/23	42	18	13	11	65	58	49	6th
1923/24	42	21	7	14	55	49	49	6th
1924/25	28	12	5	11	45	41	29	7th
1925/26	40	19	9	12	86	78	47	7th
1926/27	38	28	4	6	121	44	60	Champions
1927/28	44	23	4	17	118	85	50	9th
1928/29	50	20	14	16	98	96	54	11th
1929/30	50	26	6	18	124	98	58	7th
1930/31	46	19	11	16	98	101	49	11th
1931/32	46	18	9	19	83	99	45	9th
1932/33	44	23	5	16	104	100	51	8th
1933/34	32	14	5	13	76	73	33	7th
1934/35	38	17	3	18	67	82	37	11th
1935/36	40	16	8	16	73	77	40	11th
1936/37	42	19	3	20	77	86	41	14th
1937/38	42	22	5	15	109	78	49	6th
1938/39	42	28	8	6	133	57	64	Champions
1939-45	*Competition suspended because of WWII*							
1945/46	36	17	6	13	82	65	40	6th
1946/47	42	24	9	9	121	61	57	4th
1947/48	42	23	9	10	89	57	55	2nd
1948/49	42	24	6	12	104	56	54	4th
1949/50	46	29	6	11	99	44	64	3rd

The players for Scunthorpe's first Midland League game, 14th September 1912

SCUNTHORPE IN THE MIDLAND LEAGUE, 1912/13 to 1949/50

1912/13

Sep	7	Leeds City Res.	0-1	
	14	NOTTS COUNTY RES.	0-1	
	21	Lincoln City Res.	1-7	Bell
Oct	3	CHESTERFIELD TOWN	0-1	
	5	LEEDS CITY RES.	1-2	Henderson
	10	Notts County Res.	1-9	Henderson
	19	MEXBOROUGH TOWN	5-3	Walden 3, Bell 2
	26	GAINSBOROUGH TRINITY	2-2	Bell, Pearce
	28	Rotherham Town	1-2	Higgins
Nov	9	YORK CITY	4-3	Bell, Walden 3
	11	DONCASTER ROVERS	1-3	Walden
	23	THE WEDNESDAY RES.	1-3	Pearce
Dec	14	Mexborough Town	0-3	
	25	HALIFAX TOWN	3-0	Spelvins, Pearce, Walden
	26	Grimsby Town Res.	1-1	Wagstaffe
	28	Halifax Town	1-4	Spelvins
Jan	18	ROTHERHAM TOWN	3-3	Jackson 2, Spelvins
	25	York City	0-4	
	30	HULL CITY RES.	3-2	Jackson 2, Barrick
Feb	1	Goole Town	0-2	
	8	GRIMSBY TOWN RES.	2-2	Oates, Spelvins
	20	WORKSOP TOWN	3-1	Spelvins 2, Walden
	22	Sheffield United Res.	2-3	Bell, Walden
	27	ROTHERHAM COUNTY	1-5	Walden
Mar	1	GOOLE TOWN	1-1	Walden
	8	Doncaster Rovers	2-2	Cox, Walden
	13	Castleford Town	0-0	
	15	LINCOLN CITY RES.	2-1	Cox, Spelvins
	22	Hull City Res.	1-0	Walden
	26	Gainsborough Trinity	1-0	Cox
	29	Denaby United	3-1	Bell 3
Apr	3	Worksop Town	0-0	
	7	Rotherham County	0-3	
	12	SHEFFIELD UTD RES.	3-1	Walden, Bell, Higgins
	16	Chesterfield Town	4-2	Higgins, Walden, Bell, Roberts
	19	DENABY UNITED	3-0	Walden, Bell, Higgins
	24	CASTLEFORD TOWN	1-0	Walden
	26	The Wednesday Res.	0-1	

1913/14

Sep	1	Lincoln City Res.	0-0	
	6	LEEDS CITY RES.	2-1	Bradbury, Root
	13	Rotherham County	0-7	
	20	CHESTERFIELD TOWN	4-0	Bradbury, Root, Mulholland, Smelt (OG)
Oct	4	Mexborough Town	1-1	Bradbury
	18	THE WEDNESDAY RES.	1-2	Walden
	25	The Wednesday Res.	0-1	
Nov	1	ROTHERHAM TOWN	3-1	Root, Walden 2
	8	Leeds City Res.	4-1	Bradbury 2, Walden, Mulholland
	15	WORKSOP TOWN	3-1	Morris, Walden, Mulholland
	22	MEXBOROUGH TOWN	3-1	Root, Walden, Mulholland
	29	CASTLEFORD TOWN	2-0	Bradbury, Clark
Dec	6	Castleford Town	3-2	Root 2, Mulholland
	13	Worksop Town	0-1	
	20	GOOLE TOWN	1-0	Bradbury
	25	Hull City Res.	1-0	Mulholland
	26	Chesterfield Town	0-6	
	27	SHEFFIELD UTD RES.	2-2	Mulholland 2
Jan	3	York City	1-2	Mulholland
	10	Halifax Town	3-1	Goates 3
	17	GAINSBOROUGH TRINITY	1-1	Morris
Feb	14	Doncaster Rovers	0-2	
	21	DONCASTER ROVERS	1-0	Roberts
	28	HALIFAX TOWN	2-1	Walden, Hollin
Mar	7	Rotherham Town	1-2	Wood
	14	Sheffield Utd Res.	3-2	Wood 3
	21	YORK CITY	4-1	Wood 3, Roberts
	28	ROTHERHAM COUNTY	0-2	
Apr	2	Goole Town	0-1	
	4	GRIMSBY TOWN RES.	3-4	Wood, Clark 2
	10	Gainsborough Trinty	0-2	
	11	Grimsby Town Res.	1-2	Thompson
	13	HULL CITY RES.	1-3	Thompson
	18	LINCOLN CITY RES.	4-2	Wood 2, Thompson, Root

1914/15

Sep	3	GRIMSBY TOWN RES.	3-2	Wood, Clark, Platts
	5	Leeds City Res.	0-5	
	12	ROTHERHAM COUNTY	1-1	Hill
	19	HULL CITY RES.	3-0	Robinson, Clark, Monaghan
Oct	3	York City	0-0	
	8	HECKMONDWIKE	4-0	Robinson, Rusling, Ibbotson, Hill
	17	SHEFFIELD UTD RES.	2-2	Robinson, Clark
	19	Mexborough Town	1-1	Robinson
	31	Castleford Town	2-6	Robinson, Armitage
Nov	21	Worksop Town	2-0	Robinson, Armitage
	28	Rotherham Town	1-3	Platts
Dec	5	WORKSOP TOWN	1-1	Robinson
	10	The Wednesday Res.	1-3	Platts
	12	GAINSBOROUGH TRINITY	2-0	Robinson, Armitage
	19	Bradford Park Ave Res.	1-5	Robinson
	25	GOOLE TOWN	0-0	
	26	Goole Town	0-4	
Jan	2	LINCOLN CITY RES.	2-5	Wood 2
	9	Gainsborough Trinity	0-5	
	14	Halifax Town	1-2	Wood
	16	CHESTERFIELD TOWN	3-1	Wood, Monaghan, Platts
	23	Hull City Res.	4-1	Wood, Robinson, Hill, Leaning
Feb	6	Sheffield United Res.	0-3	
	20	Rotherham County	1-4	Wood
	27	BRADFORD PARK AVE RES	2-3	Robinson 2
Mar	6	Chesterfield Town	2-2	Robinson, Wood
	13	YORK CITY	2-0	Wood 2
	15	Heckmondwike	6-0	Wood 2, Watson 2, Rusling 2
	20	THE WEDNESDAY RES.	2-3	Wood, Platts
	27	LEEDS CITY RES.	2-2	Wood, Rusling
Apr	2	Grimsby Town Res.	0-1	
	3	DONCASTER ROVERS	3-2	Robinson, Ibbotson 2
	5	Doncaster Rovers	0-2	
	10	HALIFAX TOWN	2-1	Ibbotson, Hill
	17	Lincoln City Res.	0-4	
	24	ROTHERHAM TOWN	5-5	Root, Taylor, Ibbotson 2, Chantry
	29	MEXBOROUGH TOWN	5-0	Root, Ibbotson 2, Chantry, Leaning
May	1	CASTLEFORD TOWN	4-0	Ibbotson, Root, Platts, Wood

1915 to 1919 - no Midland League due to War

1919/20

Aug	30	ROTHERHAM COUNTY RES	4-1	Spavin 2, Butler, Hobson
Sep	6	Rotherham County Res	1-3	Charlesworth
	13	Halifax Town	1-2	Spavin
	20	SHEFFIELD UTD RES	0-0	
Oct	4	CASTLEFORD TOWN	1-0	Mahon
	18	Grimsby Town Res	2-1	Spavin, Lemon
Nov	1	Sheffield Utd Res.	1-1	Butler
	8	HALIFAX TOWN	4-1	Spavin, Butler, Lemon, Booth
	15	Castleford Town	1-3	Mahon
	22	WORKSOP TOWN	1-0	Butler
	29	Barnsley Res.	3-3	Booth 2, Cox
Dec	6	HULL CITY RES.	4-1	Butler, Lemon 2, Cox
	13	Gainsborough Trinty	4-1	Booth, Robson, Butler, Spavin
	20	Notts County Res.	1-1	Wield
	25	LINCOLN CITY RES	6-0	Spavin 4, Lemon 2
	26	Lincoln City Res.	2-0	Lemon, Cox
Jan	3	GRIMSBY TOWN RES	4-1	Spavin, Amos, Robinson, Booth
	10	Worksop Town	1-3	Spavin
	31	GAINSBOROUGH TRINITY	5-0	Spavin, Butler, Lemon, Booth, Atkinson
Feb	7	SILVERWOOD COLLIERY	5-1	Spavin 2, Amos 2, Lemon
	14	BARNSLEY RES.	4-0	Spavin 2, Atkinson 2
	21	Hull City Res.	1-2	Butler
	28	Silverwood Colliery	3-0	Lemon 2, Atkinson
Mar	6	Mexborough	0-1	
	13	MEXBOROUGH	0-0	
	20	Rotherham Town	1-3	Mahon
	27	THE WEDNESDAY RES.	1-0	Mahon
Apr	3	CHESTERFIELD MUNICIPAL	1-2	Broadhead
	5	Chesterfield Municipal	1-3	Mahon
	8	LEEDS UNITED RES	3-2	Lemon 2, Butler
	10	ROTHERHAM TOWN	3-2	Lemon 2, Atkinson
	17	The Wednesday Res.	1-1	Lemon
	24	NOTTS COUNTY RES	1-0	Lemon
	28	Leeds United Res.	0-0	

1920/21

Aug	28	NOTTS COUNTY RES	1-3	Lemon
Sep	4	Sheffield United Res.	1-0	J.Duffus
	11	GAINSBOROUGH TRINITY	1-1	Lemon
	18	ROTHERHAM TOWN	2-0	J.Duffus 2
Oct	2	DONCASTER ROVERS	1-0	J.Duffus
	16	SHEFFIELD UNITED RES	1-1	J.Duffus
	30	LEEDS UNITED RES	2-0	Tunstall, Simpson
Nov	13	NOTTM FOREST RES	4-0	Lemon, Tunstall, Simpson 2
	27	The Wednesday Res.	2-3	Lemon, Harvey
Dec	4	Rotherham Town	1-3	Harvey
	11	CHESTERFIELD	1-2	Broadhead
	18	Chesterfield	3-3	Mayo 2, Lloyd
	25	Hull City Res.	3-1	Roebuck, Harvey, Simpson
	27	HULL CITY RES.	4-1	Ackroyd, Jenkins, Simpson 2
	30	Nottm Forest Res.	5-3	Roebuck 2, Jenkins, Robson, Simpson
Jan	1	Gainsborough Trinity	4-1	Roebuck 3, Simpson
	8	Rotherham County Res.	1-0	Lemon
	15	WORKSOP TOWN	0-0	
	29	Denaby United	2-0	Roebuck, Lemon
Feb	5	DENABY UNITED	4-1	Roebuck, Lemon, Crofts 2
	12	CASTLEFORD TOWN	1-3	Butler
	19	Halifax Town	0-1	
	26	Castleford Town	0-0	
Mar	5	MEXBOROUGH	3-0	Lemon 2, Ackroyd
	10	Worksop Town	0-0	
	12	Leeds United Res.	1-0	Ackroyd
	19	Lincoln City	0-2	
	26	GRIMSBY TOWN RES	3-1	Lemon, Jones, Broadhead
	28	Grimsby Town Res.	0-1	
Apr	2	LINCOLN CITY	1-0	Jenkins
	9	Doncaster Rovers	1-1	Roebuck
	14	THE WEDNESDAY RES.	0-2	
	16	ROTHERHAM COUNTY RE	1-1	Lemon
	21	Barnsley Res.	1-0	Meredith
	23	Mexborough	0-0	
	27	Notts County Res.	3-5	Lemon, Harvey 2
	30	BARNSLEY RES.	1-3	Broadhead
Ma	7	HALIFAX TOWN	5-0	Lemon 2, Broadhead 2, Meredith

1921/22

Aug	27	ROTHERHAM COUNTY RE	2-2	Maycock 2
Sep	3	WATH ATHLETIC	2-1	Gibson 2
	8	Nottm Forest Res.	1-0	Maycock
	10	HULL CITY RES.	2-0	Richards, Maycock
	17	Gainsborough Trinity	0-3	
	20	Wombwell	1-1	Gibson
Oct	1	Barnsley Res.	2-3	Whitham, Gibson
	15	Mexborough	0-2	
	27	MANSFIELD TOWN	3-1	Gibson, Reed, Maycock
	29	WORKSOP TOWN	2-2	Ackroyd, Whitham
Nov	12	Rotherham Town	1-5	Gibson
	19	Denaby United	3-4	Duke, Broadhead, Maycock
	26	NOTTS COUNTY RES	1-2	Clark
Dec	3	Boston	0-2	
	10	Hull City Res.	1-3	Lloyd
	17	THE WEDNESDAY RES.	3-1	Lloyd, Meredith, Whitham
	24	BARNSLEY RES.	4-1	Whittingham, Whitham, Maycock 2
	26	LINCOLN CITY RES	4-1	Whittingham, Whitham, Maycock, Meredith
	28	Lincoln City Res.	1-0	Lloyd
	31	DONCASTER ROVERS	2-1	Whitham, Maycock
Jan	7	Doncaster Rovers	1-0	Whittingham
	14	GRIMSBY TOWN RES	6-0	Meredith, Chambers, Whitham, Lloyd, Maycock 2
	26	Notts County Res.	3-1	Whitham, Lloyd, Maycock
	28	NOTTM FOREST RES	5-3	Lloyd, Ackroyd, Whitham 2, Maycock
Feb	4	Worksop Town	3-4	Ackroyd, Whittingham, Maycock
	11	BOSTON	4-1	Meredith, Ackroyd, Whittingham, Whitham
	15	Wakefield City	1-1	Maycock
	18	DENABY UNITED	3-0	Meredith, Whittingham, Maycock
	25	Wath Athletic	4-1	Whitham 2, Maycock 2
	27	Rotherham County Res.	3-0	Lloyd, Whitham, Maycock
Mar	4	Grimsby Town Res.	1-1	Lloyd
	8	WAKEFIELD CITY	3-0	Crooks, Whitham 2
	18	WOMBWELL	4-0	Meredith 2, Ackroyd, Lloyd
	22	Mansfield Town	1-3	Ackroyd
	25	MEXBOROUGH	1-1	Maycock
Apr	1	The Wednesday Res.	0-5	
	8	GAINSBOROUGH TRINITY	2-1	Whitham 2
	15	CASTLEFORD TOWN	3-0	Yarrow, Maycock 2
	17	Castleford Town	0-0	
	22	ROTHERHAM TOWN	3-1	Whitham 3
	29	Harrogate	0-1	
Ma	6	HARROGATE	1-1	Broadhead

1921/22. Back: C White (trainer), R Smith, H Lloyd, J Wogin, J Ackroyd, J Duke, J Broadhead, W Richards.
Front: J Meredith, R Whittingham, V Whitham, H Maycock, A Chambers.

1922/23

Aug	26	NOTTS COUNTY RES	2-0	Whitham, Hargreaves
Sep	2	HULL CITY RES.	1-2	Whitham
	9	Rotherham County Res	2-1	Whitham, Talbot
	16	ROTHERHAM COUNTY RES	2-1	Rushby, Maycock
	23	Castleford Town	0-0	
	25	The Wednesday Res.	0-2	
Oct	9	Denaby United	0-6	
	14	Gainsborough Trinity	2-2	Gittos 2
Nov	11	WOMBWELL	3-0	Rushby 2, Gittos
	25	BARNSLEY RES.	1-1	Gittos
Dec	9	NOTTM FOREST RES	3-0	Lloyd, Talbot, Hill
	16	Boston	0-3	
	23	WORKSOP TOWN	3-2	Gittos 3
	25	DONCASTER ROVERS	2-2	Gittos, Whitham
	26	Lincoln City Res.	2-1	Meredith, Gittos
	30	Mexborough	0-0	
Jan	1	Rotherham Town	2-1	Gittos, Whitham
	7	MANSFIELD TOWN	2-1	Gittos, Rushby
	13	Wombwell	2-2	Gittos, Whitham
	17	York City	2-2	Gittos, Meredith
	20	LINCOLN CITY RES.	2-0	Moore, Smith
	27	Wath Athletic	0-4	
Feb	3	GRIMSBY TOWN RES	4-2	Gittos 3, Meredith
	8	Nottm Forest Res.	2-2	Whitham, Maycock
	10	Chesterfield Res.	0-0	
	15	Hull City Res.	4-3	Gittos, Crooks, Meredith, Rushby
	17	MEXBOROUGH	4-0	Rushby 2, Whitham, Maycock
	24	Mansfield Town	1-1	Maycock
Mar	1	Notts County Res.	1-1	Maycock
	3	GAINSBOROUGH TRINITY	3-0	Meredith, Gittos 2
	10	Grimsby Town Res.	0-3	
	12	Barnsley Res.	0-3	
	17	WATH ATHLETIC	2-1	Meredith, Maycock
	31	ROTHERHAM TOWN	5-0	Talbot 3, Gittos 2
Apr	2	Doncaster Rovers	0-0	
	7	BOSTON	0-0	
	14	THE WEDNESDAY RES.	0-1	
	19	YORK CITY	3-0	Whitham, Gittos, Own goal (Thorpe)
	21	Worksop Town	0-3	
	26	DENABY UNITED	0-3	
	28	CASTLEFORD TOWN	0-2	
May	5	CHESTERFIELD RES	3-0	Meredith, Whitham, Talbot

1923/24

Aug	25	York City	0-0	
Sep	1	DENABY UNITED	1-2	Burkinshaw
	8	Gainsborough Trinity	2-2	White, Foster
	13	Notts County Res.	1-4	Kitchen
	15	SUTTON TOWN	2-1	Burkinshaw, Kitchen
	29	YORK CITY	4-1	Kitchen 2, Raby 2
Oct	13	NOTTS COUNTY RES	0-0	
	27	BARNSLEY RES.	0-0	
Nov	10	GRIMSBY TOWN RES.	3-0	White, Kitchen 2
	24	HULL CITY RES.	1-2	Wilson
Dec	8	NOTTM FOREST RES	2-0	Kitchen 2
	15	CASTLEFORD TOWN	3-1	Kitchen 2, Ashmore
	22	Wombwell	0-0	
	25	LINCOLN CITY RES.	1-0	Raby
	26	Lincoln City Res.	3-1	Burkinshaw, Kitchen, Raby
	29	Mexborough	0-3	
Jan	1	Barnsley Res.	1-0	Raby
	5	MEXBOROUGH	0-2	
	12	Rotherham Town	3-0	Raby 3
	19	ROTHERHAM TOWN	2-0	Raby 2
	26	Hull City Res.	2-0	Raby 2
Feb	2	CHESTERFIELD RES.	2-0	Green, Kitchen
	9	Chesterfield Res.	1-0	Ashmore
	16	Worksop Town	0-3	
	18	Nottm Forest Res.	1-0	Raby
	23	WATH ATHLETIC	1-0	Kitchen
	25	Denaby United	1-5	Raby
Mar	1	GAINSBOROUGH TRINITY	3-0	Raby 3
	8	Rotherham County Res.	1-1	Burkinshaw
	13	ROTHERHAM COUNTY RES	1-0	Bradbury
	15	WOMBWELL	1-0	Raby
	22	Boston	0-1	
	27	Doncaster Rovers Res.	0-4	
	29	BOSTON	2-0	Raby, Foster
Apr	5	Sutton Town	1-3	Raby
	9	Castleford Town	1-1	Ashmore
	12	Wath Athletic	0-3	
	19	MANSFILED TOWN	0-2	
	21	Grimsby Town Res.	0-1	
	22	Mansfiled Town	0-6	
	26	WORKSOP TOWN	4-0	Burkinshaw, Kitchen, Raby 2
May	3	DONCASTER ROVERS RES	4-0	Broksom, Kitchen, Raby 2

1924/25

Aug	30	Wombwell	0-1	
Sep	4	CASTLEFORD TOWN	0-3	
	6	DENABY UNITED	1-0	Needham
	10	York City	0-1	
	13	GAINSBOROUGH TRINITY	2-1	Cammack, Shaw
	27	Lincoln City Res.	0-1	
Oct	11	Gainsborough Trinity	2-2	Lees, Fenwick
	25	Sutton Town	5-0	Shaw 3, Fenwick, Lees
Nov	8	WATH ATHLETIC	1-0	Shaw
	15	Worksop Town	0-3	
	22	WORKSOP TOWN	1-1	Burnham
	29	Mansfield Town	0-3	
Dec	6	MANSFIELD TOWN	2-3	Shaw 2
	13	Frickley Colliery	4-1	Shaw 3, Green
	20	BOSTON	2-4	Shaw 2
	25	WOMBWELL	3-0	Shaw, Skull, Dawson
	26	MEXBOROUGH	3-1	Shaw, Geaves, Dawson
	27	ROTHERHAM TOWN	3-2	Shaw 2, Burnham
Jan	3	SUTTON TOWN	0-0	
	10	Mexborough	3-1	Shaw 2, Green
	17	FRICKLEY COLLIERY	2-0	Shaw 2,
	24	Rotherham Town	1-3	Shaw
	31	Boston	1-3	Shaw
Feb	7	YORK CITY	1-1	Shaw
	14	LINCOLN CITY RES	2-0	Shaw 2
	16	Denaby United	1-2	Own goal (Rhodes)
	21	Castleford Town	0-0	
	28	Wath Athletic	5-4	Shaw 4, Todd

As only 15 teams were in the Midland League the following fixtures were played as a subsidiary competition.

Mar	12	SUTTON TOWN	1-1	Woulds
	14	Lincoln City Res.	0-2	
	21	BOSTON	1-2	J.Hill
	28	Boston	0-2	
Apr	4	GAINSBOROUGH TRINITY	0-2	
	6	SUTTON TOWN	3-0	Shaw, Green, Burnham
	11	WORKSOP TOWN	1-0	Shaw
	13	Worksop Town	1-2	McDonald
	20	LINCOLN CITY RES	1-3	J.Hill
	23	MANSFIELD TOWN	0-1	
	25	Gainsborough Trinity	0-2	
May	2	Mansfield Town	3-4	Shaw, Skull, Burnham

1925/26

Aug	29	ALFRETON TOWN	2-1	Dawson, Briggs
Sep	2	Alfreton Town	1-4	Briggs
	5	Gainsborough Trinity	0-0	
	12	GAINSBOROUGH TRINITY	0-0	
	14	Frickley Colliery	3-1	Whitham, Volwes
	24	FRICKLEY COLLIERY	5-0	Lawrie, Volwes 3, Clarkson
	26	MANSFIELD TOWN	3-0	Whitham, Volwes, Cawley
Oct	10	Mansfield Town	1-3	Volwes
	24	LINCOLN CITY RES.	1-1	J.Hill
	31	Mexborough	1-4	Whitham
Nov	7	Denaby United	0-0	
	21	WATH ATHLETIC	4-1	Whitham, Cawley 2, Wilson
	28	Newark Town	0-4	
DEc	5	DENABY UNITED	3-1	Volwes, Cawley 2
	12	York City	1-1	Volwes
	19	YORK CITY	2-1	Whitham, Cawley
	25	Long Eaton	1-5	Volwes
	26	LONG EATON	5-3	Whitham 2, Volwes 2, Cawley
	28	Wath Athletic	2-6	Volwes 2
Jan	9	LOUGHBOROUGH COR.	3-0	Lawrie, Whitham, Cawley
	16	Lincoln City Res.	2-9	Whitham, Volwes
	23	WOMBWELL	3-1	Whitham, Cawley 2
	30	Loughborough Corinthians	1-6	Kemp
Feb	6	Castleford Town	5-1	Volwes 4, Cawley
	13	MEXBOROUGH	1-2	Lawrie
	20	SHIREBROOK	4-1	Whitham, Volwes 3
	27	SUTTON TOWN	5-0	Lawrie, Whitham 2, Clarkson 2
Mar	6	GRANTHAM	1-1	Volwes
	13	BOSTON	1-1	Volwes
	20	Boston	1-5	Lawrie
	22	Ilkeston United	1-1	Volwes
	27	Grantham	2-1	Volwes 2
Apr	3	WORKSOP TOWN	2-1	Volwes 2
	5	Worksop Town	2-1	Cawley, Own goal (Marsh)
	10	Shirebrook	2-5	Volwes, Whitham
	15	ILKESTON UNITED	4-1	Volwes, Whitham, Green 2
	17	Sutton Town	1-1	Green
	22	CASTLEFORD TOWN	5-2	R.Webb, Volwes, Cawley 2, G.Webb
	24	Wombwell	0-2	
May	1	NEWARK TOWN	5-0	Volwes 3, Whitham 2

1926/27

Aug	28	FRICKLEY COLLIERY	3-1	Allen, Hunter, Smith
Sep	4	Heanor Town	2-0	Thompson 2
	11	Mexborough Athletic	0-4	
	13	LINCOLN CITY RES.	4-1	Johnson, Simms 3
	20	Wombwell	2-0	Johnson, Hunter
	25	GAINSBOROUGH TRINITY	0-0	
Oct	9	NEWARK TOWN	1-0	Simms
	23	Newark Town	1-1	Allen
Nov	6	WATH ATHLETIC	3-0	Simms 2, Allen
	20	ILKESTON UNITED	5-3	Johnson 2, Simms, Allen 2
	27	Alfreton Town	6-1	Johnson 2, Simms 2, Allen, Alford
Dec	4	LONG EATON	6-1	Johnson 2, Simms 2, Allen, Smith
	11	Sutton Town	3-2	Johnson, Simms, Allen
	18	MEXBOROUGH ATHLETIC	5-2	Johnson, Simms 3, Allen
	25	YORK CITY	2-2	Allen 2
	27	York City	2-1	Simms 2
Jan	1	Grantham	3-0	Johnson, Simms 2
	8	WOMBWELL	5-1	Johnson, Simms 3, Allen
	15	Gainsborough Trinity	1-0	Simms
	22	SHIREBROOK	8-1	Johnson 2, Simms 3, Allen 3
Feb	5	GRANTHAM	7-1	Simms 4, Allen 3
	12	Loughborough Corinthians	3-2	Johnson, Simms, Allen
	19	LOUGHBOROUGH COR.	3-0	Johnson, Simms 2
	24	Frickley Colliery	3-4	Johnson, Allen, Hunter
	26	Lincoln City Res.	2-0	Johnson, Simms
Mar	5	BOSTON	2-1	Johnson, Allen
	12	Denaby United	2-3	Simms, Alford
	19	ALFRETON TOWN	6-1	Skull, Johnson, Simms 2, Smith, Allen
	26	Long Eaton	0-1	
Apr	2	SUTTON TOWN	10-0	Simms 6, Johnson, Allen, Alford, Smith
	9	Boston	2-1	Simms 2
	16	WORKSOP TOWN	6-1	Johnson, Simms 2, Allen 2, Smith
	18	Worksop Town	2-2	Johnson, Alford
	19	Shirebrook	1-2	Allen
	23	Wath Athletic	1-2	Moore
	27	Ilkeston United	3-1	Simms 3
	30	DENABY UNITED	1-0	Allen
May	6	HEANOR TOWN	5-1	Simms 2, Allen 3

1927/28

Aug	27	Newark Town	5-2	Simms, Brooks 2, Allen 2
Sep	1	SCARBOROUGH	2-3	Simms, Wainwright
	3	NOTTM FOREST RES.	2-1	Simms, Brooks
	10	GAINSBOROUGH TRINITY	4-2	Simms 2, Wainwright, Own goal (Vincent)
	19	Heanor Town	7-4	Simms 4, Brooks 2, Allen 2
	24	Gainsborough Trinity	1-1	Green
	26	WOMBWELL	3-0	Allen 2, Hunter
Oct	8	Scarborough	2-3	Simms, Brooks
	15	STAVELEY TOWN	7-2	Simms, Brooks 2, Allen 3, Hunter
	20	Wombwell	4-2	Simms, Brooks, Allen 2
	22	Lincoln City Res.	2-2	Simms 2
	29	HEANOR TOWN	5-0	Simms 4, Brooks
Nov	5	Mansfield Town	1-5	Allen
	12	LINCOLN CITY RES	1-3	Brooks
	19	Grantham	5-4	Simms, Brooks 2, Allen 2
	26	Staveley Town	1-2	Foster
Dec	3	Ilkeston United	1-4	Simms
	10	BOSTON	4-2	Simms 2, Allen, Noble
	17	Boston	2-2	Allen, Foster
	24	NOTTS COUNTY RES	4-4	Simms, Maw 2, Moore
	26	GRIMSBY TOWN RES	0-1	
	27	Grimsby Town Res.	1-3	Moore
	31	GRANTHAM	2-0	Maw, Foster
Jan	2	Shirebrook	0-3	
	7	Nottm Forest Res.	0-4	
	14	NEWARK TOWN	7-2	Simms 3, Maw 2, Allen, Skull
	21	WATH ATHLETIC	0-2	
Feb	11	York City	1-2	Maw
	16	Frickley Colliery	2-0	Hunter, Skull
	18	MEXBOROUGH ATHLETIC	5-0	Maw, Allen 2, Foster 2
	25	Mexborough Athletic	1-4	Bowers
Mar	3	YORK CITY	0-1	
	8	FRICKLEY COLLIERY	2-1	Bowers, Maw
	10	Denaby United	0-1	
	24	Wath Athletic	2-3	Bowers, Wainwright
	31	LOUGHBOROUGH COR.	4-0	Bowers 2, Maw, Holland
Apr	7	WORKSOP TOWN	4-1	Bowers, Maw, Wainwright 2
	9	Worksop town	0-3	
	10	Loughborough Corinthians	2-1	Maw, Allen
	14	ILKESTON UNITED	4-1	Maw 2, Holland, Green
	19	MANSFIELD TOWN	5-1	Maw 2, Allen 2, Green
	23	Notts County Res.	3-2	Bowers 2, Maw

?	SHIREBROOK	?	?
?	DENABY UNITED	?	?

The details of these two games are missing, but the final record shows that they were both won with a total of 10 goals scored and only one conceded.

1928/29

Aug	25	HULL CITY RES.	0-0	
	30	NEWARK TOWN	1-2	Allen
Sep	1	DONCASTER ROVERS	5-1	King 3, Allen, Moore
	5	Shirebrook	0-7	
	8	Gainsborough Trinity	0-2	
	22	GAINSBOROUGH TRINITY	2-2	Brandon 2
Oct	3	York City	1-3	Webb
	6	Lincoln City Res.	1-2	Maw
	20	FRICKLEY COLLIERY	2-1	Skull, Allen
Nov	3	CHESTERFIELD RES.	4-0	Wadsworth, Allen, Maw, Webb
	12	Rotherham Utd Res.	2-3	King, Whaley
	17	STAVELEY TOWN	6-1	Drury 3, Allen, Maw 2
	24	DENABY UNITED	2-0	Wadsworth, Maw
Dec	1	SCARBOROUGH	2-2	Maw 2
	8	Hull City Res.	1-1	Wadsworth
	15	GRANTHAM	2-1	Wadsworth, Allen
	22	BARNSLEY RES.	3-1	Allen, Maw, Bailey
	25	GRIMSBY TOWN RES	2-1	Allen 2
	26	Grimsby Town Res.	2-1	Wadsworth, Goy
	29	MEXBOROUGH ATHLETIC	4-2	Allen 2, Hall 2
Jan	1	Mexborough Athletic	0-0	
	5	Mansfield Town	0-5	
	12	BOSTON	1-2	Allen
	16	Chesterfield Res.	1-0	Allen
	19	Denaby United	2-2	Wadsworth, Maw
	26	WOMBWELL	2-2	Wadsworth, Brandon
	31	YORK CITY	3-2	Mooney, Smalley, Maw
Feb	2	Wombwell	1-1	Allen
	9	MANSFIELD TOWN	0-3	
	14	ROTHERHAM UTD RES	1-1	Smalley
	16	Doncaster Rovers Res.	1-3	Webb
	23	NOTTM FOREST RES	3-1	Smith, Maw, Webb
	28	Notts County Res.	2-6	Maw, Allen
Mar	2	Grantham	2-3	Maw, Allen
	7	Frickley Colliery	3-3	Smith, Maw 2
	9	NOTTS COUNTY RES	3-1	Smith 2, Maw
	14	SHIREBROOK	1-1	Smith
	16	Newark Town	2-1	Wadsworth, Maw
	23	Barnsley Res.	1-1	Webb
	25	Loughborough Corinthians	1-5	Courtney
	30	WORKSOP TOWN	4-0	Smith 2, Whaley, Naylor
Apr	1	Worksop Town	1-0	Smith
	2	Wath Athletic	0-4	
	11	LOUGHBOROUGH COR.	3-1	Smith 2, Mooney
	13	Boston	2-4	Smith 2
	17	Nottm Forest Res.	1-1	Smith
	20	LINCOLN CITY RES	5-2	Smith 2, Wadsworth 2, Webb
	27	Scarborough	2-2	Smalley 2
May	1	Staveley Town	1-4	Smith
	4	WATH ATHLETIC	7-2	Smith 3, Calladine 3, Allen

1929/30

Aug	31	HULL CITY RES.	3-1	Smalley, Calladine 2
Sep	5	Newark Town	1-1	Bailey
	7	Lincoln City Res.	0-2	
	14	GAINSBOROUGH TRINITY	5-0	Stringfellow, Smalley, Calladine 2, Beynon
	25	Shirebrook	3-1	Smalley 2, Bailey
	28	ROTHERHAM UTD RES	4-0	Simmons, Smalley, Calladine, Beynon
	30	Staveley Town	1-1	Simmons
Oct	7	LOUGHBOROUGH COR.	2-0	Calladine 2
	12	Gainsborough Trinity	1-4	Hackett
	26	Rotherham Utd Res.	1-3	Beynon
Nov	11	Chesterfield Res.	2-3	Kennedy, Beynon
	18	Wombwell	5-1	Stringfellow, Kennedy, Calladine 2, Beynon
	23	Grantham	1-2	Beynon
Dec	7	Worksop Town	5-3	Simmons, Beynon, Cross, Stanyon, Calladine
	21	HULL CITY RES.	4-1	Cross, Calladine 3
	25	GRIMSBY TOWN RES	1-1	Simmons
	26	Grimsby Town Res.	2-6	Baldwin 2
	28	MEXBOROUGH ATHLETIC	6-0	Simmons, Stringfellow, Baldwin, Calladine 2, Cooke
Jan	1	Frickley Colliery	5-1	Baldwin 2, Calladine 2, Cooke
	4	WOMBWELL	4-1	Simmons, Calladine, Baldwin, Cooke
	11	CHESTERFIELD RES.	3-0	Stringfellow, Baldwin, Calladine
	16	Nottm Forest Res.	3-5	Stringfellow, Baldwin, Beynon
	18	Barnsley Res.	1-5	Stringfellow
	23	DENABY UNITED	5-1	Stringfellow, Baldwin 3, Calladine
	25	NOTTM FOREST RES	5-3	Baldwin 2, Calladine, Beynon 2
	30	NOTTS COUNTY RES	1-2	Baldwin
Feb	1	Scarborough	1-1	Stringfellow
	8	GRANTHAM	4-1	Baldwin, Calladine, Beynon 2
	10	Denaby United	2-0	Cross, Calladine
	15	BARNSLEY RES.	2-2	Baldwin, Calladine
	20	WATH ATHLETIC	3-0	Stringfellow, Calladine, Beynon
	22	Doncaster Rovers Res	0-3	
	27	Wath Athletic	1-3	Osborne
Mar	1	WORKSOP TOWN	3-0	Crawford, Calladine, Beynon
	8	Boston	1-1	Baldwin
	12	Loughborough Corinthians	1-7	Calladine
	15	BOSTON	3-5	Baldwin, Calladine, Beynon
	17	FRICKLEY COLLIERY	2-0	Baldwin, Beynon
	22	Mansfield Town	3-1	Calladine, Beynon 2
	24	DONCASTER ROVERS RES	4-0	Whittingham, Crawford, Beynon 2
	27	Notts County Res.	0-3	
	29	LINCOLN CITY RES	2-1	Whittingham, Hackett
Apr	3	SHIREBROOK	1-0	Stringfellow
	5	Mexborough Athletic	1-3	Kennedy
	10	STAVELEY TOWN	9-0	Staniforth 2, Moore 2, Baldwin 3, Shaw, Benyon
	12	MANSFIELD TOWN	2-1	Stringfellow, Baldwin
	19	BRADFORD PARK AVE RES	2-5	Baldwin, Beynon
	21	Bradford Park Avenue Res	0-9	
	26	SCARBOROUGH	1-4	Kennedy
May	3	NEWARK TOWN	2-0	Simmons, Beynon

1930/31

Aug	30	Wombwell	1-3	Rawlings
Sep	1	WOMBWELL	2-1	Rawlings, Beynon
	6	BARNSLEY RES.	0-2	
	13	Lincoln City Res.	4-4	Whittingham, Green, Beynon, Oakton
	18	SCARBOROUGH	1-1	Green
	20	ROTHERHAM UTD RES	7-2	Rawlings 2, Stringfellow, Green 2, Pattison, Oakton
	27	GAINSBOROUGH TRINITY	2-1	Stringfellow, Richards
Oct	4	Doncaster Rovers Res	2-0	Rawlings, Stringfellow
	9	NEWARK TOWN	0-2	
	11	DENABY UNITED	4-0	Stringfellow, Whittingham 2, Green
	18	Barnsley Res.	2-6	Stringfellow, Oakton
	22	Gainsborough Trinity	0-4	
	25	LOUGHBOROUGH COR.	4-2	Pattison 2, Stringfellow, Beynon
Nov	1	Scarborough	4-2	Pattison 2, Stringfellow, Green
	8	NOTTS COUNTY RES	5-1	Pattison 3, Oakton, Beynon
Dec	6	Chesterfield Res.	4-4	Pattison 3, Foster
	13	SHIREBROOK	1-0	Beynon
	25	GRIMSBY TOWN RES	2-2	Pattison, Beynon
	27	Frickley Colliery	6-0	Pattison 4, Green, Oakton
Jan	1	Rotherham Utd Res.	2-2	Pattison, Green
	10	HULL CITY RES	1-2	Pattison
	17	LINCOLN CITY RES	0-5	
	24	Newark Town	0-1	
	31	BRADFORD PARK AVE RES	1-0	Beynon
Feb	7	DONCASTER ROVERS RES	3-1	Wainwright, Beynon 2
	12	Grimsby Town Res.	4-3	Rawlings 2, Wainwright, Stringfellow
	14	Boston	3-0	Oakton, Johnson, Beynon
	19	Hull City Res.	2-2	Rawlings 2
	21	BOSTON	1-1	Rawlings
	26	Mexborough Athletic	3-3	Rawlings 2, Pattison
Mar	5	Nottm Forest Res.	0-9	
	7	NOTTM FOREST RES	1-0	Pattison
	12	MEXBOROUGH ATHLETIC	5-2	Pattison 3, Stringfellow, Oakton
	14	Shirebrook	0-3	
	18	Bradford City Res.	1-4	Pattison
	21	GRANTHAM	2-2	Rawlings, Oakton
	23	Denaby United	2-2	Oakton 2
	28	Notts County Res.	2-6	Rawlings 2
	30	Grantham	1-3	Johnson
Apr	4	Bradford Park Ave Res.	1-1	Cross
	6	Mansfield Town	4-3	Rawlings, Johnson 3
	11	Loughborough Corinthians	1-1	Pattison
	18	BRADFORD CITY RES	3-1	Stringfellow, Pattison 2
	20	FRICKLEY COLLIERY	3-1	Rawlings, Pattison 2
	25	CHESTERFIELD RES.	1-2	Pattison
May	2	MANSFIELD TOWN	0-2	

1931/32

Aug	29	MANSFIELD TOWN RES	3-2	Adams 2, Dawson
	31	BOSTON	2-1	Dawson, Isaac
Sep	5	SCARBOROUGH	0-2	
	7	Denaby United	2-2	Smith, Edding
	12	NOTTS COUNTY RES	0-3	
	19	Gainsborough Trinity	0-3	
	21	MEXBOROUGH ATHLETIC	4-1	Adams 2, Reed, Baynham
	26	GAINSBOROUGH TRINITY	2-4	Methven, Hubbard
Oct	3	Rotherham Utd Res.	4-0	Methven, Reed 2, Welbourne
	10	FRICKLEY COLLIERY	4-2	Methven 2, Hubbard 2
	17	BARNSLEY RES.	4-2	Methven, Dawson, Baynham, Smith(og)
	24	Notts County Res.	0-3	
	31	LINCOLN CITY RES	1-0	Dawson
Nov	7	Mexborough Athletic	6-1	Dawson, Reed 3, Daws 2
	21	Barnsley Res.	1-6	Hubbard
Dec	5	Lincoln City Res.	4-4	Cross, Reed, Daws 2
	19	NOTTM FOREST RES	2-1	Baynham, Osbourne
	25	GRIMSBY TOWN RES	2-4	Stimpson, Whittingham
	26	Grimsby Town Res.	0-3	
Jan	1	Wombwell	3-5	Cross, Baynham, Reed
	2	Bradford Park Ave Res.	0-6	
	9	Frickley Colliery	3-2	Methven 2, Dawson
	16	GRANTHAM	4-1	Cross, Hubbard 3
	23	CHESTERFIELD RES	3-1	Hubbard 2, Reed
	30	DONCASTER ROVERS RES	1-3	Reed
Feb	6	Grantham	0-3	
	13	ROTHERHAM UTD RES	3-0	Smelt, Dawson, Reed
	20	Doncaster Rovers Res	0-3	
	27	Bradford City Res	3-1	Methven 2, Reed
Mar	5	LOUGHBOROUGH COR	0-0	
	9	York City Res.	0-6	
	12	Boston	2-3	Methven, Reed
	19	BRADFORD CITY RES	2-2	Hubbard 2
	25	Hull City Res.	1-1	Methven
	26	BRADFORD PARK AVE RES	1-0	Hubbard
	28	HULL CITY RES	3-2	Methven, Hubbard 2
Apr	2	Nottm Forest Res.	1-3	Hubbard
	9	NEWARK TOWN	1-0	Smelt
	11	Loughborough Corinthians	1-1	Smelt
	13	Mansfield Town Res.	0-0	
	16	Chesterfield Res.	2-4	Methven, Hubbard
	23	Scarborough	0-1	
	25	WOMBWELL	2-2	Cross, Meadows
	30	DENABY UNITED	3-3	Brown, Hubbard, Tucker
May	5	YORK CITY RES.	2-0	Methven, Hubbard
	7	Newark Town	1-2	Hubbard

1932/33

Aug	27	Wombwell	3-2	Tucker 2, Chapman
	29	WOMBWELL	3-0	Tucker, Patton, Chapman
Sep	3	SCARBOROUGH	0-4	
	10	Scarborough	0-6	
	17	GAINSBOROUGH TRINITY	3-0	Hubbard, Baynham, Murfin
	24	Chesterfield Res.	3-3	Price 2, Chapman
	26	BRADFORD PARK AVE RES	3-0	Price, Hubbard, Murfin
Oct	1	Mansfield Town Res.	2-1	Hubbard, Chapman
	8	NOTTS COUNTY RES.	2-2	Hubbard, Milson
	12	Bradford Park Ave Res.	0-7	
	15	Gainsborough Trinity	4-4	Price 2, Baynham, Murfin
	22	Doncaster Rovers Res.	3-1	Price, Hubbard, Murfin
	29	Rotherham Utd Res.	2-2	Price 2
Nov	5	Barnsley Res.	1-4	Sumpter
	19	YORK CITY RES.	2-3	Price, Murfin
Dec	3	ROTHERHAM UTD RES	5-0	Price, Hubbard 2, Murfin
	10	York City Res.	4-2	Price, Hubbard 2, Murfin
	17	Lincoln City Res.	1-7	Hubbard
	24	BRADFORD CITY RES	4-2	Price, Chapman 2, Murfin
	27	Grimsby Town Res.	0-1	
	31	GRANTHAM	4-1	Price 2, Hubbard, Baynham
Jan	2	Mexborough Athletic	3-2	Sharman, Baynham, Murfin
	21	BARNSLEY RES.	4-1	Price 3, Chapman
	28	Grantham	3-2	Price, Oates, Chapman
Feb	2	Frickley Colliery	3-1	Price, Hubbard, Chapman
	4	LINCOLN CITY RES	1-2	Price
	16	DENABY UNITED	3-1	Price, Chapman, Tucker
	18	Boston	2-5	Chapman, Tucker
	25	DONCASTER ROVERS RES	4-1	Hubbard 2, Chapman, Murfin
Mar	4	BOSTON	3-2	Hubbard, Tucker 2
	6	Denaby United	1-5	Hubbard
	11	Notts County Res.	0-4	
	18	MEXBOROUGH ATHLETIC	3-1	Hubbard, Chapman, Price
	22	Loughborough Corinthians	1-5	Chapman
	25	Bradford City Res.	0-2	
Apr	3	LOUGHBOROUGH COR	3-1	Hubbard 2, Chapman
	8	MANSFIELD TOWN RES	0-1	
	14	Hull City Res.	3-1	Price, Hubbard, Tucker
	15	FRICKLEY COLLIERY	0-0	
	17	HULL CITY RES.	6-0	Hubbard 4, Chapman 2
	22	Newark Town	6-3	Price, Hubbard 2, Oates, Tucker, Murfin
	27	GRIMSBY TOWN RES	0-1	
	29	CHESTERFIELD RES.	2-5	Hubbard, Chapman
May	6	NEWARK TOWN	4-2	Oates 3, Chapman

1933/34

Aug	26	BARNSLEY RES.	5-0	Pattison 3, Smalley, Allen
	30	Scarborough	2-2	Pattison 2
Sep	2	Boston United	2-0	Pattison, Sumpter
	9	Gainsborough Trinity	2-1	Pattison, Smalley
	16	CHESTERFIELD RES.	6-0	Pattison 2, Barry 2, Swain, Allen
	23	Rotherham Utd Res.	0-2	
Oct	7	GAINSBOROUGH TRINITY	2-1	Smalley, Starkey
	21	DENABY UNITED	3-0	Smalley, Mills 2
Nov	4	LINCOLN CITY RES	3-1	Pattison 3
	18	ROTHERHAM UTD RES	8-1	Pattison, Sumpter 3, Oates 2, Nicholson, Mills
Dec	2	BRADFORD CITY RES	3-2	Pattison 2, Mills
	9	Notts County Res.	2-4	Pattison, Sumpter
	23	Doncaster Rovers Res	2-4	Smalley, Allen
	25	Grimsby Town Res.	1-5	Pattison
	26	GRIMSBY TOWN RES	3-9	Pattison, Reed, Mills
Jan	13	DONCASTER ROVERS RES	1-1	Pattison
	20	YORK CITY RES.	6-1	Pattison 2, Sumpter, Allen, Reed 2
	27	Denaby United	1-1	Pattison
Feb	3	NOTTS COUNTY RES	3-1	Pattison 2, Allen
	10	Lincoln City Res.	2-2	Pattison, Reed
	17	Barnsley Res.	2-3	Cross 2
Mar	3	Mexborough Athletic	2-6	Barry, Smalley
	17	BOSTON UNITED	1-0	Burton
	24	SCARBOROUGH	1-1	Oates
	30	Hull City Res.	0-4	
	31	BRADFORD PARK AVE RES	5-3	Sumpter 2, Allen, Mills, Roberts
Apr	2	HULL CITY RES.	0-3	
	7	Chesterfield Res.	0-4	
	14	Bradford City Res.	1-4	Barry
	21	Bradford Park Avenue	0-3	
	26	York City Res.	1-4	Smalley
	28	MEXBOROUGH ATHLETIC	6-0	Sumpter 3, Davidson, Allen, Reed

1934/35

Aug	25	Mexborough Athletic	3-1	Pattison, Allen, Lax
Sep	3	PETERBOROUGH UNITED	0-0	
	8	DENABY UNITED	4-2	Fenwick, Pattison, Cross, Lax
	15	GAINSBOROUGH TRINITY	2-3	Barley, Lax
	22	Lincoln City Res.	1-1	Roberts
	29	NOTTS COUNTY RES.	2-1	Pattison, Lax
Oct	6	Denaby United	4-1	Mills 2, Allen 2
	13	BRADFORD CITY RES	0-1	
	20	BOSTON UNITED	4-2	Barley, Lynch 2, Barkley
	27	Gainsborough Trinity	0-2	
Nov	3	CHESTERFIELD RES.	4-2	Lynch, Pattison 2, Lax
	17	Bradford City Res.	0-1	
Dec	1	LINCOLN CITY RES	1-1	Roberts
	8	Norwich City Res.	0-5	
	15	BRADFORD PARK AVE RES	1-1	Noble
	22	Hull City Res.	1-7	Barkley
	25	GRIMSBY TOWN RES	1-0	Allen
	26	Grimsby Town Res.	0-3	
	29	NORWICH CITY RES	3-2	Barley, Rushby, Barkley
Jan	5	ROTHERHAM UTD RES	2-0	Mills, Lax
	12	MEXBOROUGH ATHLETIC	4-1	Barkley, Mills, Allen, Lax
	26	Doncaster Rovers Res	1-2	Noble
Feb	2	Boston United	2-1	Pattison, Lax
	9	Barnsley Res.	0-4	
	16	DONCASTER ROVERS RES	0-2	
	23	Frickley Colliery	0-4	
	28	Notts County Res.	1-0	Barley
Mar	2	Rotherham Utd Res.	1-4	Noble
	16	Chesterfield Res.	0-4	
	21	GRANTHAM	2-0	Pattison 2
	30	BARNSLEY RES.	2-3	Mills, Nicholson
Apr	4	Peterborough United	0-2	
	9	Grantham	0-5	
	19	Scarborough	5-3	Mills 3, Allen, Lax
	20	HULL CITY RES.	4-2	Noble 2, Fenwick, Allen
	23	SCARBOROUGH	6-2	Barley, Noble 3, Fenwick 2
	27	Bradford Park Ave Res	1-3	Noble
May	4	Frickley Colliery	5-1	Barley, Pattison 2, Mills 2

1935/36

Aug	31	MEXBOROUGH ATHLETIC	2-2	Snaith, Roberts
Sep	7	Gainsborough Trinity	0-3	
	14	BRADFORD CITY RES.	2-0	Snaith, Roberts
	16	GAINSBOROUGH TRINITY	2-1	Barker, Davies
	21	Lincoln City Res.	8-5	Kilsby 2, Barker, Snaith 3, Roberts, Davies
	23	Burton Town	1-6	Roberts
	28	ROTHERHAM UTD RES	3-3	Kilsby 2, Barker
Oct	5	BOSTON UNITED	2-0	Roberts, Davies
	12	Notts County Res.	0-3	
	19	BARNSLEY RES.	1-2	Lewis
	26	Chesterfield Res.	3-2	Lewis, Snaith 2
Nov	2	NOTTS COUNTY RES.	0-2	
	9	PETERBOROUGH UNITED	1-0	Snaith
	23	NORWICH CITY RES	2-0	Snaith, Roberts
Dec	7	Bradford City Res.	1-2	Allen
	21	Denaby United	1-5	Davies
	25	GRIMSBY TOWN RES	5-0	Kilsby, Lewis, Snaith 2, Roberts
	26	Grimsby Town Res.	3-2	Kilsby, Lewis, Roberts
	28	Barnsley Res.	2-6	Allen 2
Jan	1	Frickley Colliery	3-3	Snaith 2, Roberts
	4	LINCOLN CITY RES.	1-4	Snaith
	11	DENABY UNITED	1-1	Allen
	25	DONCASTER ROVERS RES	0-0	
Feb	1	Rotherham Utd Res	2-2	Roberts, Allen
	8	Grantham	0-2	
	15	SCARBOROUGH	2-0	Barker, Allen
	22	Mexborough Athletic	8-3	Kilsby, Noble 2, Snaith 3, Roberts, Allen
	29	CHESTERFIELD RES.	2-3	Snaith, roberts
Mar	14	GRANTHAM	1-0	Kilsby
	21	Peterborough United	1-3	Noble
	25	Norwich City Res.	2-2	Kilsby, Noble
	28	Doncaster Rovers Res.	1-0	Allen
Apr	2	Boston United	1-3	Kilsby
	4	BRADFORD PARK AVE RES	4-1	Kilby, Lewis 3
	10	Hull City Res.	0-1	
	11	FRICKLEY COLLIERY	2-1	Snaith, Oates
	13	HULL CITY RES.	0-0	
	18	Scarborough	1-0	Snaith
	25	BURTON TOWN	2-3	Chapman 2
May	2	Bradford Park Ave Res	0-1	

1936/37

Aug	29	Newark Town	1-3	Porter
	31	HULL CITY RES.	1-1	Barker
Sep	5	GAINSBOROUGH TRINITY	2-0	Porter, Beckett
	7	Denaby United	3-1	Porter, Norris, Barker
	16	Scarborough	1-2	Moore
	19	NOTTM FOREST RES.	1-3	Norris
	26	MANSFIELD TOWN RES	2-1	Norris, Barker
Oct	3	Gainsborough Trinity	0-3	
	12	NEWARK TOWN	0-2	
	17	Burton Town	1-3	Norris
	24	Grimsby Town Res.	0-3	
	29	Nottm Forest Res.	1-2	Smithson
	31	GRIMSBY TOWN RES.	0-3	
Nov	7	FRICKLEY COLLIERY	5-1	Chapman, Pattison, Smithson 2, Bartley
	21	SCARBOROUGH	2-0	Norris, Allen
Dec	12	Peterborough United	5-3	Norris, Smithson 4
	19	CHESTERFIELD RES.	0-0	
	25	BURTON TOWN	2-0	Porter, Smithson
Jan	2	Grantham	0-7	
	9	Bradford Park Ave Res.	1-6	Smithson
	23	BRADFORD PARK AVE RES	1-0	Moses
	30	Mansfield Town Res.	1-4	Porter
Feb	6	BARNSLEY RES.	2-1	Norris 2
	11	Doncaster Rovers Res	0-2	
	13	Barnsley Res.	2-1	Porter, Jones
	20	GRANTHAM	1-1	Norris
	27	Boston United	0-1	
Mar	6	DENABY UNITED	7-2	Porter 4, Gardiner, Moses 2
	15	Chesterfield Res.	2-3	Porter, Horton
	20	BRADFORD CITY RES	3-2	Porter 2, Norris
	26	Lincoln City Res.	2-3	Porter, Norris
	27	PETERBOROUGH UNITED	4-0	Porter 2, Norris, Horton
	29	LINCOLN CITY RES	3-2	Porter 2, Moses
	30	Rotherham Utd Res.	1-6	Porter
Apr	3	BOSTON UNITED	3-0	Norris, Moses 2
	5	DONCASTER ROVERS RES	1-4	Norris
	10	Bradford City Res.	4-1	Smithson 4
	15	Hull City Res.	0-2	
	17	Notts County Res.	5-2	Smithson 3, Horton 2
	21	Frickley Colliery	0-2	
	24	NOTTS COUNTY RES.	3-1	Smithson, Norris, Horton
May	1	ROTHERHAM UTD RES	3-2	Smithson, Bett, Horton

1937/38

Aug	28	DENABY UNITED	5-0	Johnson 2, Bett 2, Wilkinson
Sep	1	NOTTM FOREST RES	3-2	Norris, Bett, Wilkinson
	4	Peterborough United	3-3	Whittaker, Stocks, Wilkinson
	6	SCARBOROUGH	1-2	Lewis
	11	GRIMSBY TOWN RES	3-0	Lewis 2, Stocks
	16	Grantham	0-0	
	18	BARNSLEY RES.	4-3	Lewis, Johnson 2, Bett
	25	Gainsborough Trinity	0-1	
	27	PETERBOROUGH UNITED	5-0	Lewis 2, Johnson 2, Bett
Oct	2	GAINSBOROUGH TRINITY	2-3	Baldry, Bett
	6	Lincoln City Res.	3-4	Johnson 3
	9	Denaby United	3-2	Lewis, Proctor, Wilkinson
	16	Grimsby Town Res.	3-2	Baldry 2, Wilkinson
	23	Boston United	3-6	Baldry, Johnson 2
Nov	6	Frickley Colliery	1-2	Johnson
	20	ROTHERHAM UNITED RES	6-0	Baldry 2, Lewis, Johnson 2, Bett
Dec	4	MANSFIELD TOWN RES	4-1	Baldry, Johnson, Lewis, Butler
	11	Barnsley Res.	2-4	Wilkinson 2
	18	Bradford Park Ave Res	0-3	
	27	DONCASTER ROVERS RES	1-2	Wilkinson
	27	SHREWSBURY TOWN	2-1	Norris, Allen
Jan	1	Newark Town	5-2	Norris 2, Johnson 3,
	15	FRICKLEY COLLIERY	4-0	Baldry, Johnson, Allen, Wilkinson
	22	Mansfield Town Res.	1-1	Johnson
	29	Bradford City Res.	6-4	Norris, Lewis 2, Johnson, Stocks, Wilkinson
Feb	12	BOSTON UNITED	3-0	Baldry, Johnson 2
	19	Rotherham United Res	0-0	
	26	Notts County Res.	2-2	Johnson 2
Mar	5	BURTON TOWN	4-3	Lloyd 2, Stocks, Wilkinson
	12	Shrewsbury Town	1-5	Johnson
	19	NOTTS COUNTY RES	4-0	Johnson 2, wilkinson 2
	26	BRADFORD CITY RES	1-3	Lloyd
Apr	2	BRADFORD PARK AVE RES	3-1	Johnson 3
	7	LINCOLN CITY RES	4-2	Lewis 3, Johnson
	9	Burton Town	1-2	Johnson
	15	Hull City Res.	2-1	Wilkinson 2
	18	HULL CITY RES.	7-1	Norris, Lewis, Johnson 3, Clarvis, Wilkinson
	21	Doncaster Rovers Res	0-1	
	23	Scarborough	1-1	Lewis
	30	NEWARK TOWN	2-1	Lewis, Wilkinson
May	2	GRANTHAM	4-3	Johnson 2, Proctor, Wilkinson
	7	Nottm Forest Res.	0-1	

1938/39

Aug	27	Mansfield Town Res.	2-0	Johnson, Fleetwood
	29	NEWARK TOWN	10-3	Johnson 5, Norris, Fleetwood 2, Nightingale, Own goal (Hunt)
Sep	5	MANSFIELD TOWN RES	3-1	Norris, Allen, Nightingale
	10	Bradford Park Ave Res	3-3	Johnson 2, Nightingale
	15	Grantham	3-1	Johnson 3
	17	SHREWSBURY TOWN	3-1	Johnson 2, Norris
	19	Gainsborough Trinity	1-1	Wilkinson
	24	GAINSBOROUGH TRINITY	2-0	Johnson, Fleetwood
	28	Scarborough	2-2	Johnson 2
Oct	8	GRANTHAM	4-1	Johnson 2, Norris, Nightingale
	20	NOTTM FOREST RES	2-3	Fleetwood 2
	22	Peterborough United	3-0	Johnson, Norris 2
Nov	5	Newark Town	3-0	Johnson, Fleetwood, Nightingale
	19	GRIMSBY TOWN RES.	5-0	Johnson 3, Oxley, Nightingale
Dec	3	NOTTS COUNTY RES.	8-0	Johnson 2, Norris 2, Fleetwood, Nightingale 2, Oxley
	17	Bradford City Res.	0-5	
	24	BRADFORD PARK AVE RES	5-2	Johnson 2, Nightingale 2, Wilkinson
	27	DENABY UNITED	9-1	Johnson 6, Fleetwood, Lacy, Nightingale
	31	Shrewsbury Town	2-4	Fleetwood, Nightingale
Jan	2	Denaby United	10-0	Johnson 2, Norris 2, Fleetwood 2, Nightingale 2, Wilkinson 2
	14	LINCOLN CITY RES	4-1	Johnson, Norris, Wilkinson 2
	28	BOSTON UNITED	3-1	Johnson, Wilkinson, Nightingale
Feb	4	Barnsley Res.	4-3	Johnson, Fleetwood, Nightingale, Staniland
	9	BARNSLEY RES.	5-1	Johnson 3, Fleetwood 2
	11	Doncaster Rovers Res.	0-0	
	16	Notts County Res.	2-2	Johnson, Wilkinson
	18	ROTHERHAM UTD RES	0-0	
	25	Grimsby Town Res.	2-2	Fleetwood, Nightingale
Mar	4	DONCASTER ROVERS RES	5-2	Johnson 4, Nightingale
	6	PETERBOROUGH UNITED	2-1	Fleetwood, Nightingale
	18	Nottm Forest Res.	2-1	Fleetwood, Wilkinson
	22	Burton Town	1-2	Nightingale
	25	BRADFORD CITY RES	4-0	Norris, Nightingale 2, Wilkinson
Apr	1	LINCOLN CITY RES	1-0	Harris
	7	HULL CITY RES.	2-0	Harris, Nightingale
	8	Boston United	4-3	Johnson 2, Harris, Nightingale
	10	Hull City Res.	2-4	Harris, Norris
	15	BURTON TOWN	2-0	Johnson, Wilkinson
	17	SCARBOROUGH	0-1	
	24	FRICKLEY COLLIERY	4-2	Johnson 2, Fleetwood, Harris
	27	Rotherham Utd Res.	2-2	Fleetwood, Nightingale
	29	Frickley Colliery	2-1	Nightingale 2

1939/40

Aug	26	Rotherham Utd Res.	3-1	Campbell, Maw, J.Millington
	28	SHREWSBURY TOWN	4-2	Campbell 2, Maw, Rickards
Sep	1	GRIMSBY TOWN RES	1-2	Campbell

The official competition was suspended at this stage due to the outbreak of war.
An unofficial wartime competition was introduced, split into two parts.

Part 1

Oct	28	Newark Town	5-2	Nightingale 2, Maw, Norris 2
Nov	4	GRANTHAM	5-2	Nightingale 3, Swain, Maw
	11	Frickley Colliery	3-5	Maw, Norris 2
	18	NEWARK TOWN	2-1	Robertshaw, Fleetwood
	25	BOSTON UNITED	7-0	Nightingale 5, Maw, Norris
Dec	9	FRICKLEY COLLIERY	3-0	Nightingale 2, Norris
	16	Grantham	2-2	Maw, Fleetwood
	23	DENABY UNITED	6-1	Nighhtingale 2, Johnson, Fleetwood 3
	25	GAINSBOROUGH TRINITY	7-3	Nightingale 2, Johnson 2, Maw, Norris, Fleetwood
	26	Gainsborough Trinity	8-2	Nightingale 6, Norris, Fleetwood
	30	Boston United	1-0	Nightingale
Jan	6	Peterborough United	1-1	Nightingale
	13	PETERBOROUGH UNITED	3-6	Nightingale 2, Fleetwood
	20	Denaby United	2-2	Nightingale, Fleetwood

Part 2

Feb	24	BOSTON UNITED	8-2	Nightingale 2, Maw 2, Fleetwood 2, Johnson, Greaves
Mar	2	Boston United	0-2	
	9	DENABY UNITED	3-0	Nightingale 2, Johnson
	16	Frickley Colliery	3-1	Johnson 3
	22	GAINSBOROUGH TRINITY	5-1	Nightingale, Maw, Johnson 2, Greaves
	25	Gainsborough Trinity	3-2	Nightingale, Johnson, Own goal (Carter)
	30	Peterborough United	3-5	Johnson 2, Fleetwood
Apr	6	PETERBOROUGH UNITED	4-1	Nightingale 2, Fleetwood 2
	13	Grantham	8-0	Nightingale 4, Johnson 2, Swain, Fleetwood
	27	FRICKLEY COLLIERY	3-3	Nightingale, Johnson, Swain
May	4	Newark Town	2-1	Maw, Johnson
	11	GRANTHAM	5-0	Nightingale, Johnson 2, Swain, Own goal (Archer)
	13	Denaby United	2-0	Johnson 2

Fixtures for Part 2 were never completed. The second half of the competition was abandoned and the first half counted as the unofficial Championship.

Friendlies played by the club were as follows:

Sep	23	BARNSLEY RES.	5-3	Norris, Maw, Fleetwood 2, Nightingale
	30	GAINSBOROUGH TRINITY	3-2	Maw, Johnson, Norris
Oct	7	Gainsborough Trinity	2-1	Maw, Norris
	14	LINCOLN CITY	5-2	Nightingale 3, Norris, Fleetwood
	21	GRIMSBY TOWN RES	5-2	Maw 2, Nightingale 2, Fleetwood
Dec	12	BRADFORD PARK AVENUE	2-1	Nightingale, Own goal (Stephens)
May	18	Peterborough United	2-3	Johnson 2

This latter match was described as "Champions versus Runners Up"

1940/41 to 1944/45: Second World War

1945/46

Aug	25	MANSFIELD TOWN RES	6-1	Marriott, Leeman 2, Carver 3
Sep	1	Notts County Res.	0-3	
	8	Lincoln City Res.	3-0	Fleetwood 2, Redhead
	15	GAINSBOROUGH TRINITY	4-1	Leeman 3, Carver
	22	BRADFORD PARK AVE RES	3-1	Fleetwood, Carver 2
	29	Gainsborough Trinity	2-3	Johnson, Marriott
Oct	6	NOTTS COUNTY RES	3-3	Johnson 2, Proctor
	13	RANSOME & MARLES	1-2	Johnson
	27	Barnsley Res.	3-1	Leeman, Carver 2
Nov	10	BARNSLEY RES.	2-1	Gratton, Carver
	17	OLLERTON COLLIERY	5-1	Marriott, Fleetwood, Swain, Carver 2
	24	Boston United	2-1	Leeman, Swain
Dec	1	Ransome & Marles	0-2	
	15	Rotherham United Res	1-1	Carver
	22	ROTHERHAM UTD RES	1-1	Redhead
	25	GRIMSBY TOWN RES	2-2	Carver 2
	26	Grimsby Town Res.	3-4	Marriott, Sheen 2
	29	Lincoln City Res.	4-2	Johnson 3, Wilson
Jan	5	Frickley Colliery	4-5	Johnson 2, Wilson, Marriott
	12	PETERBOROUGH UNITED	1-0	Sheen
	19	Shrewsbury Town	0-0	
	26	Denaby United	4-2	Carver 4
Feb	2	GRANTHAM	3-1	Stewart, Carver 2
	9	NOTTM FOREST RES	2-0	Heath 2
	16	Peterborough United	1-3	Heath
Mar	2	SHREWSBURY TOWN	2-3	Sheen, Robertshaw
	16	Nottm Forest Res.	4-0	Priestley 3, Robertshaw
	23	FRICKLEY COLLIERY	3-1	Sheen 3
	30	Grantham	0-3	
Apr	6	Bradford Park Ave Res	0-4	
	10	Mansfield Town Res.	0-4	
	13	DENABY UNITED	4-1	Burton 3, Wallace
	19	Donacster Rovers' Res	4-1	Stock, Empson, Leeman, Wallace
	22	DONCASTER ROVERS RES	1-3	Johnson
	27	BOSTON UNITED	2-2	Robertshaw 2
	28	Ollerton Colliery	2-3	Robertshaw 2

1946/47

Aug	31	MANSFIELD TOWN RES	5-4	Bowers, Wynne 3, Wallace
Sep	5	SCARBOROUGH	4-1	Marriott, Bowers, Wynne, Robertshaw
	7	Shrewsbury Town	1-3	Wallace
	14	BARNSLEY RES.	2-3	Marriott, Wynne
	19	Boston United	2-2	Bowers, Wynne
	23	Gainsborough Trinity	2-0	Bowers, Wallace
	28	DONCASTER ROVERS RES	3-3	Bowers, Robertshaw
Oct	12	GAINSBOROUGH TRINITY	0-3	
	26	Rotherham United Res	2-0	Wallace 2
Nov	9	Bradford Park Ave Res	1-3	Marriott
	23	NOTTS COUNTY RES	6-1	Bowers 3, Wynne 3
Dec	7	FRICKLEY COLLIERY	9-0	Marriott, Bowers 4, Wynne 3, R.Jones
	21	Lincoln City Res.	3-0	Wynne, Robertshaw 2
	25	GRIMSBY TOWN RES	3-3	Bowers 3
	26	Grimsby Town Res.	1-1	Wynne
	28	Mansfield Town Res.	3-3	Bowers 2, Robertshaw
Jan	1	Denaby United	2-3	Norris, Robertshaw
	4	Notts County Res.	5-1	Bowers 3, Harper, R.Jones
	11	BRADFORD PARK AVE RES	5-1	Norris 2, Bowers, Rodi, Wallace
	16	DENABY UNITED	7-1	Norris 3, Bowers 2, Rodi, Harper
	18	Barnsley Res.	1-2	Bowers
	25	Scarborough	2-1	Bowers, Marriott
Feb	1	PETERBOROUGH UNITED	3-0	Bowers, Marriott, Own goal (Wilson)
	20	BOSTON UNITED	1-0	Bowers
Mar	6	RANSOME & MARLES	5-1	Bowers 2, Robertshaw 3
	29	SHREWSBURY TOWN	6-2	Bowers 3, Norris 2, Hydes
Apr	4	Hull City Res.	2-0	Robertshaw 2
	5	NOTTM FOREST RES	1-1	Bowers
	7	HULL CITY RES.	3-3	Bowers 2, Wynne
	12	ROTHERHAM UTD RES	6-1	Bowers 3, Norris 2, Hydes
	19	Grantham	1-0	Bowers
	21	OLLERTON COLLIERY	1-0	Wynne
	26	Bradford City Res.	4-1	Bowers 3, Robertshaw
May	3	BRADFORD CITY RES	4-0	Bowers 3, Robertshaw
	10	GRANTHAM	5-2	Bowers 2, Hydes 3
	15	Doncaster Rovers Res	0-2	
	17	Peterborough United	0-1	
	24	LINCOLN CITY RES	3-0	Norris, Hydes, Robertshaw
	26	Ransome & Marles	2-1	Hydes, Robertshaw
	31	Frickley Colliery	1-3	Bowers
Jun	2	Nottm Forest Res.	2-2	Bowers, Wallace
	14	Ollerton Colliery	1-3	Bowers

1947/48

Aug	23	Bradford City Res.	4-3	Bowers 2, Wallace, Norris
	28	SCARBOROUGH	1-0	Brownsword (pen)
	30	BRADFORD CITY RES	3-1	Hydes 2, Norris
Sep	1	Denaby United	2-4	Wynne, Pinchbeck
	6	Notts County Res.	2-2	Robertshaw, Wallace
	10	GAINSBOROUGH TRINITY	3-1	Bowers, Rowney, Norris
	13	Shrewsbury Town	1-1	Bowers
	22	Gainsborough Trinity	1-2	Robertshaw
	27	Nottm Forest Res.	1-2	Bowers
Oct	11	York City Res.	1-1	Bowers
	25	NOTTS COUNTY RES	3-0	Bowers 2, Pinchbeck
Nov	8	Rotherham United Res	2-1	Pinchbeck, Robertshaw
Dec	6	OLLERTON COLLIERY	7-1	Bowers 6, Rowney
	13	Lincoln City Res.	1-2	Crack
	20	Mansfield Town Res	1-1	Bowers
	25	GRIMSBY TOWN RES	2-1	Bowers, Robertshaw
	26	Grimsby Town Res.	1-2	Robertshaw
	27	PETERBOROUGH UNITED	7-1	Norris, Rowney 2, Wallace, Bowers 3
Jan	3	Scarborough	1-1	Bowers
	10	Ransome & Marles	2-2	Robertshaw, Wallace
	17	Donacster Rovers Res.	2-1	Rowney, Bowers
	24	Bradford Park Ave Res	2-1	Bowers 2
	31	GRANTHAM	1-0	Robertshaw
Feb	7	Peterborough United	1-2	Rowney
	14	BRADFORD PARK AVE RES	1-0	Smith
	19	ROTHERHAM UTD RES	3-2	Rowney 2, Smith
	28	NOTTM FOREST RES	0-0	
Mar	6	BOSTON UNITED	2-1	Wallace, Rowney
	13	Ollerton Colliery	5-1	Smith, Bowers 2, Johnson 2
	18	DENABY UNITED	0-0	
	20	Grantham	1-5	Bowers
	26	Hull City Res.	1-3	Rowney
	27	RANSOME & MARLES	4-3	Johnson, Bowers 2, Wallace
	29	HULL CITY RES.	2-0	Rowney 2
Apr	1	MANSFIELD TOWN RES	1-1	Bowers
	3	SHREWSBURY TOWN	2-0	Johnson 2
	10	YORK CITY RES.	3-0	Own goal (Andrews), Rowney, Wallace
	14	Frickley Colliery	3-1	Johnson 2, Bowers
	17	Boston United	2-3	Johnson, Wallace
	22	FRICKLEY COLLIERY	2-0	Wallace, Bowers
	24	DONCASTER ROVERS RES	3-0	Johnson 2, Norris
	26	LINCOLN CITY RES	2-4	Robertshaw, Rowney

1948/49

Aug	21	Lincoln City Res.	4-1	J.Taylor 2, Murphy 2
	25	Scarborough	3-0	Murphy 2, Little
	28	RANSOME & MARLES	1-0	Wallace
Sep	4	SHREWSBURY TOWN	0-1	
	6	Gainsborough Trinity	2-5	Rowney, Wallace
	11	Nottm Forest Res.	5-0	Murphy 2, Watford, J.Taylor, Whitehead
	18	York City Res.	4-3	Murphy 2, J.Taylor, Barker
	23	GAINSBOROUGH TRINITY	7-0	Murphy 4, J.Taylor 2, Wallace
	30	FRICKLEY COLLIERY	2-1	J.Taylor, Barker
Oct	2	NOTTM FOREST RES	3-1	Murphy 2, Rowney
	9	Mansfield Town Res	0-2	
	14	GOOLE TOWN	3-0	Murphy 2, Wallace
	16	NOTTS COUNTY RES	3-0	Murphy 2, J.Taylor
	23	Boston United	2-1	Rowney, Wallace
	30	MANSFIELD TOWN RES	5-1	Little, Rowney, Murphy, Wallace, Barker
Nov	6	Denaby United	2-0	Murphy 2
	20	Doncaster Rovers Res	3-1	Murphy, Rowney, Barker
Dec	18	LINCOLN CITY RES	3-3	Little, Rowney, Barker
	25	GRIMSBY TOWN RES	0-1	
	27	Grimsby Town Res.	1-1	Rowney
Jan	1	Notts County Res.	0-1	
	8	PETERBOROUGH UNITED	4-1	Murphy, Little 2, Barker
	15	DENABY UNITED	4-1	Murphy 2, Little, Dale
	22	Rotherham United Res	1-2	Lindley
	29	GOOLE TOWN	3-2	Little, J.Taylor 2
Feb	5	BRADFORD APRK AVE RES	5-1	Murphy 3, J.Taylor 2
	12	Grantham	1-2	Whitehead
	19	Bradford Park Ave Res	2-4	Murphy 2
	26	YORK CITY RES.	3-0	Murphy 2, Bowers
Mar	5	Peterborough United	3-4	Whitfield, Bowers 2
	19	ROTHERHAM UTD RES	1-1	Bowers
	26	Raansome & Marles	4-1	Little, Whitfield, Bowers, J.Taylor
	30	Frickley Colliery	5-0	Whitfield, Bowers 2, J.Taylor, R.E.Taylor
Apr	2	GRANTHAM	1-3	Barker
	9	Bradford City Res.	1-1	Whitfield
	15	HULL CITY RES.	3-0	Whitfield 2, Bowers
	16	DONCASTER ROVERS RES	0-0	
	18	Hull City Res.	1-1	Watson
	23	Shrewsbury Town	1-5	Bowers
	28	SCARBOROUGH	2-1	Bowers, Whitfield
	30	BRADFORD CITY RES	5-0	Bowers 3, Dale, Watson
May	2	BOSTON UNITED	1-2	Bowers

1949/50

Aug	20	LINCOLN CITY RES	3-0	Barker 2, Heseltine
	27	Shrewsbury Town	1-1	Whitfield
Sep	1	GAINSBOROUGH TRINITY	3-0	Bowers 2, Conroy
	3	GRANTHAM	5-0	Bowers 3, Wallace, Barker
	8	GOOLE TOWN	5-0	Wilson, Bowers 4
	10	Denaby United	1-1	Whitfield
	14	Gainsborough Trinity	1-0	Whitfield
	17	NOTTS COUNTY RES	1-0	Whitfield
	24	York City Res.	0-1	
	28	Goole Town	1-2	Wallace
Oct	1	BRADFORD CITY RES	1-0	Malcolm
	8	Lincoln City Res.	2-0	Lindley, Wilson
	13	Notts County Res.	2-1	Wallace, Whitfield
	15	YORK CITY RES.	1-3	Wilson
	22	Bradford Park Ave Res	2-1	Whitfield 2
	27	Nottm Forest Res.	3-2	Wallace, Barkas, Wilson
	29	MANSFIELD TOWN RES	5-1	Barkas 2, Whitfield 2, Wilson
Nov	5	DONCASTER ROVERS RES	7-0	Barkas 2, Whitfield 3, Wilson, Conroy
	26	NOTTM FOREST RES.	0-2	
Dec	3	Frickley Colliery	1-2	Whitfield
	10	HALIFAX TOWN RES	2-0	Whitfield, Lodge
	17	Rotherham United Res	1-1	Sharpe
	26	GRIMSBY TOWN RES	2-1	Bowers, Whitfield
	27	Grimsby Town Res.	0-1	
	31	Grantham	2-4	Whitfield, Lodge
Jan	7	PETERBOROUGH UNITED	1-0	Conroy
	14	DENABY UNITED	1-1	Whitfield
	21	Bradford City Res.	0-3	
	28	BRADFORD PARK AVE RES	6-1	McCormick, Wilson, Whitfield 3, Lennon
Feb	4	RANSOME & MARLES	3-0	Whitfield 2, McCormick
	11	SCARBOROUGH	1-0	Whitfield
	18	Peterborough United	1-3	Lennon
	28	BOSTON UNITED	3-0	Lennon, Whitfield 2
Mar	4	Mansfield Town Res.	0-1	
	16	Halifax Town Res.	3-3	Wallace, Barker, Heseltine
	18	Worksop Town	3-0	Wallace, Heseltine 2
	25	ROTHERHAM UTD RES	2-1	Whitfield, Wallace
Apr	1	Ransome & Marles	5-0	Heseltine 3, Wilson 2
	10	HULL CITY RES.	5-0	Heseltine, Wilson 3, Lodge
	14	Hull City Res.	0-1	
	15	SHREWSBURY TOWN	4-1	Wallace 2, Heseltine, Brownsword (pen)
	20	FRICKLEY COLLIERY	1-1	Heseltine
	22	Doncaster Rovers Res	2-1	Whitfield 2
	26	Scarborough	2-1	Wilson, Malcolm
	29	Boston United	2-1	Heseltine, Whitfield
May	3	WORKSOP TOWN	2-1	Malcolm, McCormick

1950/51   12th in Division 3(N)

No		Date	Opponent	Score	Scorers	Att	Thompson GH	Barker, Jeff	Brownsword NJ	Allen W	Taylor RE	McCormick JM	Mosby H	Payne IEH	Gorin ER	Rees MJF	Boyes WE	Whitfield J	Clelland D	Hubbard J	Bowen D	White R	Babes J	Cumner RH	Mulholland JR	Malan NF	Comley LG	Jones RJ	Conroy RM
1	Aug	19	SHREWSBURY TOWN	0-0		11847	1	2	3	4	5	6	7	8	9	10	11												
2		23	Lincoln City	1-2	Gorin	16857	1	2	3	4	5	6	7		9	10		8	11										
3		26	Mansfield Town	1-1	Whitfield	11531	1	2	3	6	5				9	10	11	8		4	7								
4		30	LINCOLN CITY	1-1	Whitfield	14840	1	2	3	6	5				9	10	11	8		4	7								
5	Sep	2	ROTHERHAM UNITED	0-0		14858	1	2	3	6	5			11	9	10		8		4	7								
6		6	OLDHAM ATHLETIC	1-0	Whitfield	7994	1	2	3		5			11	9	10		8		4	7	6							
7		9	Barrow	0-1		9601	1	2	3		5			11	9	10		8		4	7	6							
8		12	Oldham Athletic	4-3	Gorin 2, Whitfield, Mosby	12239	1	2	3		5	6	11	7	9	10		8		4									
9		16	YORK CITY	0-1		12101	1	2	3		5	6	11	7	9	10		8		4									
10		23	Carlisle United	1-3	Gorin	11961	1	4	3	6	5			11	10	9		8		7			2						
11		30	ACCRINGTON STANLEY	3-0	Gorin 3	7861	1	2	3	6	5		7	10	9			8		4				11					
12	Oct	7	Gateshead	0-1		11903	1	2	3	6	5		7	10	9	8				4				11					
13		14	CREWE ALEXANDRA	1-1	Gorin	11307	1	2	3	6	5		7	10	9			8		4				11					
14		21	Halifax Town	3-3	Mulholland, Cumner, Rees	9512	1	2	3	6	5			10	9	8				4				11	7				
15		28	HARTLEPOOLS UNITED	0-0		10576	1	2	3	6	5			10	9	8				4				11	7				
16	Nov	4	Darlington	2-3	Gorin, Barker (pen)	5496	1	2	3	6	5			11	10	9	8			4					7				
17		18	New Brighton	2-1	Gorin 2	3060		2	3	4		6		7	10	9	8				5			11		1			
18	Dec	2	Rochdale	0-2		5213	1	2	3	4		6		7	10	9	8				5			11					
19		9	CHESTER	2-0	Mosby, Boyes	7989	1	2	3	6	5		7	10	9		8			4				11					
20		16	Shrewsbury Town	1-3	Gorin	6620	1	2	3	6	5		7	10	9		8			4				11					
21		23	MANSFIELD TOWN	0-0		7459	1	2	3	6	5		7	10	9		8			4				11					
22		25	WREXHAM	2-0	Cumner, Own goal (Turney)	8933	1	2	3	6	5		7	10	9		8			4				11					
23		26	Wrexham	1-3	Mosby	9712	1	2	3	6	5		7	10	9		8			4				11					
24		30	Rotherham United	1-4	Cumner	10169	1		3	6	5		7	10	9		8			4		2		11					
25	Jan	6	BRADFORD PARK AVE.	1-1	Own goal (James)	6760	1		2	6	5			8	9		10			4		3		11	7				
26		13	Barrow	1-0	Boyes	7850	1	2	3	6	5			7	8		10			4				11					
27		20	York City	0-0		7187	1	2	3	6	5			7	8		10		9	4				11					
28		27	Bradford Park Avenue	2-2	Clelland 2	10246	1	2	3		5			7	8	10			9	6		4		11					
29	Feb	3	CARLISLE UNITED	1-1	Clelland	9247	1	2	3		5			7	8	10			9	6		4		11					
30		10	TRANMERE ROVERS	1-1	Payne	10495	1	2	3		5			7	10				9	8		4		11					
31		17	Accrington Stanley	0-0		3433	1	2	3	6	5			7	8			10	9	4				11					
32		24	GATESHEAD	2-1	Cumner, Whitfield	9688	1	2	3	6	5			7	8			10	9	4				11					
33	Mar	3	Crewe Alexandra	0-2		6390	1	2	3	6	5			7	8			10	9	4				11					
34		10	HALIFAX TOWN	2-2	Mosby, Cumner	8447	1	2	3	6	5		11	9	8					4				10	7				
35		17	Hartlepools United	2-4	Comley, Whitfield	5365	1	2	3		5	6	7					9		4				11			10		
36		23	Southport	2-2	Comley, Clelland	8206	1	2	3	6	5		7	8					9	4				11			10		
37		24	DARLINGTON	2-0	Clelland, Mosby	8888	1	2	3	6	5		7	8					9	4				11			10		
38		26	SOUTHPORT	0-0		5038	1	2	3	6	5		7	8				9		4				11			10		
39		31	Stockport County	2-1	Cumner, Clelland	6401	1	2	3	6	5		7	8					9	4				11			10		
40	Apr	7	NEW BRIGHTON	6-0	Clelland 2, Comley 2, Payne, Cumner(p)	8588		2	3	6	5		7	8					9	4				11		1	10		
41		14	Bradford City	0-2		13001		2	3	6	5		7	8					9	4				10		1	11		
42		18	BRADFORD CITY	0-0		10287	1		3	6	5		7	8						4		2		11			10	9	
43		21	ROCHDALE	3-0	Cumner 2, Comley	9229	1		3	6	5		7	8						4		2		11			10	9	
44		28	Chester	1-4	Cumner	3778	1	2	3	6	5		7			8				4				11			10	9	
45		30	STOCKPORT COUNTY	3-0	Mosby, Hubbard, White	9175		2	3	6	5		7					9		8		4		11			10		
46	May	5	Tranmere Rovers	0-1		6990		2	3	6	5									9		4		11	7	1	10		8
			Apps				41	42	46	39	44	7	37	40	26	18	13	16	16	42	5	9	3	35	6	5	12	3	1
			Goals					1					6	2	12	1	2	6	8	1		1		10	1		5		

Two own goals

F.A. Cup

No		Date	Opponent	Score		Att	Thompson GH	Barker, Jeff	Brownsword NJ	Allen W	Taylor RE	McCormick JM	Mosby H	Payne IEH	Gorin ER	Rees MJF	Boyes WE	Whitfield J	Clelland D	Hubbard J	Bowen D	White R	Babes J	Cumner RH	Mulholland JR	Malan NF	Comley LG	Jones RJ	Conroy RM
Q4	Nov	11	Hereford United	0-1		10527		2	3	4	5	6	11	10	9	8								7	1				

		P	W	D	L	F	A	W	D	L	F	A	Pts
1	Rotherham United	46	16	3	4	55	16	15	6	2	48	25	71
2	Mansfield Town	46	17	6	0	54	19	9	6	8	24	29	64
3	Carlisle United	46	18	4	1	44	17	7	8	8	35	33	62
4	Tranmere Rovers	46	15	5	3	51	26	9	6	8	32	36	59
5	Lincoln City	46	18	1	4	62	23	7	7	9	27	35	58
6	Bradford Park Ave.	46	15	3	5	46	23	8	5	10	44	49	54
7	Bradford City	46	13	4	6	55	30	8	6	9	35	33	52
8	Gateshead	46	17	1	5	60	21	4	7	12	24	41	50
9	Crewe Alexandra	46	11	5	7	38	26	8	5	10	23	34	48
10	Stockport County	46	15	3	5	45	26	5	5	13	18	37	48
11	Rochdale	46	11	6	6	38	18	6	5	12	31	44	45
12	SCUNTHORPE UNITED	46	10	12	1	32	9	3	8	14	26	48	44
13	Chester	46	11	6	6	42	30	6	3	14	20	34	43
14	Wrexham	46	12	6	5	37	28	6	4	14	18	43	42
15	Oldham Athletic	46	10	5	8	47	36	6	3	14	26	37	40
16	Hartlepools United	46	14	5	4	55	26	2	2	19	9	40	39
17	York City	46	7	12	4	37	24	5	3	15	29	53	39
18	Darlington	46	10	8	5	35	29	3	5	15	24	48	39
19	Barrow	46	12	3	8	38	27	4	3	16	13	49	38
20	Shrewsbury Town	46	11	3	9	28	30	4	4	15	15	44	37
21	Southport	46	9	4	10	29	25	4	6	13	27	47	36
22	Halifax Town	46	11	6	6	36	24	0	6	17	14	45	34
23	Accrington Stanley	46	10	4	9	28	29	1	6	16	14	72	32
24	New Brighton	46	7	6	10	22	32	4	2	17	18	58	30

1951/52   14th in Division 3(N)

No	Date	Opponent	Score	Scorers	Att	Thompson GH	Barker, Jeff	Brownsword NJ	Stirland CJ	Taylor RE	Allen W	Mosby H	Hubbard J	Powell R	Hall A	Cumner RH	McLaren R	Gray G	Wallace G	Babes J	Platts P	Malan NF	Lockwood E	Sharpe LT	Rudd JJ	White R	Whitfield J	Ottewell S
1	Aug 18	BRADFORD CITY	1-0	Cumner	10315	1	2	3	4	5	6	7	8	9	10	11												
2	22	Chester	1-3	Hall	7045	1	2	3	4	5	6		8	9	10	11	7											
3	25	Hartlepools United	1-3	Powell	9028	1	2	3		5	6		4	9	8	11		7	10									
4	30	CHESTER	2-2	Cumner 2	6042	1	2	3	4	5	6	7	8	9		11			10									
5	Sep 1	OLDHAM ATHLETIC	2-2	Cumner, Wallace	10389	1		3	4	5	6	7	8	9		11			10	2								
6	6	LINCOLN CITY	1-3	Allen	12967	1		3	4	5	6	7	8	9		11			10	2								
7	8	Darlington	3-2	Cumner, Platts, Wallace	6169	1		3		5	6	7	4	8		11			10	2	9							
8	12	Lincoln City	1-4	Platts	14220	1		3		5	6	7	4	8		11			10	2	9							
9	15	GATESHEAD	1-1	Hall	8539			3		5		7	4		8	11		9	10	2		1	6					
10	22	Crewe Alexandra	2-2	Hall, Gray	5632	1	2	3		5			4	9	8	11		7	10					6				
11	29	SOUTHPORT	1-1	Gray	9297	1	2	3		5	6	11		9	8			7	10					4				
12	Oct 6	Wrexham	2-1	Powell 2	8219	1	2	3		5	6			9				7	10					4	11			
13	13	CHESTERFIELD	1-1	Powell	9833	1	2	3		5	6		9	7	8				10					4	11			
14	20	Bradford Park Avenue	2-2	Wallace 2	11207	1	2	3		5	6	7		9	8				10					4	11			
15	27	HALIFAX TOWN	2-1	Wallace, Powell	8729	1	2	3		5	6	7		9	8				10					4	11			
16	Nov 3	Mansfield Town	1-4	Mosby	10301	1	2	3		5	6	7		9		10			8					4	11			
17	10	ROCHDALE	3-1	Powell, Cumner, Taylor (pen)	8374	1	2	3		5	6	7		9		11			8					4	10			
18	17	Accrington Stanley	2-2	Martin(og), Powell	6381	1	2	3		5	6	7	4	9		11			8						10			
19	Dec 1	Stockport County	1-1	Wallace	10398	1	2	3		5		7	4	9		11			8					6	10			
20	8	WORKINGTON	3-1	Mosby, Rudd, Powell	7103	1	2	3		5		7	4	9		11			8					6	10			
21	22	HARTLEPOOLS UNITED	2-0	Powell, Cumner	7320	1	2	3		5		7	4	9		11			8					6	10			
22	25	Grimsby Town	2-3	Powell 2	19351	1	2	3		5		7	4	9		11			8					6	10			
23	26	GRIMSBY TOWN	1-3	Powell	15734	1	2	3		5	8	7	4	9		11								6	10			
24	29	Oldham Athletic	0-2		16332	1	2	3		5		7	4	9	8	11								6	10			
25	Jan 5	DARLINGTON	5-2	Hall 2, Powell, Mosby, Rudd	7223	1	2	3		5		7	4	9		11								6	10			
26	17	YORK CITY	1-1	Rudd	4046	1	2	3			10	7	4	9	8									6	11	5		
27	19	Gateshead	1-2	Cumner	5586	1	2	3				7	4	9	8									6	10	5		
28	26	CREWE ALEXANDRA	2-0	Cumner, Powell	6404	1	2	3		5			4	9	8		7							6	10			
29	Feb 9	Southport	1-5	Gray	4592	1	2	3		5			4	9	8		7							6	10			
30	16	WREXHAM	0-0		6923	1	2	3					4	9	8	11	10	7						6		5		
31	23	Barrow	1-2	Hubbard	7062		2	3					4			11	10	7				1		6	8	5		9
32	Mar 1	Chesterfield	0-3		10152			3	6			7	4			11	10			2		1			8	5		9
33	8	BRADFORD PARK AVE.	0-0		8445	1	2	3					4	9		11								6	7	5	8	10
34	15	Halifax Town	1-2	Whitfield	8418	1	2	3				7	4			11								6	8	5	9	10
35	22	MANSFIELD TOWN	4-1	Mosby, Cumner, Ottewell, Rudd	7552	1	2	3	4		6	7				10									11	5	9	8
36	26	Bradford City	0-1		3823	1	2	3	4		6					10			7						11	5	9	8
37	29	Rochdale	2-1	Ottewell, Wallace	1226	1	2	3	4		6					10			7						11	5	9	8
38	Apr 5	ACCRINGTON STANLEY	3-1	Cumner, Whitfield, Ottewell	4801	1		3			6	7	4	2		10									11	5	9	8
39	11	Tranmere Rovers	1-3	Ottewell	9075			3			6	7	4	2		10						1			11	5	9	8
40	12	Carlisle United	0-3		6981			3			6		4	2		10			7			1			11	5	9	8
41	14	TRANMERE ROVERS	2-0	Ottewell, Wallace	8066			3			6		4	2		10	11		7			1				5	9	8
42	19	STOCKPORT COUNTY	1-1		8305			3					4	2		10	11		7			1		6		5	9	8
43	24	CARLISLE UNITED	1-1	Ottewell	7453			3						2		10			7			1		6	11	5	9	8
44	26	Workington	0-0		5133			3						2		10			7			1		6	11	5	9	8
45	28	York City	1-0	Ottewell	7827			3						2	9	10			7			1		6	11	5		8
46	May 1	BARROW	0-0		7103			3						2	9	10			7			1		6	11	5		8
		Apps				36	31	46	17	28	25	27	36	31	15	44	6	9	29	6	2	10	1	28	32	19	14	14
		Goals								1	1	4	1	14	5	11		3	8		2				4		2	8

One own goal

F.A. Cup

No	Date	Opponent	Score	Scorers	Att	Thompson GH	Barker, Jeff	Brownsword NJ	Stirland CJ	Taylor RE	Allen W	Mosby H	Hubbard J	Powell R	Hall A	Cumner RH	McLaren R	Gray G	Wallace G	Babes J	Platts P	Malan NF	Lockwood E	Sharpe LT	Rudd JJ	White R	Whitfield J	Ottewell S
R1	Nov 24	BILLINGHAM SYNTH.	5-0	Wallace 2, Powell 2, Hubbard	9861	1	2	3		5	6	7	4	9		11			8						10			
R2	Dec 15	Millwall	0-0		22702	1	2	3		5		7	4	9		11			8					6	10			
rep	20	MILLWALL	3-0	Powell 2, Rudd	13580	1	2	3		5		7	4	9		11			8					6	10			
R3	Jan 12	TOTTENHAM HOTSPUR	0-3		22652	1	2	3		5		7	4	9	8	11								6	10			

		P	W	D	L	F	A	W	D	L	F	A	Pts
1	Lincoln City	46	19	2	2	80	23	11	7	5	41	29	69
2	Grimsby Town	46	19	2	2	59	14	10	6	7	37	31	66
3	Stockport County	46	12	9	2	47	17	11	4	8	27	23	59
4	Oldham Athletic	46	19	2	2	65	22	5	7	11	25	39	57
5	Gateshead	46	14	7	2	41	17	7	4	12	25	32	53
6	Mansfield Town	46	17	3	3	50	23	5	5	13	23	37	52
7	Carlisle United	46	10	7	6	31	24	9	6	8	31	33	51
8	Bradford Park Ave.	46	13	6	4	51	28	6	6	11	23	36	50
9	Hartlepools United	46	17	3	3	47	19	4	5	14	24	46	50
10	York City	46	16	4	3	53	19	2	9	12	20	33	49
11	Tranmere Rovers	46	17	2	4	59	29	4	4	15	17	42	48
12	Barrow	46	13	5	5	33	19	4	7	12	24	42	46
13	Chesterfield	46	15	7	1	47	16	2	4	17	18	50	45
14	SCUNTHORPE UNITED	46	10	11	2	39	23	4	5	14	26	51	44
15	Bradford City	46	12	5	6	40	32	4	5	14	21	36	42
16	Crewe Alexandra	46	12	6	5	42	28	5	2	16	21	54	42
17	Southport	46	12	6	5	36	22	3	5	15	17	49	41
18	Wrexham	46	14	5	4	41	22	1	4	18	22	51	39
19	Chester	46	13	4	6	46	30	5	1	16	26	55	39
20	Halifax Town	46	11	4	8	31	23	3	3	17	30	74	35
21	Rochdale	46	10	5	8	32	34	1	4	14	15	45	35
22	Accrington Stanley	46	6	8	9	30	34	4	4	15	31	58	32
23	Darlington	46	10	5	8	39	34	1	4	18	25	69	31
24	Workington	46	8	4	11	33	34	3	3	17	17	57	29

No	Date	Opponent	Res	Scorers	Att	Thompson GH	Cox S	Brownsword N.J	McGill A	White R	Sharpe LT	Mosby H	Haigh J	Mynard LD	Cumner RH	Daley AJ	Hubbard J	Broadley L	Ottewell S	Taylor RE	Whitfield J	Wallace G	Bushby A	Malan NF	Taylor R	Brown GA	Lockwood E	Charlesworth T
1	Aug 23	Barrow	1-2	Mynard	6289	1	2	3	4	5	6	7	8	9	10	11												
2	28	GRIMSBY TOWN	0-1		18974	1		3	4	5	6		8	7	10	11	2	9										
3	30	STOCKPORT COUNTY	2-2	Broadley, Ottewell	8892	1		3	4	5	6		8	7		11	2	9	10									
4	Sep 3	Grimsby Town	0-1		22213	1		3	4				8	7		11	2	9	10	5	6							
5	6	Bradford City	0-0		11525	1		3	4				8			11	2	9	10	5	6	7						
6	11	CHESTER	1-1	Broadley	6695	1		3	4			7	8			11	2	9	10	5	6							
7	13	ROCHDALE	5-1	McGill, Mynard, Whitfield, Mosby, Haigh	7381	1		3	4		6	7	8	9		11	2			5	10							
8	17	Chester	1-1	Haigh	5004	1		3	4		6	7	8	9		11	2			5	10							
9	20	Darlington	0-1		5904	1		3	4		6	7	8	9	10	11	2			5								
10	25	MANSFIELD TOWN	0-1		7252	1		3	4		6	7	8	9	11		2			5	10							
11	27	GATESHEAD	0-0		6940	1		3	4			7	8	9	11		2			5	10		6					
12	Oct 2	SOUTHPORT	3-0	Daley, Haigh, Whitfield	5105	1		3	4				8	11	10	7	2			5	9		6					
13	4	Hartlepools United	1-1	Daley	9060	1		3	4				8	11	10	7	2			5	9		6					
14	11	YORK CITY	2-0	Daley, Brownsword (p)	7850	1		3	4				8	11		7	2		10	5	9		6					
15	18	Tranmere Rovers	1-0	Mynard	9156	1		3	4				8	11		7	2		10	5	9		6					
16	25	CHESTERFIELD	1-0	Daley	8319			3	4				8	11		7	2		10	5	9		6	1				
17	Nov 1	Workington	3-0	Whitfield, Haigh, McGill	7348			3	4	9			8	11		7	2			5	10		6	1				
18	8	ACCRINGTON STANLEY	5-2	White 2, Daley 2, Brownsword (p)	7334			3	4	9			8	11		7	2			5	10		6	1				
19	15	Halifax Town	1-2	White	7247			3	4	9			8	11		7	2			5	10		6	1				
20	29	Oldham Athletic	1-0	White	14314			3	4	9		11	8			7	2			5	10		6	1				
21	Dec 13	Wrexham	3-2	Hubbard, Haigh, Brownsword (p)	9266			3	4	9		11	8			7	2			5	10		6	1				
22	20	BARROW	1-2	White	5434		3		4	9		11	8			7	2			5	10		6	1				
23	25	Carlisle United	0-8		9518		2	3	4	9		11	8			7				5	10		6	1				
24	27	CARLISLE UNITED	1-2	White	7325			3	4	9		7	8	11			2			5	10		6	1				
25	Jan 1	Southport	3-2	Haigh, Mosby, Ottewell	4727			3	4			11	8			7	2		9	5	10		6	1				
26	3	Stockport County	1-1	Whitfield	7999			3	4			11	8			7	2		9	5	10		6	1				
27	17	BRADFORD CITY	4-0	Haigh 2, Whitfield, Daley	7356			3	4			7	8			11	2		9	5	10		6	1				
28	24	Rochdale	2-2	Ottewell, Brownsword (p)	5050			3	4			7	8			11	2		9	5	10		6	1				
29	31	PORT VALE	1-2	Mosby	6984			3	4			7	8			11	2		9	5	10		6	1				
30	Feb 7	DARLINGTON	2-0	Haigh, Whitfield	5922			3	4			7	8			11	2		9	5	10		6	1				
31	18	Gateshead	1-1	Ottewell	4126			3	4			7	8			11	2		9	5	10		6	1				
32	21	HARTLEPOOLS UNITED	0-0		7076			3	4			7	8			11	2		9	5	10		6	1				
33	28	York City	2-0	Haigh, Brownsword (p)	7480			3	4			7	8		10	11	2			5	9		6	1				
34	Mar 7	TRANMERE ROVERS	2-0	Haigh, Daley	6796			3	4			7	8		10	11	2			5	9		6	1				
35	14	Chesterfield	1-1	Whitfield	8337			3	4			7	8		10	11	2			5	9		6	1				
36	16	Port Vale	0-4		11371			3	4			7	8			11	2		9	5	10		6	1				
37	21	WORKINGTON	2-1	Bushby 2	6529			3	4				8		10	11	2			5	9		6	1	7			
38	26	BRADFORD PARK AVE.	1-2	Haigh	6119			3	4				8	11	10		2			5	9		6	1	7			
39	28	Accrington Stanley	1-2	Brown	2903				4				8	11	10		2			5	9		6	1		3	7	
40	Apr 3	Crewe Alexandra	0-2		9379				4				8	11	10		2			5	9		6	1		3	7	
41	4	HALIFAX TOWN	1-1	Whitfield	6451				4				8	11			2			5	9	10	6	1		3	7	
42	6	CREWE ALEXANDRA	2-0	Haigh, Brown	5989				4				8	11			2			5	9	10	6	1		3	7	
43	11	Mansfield Town	0-1		7310				4				8	11			2			5	9	10	6			3	7	1
44	18	OLDHAM ATHLETIC	1-1	Bushby	9399				4	6			8	11			2			5	9		10	1		3	7	
45	25	Bradford Park Avenue	1-1	Brown	8571				4	6			8	11	9		2			5			10	1		3	7	
46	27	WREXHAM	1-2	Brown	4250				4	6			8	11	9		2			5			10			3	7	1
		Apps				15	3	38	46	11	10	24	46	18	23	35	44	5	16	43	40	4	36	27	2	10	8	2
		Goals						5	2	6		3	13	3		8	1	2	4		8		3			4		

F.A. Cup

Rd	Date	Opponent	Res	Scorers	Att	Thompson GH	Cox S	Brownsword N.J	McGill A	White R	Sharpe LT	Mosby H	Haigh J	Mynard LD	Cumner RH	Daley AJ	Hubbard J	Broadley L	Ottewell S	Taylor RE	Whitfield J	Wallace G	Bushby A	Malan NF	Taylor R	Brown GA	Lockwood E	Charlesworth T
R1	Nov 22	CARLISLE UNITED	1-0	Whitfield	9028			3	4	9		11	8			7	2			5	10		6	1				
R2	Dec 6	Hereford United	0-0		8765			3	4	9		11	8			7	2			5	10		6	1				
rep	11	HEREFORD UNITED	2-1	White, Whitfield	10631			3	4	9		11	8			7	2			5	10		6	1				
R3	Jan 10	Sunderland	1-1	McGill	56507			3	4			7	8			11	2		9	5	10		6	1				
rep	15	SUNDERLAND	1-2	Daley	21626			3	4			7	8			11	2		9	5	10		6	1				

		P	W	D	L	F	A	W	D	L	F	A	Pts
1	Oldham Athletic	46	15	4	4	48	21	7	11	5	29	24	59
2	Port Vale	46	13	9	1	41	10	7	9	7	26	25	58
3	Wrexham	46	18	3	2	59	24	6	5	12	27	42	56
4	York City	46	14	5	4	35	16	6	8	9	25	29	53
5	Grimsby Town	46	15	5	3	47	19	6	5	12	28	40	52
6	Southport	46	16	4	3	42	18	4	7	12	21	42	51
7	Bradford Park Ave.	46	10	8	5	37	23	9	4	10	38	38	50
8	Gateshead	46	13	6	4	51	24	4	9	10	25	36	49
9	Carlisle United	46	13	7	3	57	24	5	6	12	25	44	49
10	Crewe Alexandra	46	13	5	5	46	28	7	3	13	24	40	48
11	Stockport County	46	13	8	2	61	26	4	5	14	21	43	47
12	Tranmere Rovers	46	16	3	4	45	16	5	1	17	20	47	47
13	Chesterfield	46	13	6	4	40	23	4	5	13	25	40	47
14	Halifax Town	46	13	5	5	47	31	3	10	10	21	37	47
15	SCUNTHORPE UNITED	46	10	6	7	38	21	6	8	9	24	35	46
16	Bradford City	46	14	7	2	54	29	0	11	12	21	51	46
17	Hartlepools United	46	14	6	3	39	16	2	8	13	18	45	46
18	Mansfield Town	46	11	9	3	34	25	5	5	13	21	37	46
19	Barrow	46	15	6	2	48	20	1	6	16	18	51	44
20	Chester	46	10	7	6	39	27	1	8	14	25	58	37
21	Darlington	46	13	4	6	33	27	1	2	20	25	69	34
22	Rochdale	46	12	5	6	41	27	2	0	21	21	56	33
23	Workington	46	9	5	9	40	33	2	5	16	15	58	32
24	Accrington Stanley	46	7	9	7	25	29	1	2	20	14	60	27

1953/54   3rd in Division 3(N)

#	Date	Opponent	Score	Scorers	Att	Malan NF	Hubbard J	Brownsword NJ	McGill A	Taylor RE	Bushby A	Brown GA	Haigh J	Whitfield J	Gregory JE	Jones JM	Roberts H	Barley PJ	Sharpe LT	White R	Mosby H	Underwood GR	Heward B
1	Aug 22	Grimsby Town	1-0	Gregory	18246	1	2	3	4	5	6	7	8	9	10	11							
2	24	Gateshead	0-0		8727	1	2	3	4	5	6	7	8	9	10	11							
3	29	YORK CITY	3-0	Brown 2, Bushby	7494	1	2	3	4	5	6	7	8	9	10	11							
4	Sep 3	GATESHEAD	1-1	Brownsword (p)	11302	1	2	3	4	5	6	7	8	9	10	11							
5	5	Southport	3-4	Brown, Haigh, Whitfield	5821	1	2	3	4	5	6	7	8	9	10	11							
6	7	Workington	3-1	Whitfield 2, Haigh	7367	1	2	3	4	5	6	7	8	9		11	10						
7	12	CHESTER	1-0	Whitfield	10234	1	2	3	4	5	6	7	8	9		11	10						
8	17	WORKINGTON	4-1	Brown, Taylor, Roberts, Jones	10013	1	2	3	4	5	6	7	8	9		11	10						
9	19	Crewe Alexandra	1-1	Haigh	8717	1	2	3	4	5	6	7	8	9		11	10						
10	21	Hartlepools United	2-3	McGill, Jones	6174	1	2	3	4	5	6	7	8	9		11	10						
11	26	PORT VALE	0-2		12630	1	2	3	4	5	6	7	8	9		11	10						
12	Oct 1	HARTLEPOOLS UNITED	0-0		9102		2	3			6	7	8	9		11	10	1	4	5			
13	3	Bradford Park Avenue	2-2	Jones, Gregory	13686		2	3			6		8	9	10	11		1	4	5	7		
14	10	Rochdale	1-1	Mosby	7873		2	3			6		8	9	10	11		1	4	5	7		
15	17	WREXHAM	3-1	Whitfield 2, Gregory	8402		2	3			6		8	9	10	11		1	4	5	7		
16	24	Mansfield Town	1-2	Brownsword (p)	8539		2	3			6		8	9	10	11		1	4	5	7		
17	31	BARROW	3-2	Jones 2, Sharpe	7008	1	2	3			6		8		10	11			4	5	7		
18	Nov 7	Bradford City	3-1	Jones, Whitfield, Brownsword (p)	8093	1	2	3			6		8	9	10	11			4	5	7		
19	14	CHESTERFIELD	2-1	Whitfield, Brownsword (p)	8247	1	2	3			6		8	9	10	11			4	5	7		
20	28	HALIFAX TOWN	3-2	Haigh, Brownsword (p), Bushby	8151	1	2	3			6		8	9	10		11		4	5	7		
21	Dec 5	Carlisle United	1-5	Gregory	6169	1	2	3			6		8	9	10	11			4	5	7		
22	19	GRIMSBY TOWN	2-1	Whitfield, Gregory	9985	1	2	3			6		8	9	10	11			4	5	7		
23	25	DARLINGTON	1-1	Brownsword (p)	8035	1	2	3			6		8	9	10	11			4	5	7		
24	26	Darlington	0-3		4518	1	2	3			6	7	8	9	10	11			4	5			
25	Jan 1	Accrington Stanley	1-0	Gregory	8729	1		3	4	5	6	7	8	9	10	11						2	
26	2	York City	0-2		5355	1		3	4		6	7	8	9	10	11				5		2	
27	16	SOUTHPORT	1-1	Brownsword (p)	6870	1	2	3	4		6		8	9	10	11				5	7		
28	23	Chester	0-0		5180	1	2	3	4		6		8	9	10	11				5	7		
29	Feb 6	CREWE ALEXANDRA	2-2	Mosby, Haigh	7962	1	2	3	4		6		8	9	10	11				5	7		
30	13	Port Vale	0-0		17240	1	2	3			6		8	9	10	11			4	5	7		
31	20	BRADFORD PARK AVE.	4-1	Brown 2, Mosby, Wright (og)	8097	1	2	3			6	9	8	4	10	11				5	7		
32	27	ROCHDALE	1-1	Brown	7260	1	2	3			6	9	8	4	10	11				5	7		
33	Mar 6	Wrexham	1-3	Gregory	6522	1	2	3			6	9	8	4	10	11				5	7		
34	10	Stockport County	1-1	Brownsword (p)	2939	1	2	3	4	5	6	7	8	9							11		
35	13	MANSFIELD TOWN	2-2	Gregory, Haigh	6516	1	2	3	4		6	9	8		10	11				5	7		
36	18	ACCRINGTON STANLEY	1-2	McGill	5191	1	2	3	4	5	6		8	9	10	11					7		
37	20	Barrow	2-1	Gregory 2	4486	1	2	3	4				8	9	10	11				5	7		6
38	27	BRADFORD CITY	2-1	Haigh, Mosby	7035	1	2	3	4		6		8	9	10	11				5	7		
39	Apr 1	STOCKPORT COUNTY	2-0	Mosby, Jones	5868	1	2	3	4	5	6		8	9	10	11					7		
40	3	Chesterfield	0-1		5769	1	2	3	4		6	9	8		10	11				5	7		
41	10	TRANMERE ROVERS	3-1	Gregory 3	6213	1	4	3			6	9	8		10	11				5	7	2	
42	16	BARNSLEY	6-0	Gregory 2, Haigh, Brown, Jones, Thomas (og)	10302	1	6	3	4			9	8		10	7	11			5		2	
43	17	Halifax Town	3-0	Brown 2, Haigh	4674	1	6	3	4			9	8		10	11	7			5		2	
44	19	Barnsley	1-0	Haigh	10867	1	6	3	4			9	8		10	7	11			5		2	
45	24	CARLISLE UNITED	2-1	Hubbard, Gregory	7731	1	6	3	4			9	8		10	7	11			5		2	
46	27	Tranmere Rovers	1-1	Jones	4826	1	6	3	4	5		9	8		10	7	11					2	
		Apps				41	44	46	28	16	40	30	43	38	39	44	13	5	14	30	26	8	1
		Goals					1	8	2	1		2	10	10	9	16	9		1		5		

Two own goals

F.A. Cup

Rd	Date	Opponent	Score	Scorers	Att	Malan NF	Hubbard J	Brownsword NJ	McGill A	Taylor RE	Bushby A	Brown GA	Haigh J	Whitfield J	Gregory JE	Jones JM	Roberts H	Barley PJ	Sharpe LT	White R	Mosby H	Underwood GR	Heward B
R1	Nov 21	BOSTON UNITED	9-0	Haigh 3, Whitfield 2, Jones 2, Mosby, Gregory	8894	1	2	3			6		8	9	10	11			4	5	7		
R2	Dec 12	BOURNEMOUTH	1-0	Brown	12005	1	2	3			6	7	8	9	10	11			4	5			
R3	Jan 9	Wrexham	3-3	Bushby 2, Mosby	17287	1	2	3	4		6		8	9	10	11				5	7		
rep	14	WREXHAM	3-1	Whitfield, Gregory, Brownsword (p)	12862	1	2	3	4		6		8	9	10	11				5	7		
R4	30	PORTSMOUTH	1-1	Jones	23735	1	2	3	4		6		8	9	10	11				5	7		
rep	Feb 3	Portsmouth	2-2	Jones 2	30247	1	2	3	4		6		8	9	10	11				5	7		
rep2	8	Portsmouth	0-4		24556	1	2	3	4		6		8	9	10	11				5	7		

R4 replay a.e.t. R4 replay 2 at Highbury.

		P	W	D	L	F	A	W	D	L	F	A	Pts
1	Port Vale	46	16	7	0	48	5	10	10	3	28	16	69
2	Barnsley	46	16	3	4	54	24	8	7	8	23	33	58
3	SCUNTHORPE UNITED	46	14	7	2	49	24	7	8	8	28	32	57
4	Gateshead	46	15	4	4	49	22	6	9	8	25	33	55
5	Bradford City	46	15	6	2	40	14	7	3	13	20	41	53
6	Chesterfield	46	13	6	4	41	19	6	8	9	35	45	52
7	Mansfield Town	46	15	5	3	59	22	5	6	12	29	45	51
8	Wrexham	46	16	4	3	59	19	5	5	13	22	49	51
9	Bradford Park Ave.	46	13	6	4	57	31	5	8	10	20	37	50
10	Stockport County	46	14	6	3	57	20	4	5	14	20	47	47
11	Southport	46	12	5	6	41	26	5	7	11	22	34	46
12	Barrow	46	12	7	4	46	26	4	5	14	26	45	44
13	Carlisle United	46	10	8	5	53	27	4	7	12	30	44	43
14	Tranmere Rovers	46	11	4	8	40	34	7	3	13	19	36	43
15	Accrington Stanley	46	12	7	4	41	22	4	3	16	25	52	42
16	Crewe Alexandra	46	9	8	6	30	26	5	5	13	19	41	41
17	Grimsby Town	46	14	5	4	31	15	2	4	17	20	62	41
18	Hartlepools United	46	10	8	5	40	21	3	6	14	19	44	40
19	Rochdale	46	12	5	6	40	20	4	5	15	19	57	40
20	Workington	46	10	9	4	36	22	3	5	15	23	58	40
21	Darlington	46	11	3	9	31	27	1	11	11	19	44	38
22	York City	46	8	7	8	39	32	4	6	13	25	54	37
23	Halifax Town	46	9	6	8	26	21	3	4	16	18	52	34
24	Chester	46	10	7	6	39	22	1	3	19	9	45	32

1954/55   3rd in Division 3(N)

#	Date		Opponent	Score	Scorers	Att	Malan NF	Hubbard J	Brownsword NJ	McGill A	White R	Bushby A	Mosby H	Haigh J	Brown GA	Gregory JE	Jones JM	Lamb HT	Roberts H	Turner PS	Whitfield J	Lloyd WS	Sharpe LT	Barrett J	Marshall PW	Fawcett B
1	Aug	21	HALIFAX TOWN	2-2	Haigh 2	10388	1	2	3	4	5	6	7	8	9	10	11									
2		24	Grimsby Town	4-1	Brown 2, McGill, Gregory	19736	1	6	3	4	5		7	8	9	10	11	2								
3		28	York City	3-2	Gregory 3	12911	1	6	3	4	5		7	8	9	10	11	2								
4	Sep	2	GRIMSBY TOWN	1-0	Jones	15547	1	6	3	4	5		7	8	9	10	11	2								
5		4	SOUTHPORT	2-0	Brown 2	9406	1	6	3	4	5		7	8	9	10	11	2								
6		9	BARNSLEY	1-0	Gregory	12158	1	6	3	4	5		7	8	9	10	11	2								
7		11	Barrow	3-1	Gregory, Brown, Haigh	6307	1	6	3	4	5		7	8	9	10	11	2								
8		15	Barnsley	0-1		16431	1	6	3	4	5		7	8	9	10	11	2								
9		18	WORKINGTON	1-1	Haigh	9403	1	6	3	4	5		7	8	9	10	11	2								
10		22	Wrexham	1-0	Gregory	8139	1	6	3	4	5			8	9	10	11	2		7						
11		25	Mansfield Town	1-2	McGill (p)	11809	1	6	3	4	5			8	9	10	11	2		7						
12		30	WREXHAM	1-0	Gregory	8810	1		3	4	5	6	7	8	9	10	11	2								
13	Oct	2	ACCRINGTON STANLEY	4-0	Brown 2, Turner, Haigh	11370	1	2		4	5	6		8	9	10	11	3		7						
14		9	Bradford Park Avenue	0-0		14402	1	2	3	4	5	6		8	9	10	11				7					
15		16	ROCHDALE	2-2	Brown 2	10331	1	2	3	4	5	6		8	9	10	11				7					
16		23	Tranmere Rovers	2-1	Brown, Haigh	5493	1	2	3	4	5	6	7	8	9	10	11									
17		30	STOCKPORT COUNTY	3-0	Brown, Bushby, Brownsword (p)	9956	1	2	3	4	5	6	7	8	9	10	11									
18	Nov	6	Hartlepools United	2-4	Gregory 2	7621	1	2	3	4	5	6	7	8	9	10	11									
19		13	GATESHEAD	0-2		9159	1	2	3	4	5	6		8	9	10	11					7				
20		27	CHESTERFIELD	2-1	Brown, Brownsword (p)	8739	1	2	3	4	5	6	7	8	9	10	11									
21	Dec	4	Crewe Alexandra	1-1	Gregory	3651	1	2	3	4	5	6	7	8	9	10	11									
22		18	Halifax Town	1-3	McGill	10981	1	2	3	4	5	6	7	8	9	10	11									
23		25	Bradford City	4-2	Brown 2, Gregory, Mosby	12587	1	2	3		5	6	7	8	9	10	11						4			
24		27	BRADFORD CITY	1-0	Brown	11016	1	2	3		5	6	7	8	9	10	11						4			
25	Jan	1	YORK CITY	1-2	Brownsword (p)	10593	1	2	3		5	6	7	8	9	10	11							4		
26		8	Chester	4-2	Whitfield 3, Brown	4083	1	2	3	4	5	6	7	8	9		11				10					
27		22	BARROW	3-0	Whitfield 2, Mosby	7348		2	3	4	5	6	7		9	10			11		8				1	
28		29	CHESTER	1-1	Brown	8328		2	3	4	5	6	7	8	9				11		10				1	
29	Feb	5	Workington	1-1	Gregory	8601		2	3	4	5	6	7		9	10	11				8				1	
30		12	MANSFIELD TOWN	2-0	Jones, Gregory	7132		2	3	4	5	6	7		9	10	11				8				1	
31		19	Accrington Stanley	1-2	Turner	10926		2	3	4	5	6			9	10	11			7	8				1	
32	Mar	5	Rochdale	0-2		6078		2	3	4	5	6			9	10	11				8				1	7
33		12	TRANMERE ROVERS	1-2	Gregory	7817	1	2	3	4	5	6	7		9	10	11				8					
34		19	Stockport County	2-4	Gregory, Brown	7005	1	6	3	4	5		7	8	9	10	11	2								
35		26	HARTLEPOOLS UNITED	5-1	Hubbard 4, Gregory	4155	1	8	3	4	5	6	7		9	10	11	2								
36	Apr	2	Gateshead	1-0	Brown	4217	1	8	3	4	5	6	7		9	10	11	2								
37		8	Oldham Athletic	1-1	Hubbard	9396	1	8	3	4	5	6	7		9	10	11	2								
38		9	DARLINGTON	1-0	McGill	8268	1	8	3	4	5	6	7		9	10	11	2								
39		11	OLDHAM ATHLETIC	6-1	Brown 2, Hubbard 2, Gregory 2	8471	1	8	3	4	5	6	7		9	10	11	2								
40		16	Chesterfield	0-2		7304	1	8	3	4	5	6	7		9	10	11	2								
41		18	CARLISLE UNITED	1-1	Gregory	7263	1	8	3	4	5	6	7		9	10	11	2								
42		23	CREWE ALEXANDRA	3-1	Gregory, Brown, McGill	5316	1	8	3	4	5	6			9	10	11	2			7					
43		27	Darlington	1-1	Whitfield	3395	1	8	3	4	5	6			9	10	11	2			7					
44		30	Carlisle United	2-1	Brown, Brownsword (p)	4636	1	2	3	4	5	6	7		9	10	11				8					
45	May	5	BRADFORD PARK AVE.	1-1	Gregory	5136	1	2	3	4	5	6	7		9	10	11				8					
46		7	Southport	1-1	Mosby	2407	1	2	3	4	5	6	7		9	10	11				8					
			Apps				40	45	45	43	46	36	35	28	46	44	44	22	4	5	12	1	2	1	6	1
			Goals					7	4	5		1	3	6	23	22	2			2	6					

F.A. Cup

#	Date		Opponent	Score	Scorers	Att	Malan NF	Hubbard J	Brownsword NJ	McGill A	White R	Bushby A	Mosby H	Haigh J	Brown GA	Gregory JE	Jones JM	Lamb HT	Roberts H	Turner PS	Whitfield J
R1	Nov	20	Horden Colliery	1-0	McGill	5949	1	2	3	4	5		7	8	10	9	11				6
R2	Dec	11	Coventry City	0-4		21360	1	2	3	4	5	6	7	8	9	10	11				

		P	W	D	L	F	A	W	D	L	F	A	Pts
1	Barnsley	46	18	3	2	51	17	12	2	9	35	29	65
2	Accrington Stanley	46	18	2	3	65	32	7	9	7	31	35	61
3	SCUNTHORPE UNITED	46	14	6	3	45	18	9	6	8	36	35	58
4	York City	46	13	5	5	43	27	11	5	7	49	36	58
5	Hartlepools United	46	16	3	4	39	20	9	2	12	25	29	55
6	Chesterfield	46	17	1	5	54	33	7	5	11	27	37	54
7	Gateshead	46	11	7	5	38	26	9	5	9	27	43	52
8	Workington	46	11	7	5	39	23	7	7	9	29	32	50
9	Stockport County	46	13	4	6	50	27	5	8	10	34	43	48
10	Oldham Athletic	46	14	5	4	47	22	5	5	13	27	46	48
11	Southport	46	10	9	4	28	18	6	7	10	19	26	48
12	Rochdale	46	13	7	3	39	20	4	7	12	30	46	48
13	Mansfield Town	46	14	4	5	40	28	4	5	14	25	43	45
14	Halifax Town	46	9	9	5	41	27	6	4	13	22	40	43
15	Darlington	46	10	7	6	41	28	4	7	12	21	45	42
16	Bradford Park Ave.	46	11	7	5	29	21	4	4	15	27	49	41
17	Barrow	46	12	4	7	39	34	5	2	16	31	55	40
18	Wrexham	46	9	6	8	40	35	4	6	13	25	42	38
19	Tranmere Rovers	46	9	6	8	37	30	4	5	14	18	40	37
20	Carlisle United	46	12	1	10	53	39	3	5	15	25	50	36
21	Bradford City	46	9	9	5	30	26	4	5	14	17	29	36
22	Crewe Alexandra	46	8	10	5	45	35	2	4	17	23	56	34
23	Grimsby Town	46	10	4	9	28	32	3	4	16	19	46	34
24	Chester	46	10	3	10	23	25	2	6	15	21	52	33

1955/56 9th in Division 3(N)

#	Date		Opponent	Score	Scorers	Att	Malan NF	Hubbard J	Brownsword NJ	McGill A	White R	Bushby A	Davies JR	Haigh J	Brown GA	Gregory JE	Jones JM	Barrett J	Callaghan R	Marshall PW	Thompson D	Sharpe LT	Benson JR	Lamb HT	Heward B	Parrott JF	Mullen A	Wainwright L
1	Aug	20	Bradford Park Avenue	0-2		12624	1	2	3	4	5	6	7	8	9	10	11											
2		22	Mansfield Town	2-3	Haigh, Gregory	9729	1	2	3	4	5	6	7	8	9	10	11											
3		27	OLDHAM ATHLETIC	2-1	Haigh, Callaghan	8839	1	2	3		5	6		8	9	10	11	4	7									
4		31	MANSFIELD TOWN	3-0	Gregory 2, Plummer (og)	8923	1	2	3		5	6		8	9	10	11	4	7									
5	Sep	3	Workington	2-1	Callaghan, Gregory	7087		2	3		5	6		8	9	10	11	4	7	1								
6		7	WREXHAM	1-1	Brown	9566		2	3		5	6		8	9	10	11	4	7	1								
7		10	YORK CITY	1-1	Callaghan	9720		2	3		5	6		8	9	10	11	4	7	1								
8		14	Wrexham	1-0	Brownsword (p)	8902		2	3		5	6		8	9	10	11	4	7	1								
9		17	Derby County	2-2	Callaghan 2	18237		2	3		5	6	11		9	10		4	7	1		8						
10		21	HALIFAX TOWN	1-0	Davies	8434		2	3		5	6	11	8	9	10		4	7	1								
11		24	CREWE ALEXANDRA	1-1	Brown	8271		2	3		5		7	8	9	10	11	4		1			6					
12		26	Stockport County	2-3	Brown, Jones	4146		2	3	4	5		7	8	9	10	11			1			6					
13	Oct	1	Hartlepools United	2-0	Gregory, Jones	8170		2	3	4	5		7	8	9	10	11			1			6					
14		8	CARLISLE UNITED	4-0	Gregory 2, Davies, Haigh	8623		2	3	4	5	6	7	8	9	10	11			1								
15		15	Rochdale	2-3	Brown, Gregory	6110		2	3	4	5	6	7	8	9	10	11			1								
16		22	BARROW	2-0	Gregory, Brownsword (p)	7050	1	2	3	4	5		7	8		10	11					9						
17		29	Accrington Stanley	0-2		7443	1	2	3	4	5		7	8		10	11	6	9									
18	Nov	5	DARLINGTON	0-1		7877	1	2		4	5			8	7	10	11	6	9					3				
19		12	Gateshead	0-1		3765	1	10	3	4			7	8		9	11	6						2	5			
20		26	Tranmere Rovers	1-2	Brown	4748	1	6	3	4			7	8		9	10	11						2	5			
21	Dec	3	CHESTERFIELD	2-0	Jones, Brownsword (p)	7114	1	6	3	4				8	9		11		7					2	5		10	
22		17	BRADFORD PARK AVE.	4-2	Brown 3, Gregory	5942	1	6	3	4			7	8	10	9	11							2	5			
23		24	Oldham Athletic	1-2	Jones	5852	1	6	3	4			7	8	10	9	11							2	5			
24		26	Bradford City	3-4	Gregory 2, Brown	7896	1	6	3	4			7	8	10	9	11							2	5			
25		27	BRADFORD CITY	2-0	Haigh, McGill	7978		6	3	4			7	8	10	9	11			1				2	5			
26		31	WORKINGTON	3-1	Brown 2, Davies	7446		6	3	4			7	8	10	9	11			1				2	5			
27	Jan	21	DERBY COUNTY	0-2		10361		6	3	4			7	8	10	9	11			1				2	5			
28	Feb	4	Crewe Alexandra	2-1	Gregory, Jones	2432		2	3	4		6	7	8	10	9	11			1					5			
29		11	HARTLEPOOLS UNITED	5-1	Jones 2, Brown, Bushby, McGill(p)	5614		2	3	4		6	7	8	10	9	11			1					5			
30		18	Carlisle United	2-1	Haigh, Gregory	4928		2	3	4		6	7	8	10	9	11			1					5			
31	Mar	3	Barrow	2-2	Callaghan, Haigh	4001		2	3	4		6		8	10	9	11		7	1					5			
32		10	ACCRINGTON STANLEY	2-3	Brown 2	10049		2	3	4		6	7	8	10	9	11			1					5			
33		17	Southport	2-2	Brown, Mullen	5610		2	3	4		6	7	8	10	9				1					5		11	
34		22	ROCHDALE	1-2	Gregory	4865		2	3	4		6	7	8	10	9				1					5		11	
35		24	GATESHEAD	1-1	Brown	4702		2	3	4		6		8	10	9					7	1			5		11	
36		30	Grimsby Town	1-0	Brown	23399		2	3	4		6		8	10	9					7	1			5		11	
37		31	Darlington	0-1		4797			3	4		6	7	8	10	9						1		2	5		11	
38	Apr	2	GRIMSBY TOWN	0-1		19067			3	4		6		8	10	9	11				7	1		2	5			
39		7	TRANMERE ROVERS	2-1	Brown, Gregory	4343		2	3			6		8	10	9			4	7	1				5		11	
40		9	York City	0-0		9045		2	3			6		8	10	9			4	7	1				5		11	
41		14	Chesterfield	0-2		5592		2	3			6		8	10	9			4	7	1				5		11	
42		18	SOUTHPORT	0-1		4333		2	3			6	7	8	10	9	11			1		4			5			
43		21	CHESTER	2-1	Gregory, Haigh	4452		6	3				7	8		10	11	9		1		4			5			2
44		26	STOCKPORT COUNTY	1-5	Gregory	3780		6	3				7	8		9	10			1		4			5		11	2
45		28	Halifax Town	3-0	Haigh, Gregory, Brown	2839			3	4			7	8	10	9	11			1		6		2	5			
46	May	2	Chester	5-3	Brown 2, Gregory, McGill(p), Bushby	3253			3	8		6	7		10	9	11			1		4		2	5			
			Apps				13	42	45	31	18	28	31	44	40	45	36	16	19	33	3	6	2	14	28	1	9	2
			Goals						3	3		2	3	8	21	20	7		6								1	

One own goal

F.A. Cup

	Date		Opponent	Score	Scorers	Att	Malan NF	Hubbard J	Brownsword NJ	McGill A	White R	Bushby A	Davies JR	Haigh J	Brown GA	Gregory JE	Jones JM	Barrett J	Callaghan R	Marshall PW	Thompson D	Sharpe LT	Benson JR	Lamb HT	Heward B	Parrott JF	Mullen A	Wainwright L
R1	Nov	19	SHILDON COLLIERY	3-0	Davies, Brown, Gregory	7114	1	8	3	4			7		9	10	11	6						2	5			
R2	Dec	10	Bishop Auckland	0-0		12440	1	6	3	4				8	10		11			7				2	5	9		
rep		15	BISHOP AUCKLAND	2-0	Davies, Hubbard	9923	1	6	3	4			7	8	10	9	11							2	5			
R3	Jan	7	Rotherham United	1-1	Brown	16104		6	3	4			7	8	10	9	11			1				2	5			
rep		12	ROTHERHAM UNITED	4-2	Brown 3, Davies	13222		6	3	4			7	8	10	9	11			1				2	5			
R4		28	Liverpool	3-3	Davies 2, Gregory	53393		2	3	4		6	7	8	10	9	11			1					5			
rep	Feb	6	LIVERPOOL	1-2	Davies	19602		2	3	4		6	7	8	10	9	11			1					5			

R4 replay a.e.t.

		P	W	D	L	F	A	W	D	L	F	A	Pts
1	Grimsby Town	46	20	1	2	54	10	11	5	7	22	19	68
2	Derby County	46	18	4	1	67	23	10	3	10	43	32	63
3	Accrington Stanley	46	17	4	2	61	19	8	5	10	31	38	59
4	Hartlepools United	46	18	2	3	47	15	8	3	12	34	45	57
5	Southport	46	12	9	2	39	18	11	2	10	27	35	57
6	Chesterfield	46	18	1	4	61	21	7	3	13	33	45	54
7	Stockport County	46	16	4	3	65	22	5	5	13	25	39	51
8	Bradford City	46	16	5	2	57	25	2	8	13	21	39	49
9	SCUNTHORPE UNITED	46	12	4	7	40	26	8	4	11	35	37	48
10	Workington	46	13	4	6	47	20	6	5	12	28	43	47
11	York City	46	12	4	7	44	24	7	5	11	41	48	47
12	Rochdale	46	13	5	5	46	39	4	8	11	20	45	47
13	Gateshead	46	15	4	4	56	32	2	7	14	21	52	45
14	Wrexham	46	11	5	7	37	28	5	5	13	29	45	42
15	Darlington	46	11	6	6	41	28	5	3	15	19	45	41
16	Tranmere Rovers	46	11	4	8	33	25	5	5	13	26	59	41
17	Chester	46	10	8	5	35	33	3	6	14	17	49	40
18	Mansfield Town	46	13	6	4	59	21	1	5	17	25	60	39
19	Halifax Town	46	10	6	7	40	27	4	5	14	26	49	39
20	Oldham Athletic	46	7	12	4	48	36	3	6	14	28	50	38
21	Carlisle United	46	11	3	9	45	36	4	5	14	26	59	38
22	Barrow	46	11	6	6	44	25	1	3	19	17	58	33
23	Bradford Park Ave.	46	13	4	6	47	38	0	3	20	14	84	33
24	Crewe Alexandra	46	9	4	10	32	35	0	6	17	18	70	28

40

1956/57   14th in Division 3(N)

Players (columns, left to right):
Whitnall B · Hubbard J · Brownsword NJ · McGill A · Hussey FM · Bushby A · Whiteside WR · Haigh J · Brown GA · Fletcher D · Jones JM · Gregory JE · Sharpe LT · Luke GB · Heward B · Lewis K · Charlesworth T · Davies JR · Horstead JB · Waldock R · Mullen A · Gleadall E · Hardwick K · Whitnall B

#		Date	Opponent	Score	Scorers	Att	Hub	Brw	McG	Hus	Bus	Whi	Hai	Brn	Fle	Jon	Gre	Sha	Luk	Hew	Lew	Cha	Dav	Hor	Wal	others
1	Aug	18	DARLINGTON	1-2	Brown	7923	2	3	4	5	6	7	8	9	10	11										
2		21	Southport	2-2	Brown 2	6625	2	3	4	5	6	7	8	9	10	11										
3		25	Barrow	2-1	Brown, Fletcher	8455	2	3	4	5	6		8	9	10	11	7									
4		30	SOUTHPORT	1-0	Brown	7788	2	3	4	5	6		8	9	10	11	7									
5	Sep	1	HULL CITY	1-1	Brown	11004	2	3		5	6		8	9	10	11	7	4								
6		3	Bradford Park Avenue	2-1	Haigh, Gregory	8564	2	3		5	6		8	9	10	11	7	4								
7		8	Workington	2-2	Haigh, Jones	11073	2	3		5	6		8	7	10	11		4	9							
8		13	BRADFORD PARK AVE.	2-2	Brown, Luke	7855	2	3		5	6		8	7	10	11		4	9							
9		15	HALIFAX TOWN	6-1	Luke 2, Jones 2, Fletcher, Brown	7143	2	3		5	6		8	7	10	11		4	9							
10		19	Crewe Alexandra	1-2	Luke	5425	2	3		5	6		8	7	10	11		4	9							
11		22	Rochdale	0-3		6320	2	3		5	6		8	7	10	11		4	9							
12		27	CREWE ALEXANDRA	5-1	Gregory 2, Haigh, Fletcher, Brown	5778	2	3	4	5	6		8	7		11	10		9							
13		29	MANSFIELD TOWN	0-1		7774	2	3	4	5	6		8	7		11	10		9							
14	Oct	6	Chesterfield	0-1		9017	2	3	4		6		8		11	7	10		9			5				
15		13	CHESTER	3-0	Brown, McGill, Gill (og)	6377	2	3	4		6		8	7		11	10		9			5				
16		20	York City	2-0	Gregory, Hubbard	8881	2	3	4		6		8	7		11	10		9			5				
17		27	BRADFORD CITY	1-1	Brown	6837	2	3	4		6		8		7	11	10		9			5				
18	Nov	3	Stockport County	3-1	Brown, Bushby, Jones	12313	2	3	4		6		8		7	11	10		9			5				
19		10	CARLISLE UNITED	1-2	Luke	5546	2	3	4		6		8			11	10		9			5	7			
20		24	TRANMERE ROVERS	1-4	Gregory	5228	2	3	4		6		8		7	11	10		9			5				
21	Dec	1	Hartlepools United	0-0		7881	2	3	4		6		8		10	11			9			5	1	7		
22		15	Darlington	2-1	Fletcher 2	3421	2	3			6		8	9		11		10	4			5	1	7		
23		22	BARROW	1-1	Haigh	3234	2	3			6		8	9		11		10	4			5	1	7		
24		25	Derby County	0-4		11266	2	3	4		6		8	9	7	11			10			5	1			
25		26	DERBY COUNTY	1-4	McGill (pen)	4103	2	3	4		6		8	9	7	11			10			5	1			
26		29	Hull City	2-2	Fletcher 2	12873		3	4		6		8	9	7	11	10					5	1	2		
27	Jan	1	Accrington Stanley	1-0	Brown	8880	3		4		6		8	9	7	11	10					5	1	2		
28		12	WORKINGTON	2-1	Brown, R Brown (og)	5707		3	4		6		8	9	7	11	10					5	1	2		
29		19	Halifax Town	0-1		4496		3	4		6		8	9		11	10					5	1	7	2	
30	Feb	2	ROCHDALE	1-0	Haigh	6080		3	4		6		10	9						11		5	7	2	8	
31		9	Mansfield Town	1-1	Davies	8823		3	4		6		10	9		11						5	7	2	8	
32		16	CHESTERFIELD	5-1	Waldock 3, Fletcher, McGill	6854		3	4		6		10	9		11						5	7	2	8	
33		23	Chester	2-2	Waldock, Haigh	2691		3	4		6		10	9		11						5	7	2	8	
34	Mar	2	YORK CITY	2-1	Davies, Jones	7848		3	4	5	6		10	9		11							7	2	8	
35		9	Bradford City	1-3	Waldock	13475		3	4		6		10	9								5	7	2	8	Hardwick 7
36		16	STOCKPORT COUNTY	2-3	Waldock, Bushby (p)	6829		3	4	5	6		10	9								1	7	2	8	Hardwick 7
37		23	Carlisle United	0-0		8165	3		4	5	6			9		11						1	7	2	10	Hardwick 8
38		30	ACCRINGTON STANLEY	2-3	Fletcher, Haigh	6602		3	4	5	6		10	9								1	7	2	8	
39	Apr	4	WREXHAM	4-3	Haigh, Waldock, Fletcher, Davies	4196	3		4	5	6		10	9								1	7	2	8	
40		6	Tranmere Rovers	2-4	Waldock, Haigh	5491	9	3	4	5	6		10									1	7	2	8	
41		10	Wrexham	1-1	Luke	4340	2	3	4	5	6			10					9			1	7		8	
42		13	HARTLEPOOLS UNITED	1-2	Fletcher	4599		3	4	5	6		10	9									7	2	8	
43		19	GATESHEAD	1-2	Waldock	4044		3	4	5	6		10	9									7	2	8	Hardwick 1
44		20	Oldham Athletic	1-1	Fletcher	5897	2	3	4		6		10	9						5			7		8	Hardwick 1
45		22	Gateshead	0-0		3324	2	3			6		10	9		11		4		5			7		8	Hardwick 1
46		27	OLDHAM ATHLETIC	0-0		3903	3	2			6		10	9		11		4		5			7		8	Whitnall 1, 3

	Whitnall B	Hubbard J	Brownsword NJ	McGill A	Hussey FM	Bushby A	Whiteside WR	Haigh J	Brown GA	Fletcher D	Jones JM	Gregory JE	Sharpe LT	Luke GB	Heward B	Lewis K	Charlesworth T	Davies JR	Horstead JB	Waldock R	Mullen A	Gleadall E	Hardwick K	Whitnall B
Apps	1	32	43	35	22	46	2	45	38	28	38	19	11	18	24	1	17	19	17	17	1	3	4	1
Goals		1		3		2		9	14	12	5	5		6				3		9				

Two own goals

F.A. Cup

		Date	Opponent	Score	Scorers	Att	Hub	Brw	McG	Bus	Hai	Brn	Fle	Jon	Gre	Luk	Cha	Dav	Hor
R1	Nov	17	ROCHDALE	1-0	Brown	8655	2	3	4	6	8		7	11	10	9	5		
R2	Dec	8	WREXHAM	0-0		9153	2	3	4	6	8		10	11	9		5	1	7
rep		11	Wrexham	2-6	Gregory 2	11549	2	3	4	6	8	9		11	10		5	1	7

R2 replay a.e.t.

		P	W	D	L	F	A	W	D	L	F	A	Pts
1	Derby County	46	18	3	2	69	18	8	8	7	42	35	63
2	Hartlepools United	46	18	4	1	56	21	7	5	11	34	42	59
3	Accrington Stanley	46	15	4	4	54	22	10	4	9	41	42	58
4	Workington	46	16	4	3	60	25	8	6	9	33	38	58
5	Stockport County	46	16	3	4	51	26	7	5	11	40	49	54
6	Chesterfield	46	17	5	1	60	22	5	4	14	36	57	53
7	York City	46	14	4	5	43	21	7	6	10	32	40	52
8	Hull City	46	14	6	3	45	24	7	4	12	39	45	52
9	Bradford City	46	14	3	6	47	31	8	5	10	31	37	52
10	Barrow	46	16	2	5	51	22	5	7	11	25	40	51
11	Halifax Town	46	16	2	5	40	24	5	5	13	25	46	49
12	Wrexham	46	12	7	4	63	33	7	3	13	34	41	48
13	Rochdale	46	14	6	3	38	19	4	6	13	27	46	48
14	SCUNTHORPE UNITED	46	9	5	9	44	36	6	10	7	27	33	45
15	Carlisle United	46	9	9	5	44	36	7	4	12	32	49	45
16	Mansfield Town	46	13	3	7	58	38	4	7	12	33	52	44
17	Gateshead	46	9	6	8	42	40	8	4	11	30	50	44
18	Darlington	46	11	5	7	47	36	6	3	14	35	59	42
19	Oldham Athletic	46	9	7	7	35	31	3	8	12	31	43	39
20	Bradford Park Ave.	46	11	2	10	41	40	5	1	17	25	53	35
21	Chester	46	8	7	8	40	35	2	6	15	15	49	33
22	Southport	46	7	8	8	31	34	3	4	16	21	60	32
23	Tranmere Rovers	46	5	9	9	33	38	2	4	17	18	53	27
24	Crewe Alexandra	46	5	7	11	31	46	1	2	20	12	64	21

#	Date	Opponents	Score	Scorers	Att	Hardwick K	Horstead JB	Brownsword NJ	Marshall F	Heward B	Bushby A	Marriott JL	Waldock R	Fletcher D	Haigh J	Jones JM	Hussey FM	Hubbard J	Stokes AW	Whitnall B	Sharpe LT	Davies JR	Gleadall E	Davis EWC	Maw J	Minton AE
1	Aug 24	Chesterfield	1-1	Marriott	10768	1	2	3	4	5	6	7	8	9	10	11										
2	26	Tranmere Rovers	4-1	Waldock 3, Fletcher	13197	1	2	3	4	5	6	7	8	9	10	11										
3	31	DARLINGTON	5-0	Marriott 2, Waldock 2, Fletcher	8506	1	2	3	4	5	6	7	8	9	10	11										
4	Sep 5	TRANMERE ROVERS	1-0	Fletcher	10480	1	2	3	4	5	6	7	8	9	10	11										
5	7	Gateshead	2-1	Waldock, Fletcher	5666	1	2	3	4	5	6	7	8	9	10	11										
6	12	CREWE ALEXANDRA	3-2	Marriott, Haigh, Brownsword (pen)	9674	1	2	3	4	5	6	7	8	9	10	11										
7	14	MANSFIELD TOWN	3-3	Haigh, Brownsword(p), Chamberlain(og)	9533	1	2	3	4		6	7	8	9	10	11	5									
8	18	Crewe Alexandra	2-0	Haigh, Williams (og)	4159	1	5	3	4		6	7	8	9	10	11		2								
9	21	Workington	2-3	Haigh, Fletcher	8839	1	5	3	4		6	7	8	9	10	11		2								
10	25	Rochdale	4-1	Haigh, Waldock, Marriott, Fletcher	5278	1	5	3	4		6	7	8	9	10	11		2								
11	28	BRADFORD CITY	0-2		9576	1	5	3	4		6	7	8	9	10	11		2								
12	Oct 3	ROCHDALE	2-0	Haigh, Stokes	11638	1	5	3	4		6	7	8		10	11		2	9							
13	5	Hull City	0-2		12009	1	5	3	4		6	7	8		10	11		2	9							
14	12	Accrington Stanley	1-2	Fletcher	7388	1	5		4		6	7	8		10	11		3	9	2						
15	19	BRADFORD PARK AVE.	6-2	Davies 2, Fletcher 2, Brownsword 2(2p)	7591	1	5	3	4		6	11	8	9	10			2				7				
16	26	Carlisle United	4-3	Gleadall 2, Fletcher, Marriott	10579	1	5	3	4		6	11		9	10			2				7	8			
17	31	HALIFAX TOWN	1-1	Davies	9373	1	5	3	4		6	11		9	10			2				7	8			
18	Nov 2	SOUTHPORT	1-0	Fletcher	8305	1	5	3	4		6	11	8	9	10			2				7				
19	9	York City	0-0		8276	1	5	3	4		6	11	8	9				2				7				
20	23	Oldham Athletic	1-2	Davis	8150	1	5	3	4		6		8		10	11		2				7		9		
21	30	BURY	1-0	Waldock	10926	1	5	3	4		6	7	8	9	10	11		2								
22	Dec 14	Chester	2-1	Fletcher 2	4604	1	5	3	4		6	7	8	9	10	11		2								
23	21	CHESTERFIELD	1-1	Fletcher	7741	1	5	3	4		6		8	9	10	11		2				7				
24	26	Halifax Town	1-0	Waldock	9942	1	5	3	4		6		8	9	10	11		2				7				
25	28	Darlington	1-1	Waldock	7833	1	5	3	4		6		8		10	11		2				7		9		
26	Jan 11	GATESHEAD	2-1	Waldock 2	7750	1	5	3	4		6	7	8		10	11		2						9		
27	18	Mansfield Town	5-3	Davis 2, Waldock, Haigh, Marriott	8415	1	5	3	4		6	7	8		10	11		2						9		
28	Feb 1	WORKINGTON	2-2	Waldock 2	9060	1	5		4		6	7	8		10	11		2						9	3	
29	20	HULL CITY	2-0	Davis, Feasey (og)	11408	1	5	3	4		6	7	8		10	11		2						9		
30	22	OLDHAM ATHLETIC	1-1	Waldock	10036	1	5	3	4		6		8		10	11		2				7		9		
31	Mar 1	Bradford Park Avenue	2-1	Waldock 2	13467	1	5	3	4		6		8		10	11					2	7		9		
32	13	STOCKPORT COUNTY	4-0	Waldock 2, Davis 2	8446	1	5	3	4	6			8		10	11					2	7		9		
33	15	Southport	2-1	Waldock, Davis	3366	1	5	3	4	6			8		10	11					2	7		9		
34	22	ACCRINGTON STANLEY	1-0	Davis	11304	1	5	3	4	6			8		10	11					2	7		9		
35	29	Barrow	1-0	Davies	5261	1	5	3	4	6			8		10	11					2	7		9		
36	Apr 4	Wrexham	0-1		14280	1	5	3	4	6			8		10	11					2	7		9		
37	5	HARTLEPOOLS UNITED	2-0	Davis 2	8684	1	5	3	4				8		10	11		6			2	7		9		
38	7	WREXHAM	1-0	Brownsword (p)	9879	1	5	3	4			7	8		10	11		6			2			9		
39	12	Bury	1-2	Haigh	12508	1	5	3	4			7	8			11		6	10		2			9		
40	17	BARROW	1-0	Stokes	9609	1	5	3	4			7	8			11		6	10		2			9		
41	19	YORK CITY	1-2	Davis	10083	1	5	3	4			7	8			11		6	10		2			9		
42	21	Stockport County	1-2	Davis	14005	1	5	3	4			7	8		10	11		6			2			9		
43	24	Bradford City	3-2	Minton 2, Davis	18240	1	5	3	4			7			10	11		6			2			9		8
44	26	CHESTER	2-1	Haigh, Davis	10403	1	5	3	4			7			10	11		6			2			9		8
45	28	Hartlepools United	2-1	Davis 2	8159	1	5	3	4			7			10	11		6			2			9		8
46	May 1	CARLISLE UNITED	3-1	Davis, Haigh, Brownsword (p)	12555	1	5	3	4			7	8		10	11		6			2			9		
		Apps				46	46	44	46	11	31	34	33	26	45	41	1	33	5	1	16	17	3	23	1	3
		Goals						6				7	21	14	10				2			4	2	17		2

Three own goals

F.A. Cup

#	Date	Opponents	Score	Scorers	Att	Hardwick K	Horstead JB	Brownsword NJ	Marshall F	Heward B	Bushby A	Marriott JL	Waldock R	Fletcher D	Haigh J	Jones JM	Hussey FM	Hubbard J	Stokes AW	Whitnall B	Sharpe LT	Davies JR	Gleadall E	Davis EWC	Maw J	Minton AE
R1	Nov 16	GOOLE TOWN	2-1	Fletcher, Davies	8896	1	5	3	4		6	11	8	9	10			2				7				
R2	Dec 7	BURY	2-0	Waldock, Jones	12597	1	5	3	4		6	7	8	9	10	11		2								
R3	Jan 4	BRADFORD CITY	1-0	Haigh	11645	1	5	3	4		6	7	8	9	10	11					2					
R4	25	Newcastle United	3-1	Davis 2, Haigh	39230	1	5	3	4		6	7	8		10	11					2			9		
R5	Feb 15	LIVERPOOL	0-1		23000	1	5	3	4		6	7	8		10	11					2			9		

		P	W	D	L	F	A	W	D	L	F	A	Pts
1	SCUNTHORPE UNITED	46	16	5	2	46	19	13	3	7	42	31	66
2	Accrington Stanley	46	16	4	3	53	28	9	5	9	30	33	59
3	Bradford City	46	13	7	3	42	19	8	8	7	31	30	57
4	Bury	46	17	4	2	61	18	6	6	11	33	44	56
5	Hull City	46	15	6	2	49	20	4	9	10	29	47	53
6	Mansfield Town	46	16	3	4	68	42	6	5	12	32	50	52
7	Halifax Town	46	15	5	3	52	20	5	6	12	31	49	51
8	Chesterfield	46	12	8	3	39	28	6	7	10	32	41	51
9	Stockport County	46	15	4	4	54	28	3	7	13	20	39	47
10	Rochdale	46	14	4	5	50	25	5	4	14	29	42	46
11	Tranmere Rovers	46	12	6	5	51	32	6	4	13	31	44	46
12	Wrexham	46	13	8	2	39	18	4	4	15	22	45	46
13	York City	46	11	8	4	40	26	6	4	13	28	50	46
14	Gateshead	46	12	5	6	41	27	3	10	10	27	49	45
15	Oldham Athletic	46	11	7	5	44	32	3	10	10	28	52	45
16	Carlisle United	46	13	3	7	56	35	6	3	14	24	43	44
17	Hartlepools United	46	11	6	6	45	26	5	6	12	28	50	44
18	Barrow	46	9	7	7	36	32	4	8	11	30	42	41
19	Workington	46	11	6	6	46	33	3	7	13	26	48	41
20	Darlington	46	15	3	5	53	25	2	4	17	25	64	41
21	Chester	46	7	10	6	38	26	6	3	14	35	55	39
22	Bradford Park Ave.	46	8	6	9	41	41	5	5	13	27	54	37
23	Southport	46	8	3	12	29	40	3	3	17	23	48	28
24	Crewe Alexandra	46	6	5	12	29	41	2	2	19	18	52	23

1958/59   18th in Division 2

No		Date	Opponent	Score	Scorers	Att	Hardwick K	Hubbard J	Brownsword NJ	Marshall F	Horstead JB	Sharpe LT	Marriott JL	Waldock R	Davis EWC	Haigh J	Ormond W	Jones JM	Heward B	Wood BW	Minton AE	Neale P	Jones K	Harburn PAP	Ward JR	Bushby A	Pearce DG	Donnelly P	Grant J
1	Aug	23	IPSWICH TOWN	1-1	Davis	13317	1	2	3	4	5	6	7	8	9	10	11												
2		28	Swansea Town	0-3		21056	1	2	3	4	5	6	7	8	9	10	11												
3		30	Bristol Rovers	0-4		24221	1	2	3	4	5	6	7	8	9	10	11												
4	Sep	4	SWANSEA TOWN	3-1	Davis 2, Waldock	13592	1	2	3	4	5	6	7	8	9	10		11											
5		6	DERBY COUNTY	2-2	Marriott, Haigh	13318	1	2	3	4	5	6	7	8	9	10		11											
6		10	Stoke City	3-4	Waldock, Sharpe, M Jones	17824	1	2	3	4	5	6	7	8	9	10		11											
7		13	Leyton Orient	1-2	Waldock	15955	1	2	3	4	5	6	7	8	9	10		11											
8		18	STOKE CITY	1-1	M Jones	14159	1	2	3	4	10	6	7	8	9			11	5										
9		20	ROTHERHAM UNITED	2-0	Wood, Brownsword (p)	13595	1	2	3	4		6	7		9	8		11	5	10									
10		27	SHEFFIELD WEDNESDAY	1-4	Brownsword (p)	17488	1	2	3	4		6	7		9	8		11	5	10									
11	Oct	4	Fulham	1-1	Bentley (og)	24569	1	2	3	4		6	7		10	8		11	5		9								
12		11	Sheffield United	1-4	M Jones	22084	1	2	3	4		6	7	10	9	8		11	5										
13		18	BRIGHTON & HOVE ALB	2-3	Waldock, Haigh	11921	1	2	3			2	7	8	9	4		11	5		10	6							
14		25	Grimsby Town	1-1	Waldock	16979	1	2	3		5	6	7	9		8		11	4			10							
15	Nov	1	BARNSLEY	1-0	Waldock	12958	1	2	3			6	7	8	9	4		11	5			10							
16		8	Middlesbrough	1-6	Neale	23020	1	2	3			6	7	8	9	4		11	5			10							
17		15	CHARLTON ATHLETIC	3-3	Waldock, Hewie (og), Brownsword (p)	11023	1	2	3	4	5	6	7	9		8		11				10							
18		22	Bristol City	1-0	Marriott	20306	1	2	3	4	5	6	7	9		8		11				10							
19	Dec	6	Huddersfield Town	1-0	Marriott	13888	1	2	3	4	5	6	7	9		8		11				10							
20		13	LIVERPOOL	1-2	Waldock	11194	1	2	3	4	5	6	7	9		8		11				10							
21		18	CARDIFF CITY	1-0	Marriott	10365	1	2	3	4	5	6	7	9		8		11				10							
22		20	Ipswich Town	1-3	Waldock	13204	1	2	3		5	4	7	10	9	8		11				6							
23		26	SUNDERLAND	3-2	Ashurst (og), Neale, Sharpe	14509	1	2	3	4	5	6	7	9		8		11				10							
24		27	Sunderland	1-3	Neale	27550	1	2	3	4		6	7	9		8		11	5			10							
25	Jan	3	BRISTOL ROVERS	0-0		11130		2	3	4	5		7	9		8		11	6			10	1						
26		17	Derby County	1-3	Harburn	13941	1	2	3	4	5	6	7	10		8		11						9					
27		31	LEYTON ORIENT	2-0	Harburn, Waldock	10295	1	2	3	4	5	6	7	10		8		11						9					
28	Feb	7	Rotherham United	0-1		9843	1	2	3	4	5	6	7	10		8		11						9					
29		14	Sheffield Wednesday	0-2		21801	1	2	3	4	5	6	7	10		8		11						9					
30		21	FULHAM	1-2	Waldock	10086		2	3	4	5	6	7	11								8	1	9	10				
31		28	MIDDLESBROUGH	0-3		11171		2	3	4	5	6	7	10								11	1	9					
32	Mar	7	Brighton & Hove Albion	1-2	Haigh	17795		2	3	4	5		7	9		8		11					1	10		6			
33		14	GRIMSBY TOWN	1-3	Marriott	13559		2	3	4		5	7	9		8		11	6				1	10			4		
34		21	Barnsley	1-0	Harburn	6082	1	2	3	4	5		7	8		10		11						9					
35		27	Lincoln City	3-3	Harburn, Waldock, Jones M	14679	1	2	3	4	5		7	8		10		11						9					
36		28	SHEFFIELD UNITED	1-3	Harburn	12353		2	3	4			7	8		10		11	5			6	1	9					
37		30	LINCOLN CITY	3-1	Donnelly 2, Harburn	13742	1	2	3				7	8		4		11	5			6	1	9				10	
38	Apr	4	Charlton Athletic	3-2	Harburn 2, Waldock	15285	1	2	3	4			7	8		10		11	5			6		9					
39		11	BRISTOL CITY	3-3	Donnelly 2 (1 p), McCall (og)	11101	1	2	3				7	8		4		11	5			6		9				10	
40		18	Cardiff City	2-0	Haigh, Waldock	13003	1	2	3	4				8	10	7			5			6		9			11		
41		22	Liverpool	0-3		13976	1	2	3	4				8	10	7			5		11	6		9					
42		25	HUDDERSFIELD T	0-3		9035	1		3	4				8	10			11	5			6		9				2	7
Apps							35	40	42	34	27	30	39	38	17	40	3	37	19	3	2	26	7	15	1	1	2	3	1
Goals									3			2	5	14	3	4		4		1		3		8				4	

Four own goals

F.A. Cup

		Date	Opponent	Score		Att	Hardwick K	Hubbard J	Brownsword NJ	Marshall F	Horstead JB	Sharpe LT	Marriott JL	Waldock R	Davis EWC	Haigh J	Ormond W	Jones JM	Heward B	Wood BW	Minton AE	Neale P
R3	Jan	10	BOLTON WANDERERS	0-2		23706	1	2	3	4	5	6	7	9		8		11				10

		P	W	D	L	F	A	W	D	L	F	A	Pts
1	Sheffield Wed.	42	18	2	1	68	13	10	4	7	38	35	62
2	Fulham	42	18	1	2	65	26	9	5	7	31	35	60
3	Sheffield United	42	16	2	3	54	15	7	5	9	28	33	53
4	Liverpool	42	15	3	3	57	25	9	2	10	30	37	53
5	Stoke City	42	16	2	3	48	19	5	5	11	24	39	49
6	Bristol Rovers	42	13	5	3	46	23	5	7	9	34	41	48
7	Derby County	42	15	1	5	46	29	5	7	9	28	42	48
8	Charlton Athletic	42	13	3	5	53	33	5	4	12	39	57	43
9	Cardiff City	42	12	2	7	37	26	6	5	10	28	39	43
10	Bristol City	42	11	3	7	43	27	6	4	11	31	43	41
11	Swansea Town	42	12	5	4	52	30	4	4	13	27	51	41
12	Brighton & Hove A.	42	10	9	2	46	29	5	2	14	28	61	41
13	Middlesbrough	42	9	7	5	51	26	6	3	12	36	45	40
14	Huddersfield Town	42	12	3	6	39	20	4	5	12	23	35	40
15	Sunderland	42	13	4	4	42	23	3	4	14	22	52	40
16	Ipswich Town	42	12	4	5	37	27	5	2	14	25	50	40
17	Leyton Orient	42	9	4	8	43	30	5	4	12	28	48	36
18	SCUNTHORPE UNITED	42	7	6	8	32	37	5	3	13	23	47	33
19	Lincoln City	42	10	5	6	45	37	1	2	18	18	56	29
20	Rotherham United	42	9	5	7	32	28	1	4	16	10	54	29
21	Grimsby Town	42	7	7	7	41	36	2	3	16	21	54	28
22	Barnsley	42	8	4	9	34	34	2	3	16	21	57	27

1959/60 — 15th in Division 2

#	Date		Opponent	Score	Scorers	Att	Hardwick K	John DCJ	Brownsword NJ	Sharpe LT	Horstead JB	Neale P	Marriott JL	Waldock R	Harbum PAP	Haigh J	Donnelly P	Heward B	Bakes MS	Thomas BEB	Williams I	Middleton H	Jones K	Pashley R	Passmoor T	Hubbard J	Needham A
1	Aug	22	BRISTOL CITY	1-1	Brownsword (p)	10863	1	2	3	4	5	6	7	8	9	10	11										
2		24	Plymouth Argyle	0-4		25888	1	2	3	4	5	6	7	8	9	10	11										
3		29	Huddersfield Town	0-2		14370	1	2	3	6	5	10	7	11	9	8		4									
4	Sep	3	PLYMOUTH ARGYLE	2-0	Sharpe, Haigh	12165	1	2	3	6	5		7	8	9	10		4	11								
5		5	Rotherham United	1-1	Haigh	10784	1	2	3	6	5		7	8	9	10		4	11								
6		9	Liverpool	0-2		31713	1	2	3	6	5	9	7	8		10		4	11								
7		12	CARDIFF CITY	1-2	Haigh	10933	1	2	3	6	5	9	7	8		10		4	11								
8		17	LIVERPOOL	1-1	Donnelly	11822	1	2	3	4		6	7	8		10	9	5	11								
9		19	Hull City	2-0	Waldock, Donnelly	18459	1	2	3	4		6	7	8		10	9	5	11								
10		26	SHEFFIELD UNITED	1-1	Marriott	15384	1	2	3	4		6	7			10	9	5	11	8							
11	Oct	3	Middlesbrough	1-3	Thomas	27979	1	2	3	4		6	7			10	9	5	11	8							
12		10	IPSWICH TOWN	2-2	Middleton, Thomas	11408		2	3	4		6	7			10	11	5		8	1	9					
13		17	Bristol Rovers	1-1	Donnelly	15225		2	3	4		6	7			8	10	5	11		1	9					
14		24	SWANSEA TOWN	3-1	Marriott, Donnelly, Middleton	9675		2	3	4		6	7			8	10	5	11		1	9					
15		31	Brighton & Hove Albion	1-0	Middleton	18927		2	3	4		6	7			8	10	5	11		1	9					
16	Nov	7	STOKE CITY	1-1	Haigh	10827		2	3	4		6	7			8	10	5	11		1	9					
17		14	Portsmouth	0-4		14949		2	3	4		6	7			8	10	5	11		1	9					
18		21	SUNDERLAND	3-1	Donnelly 2, Thomas	11822		2	3	6			7			4	10	5	11	8	1	9					
19		28	Aston Villa	0-5		37367		2	3	6			7			4	10	5	11	8	1	9					
20	Dec	5	LINCOLN CITY	5-0	Middleton 2, Thomas, Bakes, Brownsword (p)	13945		2	3	6			7			4	10	5	11	8		9	1				
21		12	Leyton Orient	1-1	Haigh	9588		2	3	6			7			4	10	5	11	8		9	1				
22		19	Bristol City	2-0	Marriott, Middleton	9099		2	3	6			7			4	10	5	11	8		9	1				
23		26	DERBY COUNTY	3-2	Middleton 2, Donnelly	13342		2	3	6			7			4	10	5	11	8		9	1				
24		28	Derby County	0-3		17677		2	3	6			7			4	10	5	11	8		9	1				
25	Jan	2	HUDDERSFIELD T	0-2		12228		2	3	6			7			4	10	5	11	8		9	1				
26		16	ROTHERHAM UNITED	2-1	Donnelly, Middleton	12745		2	3	6			7			4	10	5	11	8		9	1				
27		23	Cardiff City	2-4	Thomas, Middleton	16759		2	3	6			7			4	10	5	11	8		9	1				
28	Feb	6	HULL CITY	3-0	Middleton, Thomas, Donnelly	10885		2	3	6			7			4	10	5	11	8		9	1				
29		13	Sheffield United	1-2	Thomas	16460		2	3	6			7			4	10	5	11	8		9	1				
30		20	MIDDLESBROUGH	1-1	Thomas	10817		2	3	6			7			4	10	5	11	8		9	1				
31		27	Ipswich Town	0-1		12829		2	3	6			7			4	10	5	11	8		9	1				
32	Mar	5	BRISTOL ROVERS	3-4	Thomas 2, Donnelly	9277		2	3	6			7			4	10	5	11	8		9	1				
33		12	Swansea Town	1-3	Donnelly	11646		2	3	6			7			4	10	5	11	8		9	1				
34		19	ASTON VILLA	1-2	Marriott	13084		2	3	4		6	7				10	5	11	8		9	1				
35		26	Stoke City	3-1	Marriott, Pashley, Bakes	6234		2	3	4		6	7				9	5	11	10			1	8			
36	Apr	2	PORTSMOUTH	1-0	Donnelly	8675		2	3	4		6	7				9	5	11	10			1	8			
37		9	Sunderland	0-1		16952		2	3	4		6	7				9		11	10			1	8	5		
38		15	CHARLTON ATHLETIC	1-1	Haigh	8741		2	3	4		6	7			8			11	9		10	1		5		
39		16	LEYTON ORIENT	2-1	Bakes, Brownsword (p)	8197		2	3	4		6				8	10		11	7		9	1		5		
40		18	Charlton Athletic	2-5	Bakes, Donnelly	10787		2	3	4		6	7			8	10		11			9	1		5		
41		23	Lincoln City	1-2	Donnelly	12691		2	3				7			8	10	5	11			9	1			4	6
42		30	BRIGHTON & HOVE ALB	1-2	Donnelly	6537			3	8	2	10				4	11	5		7		9	1				6
			Apps				11	41	42	41	8	23	40	9	5	38	36	36	38	25	8	28	23	3	4	1	2
			Goals						3	1			5	1		6	15		4	10		11		1			

F.A. Cup

	Date		Opponent	Score	Scorers	Att	Hardwick K	John DCJ	Brownsword NJ	Sharpe LT	Horstead JB	Neale P	Marriott JL	Waldock R	Harbum PAP	Haigh J	Donnelly P	Heward B	Bakes MS	Thomas BEB	Williams I	Middleton H	Jones K	Pashley R	Passmoor T	Hubbard J	Needham A
R3	Jan	9	CRYSTAL PALACE	1-0	Middleton	12651		2	3	6			7			4	10	5	11	8		9	1				
R4		30	PORT VALE	0-1		14043		2	3	4		6	7			10	9	5		8			1	11			

	P	W	D	L	F	A	W	D	L	F	A	Pts
1 Aston Villa	42	17	3	1	62	19	8	6	7	27	24	59
2 Cardiff City	42	15	2	4	55	36	8	10	3	35	26	58
3 Liverpool	42	15	3	3	59	28	5	7	9	31	38	50
4 Sheffield United	42	12	5	4	43	22	7	7	7	25	29	50
5 Middlesbrough	42	14	5	2	56	21	5	5	11	34	43	48
6 Huddersfield Town	42	13	3	5	44	20	6	6	9	29	32	47
7 Charlton Athletic	42	12	7	2	55	28	5	6	10	35	59	47
8 Rotherham United	42	9	9	3	31	23	8	4	9	30	37	47
9 Bristol Rovers	42	12	6	3	42	28	6	5	10	30	50	47
10 Leyton Orient	42	12	4	5	47	25	3	10	8	29	36	44
11 Ipswich Town	42	12	5	4	48	24	7	1	13	30	44	44
12 Swansea Town	42	12	6	3	54	32	3	4	14	28	52	44
13 Lincoln City	42	11	3	7	41	25	5	4	12	34	53	39
14 Brighton & Hove A.	42	7	8	6	35	32	6	4	11	32	44	38
15 SCUNTHORPE UNITED	42	9	7	5	38	26	4	3	14	19	45	36
16 Sunderland	42	8	6	7	35	29	4	6	11	17	36	36
17 Stoke City	42	8	3	10	40	38	6	4	11	26	45	35
18 Derby County	42	9	4	8	31	28	5	3	13	30	49	35
19 Plymouth Argyle	42	10	6	5	42	36	3	3	15	19	53	35
20 Portsmouth	42	6	6	9	36	36	4	6	11	23	41	32
21 Hull City	42	7	6	8	27	30	3	4	14	21	46	30
22 Bristol City	42	8	3	10	27	31	3	2	16	33	66	27

1960/61   9th in Division 2

		Opponent	Score	Scorers	Att	Jones K	John DCJ	Brownsword NJ	Gibson A	Heward B	Neale P	Marriott JL	Godfrey BC	Thomas BEB	Bonson J	Bakes MS	Horstead JB	Sharpe LT	Middleton H	Kaye J	Turner J	Thorpe AW	Passmoor T	Needham A	Hemstead DW
1	Aug 20	Charlton Athletic	1-1	Thomas	12590	1	2	3	4	5	6	7	8	9	10	11									
2	25	IPSWICH TOWN	4-0	Marriott, Neale, Thomas, Godfrey	11130	1	2	3	4	5	6	7	8	9	10	11									
3	27	LEYTON ORIENT	2-2	Thomas 2	10107	1	2	3	4	5	6	7	8	9	10	11									
4	30	Ipswich Town	0-2		12426	1	2	3	4	5	6	7	8	9	10	11									
5	Sep 3	Derby County	5-2	Bonson 2, Thomas, Godfrey, Brownsword (p)	16944	1	2	3	4	5	6	7	8	9	10	11									
6	10	BRISTOL ROVERS	2-1	Thomas 2	10262	1	2	3	4	5	6	7	8	9	10	11									
7	15	MIDDLESBROUGH	1-1	Thomas	13852	1	2	3	4	5	6	7	8	9	10	11									
8	17	Liverpool	2-3	Thomas, Marriott	23797	1	2	3	4	5	6	7	8	9	10	11									
9	21	Middlesbrough	3-1	Thomas 2, Bonson	19744	1	2	3	4	5	6	7	8	9	10	11									
10	24	ROTHERHAM UNITED	1-1	Marriott	12724	1	2	3	4	5	6	7	8	9	10	11									
11	Oct 1	Southampton	2-4	Thomas 2	17464	1	2	3	4	5	6	7	8	9	10	11									
12	8	Sheffield United	0-2		14160	1	2	3	4	5	6	7	8	9	10	11									
13	15	STOKE CITY	1-1	Godfrey	8777	1	2	3	4	5	6	7	8	9	10	11									
14	24	Swansea Town	2-2	Bonson 2	9599	1	2	3	4			7	8	9	10	11	5	6							
15	29	LUTON TOWN	1-0	Thomas	8643	1	2	3	4			7	8	9	10	11	5	6							
16	Nov 5	Lincoln City	2-0	Godfrey, Thomas	10262	1	2	3	4			7	8	9	10	11	5	6							
17	12	PORTSMOUTH	5-1	Thomas 2, Godfrey 2, Sharpe	8335	1	2	3	4			7	8	9	10	11	5	6							
18	19	Huddersfield Town	2-1	Thomas, McGarry (og)	8617	1	2	3			4	7	8	9	10	11	5	6							
19	26	SUNDERLAND	3-3	Thomas, Bonson, Brownsword (p)	9158	1	2	3			4	7	8	9	10	11	5	6							
20	Dec 3	Plymouth Argyle	1-3	Sharpe	11925	1	2	3	4			7	8	9	10	11	5	6							
21	10	NORWICH CITY	2-1	Thomas, Godfrey	8444	1	2	3	4			7	8	9	10	11	5	6							
22	23	BRIGHTON & HOVE ALB	2-2	Brownsword 2 (2p)	9277	1	2	3	4			7	8	9	10	11	5	6							
23	27	Brighton & Hove Albion	1-1	Godfrey	20602	1	2	3	4			7	8	9	10	11	5	6							
24	31	Leyton Orient	1-2	Bonson	8450	1	2	3	4			7	8	9	10	11	5	6							
25	Jan 14	DERBY COUNTY	1-2	Godfrey	10067	1	2	3	4				8	9	10	11	5	6	7						
26	21	Bristol Rovers	3-3	Thomas 2, Marriott	11276	1	2	3			4	7	8	9	10	11	5	6							
27	Feb 4	LIVERPOOL	2-3	Thomas, Bonson	7970	1	2	3	4	6		7		9	10	11	5			8					
28	11	Rotherham United	0-4		8225	1	2	3	4	6		7		9	10	11	5			8					
29	18	SOUTHAMPTON	2-0	Thomas, Godfrey	8268			3	4	5		7	8	9	10	11	2	6			1				
30	25	SHEFFIELD UNITED	1-1	Godfrey	10873			3	4	5		7	8	9	10	11	2	6			1				
31	Mar 4	Stoke City	0-2		12667			3	4	5		7	8	9	10		2	6			1	11			
32	11	SWANSEA TOWN	1-2	Brownsword (p)	7926			3	4			7	8	9			2			10	1	11	5	6	
33	18	Norwich City	1-0	Godfrey	20598		2	3	4			7	8	9	10	11	5	6			1				
34	25	LINCOLN CITY	3-1	Bonson 2, Marriott	6981		2	3	4			7	8	9	10		5	6			1	11			
35	Apr 1	Sunderland	0-2		18242		2	3	4			7	8	9	10		5	6			1	11			
36	3	LEEDS UNITED	3-2	Godfrey, Thomas, Bakes	8725		2	3	4			7	8	9	10	11	5	6			1				
37	8	HUDDERSFIELD T	0-1		8352		2	3	4			7	8	9	10	11	5	6			1				
38	11	CHARLTON ATHLETIC	0-0		7303		2	3	4			7	8	9		11	5	6		10	1				
39	15	Portsmouth	2-2	Kaye, Godfrey	15223		2	3	4		5		7	9	8	11		6		10	1				
40	22	PLYMOUTH ARGYLE	2-0	Thomas, Bonson	5762		2	3	4		5	7	8	9	10	11		6			1				
41	25	Leeds United	2-2	Godfrey, Thorpe	6975		2	3	4		6	7	8	9	10		5				1	11			
42	29	Luton Town	0-0		8373		2				6	7		9	10		5	4		8	1	11			3
		Apps				28	38	41	38	18	20	40	39	42	40	36	27	25	1	6	14	6	1	1	1
		Goals						5				1	5	15	26	11	1			2		1			

One own goal

F.A. Cup

		Opponent	Score	Scorers	Att	Jones K	John DCJ	Brownsword NJ	Gibson A				Godfrey BC	Thomas BEB	Bonson J	Bakes MS	Horstead JB	Sharpe LT	Middleton H						
R3	Jan 7	BLACKPOOL	6-2	Thomas 3, Bonson 3	19303	1	2	3	4				8	9	10	11	5	6	7						
R4	28	Norwich City	1-4	Bakes	15485	1	2	3	4			7	8	9	10	11	5	6							

F.L. Cup

		Opponent	Score	Scorers	Att	Jones K	John DCJ	Brownsword NJ	Gibson A	Heward B	Neale P	Marriott JL	Godfrey BC	Thomas BEB	Bonson J	Bakes MS	Horstead JB	Sharpe LT	Middleton H						
R1	Oct 10	Rochdale	1-1	Bonson	4274	1	2	3	4	5	6	7	11	9	10			8							
rep	20	ROCHDALE	0-1		5727	1	2	3	4	5		7	8	9		11		6	10						

#	Date	Opponent	Score	Scorers	Att	Jones K	John DCJ	Agnew DY	Gibson A	Horstead JB	Howells R	Marriott JL	Godfrey BC	Thomas BEB	Bonson J	Thorpe AW	Brownsword NJ	Turner J	Hemstead DW	Kaye J	Neale P	Lindsey B	Bakes MS	Wilson A	Sharpe LT	Hodgson K	McGuigan JJ	McDowall JC
1	Aug 19	BRIGHTON & HOVE ALB	3-3	Marriott (p), Godfrey, Thomas	8068	1	2	3	4	5	6	7	8	9	10	11												
2	23	Norwich City	2-2	Thomas 2	27407	1	2		4	5	6	7	8	9	10	11	3											
3	26	Bury	1-4	Gibson	11236		2		4	5	6	7	8	9	10	11	3	1										
4	29	NORWICH CITY	2-0	Thomas 2	8923				4	5	6	7	8	9	10	11	3	1	2									
5	Sep 1	CHARLTON ATHLETIC	6-1	Godfrey 2, Thomas, Marriott, Thorpe, Brownsword (p)	9639				4	5	6	7	8	9	10	11	3	1	2									
6	5	BRISTOL ROVERS	2-1	Godfrey, Thomas	9657				4	5	6	7	8	9	10	11	3	1	2									
7	9	Liverpool	1-2	Godfrey	46837				4	5	6	7	8	9	10	11	3	1	2									
8	15	ROTHERHAM UNITED	5-2	Thomas 2, Godfrey 2, Thorpe	11953	1			4		6	7	10	9		11	3		2	8	5							
9	18	Bristol Rovers	1-2	Thomas	14107	1			4		6	7		9	10	11	3		2	8	5							
10	23	Sunderland	0-4		35112				4		6	7		9			3	1	2	8	5	10	11					
11	29	STOKE CITY	2-2	Thomas, Kaye	10487				4	5	6	7		9	10	11	3	1	2	8								
12	Oct 7	Swansea Town	1-2	Thomas	12479				4	2	6	7		9	10		3	1		8	5			11				
13	13	SOUTHAMPTON	5-1	Thomas 2, Wilson, Kaye, Davies(og)	10787	1			4	2	6	7	10	9			3			8	5			11				
14	21	Luton Town	2-1	Thomas, Kaye	9766	1			4	2	6	7	10	9			3			8	5			11				
15	27	NEWCASTLE UNITED	3-2	Thomas 2, Brownsword (p)	14158	1			4	2	6	7	10	9			3			8	5			11				
16	Nov 4	Middlesbrough	2-1	Thomas 2	12142	1			4	2	6	7	10	9			3			8	5			11				
17	11	PLYMOUTH ARGYLE	5-1	Thomas 4, Thorpe	8896	1			4	2	6	7	10	9		11	3			8	5							
18	18	Derby County	2-2	Brownsword (p), Wilson	21134	1			4	2		7	10	9			3			8	5			11	6			
19	24	LEYTON ORIENT	0-2		12003	1			4	2	6	7	10	9			3			8	5			11				
20	Dec 2	Preston North End	1-4	Thomas	8326	1			4	2	6	7		9			3			10	5	8		11				
21	16	Brighton & Hove Albion	3-0	Thomas, Kaye, Sitford(og)	9377	1			4	5	6	11		9	10		3		2	8						7		
22	22	BURY	1-2	Thomas	8473	1			4	5	6	11	8	9	10		3		2							7		
23	26	Leeds United	4-1	Thomas 4	19481	1			4	5	6	11	10	9			3		2	8						7		
24	Jan 13	Charlton Athletic	3-3	Thomas, Hodgson, Hinton(og)	13872	1			4	2	6	11	10	9			3			8	5					7		
25	20	LIVERPOOL	1-1	Howells	11452	1			4	2	6	7	8				3			9	5			11		10		
26	Feb 2	Rotherham United	1-0	Kaye	12528	1			4	2	6	7	8				3			9	5					11	10	
27	10	SUNDERLAND	3-1	McGuigan, Kaye, Godfrey	11656	1			4	2	6	7	8				3			9	5					11	10	
28	17	Stoke City	0-1		16578	1			4	2	6	7					3			9	5			11		8	10	
29	20	LEEDS UNITED	2-1	Hodgson, McGuigan	9186	1			4	2	6	11	8				3			9	5					7	10	
30	23	SWANSEA TOWN	2-0	Hodgson, McGuigan	8437	1			4	2	6	11	8				3			9	5					7	10	
31	Mar 3	Southampton	4-6	McGuigan, Marriott, Brownsword (p), Kaye	10455				4	2	6	7					3			9	5			11		8	10	1
32	6	WALSALL	2-1	McGuigan, Hodgson	7198	1			4	2	6	7					3			9	5			11		8	10	
33	10	LUTON TOWN	2-0	McGuigan, Kaye	7911	1	2		4		6	7				11	3			9	5					8	10	
34	17	Newcastle United	1-2	McGuigan	37931	1	2		4		6	11					3			9	5			7		8	10	
35	23	MIDDLESBROUGH	1-1	McGuigan	8149	1			4	2	6	7	8				3			9	5			11			10	
36	31	Plymouth Argyle	1-3	Kaye	15913	1	2		4				8				3			9	5			11	6	7	10	
37	Apr 6	DERBY COUNTY	2-0	Kaye, McGuigan	7188	1	2		4		6	7	8				3			9	5			11			10	
38	14	Leyton Orient	1-0	Kaye	16867	1	2		4		6	7	8							9	5			11			10	
39	20	PRESTON NORTH END	2-1	Hodgson 2	11368	1			4		6	7					3		2	9	5			11		8	10	
40	23	Huddersfield Town	2-1	Wilson, Gibson	12397	1			4		6	7					3		2	9	5			11		8	10	
41	24	HUDDERSFIELD T	1-3	Hodgson	10812	1			4		6	7					3				5		8	11		9	10	
42	28	Walsall	1-4	McGuigan	7173	1			4	2	6	7					3				5	8		11		9	10	
				Apps		33	9	1	41	31	41	40	29	24	12	12	39	8	15	32	31	3	1	21	2	19	17	1
				Goals					2		1	3	8	31		3	4			11				3		7	10	

Three own goals

F.A. Cup

	Date	Opponent	Score		Att	Jones K	John DCJ	Agnew DY	Gibson A	Horstead JB	Howells R	Marriott JL	Godfrey BC	Thomas BEB	Bonson J	Thorpe AW	Brownsword NJ	Turner J	Hemstead DW	Kaye J	Neale P	Lindsey B	Bakes MS	Wilson A	Sharpe LT	Hodgson K	McGuigan JJ	McDowall JC
R3	Jan 6	Charlton Athletic	0-1		20694	1			4	5	6	11	10	9			3		2	8						7		

F.L. Cup

	Date	Opponent	Score		Att	Jones K	John DCJ	Agnew DY	Gibson A	Horstead JB	Howells R	Marriott JL	Godfrey BC	Thomas BEB	Bonson J	Thorpe AW	Brownsword NJ	Turner J	Hemstead DW	Kaye J	Neale P	Lindsey B	Bakes MS	Wilson A	Sharpe LT	Hodgson K	McGuigan JJ	McDowall JC
R1	Sep 13	Newcastle United	0-2		14340				4	5	6	7	8	9	10	11	3	1	2									

		P	W	D	L	F	A	W	D	L	F	A	Pts
1	Liverpool	42	18	3	0	68	19	9	5	7	31	24	62
2	Leyton Orient	42	11	5	5	34	17	11	5	5	35	23	54
3	Sunderland	42	17	3	1	60	16	5	6	10	25	34	53
4	SCUNTHORPE UNITED	42	14	4	3	52	26	7	3	11	34	45	49
5	Plymouth Argyle	42	12	4	5	45	30	7	4	10	30	45	46
6	Southampton	42	13	3	5	53	28	5	6	10	24	34	45
7	Huddersfield Town	42	11	5	5	39	22	5	7	9	28	37	44
8	Stoke City	42	13	4	4	34	17	4	4	13	21	40	42
9	Rotherham United	42	9	6	6	36	30	7	3	11	34	46	41
10	Preston North End	42	11	4	6	34	23	4	6	11	21	34	40
11	Newcastle United	42	10	5	6	40	27	5	4	12	24	31	39
12	Middlesbrough	42	11	3	7	45	29	5	4	12	31	43	39
13	Luton Town	42	12	1	8	44	37	5	4	12	25	34	39
14	Walsall	42	11	7	3	42	23	3	4	14	28	52	39
15	Charlton Athletic	42	10	5	6	38	30	4	4	12	31	45	39
16	Derby County	42	10	7	4	42	27	4	4	13	26	48	39
17	Norwich City	42	10	6	5	36	28	4	5	12	25	42	39
18	Bury	42	9	4	8	32	36	8	1	12	20	40	39
19	Leeds United	42	9	6	6	24	19	3	6	12	26	42	36
20	Swansea Town	42	10	5	6	38	30	2	7	12	23	53	36
21	Bristol Rovers	42	11	3	7	36	31	2	4	15	17	50	33
22	Brighton & Hove A.	42	7	7	7	24	32	3	4	14	18	54	31

#	Date	Opponent	Score	Scorers	Att	Jones K	Gannon MJ	Brownsword NJ	Gibson A	Neale P	Howells R	Marriott JL	Godfrey BC	Kaye J	McGuigan JJ	Hodgson K	Hemstead DW	Wilson A	Lindsey B	Horstead JB	Anderson AA	Bakes MS	Thorpe AW	Crawford I	Passmoor T	Reeves TB
1	Aug 18	SOUTHAMPTON	2-1	Hodgson, Knapp(og)	9763	1	2	3	4	5	6	7	8	9	10	11										
2	22	Chelsea	0-3		18377	1	2	3	4	5	6	7	8	9	10	11										
3	25	Grimsby Town	0-3		16533	1		3	4	5	6	7	8	9	10	11	2									
4	28	CHELSEA	3-0	Kaye 3	11196	1		3	4	5	6			9	10	11	2	7	8							
5	Sep 1	Bury	2-0	Kaye, Lindsey	8510	1		3	4	5	6			9	10	11		7	8	2						
6	4	NEWCASTLE UNITED	2-1	Wilson, McGuigan	14293	1		3	4	5	6			9	10	11		7	8	2						
7	8	ROTHERHAM UNITED	1-0	Kaye	13113	1		3	4	5	6			9	10	11		7	8	2						
8	11	SWANSEA TOWN	1-0	Hodgson	10683	1		3	4	5	6			9	10	11		7	8	2						
9	15	Charlton Athletic	0-1		13315	1		3	4	5	6			9	10	7		11	8	2						
10	18	Swansea Town	0-1		11014	1		3	4	5	6		8	9	10	11		7		2						
11	22	STOKE CITY	0-0		11861	1		3	4	5	6		8	9		11		7	10	2						
12	29	Sunderland	0-0		43230	1		3	4	5				7	10	9		11	8	2	6					
13	Oct 6	PLYMOUTH ARGYLE	2-2	Godfrey, Hodgson	8712	1			4	5			7	9	10	11	3		8	2	6					
14	13	Preston North End	1-3	Kaye	10107	1		3	4	5				7	9	10			8	2	6	11				
15	19	PORTSMOUTH	1-2	Brownsword (p)	8576	1		3	4	5				7	9	10			8	2	6	11				
16	27	Cardiff City	0-4		12003	1		3	4	5		7	8	9	10					2	6			11		
17	Nov 2	HUDDERSFIELD T	2-2	Hodgson 2	8908	1		3	4	5	6		8	9	10	7				2				11		
18	10	Middlesbrough	3-4	Thorpe, McGuigan, Brownsword (p)	10738	1		3	4	5	6	7		9	10					2			8	11		
19	16	DERBY COUNTY	2-1	Howells, Hodgson	6304	1		3	4	5	6	7		9	10	8				2				11		
20	24	Newcastle United	1-1	Marriott	25864	1		3	4	5	6	7		9	10	8				2				11		
21	30	WALSALL	2-0	Brownsword (p), McPherson(og)	7274	1		3	4	5	6	7		9	10	8				2				11		
22	Dec 8	Norwich City	3-3	Kaye 2, Howells	12708	1		3	4	5	6	7		9	10	8				2				11		
23	15	Southampton	1-1	Hodgson	11113	1		3	4	5	6	7		9	10	8				2				11		
24	21	GRIMSBY TOWN	1-1	Gibson	12698	1		3	4	5	6	7		9	10	8				2				11		
25	Feb 23	Plymouth Argyle	3-2	McGuigan, Howells, Brownsword (p)	11823	1		3	4	5	6		8	9	10	11		7		2						
26	Mar 9	Portsmouth	2-1	Hodgson, Wilson	8493	1		3	4	5	6	11	8		9			7	10	2						
27	15	CARDIFF CITY	2-2	Kaye, Brownsword (p)	8060	1		3	4	5	6		8	9		11		7	10	2						
28	23	Huddersfield Town	0-2		11002	1			4	5	6		8	9	10	7	3			2				11		
29	26	PRESTON NORTH END	4-1	McGuigan 2, Wilson, Hodgson	7239	1		3	4		6			9	10	8		7		2				11	5	
30	29	MIDDLESBROUGH	1-1	Gibson	7474	1		3	4		6			9	10	8		7		2				11	5	
31	Apr 3	Leeds United	0-1		15833	1		3	4					9	10	8		7		2	6			11	5	
32	6	Derby County	2-6	Hodgson 2	8673	1		3	4		6			9	10	8		7		2				11	5	
33	12	LUTON TOWN	2-0	McGuigan, Gibson	7739	1		3	4		6			9	10	8		7		2				11	5	
34	15	Luton Town	0-1		9091	1	6		4					9	10		3	7	8	2				11	5	
35	20	Walsall	1-1	Wilson	6828	1	6		4	5				9	10		3	7	8	2				11		
36	23	LEEDS UNITED	0-2		8042	1	6	3	4	5			8	9	10			7		2				11		
37	26	NORWICH CITY	3-1	Kaye 2, Wilson	6012		6	3	4					9	10	11		7		2			8		5	1
38	30	SUNDERLAND	1-1	Ashurst (og)	9090		6	3	4					9	10	11		7		2			8		5	1
39	May 4	Stoke City	3-2	McGuigan, Kaye, Hodgson	25569		6	3	4					9	10	11		7		2			8		5	1
40	7	CHARLTON ATHLETIC	2-0	Crawford, Tocknell (og)	6792		6	3	4					9	10	11		7		2				8	5	1
41	10	BURY	1-0	Kaye	6644		6	3						9	10	11		7	4	2			8		5	1
42	17	Rotherham United	0-1		7367		6	3	4				8	9	10			7		2				11	5	1
				Apps		36	11	38	40	30	28	11	17	39	40	36	6	26	16	38	6	2	9	15	12	6
				Goals				5	3		3	1	1	13	7	12		5	1					1	1	

Four own goals

F.A. Cup

Rd	Date	Opponent	Score	Scorers	Att	Jones K	Brownsword NJ	Gibson A	Neale P	Howells R	Marriott JL	Godfrey BC	Kaye J	McGuigan JJ	Hodgson K	Wilson A	Horstead JB	Crawford I
R3	Jan 26	Portsmouth	1-1	Godfrey	15500	1	3	4		6	11	8	9	10		7	2	5
rep	Mar 7	PORTSMOUTH	1-2	McGuigan	9765	1	3	4	5	6		8	9	10	11	7	2	

F.L. Cup

Rd	Date	Opponent	Score	Scorers	Att	Jones K	Brownsword NJ	Gibson A	Neale P	Kaye J	McGuigan JJ	Hodgson K	Wilson A	Lindsey B	Horstead JB	Anderson AA	Crawford I
R2	Sep 24	Southampton	1-1	McGuigan	5905	1	3	4	5	7	10	9	11	8	2	6	
rep	Oct 2	SOUTHAMPTON	2-2	Gibson, Godfrey	6506	1	3	4	5	7	10	9	11	8	2	6	
rep2	9	Southampton	3-0	Godfrey, McGuigan, Wimhurst (og)	4984	1	3	4	5	7	9	10		8	2	6	11
R3	17	Sunderland	0-2		18154	1	3	4	5	7	9	10		8	2	6	11

R2 replay a.e.t.   R2 replay 2 at Peterborough.

		P	W	D	L	F	A	W	D	L	F	A	Pts
1	Stoke City	42	15	3	3	49	20	5	10	6	24	30	53
2	Chelsea	42	15	3	3	54	16	9	1	11	27	26	52
3	Sunderland	42	14	5	2	46	13	6	7	8	38	42	52
4	Middlesbrough	42	12	4	5	48	35	8	5	8	38	50	49
5	Leeds United	42	15	2	4	55	19	4	8	9	24	34	48
6	Huddersfield Town	42	11	6	4	34	21	6	8	7	29	29	48
7	Newcastle United	42	11	8	2	48	23	7	3	11	31	36	47
8	Bury	42	11	6	4	28	20	7	5	9	23	27	47
9	SCUNTHORPE UNITED	42	12	7	2	35	18	4	5	12	22	41	44
10	Cardiff City	42	15	4	4	50	29	6	2	13	33	44	43
11	Southampton	42	15	3	3	52	23	2	5	14	20	44	42
12	Plymouth Argyle	42	13	4	4	48	24	2	8	11	28	49	42
13	Norwich City	42	11	6	4	53	33	6	2	13	27	46	42
14	Rotherham United	42	11	3	7	34	30	6	3	12	33	44	40
15	Swansea Town	42	13	5	3	33	17	2	4	15	18	55	39
16	Portsmouth	42	9	5	7	33	27	4	6	11	30	52	37
17	Preston North End	42	11	6	4	43	30	2	5	14	16	44	37
18	Derby County	42	10	5	6	40	29	2	7	12	21	43	36
19	Grimsby Town	42	8	6	7	34	26	3	7	11	21	40	35
20	Charlton Athletic	42	8	4	9	33	38	5	1	15	29	56	31
21	Walsall	42	7	7	7	33	37	4	2	15	20	52	31
22	Luton Town	42	10	4	7	45	40	1	3	17	16	44	29

1963/64   22nd in Division 2: Relegated

#	Date		Opponent	Score	Scorers	Att	Reeves TB	Horstead JB	Brownsword NJ	Lindsey B	Neale P	Gannon MJ	Wilson A	Hodgson K	Lawther WI	Smillie AT	Crawford I	Jones K	Hutton J	Gibson A	Passmoor T	Hemstead DW	Harper IT	Mahy B	Godfrey BC	Marriott JL	Conde JP	Needham A	Kirkman AJ	Sloan D	Mason CE	Ellis KD
1	Aug	24	Swindon Town	0-3		18620	1	2	3	4	5	6	7	8	9	10	11															
2		27	NORTHAMPTON T	1-2	Lawther	8738		2	3	4	5	6		8	9	10	11	1	7													
3		30	CARDIFF CITY	1-2	Lawther	8366		2	3		6		7	8	9	10	11	1		4	5											
4	Sep	3	Northampton Town	0-2		16032		2	3		6		7	8	9	10	11	1		4	5											
5		7	Norwich City	1-2	Lawther	16222		2	3		6		7	8	9	10	11	1		4	5											
6		9	SUNDERLAND	1-1	Smillie	10489			3		5		7		9	10	11	1		4		2	6	8								
7		12	SWANSEA TOWN	2-2	Evans (og), Brownsword (p)	8516			3		5		7	8	9	10	11	1		4		2	6									
8		18	Sunderland	0-1		36128		6	3		5		7	8	9		11	1		4		2				10						
9		21	PORTSMOUTH	1-1	Hodgson	6890		6	3		5		7	8	9		11	1		4		2				10						
10		28	Rotherham United	1-2	Crawford	8834			3	8	5	6	7		9	10	11	1		4		2										
11	Oct	1	LEYTON ORIENT	0-0		6530			3	6	5		11	9		10	8	1		4		2			7							
12		5	LEEDS UNITED	0-1		11042		4	3	6	5		11	9		10	8	1				2			7							
13		19	MIDDLESBROUGH	1-0	Wilson	7347		6	3	8	9		7			10	11	1		4	5	2										
14		26	Preston North End	0-1		15832		6	3	8	9		7			10	11	1		4	5	2										
15	Nov	2	HUDDERSFIELD T	1-0	Neale	6074		6	3	8	9		10	11				1		4	5	2			7							
16		16	PLYMOUTH ARGYLE	1-0	Neale	5731		6	3	8	9		11		10			1		4	5	2			7							
17		23	Charlton Athletic	1-0	Hodgson	19803		6	3				11	8	10			1		4	5	2			7	9						
18		30	GRIMSBY TOWN	2-2	Conde, Lawther	8403		6	3				11	8	10			1		4	5				7	9	2					
19	Dec	7	Newcastle United	1-3	Hodgson	24988		6	3				11	8	10			1		4	5				7	9	2					
20		14	SWINDON TOWN	3-0	Hodgson, Lawther, Woodruff (og)	5113		6	3		5		11	8	10			1		4		2			7	9						
21		26	Manchester City	1-8	Lawther	26365		5	3			6	11	8	10			1	7	4		2						9				
22		28	MANCHESTER CITY	2-4	Brownsword (p), Kirkman	9324		5	3				11	8	10			1	7	4		2						9	6			
23	Jan	11	NORWICH CITY	2-2	Kirkman, Hodgson	5235			3	4	5		11	8	10			1	7			2						9	6			
24		16	Swansea Town	1-4	Sloan	7357			3	4	5		11		10			1	7			2						9		8		
25		25	Derby County	2-2	Hodgson, Sloan	9134			3	4	5		7	11	9			1				2							8	10		
26		29	Southampton	2-7	Sloan, Hodgson	14221		6	3	4	5		7	11	9			1				2							8	10		
27	Feb	1	Portsmouth	4-3	Hodgson 3, Smillie	11944		2	3	4	5		7	11	6	10		1								9		8				
28		8	ROTHERHAM UNITED	4-3	Lindsey, Wilson, Sloan, Madden (og)	7656		2	3	4	5		11	9	6	10		1										7		8		
29		15	Leeds United	0-1		29118		2	3	4	5		11	9	6			1	7							10				8		
30		22	SOUTHAMPTON	1-2	Brownsword	5801		2	3	4	5		11	9	6			1	7							10				8		
31		29	Plymouth Argyle	1-3	Hodgson	10289		6	3	4	5		11	9	10			1	7			2							8			
32	Mar	7	PRESTON NORTH END	1-0	Lindsey	6492		6	3	8	5		11	7	10			1				2									4	9
33		14	Leyton Orient	2-2	Wilson, Mason	4516		6	3	8	5		11	7	10			1				2									4	9
34		20	DERBY COUNTY	3-2	Wilson, Ellis, Brownsword (p)	7058		6	3		5		11	7	10			1				2							8		4	9
35		26	BURY	0-0		7624		6	3		5		11	7	10			1				2							8		4	9
36		28	Middlesbrough	0-2		8839		6	3	8	5			11	10			1				2							7		4	9
37		31	Bury	2-3	Lindsey, Wilson	6408		6	3	10	5		11		9			1	7			2							8		4	
38	Apr	4	CHARLTON ATHLETIC	1-1	Ellis	5345			3	6	5		11		10			1	7			2							8		4	9
39		8	Cardiff City	1-3	Lawther	9618			3	6	5		7	11	10			1										8			4	9
40		11	Grimsby Town	0-2		10656			3	6	5		7	11	10			1										2	8		4	9
41		18	NEWCASTLE UNITED	2-0	Lawther, Ellis	6648			3	6	5		7		10		11	1										2	8		4	9
42		25	Huddersfield Town	2-3	Ellis 2	5158			3	6	5		7		10		11	1										2	8		4	9
			Apps				1	33	39	28	37	4	40	33	38	12	20	41	6	19	10	25	2	4	2	8	4	10	12	12	12	10
			Goals						4	2	2		5	11	9	2	1										1			2	4	1	5

3 own goals

F.A. Cup

	Date		Opponent	Score	Scorers	Att	Horstead JB	Brownsword NJ	Lindsey B	Neale P	Wilson A	Hodgson K	Lawther WI	Jones K	Hutton J	Gibson A	Hemstead DW	Marriott JL
R3	Jan	4	BARNSLEY	2-2	Wilson, Lawther	11160	6	3	8	5	11	7	10	1		4	2	9
rep		7	Barnsley	2-3	Brownsword 2 (2p)	21337	6	3	4	5	11	8	10	1	7		2	9

Replay a.e.t.

F.L. Cup

	Date		Opponent	Score	Scorers	Att	Horstead JB	Brownsword NJ	Lindsey B	Neale P	Gannon MJ	Wilson A	Hodgson K	Lawther WI	Smillie AT	Crawford I	Jones K	Gibson A	Passmoor T	Hemstead DW
R2	Sep	25	STOKE CITY	2-2	Smillie, Wilson	6945		3	8	5	6	7		9	10	11	1	4		2
rep	Oct	16	Stoke City	3-3	Horstead, Crawford, Neale	11062	6	3	8	9		7			10	11	1	4	5	2
rep2		22	Stoke City	0-1		4297	6	3	8	9		7			10	11	1	4	5	2

Replay a.e.t. Replay 2 at Hillsborough.

		P	W	D	L	F	A	W	D	L	F	A	Pts
1	Leeds United	42	12	9	0	35	16	12	6	3	36	18	63
2	Sunderland	42	16	3	2	47	13	9	8	4	34	24	61
3	Preston North End	42	13	7	1	37	14	10	3	8	42	40	56
4	Charlton Athletic	42	11	4	6	44	30	8	6	7	32	40	48
5	Southampton	42	13	3	5	69	32	6	6	9	31	41	47
6	Manchester City	42	12	4	5	50	27	6	6	9	34	39	46
7	Rotherham United	42	14	3	4	52	26	5	4	12	38	52	45
8	Newcastle United	42	14	2	5	49	26	6	3	12	25	43	45
9	Portsmouth	42	9	7	5	46	34	7	4	10	33	36	43
10	Middlesbrough	42	14	4	3	47	16	1	7	13	20	36	41
11	Northampton Town	42	10	2	9	35	31	6	7	8	23	29	41
12	Huddersfield Town	42	11	4	6	31	25	4	6	11	26	39	40
13	Derby County	42	10	6	5	34	27	4	5	12	22	40	39
14	Swindon Town	42	11	5	5	39	24	3	5	13	18	45	38
15	Cardiff City	42	10	7	4	31	27	4	3	14	25	54	38
16	Leyton Orient	42	8	6	7	32	32	5	4	12	22	40	36
17	Norwich City	42	9	7	5	43	30	2	6	13	21	50	35
18	Bury	42	8	5	8	35	36	5	4	12	22	37	35
19	Swansea Town	42	11	4	6	44	26	1	5	15	19	48	33
20	Plymouth Argyle	42	6	8	7	26	32	2	8	11	19	35	32
21	Grimsby Town	42	6	7	8	28	34	3	7	11	19	41	32
22	SCUNTHORPE UNITED	42	8	8	5	30	25	2	2	17	22	57	30

#	Date	Opponent	Score	Scorers	Att	Reeves TB	Betts JB	Horstead JB	Lindsey B	Neale P	Bannister J	Hutton J	Kirkman AJ	Lawther WI	Sloan D	Ratcliffe JB	Brownsword NJ	Needham A	Wilson A	Smillie AT	Hemstead DW	Mahy B	Brown MR	Scott RSA	Bramley JS	Thomas BEB	Harper IT	Sidebottom G	Barton F	Smith RW
1	Aug 22	BRISTOL CITY	5-2	Lawther 2, Sloan 2, Kirkman	5702	1	2	3	4	5	6	7	8	9	10	11														
2	26	Gillingham	0-0		14187	1	2		4	5	6	7	8	9	10	11	3													
3	28	Queen's Park Rangers	1-2	Kirkman	6764	1	2		4	5	6	7	8	9	10	11	3													
4	Sep 4	SHREWSBURY TOWN	3-2	Lawther, Sloan, Ratcliffe	6913	1	2		4	5	6	7	8	9	10	11		3												
5	9	Hull City	2-1	Lawther 2	8754	1	2		4	5	6		8	9	10	11		3	7											
6	12	Reading	0-2		6882	1	2			5	6		8	9	10	11		3	7	4										
7	15	HULL CITY	1-1	Ratcliffe	7525	1		3	4	5	6		8	9	10	11		3	7		2									
8	18	SOUTHEND UNITED	2-1	Sloan, Lawther	6171	1	3	2	4	5	6		8	9	10	11			7											
9	25	Barnsley	0-2		6289	1	2			5	6		8	9	10			3	11			4	7							
10	29	WORKINGTON	1-1	Scott	5205	1	2			5			8	9	10		3	6	11				7	4						
11	Oct 3	Mansfield Town	2-3	Lawther 2	7911	1	2	6		5		7	8	9	10			3	11					4						
12	6	Workington	0-2		3922	1	2	6		5		7		9	10			3	11		8			4						
13	10	PETERBOROUGH UTD.	2-3	Scott, Sloan	5340	1	2	6	4	5		7		9	10			3	11					8						
14	13	WALSALL	4-0	Lawther 2 (1pen), Scott, Hutton	4220	1		6	4	5		7	8	9				3	11		2			10						
15	17	Bournemouth	1-2	Horstead	8406	1		6	4	5		7	8	9				3	11		2			10						
16	20	Walsall	2-1	Scott, Lawther	5471	1		6	4	5		7		9				3	11		2			10	8					
17	24	EXETER CITY	0-0		4242	1		6	4	5		7		9				3	11		2			10	8					
18	28	Luton Town	1-1	Scott	3876	1		6	4	5		7		9				3	11		2			10	8					
19	31	Oldham Athletic	1-2	Lawther	9258	1		6	4	5		7		9				3	11		2			10	8					
20	Nov 3	GILLINGHAM	2-3	Scott (pen), Lawther	4290	1			5	4				9	10	11		3	7		2		6	8						
21	7	BRISTOL ROVERS	1-1	Lindsey	4213	1			5	4				9	10	11		3	7		2		6	8						
22	20	COLCHESTER UNITED	0-0		7610	1			4	5			8		10	11		3			2		6	7	9					
23	28	Port Vale	1-0	Ratcliffe	4620	1			4	5			8		10	11		3			2		6	7	9					
24	Dec 12	Bristol City	2-2	Thomas 2	8387	1		6	4	5		7				11		3						8	9	10	2			
25	18	QUEEN'S PARK RANGERS	2-1	Ratcliffe, Neale	5344	1			4	5	6	7				11		3						8	9	10	2			
26	26	GRIMSBY TOWN	2-1	Ratcliffe, Kirkman	10867	1			4	5		7	8			11		3					6		9	10	2			
27	Jan 2	Shrewsbury Town	2-3	Hutton, Scott	4707	1			4	5		7						3	11				6	8	9	10	2			
28	8	Exeter City	3-1	Thomas 2, Hutton	6092	1			4	5		7				11		3					6	8	9	10	2			
29	15	READING	1-1	Thomas	5992	1			4	5		7				11		3					6	8	9	10	2			
30	23	Southend United	1-0	Thomas	7630				4	5		7				11		3					6	8	9	10	2	1		
31	29	CARLISLE UNITED	0-1		6710				4	5		7				11		3					6	8	9	10	2	1		
32	Feb 5	BARNSLEY	2-3	Hutton, Thomas	6516			6	4	5		7						3	11					8		10	2	1	9	
33	12	MANSFIELD TOWN	0-1		6115			6	4	5		7						3	11					8		10	2	1	9	
34	26	BOURNEMOUTH	3-1	Ratcliffe, Bramley, Brown	5110			6		5		7				11		3					9	4	8	10	2	1		
35	Mar 6	Carlisle United	1-3	Thomas	9418			6		5		7	8			11		3					9			10	2	1		4
36	8	Peterborough United	2-2	Brown 2	9661	1		3	8	5		7				11							9	6		10	2			4
37	12	OLDHAM ATHLETIC	1-1	Brown	5795			3	8	5		7				11							9	6		10	2	1		4
38	20	Bristol Rovers	0-2		6650			3	8	5		7											9	11	8	10	2	1		4
39	26	BRENTFORD	2-0	Ratcliffe, Scott	5081			3	8	5		7				11							9	6		10	2	1		4
40	Apr 3	Colchester United	1-2	Lindsey	3212			3	8	5		7				11							9	6			2	1	10	4
41	6	Grimsby Town	0-3		6756			3	8	5		7	10			11							9	6			2	1		4
42	9	PORT VALE	0-0		3894	1		3	8	5		7				11							9	6			2		10	4
43	16	Watford	0-5		7140			2	10	5		7							11		3		6	8	9			1		4
44	20	WATFORD	0-2		3597			2	6	5						11					3	10		8	9			1		4
45	24	LUTON TOWN	8-1	Thomas 5, Wilson, Mahy, Bramley	2755			2	6	5						11		3	10		8	7			9			1		4
46	27	Brentford	0-4		6164			2	6	5						11		3	10		8	7			9			1		4
Apps						31	7	38	39	43	9	31	20	22	21	26	3	20	25	1	25	6	11	32	24	23	19	15	3	12
Goals							1	2	1			4	3	13	5	7			1			1	4	8	2	13				

F.A. Cup

	Date	Opponent	Score	Scorers	Att	Reeves	Betts	Horstead	Lindsey	Neale	Bannister	Hutton	Kirkman	Lawther	Sloan	Ratcliffe		Needham	Wilson		Hemstead			Scott						
R1	Nov 14	DARLINGTON	1-2	Greener (og)	5121	1		6	4	5		7	8	9				3	11		2			10						

F.L. Cup

	Date	Opponent	Score	Scorers	Att	Reeves	Betts		Lindsey	Neale	Bannister	Hutton	Kirkman	Lawther	Sloan	Ratcliffe		Needham	Wilson	Smillie										
R1	Sep 23	WORKINGTON	0-1		3910	1	2			5	6		8	9	10	11		3	7	4										

		P	W	D	L	F	A	W	D	L	F	A	Pts
1	Carlisle United	46	14	5	4	46	24	11	5	7	30	29	60
2	Bristol City	46	14	6	3	53	18	10	5	8	39	37	59
3	Mansfield Town	46	17	4	2	61	23	7	7	9	34	38	59
4	Hull City	46	14	6	3	51	25	9	6	8	40	32	58
5	Brentford	46	18	4	1	55	18	6	5	12	28	37	57
6	Bristol Rovers	46	14	7	2	52	21	6	8	9	30	37	55
7	Gillingham	46	16	5	2	45	13	7	4	12	25	37	55
8	Peterborough Utd.	46	16	3	4	61	33	6	4	13	24	41	51
9	Watford	46	13	8	2	45	21	4	8	11	26	43	50
10	Grimsby Town	46	11	10	2	37	21	5	7	11	46	49	49
11	Bournemouth	46	12	4	7	40	24	6	7	10	32	39	47
12	Southend United	46	14	4	5	48	24	5	4	14	30	47	46
13	Reading	46	12	8	3	45	26	4	6	13	25	44	46
14	Queen's Park Rgs.	46	15	5	3	48	23	2	7	14	24	57	46
15	Workington	46	11	7	5	30	22	6	5	12	28	47	46
16	Shrewsbury Town	46	10	6	7	42	38	5	6	12	34	46	42
17	Exeter City	46	8	7	8	33	27	4	10	9	18	25	41
18	SCUNTHORPE UNITED	46	9	8	6	42	27	5	4	14	23	45	40
19	Walsall	46	9	4	10	34	36	6	3	14	21	44	37
20	Oldham Athletic	46	10	3	10	40	39	3	7	13	21	44	36
21	Luton Town	46	8	8	7	32	36	5	3	15	19	58	33
22	Port Vale	46	7	6	10	27	33	2	8	13	14	43	32
23	Colchester United	46	7	6	10	30	34	3	4	16	20	55	30
24	Barnsley	46	8	5	10	33	31	1	6	16	21	59	29

No	Date	Opponent	Score	Scorers	Att	Sidebottom G	Lindsey K	Hemstead DW	Scott RSA	Horstead JB	Burkinshaw KH	Hutton J	Barton F	Brown MR	Lindsey B	Colquhoun J	Smith RW	Sloan D	Mahy B	Bedford NB	Goodwin F	Thomas BEB	Bramley JS	Neale P	Ash M	Burrows F	Clemence RN	Taylor SR	Barker J	Coatsworth FW
1	Aug 21	Hull City	2-3	Brown, Hutton	18829	1	2	3	4	5	6	7	8	9	10	11														
2	25	MANSFIELD TOWN	0-1		6894	1	2	3	4	5	6	7		9	10	11	8													
3	28	READING	2-0	Brown, Smith	4335	1	2	3	4	5	6			9	10	11	8	7	12											
4	Sep 4	Exeter City	0-4		5818	1		3	4	5	6	7		9	8	11	2			10										
5	11	PETERBOROUGH UTD.	1-1	Bedford	4828	1		3			6			9		4	2	11		10	5	7	8							
6	14	QUEEN'S PARK RANGERS	1-2	Bedford	5362	1		3			6			9		4	2	11		10	5	7	8							
7	18	Millwall	2-2	Snowdon(og), Hutton	11525	1	2	3			6	7		9	11	4	8			10				5						
8	25	GILLINGHAM	0-1		4252	1	2	3			6	7		9	11	4	8			10				5						
9	Oct 2	Oldham Athletic	3-1	Barton, Bedford, Colquhoun	6363	1	2	3			6	12		9	11	4	8			10				5	7					
10	4	Queen's Park Rangers	0-1		6726	1	2	3			6	7		9	11	4	8	12		10				5						
11	9	Brentford	1-0	Smith	7729	1		3	4		6	7		9	2	11	8			10	12			5						
12	16	BRISTOL ROVERS	3-0	Goodwin, Barton, Bedford	4219	1	2	3	4		6	7		9		11	8			10	5									
13	30	OXFORD UNITED	1-2	Smith (p)	4030	1	2	3	4		6	7		9		11	8			10	5									
14	Nov 6	Swansea Town	4-3	Ash, Thomas, Bedford, B.Lindsey	8853	1	2	3							6	11	4	7		10	5	9			8					
15	19	Workington	2-1	Thomas, Bedford	2943	1		3		5	6				2	11	4	7		10		9			8					
16	27	BOURNEMOUTH	3-0	Bedford 2, Smith	2766	1		3		5	6				2	11	4	7		10		9			8					
17	Dec 4	York City	3-1	Sloan, Bedford, Ash	4175	1		3		5	6	9			2	11	4	7		10					8					
18	11	SWINDON TOWN	2-1	Bedford 2	4483	1		3		5	6	9			2	11	4	7		10					8					
19	27	Shrewsbury Town	4-1	Bedford 3, Hutton	7520	1		3		5	6	9			2	11	4	7		10					8					
20	28	SHREWSBURY TOWN	1-4	Bedford	6249	1		3		5	6	9			2	11	4	7		10					8					
21	Jan 1	BRENTFORD	3-2	Sloan, Ash, Thomas	5738	1		3		5	6				2	11	4	7		10		9			8					
22	8	Walsall	0-3		7059	1		3		5	6	12			2	11	4	7		10		9			8					
23	15	YORK CITY	4-1	Burkinshaw, Sloan 2, Bedford	3680	1		3		5	6	9			2	11	4	7		10				12	8					
24	29	HULL CITY	2-4	Colquhoun, Ash	15570	1		3			6	9			2	11	4	7		10					8	5				
25	Feb 5	Reading	0-2		7102	1		3			6	9			2	11	4	7		10					8	5				
26	12	Brighton & Hove Albion	1-0	Bedford	12659	1		3		5	6		8		2	11	4	9		10				12	7					
27	19	EXETER CITY	2-1	Barton, Smith (p)	4566	1		3		5	6		8			11	4	9		10				2	7					
28	26	Peterborough United	1-3	Sloan	6696	1		3		5	6		8		2	11	4	9		10				12	7					
29	Mar 5	BRIGHTON & HOVE ALB	2-2	Sloan, Barton	4657	1		3	2				8		12	11	4	7		10				9	5	6				
30	7	Mansfield Town	2-2	Bedford, Smith (p)	6678	1		3	2				8		10	11	4	7		9					5	6				
31	12	MILLWALL	4-4	Snowdon(og), Smith, Colquhoun, Barton	5800	1	2	3			6		8		10	11	4	7		9					5					
32	19	Gillingham	1-0	Sloan	6110	1	2	3			6		8		10	11	4	7		9					12	5				
33	26	OLDHAM ATHLETIC	1-1	Bedford	5211	1	2	3			6		8		10	11	4	7		9						5				
34	29	Bristol Rovers	0-2		7376	1	2	3			6		8		10	11	4	7		9						5				
35	Apr 2	SWANSEA TOWN	1-1	Thomas	2914		2				6		8			11	4	7		9		10				12	5	1	3	
36	8	Grimsby Town	3-1	Sloan 3	10960	1	2				6		8			11	4	7		9					10	5	3			
37	12	GRIMSBY TOWN	2-2	Bedford, Colquhoun	7783	1			2		6					11	4	7		9	8				10	5	3			
38	16	WORKINGTON	4-1	Thomas 3, Sloan	4088	1	2				6		8			11	4	7				9			10	5	3			
39	23	Bournemouth	2-1	Burrows, Thomas	6161	1	2				6		8			11	4	7				9			10	5	3			
40	26	Watford	1-2	Barton	4072	1	2	3			6		8			11	4	7		9					10	5				
41	30	SOUTHEND UNITED	0-0		4399	1	2	3			6		8			11	4	7		9					10	5				
42	May 7	Swindon Town	0-0		9251		2	3			6					11	4	7		9					10	5		1		8
43	13	Southend United	1-0	Sloan	7326		2	3			6					11	4	7		9	8				10	5		1		
44	17	WATFORD	1-1	Colquhoun	3913			3			6					11	4	7	2	9	8				10	5		1		
45	21	WALSALL	4-2	Sloan 2, Thomas, Bedford	3429			3			6					11	4	7	2	9		8			10	5		1		
46	28	Oxford United	3-0	Thomas, Bedford, Mahy	4505	1		3			6					11	4	7	2	9		8			10	5				
		Apps				42	15	41	15	21	36	17	21	8	34	44	45	38	5	35	6	19	3	13	28	19	4	8	1	1
		Goals									1	3	6	2	1	5	7	14	1	22	1	10			4	1				

2 own goals

F.A. Cup

Round	Date	Opponent	Score	Att	Sidebottom G	Lindsey K	Hemstead DW	Burkinshaw KH	Lindsey B	Colquhoun J	Smith RW	Sloan D	Bedford NB	Goodwin F	Thomas BEB	Ash M
R1	Nov 13	Crewe Alexandra	0-3	5148	1	2	3	6	11	4	7	10	5	9	8	

F.L. Cup

Round	Date	Opponent	Score	Att	Sidebottom G	Lindsey K	Hemstead DW	Scott RSA	Horstead JB	Burkinshaw KH	Brown MR	Colquhoun J	Smith RW	Sloan D	Neale P
R1	Sep 1	DARLINGTON	0-2	2856	1	2	3	7	4	6	9	11	8	10	5

		P	W	D	L	F	A	W	D	L	F	A	Pts
1	Hull City	46	19	2	2	64	24	12	5	6	45	38	69
2	Millwall	46	19	4	0	47	13	8	7	8	29	30	65
3	Queen's Park Rgs.	46	16	3	4	62	29	8	6	9	33	36	57
4	SCUNTHORPE UNITED	46	9	8	6	44	34	12	3	8	36	33	53
5	Workington	46	13	6	4	38	18	6	8	9	29	39	52
6	Gillingham	46	14	4	5	33	19	8	4	11	29	35	52
7	Swindon Town	46	11	8	4	43	18	8	5	10	31	30	51
8	Reading	46	13	5	5	36	19	6	8	9	34	44	51
9	Walsall	46	13	7	3	48	21	7	3	13	29	43	50
10	Shrewsbury Town	46	13	7	3	48	22	6	4	13	25	42	49
11	Grimsby Town	46	15	6	2	47	25	2	7	14	21	37	47
12	Watford	46	12	4	7	33	19	5	9	9	22	32	47
13	Peterborough Utd.	46	13	6	4	50	26	4	6	13	30	40	46
14	Oxford United	46	11	3	9	38	33	8	5	10	32	41	46
15	Brighton & Hove A.	46	13	4	6	48	23	3	7	13	19	37	43
16	Bristol Rovers	46	11	10	2	38	15	3	4	16	26	49	42
17	Swansea Town	46	14	4	5	61	37	1	7	15	20	59	41
18	Bournemouth	46	9	8	6	24	19	4	4	15	14	37	38
19	Mansfield Town	46	10	5	8	31	36	5	3	15	28	53	38
20	Oldham Athletic	46	8	7	8	34	33	4	6	13	21	48	37
21	Southend United	46	15	1	7	43	28	1	3	19	11	55	36
22	Exeter City	46	9	6	8	36	28	3	5	15	17	51	35
23	Brentford	46	9	4	10	34	30	4	1	18	14	39	32
24	York City	46	5	7	11	30	44	4	2	17	23	62	27

1966/67 18th in Division 3

#		Date	Opponent	Res	Scorers	Att	Sidebottom G	Mahy B	Hemstead DW	Smith RW	Burrows F	Burkinshaw KH	Sloan D	Barton F	Thomas BEB	Ash M	Colquhoun J	Bramley JS	Horstead JB	Clemence RN	Barker J	Taylor SR	Welbourne D	Bedford NB	Neale P	Lindsey B	Rusling G	Coatsworth FW	Webster AJ	Foxon DN	Verity DA
1	Aug	20	GILLINGHAM	1-2	Thomas	5171	1	2	3	4	5	6	7	8	9	10	11														
2		27	Orient	1-3	Ash	5867	1	2	3	4	5	6	7	9		10	11	8	12												
3	Sep	3	BOURNEMOUTH	0-1		4278				4				7		10	11			5	1	2	3	6	8	9					
4		7	Grimsby Town	1-7	Bedford	8255				4					9	10	11	7		5	1	2	3	6	8						
5		10	Swansea Town	1-0	Lindsey	6185		2	3	4		6		8		10		7		5	1					9	11				
6		17	MIDDLESBROUGH	3-2	Bramley, Barton, Lindsey	4053		2	3	4		6		8		10	9	7		5	1					12	11				
7		24	Shrewsbury Town	3-4	Ash, Barton, Smith	3844		2	3	4	5	6		8		10	9	7			1						11				
8		27	GRIMSBY TOWN	0-0		11373		2	3	4	5	6	12	8		10	9	7			1						11				
9		30	COLCHESTER UNITED	3-1	Loughton(og), Thomas, Smith	5355		2	3	4	5	6		8	9	10		7			1						11				
10	Oct	8	Walsall	0-2		9236		2	3	4	5	6		8	9	10	11	7			1										
11		14	PETERBOROUGH UTD.	1-0	Smith (p)	5823			3	4	5	6	7	8	9	10	11				1	2									
12		18	Oldham Athletic	0-2		13975			3	4	5	6	7	8	9	10	11				1	2									
13		22	Torquay United	1-1	Colquhoun	5586			3	4	5	6	7	8	9	10	11				1	2									
14		24	Bristol Rovers	1-1	Thomas	11115			3	4	5	6	7	8	9	10	11				1	2									
15		28	BRIGHTON & HOVE ALB	0-1		5617			3	4	5	6	7	8	9	10	11				1	2									
16	Nov	5	Darlington	1-2	Smith	6850			3	4	5	6	7	8	9	10	11				1	2									
17		12	QUEEN'S PARK RANGERS	0-2		5052			3	4	5	6	7	8		10	11				1	2				9					
18		15	OLDHAM ATHLETIC	1-1	Colquhoun	3714	7		3	4		6	9	8		10	11			5	1	2									
19		19	Watford	1-0	Barton	7084	7		3	4		6	9	8		10	11			5	1	2									
20	Dec	3	Reading	0-4		5252	10		3	4		6	9	8			11			5	1	2									
21		9	DONCASTER ROVERS	2-1	Smith, Burkinshaw	6400	7		3	4		6	9	8		10	11			5	1	2									
22		17	Gillingham	1-0	Ash	5468	7		3	4		6	9	8		10	11			5	1	2									
23		23	MANSFIELD TOWN	2-1	Sloan, Barton	6458			3	4		6	7	8		9	11			5	1	2				10					
24		27	Mansfield Town	1-3	Lindsey	10291			3	4		6	7	8		9	11			5	1	2				10					
25		30	ORIENT	2-2	Sloan, Barton	5503			3	4		6	7	8		9	11			5	1	2				10					
26	Jan	14	SWANSEA TOWN	4-3	Hemstead, Rusling, Lindsey, Sloan	4586			3	4		6	7	9			11			5	1	2				10	8				
27		21	Middlesbrough	1-2	Burrows	19005			3	4		6	7	9			11			5	1	2				10	8				
28		28	Bournemouth	0-0		3561			3			6	7	9		10	11			5	1	2				4	8				
29	Feb	4	SHREWSBURY TOWN	2-0	Rusling 2	4562			3			6	7	9		10	11			5	1	2				4	8				
30		11	Colchester United	1-0	Sloan	3965			3			6	7	9		10	11			5	1	2				4	8				
31		18	Oxford United	1-2	Burkinshaw	7183			3			6	7	8			11			5	1	2				4	9	10			
32		24	WALSALL	2-0	Colquhoun, Barton	4959			3			6	7	8			11			5	1	2				4	9	10			
33	Mar	4	Peterborough United	0-1		5485			3			6	7	8			11	12		5	1	2				4	9	10			
34		10	OXFORD UNITED	2-2	Barton (p), Sloan	4738			3			6	7	8			11			5	1	2				4	9	10			
35		17	TORQUAY UNITED	3-1	Coatsworth, Smith(og), Sloan	4473			3			6	7	8			10			5	1	2				4	9	11			
36		25	Brighton & Hove Albion	2-2	Colquhoun, Hemstead	11524			3			6	7	8			10			5	1	2				4	9	11			
37		27	WORKINGTON	4-1	Colquhoun, Barton 2 (1 p), Sloan	5604			3			6	7	8			10			5	1	2				4	9	11			
38		28	Workington	0-1		2079			3			6	7	8			10		4	5	1	2					9	11			
39		31	DARLINGTON	2-0	Sloan, Rusling	4745			3			6	7	8			10		4	5	1	2					9	11			
40	Apr	8	Queen's Park Rangers	1-5	Rusling	13113			3			6	7	8			10		4	5	1	2					9	11			
41		14	WATFORD	1-0	Colquhoun	5047			3			6	7	8			10			5	1	2				4	9	11			
42		22	Swindon Town	1-2	Sloan	12956			3			6	7	8			10			5	1	2					9	11	4		
43		24	BRISTOL ROVERS	3-1	Barton 2, Coatsworth	4195			3			6		8			10		4	5	1	2					9	11		7	
44		28	READING	0-2		5124			3			6	7	8			10			5	1	2				4	9			11	
45	May	5	Doncaster Rovers	0-3		3948			3			6	7				10			5	1	2				4	9	11			8
46		12	SWINDON TOWN	1-2	Colquhoun	3664			3			6	7	8			10			5	1	2				4		9			
			Apps				2	7	44	25	41	44	35	44	10	21	45	8	25	44	21	27	2	2	3	23	20	14	1	2	1
			Goals						2	5	1	2	9	11	3	3	7	1						1		4	5	2			

2 own goals

F.A. Cup

	Date	Opponent	Res	Scorers	Att	Sidebottom G	Mahy B	Hemstead DW	Smith RW	Burrows F	Burkinshaw KH	Sloan D	Barton F	Thomas BEB	Ash M	Colquhoun J	Bramley JS	Horstead JB	Clemence RN	Barker J	Taylor SR	Welbourne D	Bedford NB	Neale P	Lindsey B	Rusling G	Coatsworth FW	Webster AJ	Foxon DN	Verity DA
R1	Nov 26	Lincoln City	4-3	Smith, Burrows, Barton, Mahy	6223	7		3	4		6	9	8		10	11			5	1	2									
R2	Jan 7	Mansfield Town	1-2	Foxon	9446			3	4		6	9	8			11			5	1	2				10				7	

F.L. Cup

	Date	Opponent	Res	Scorers	Att	Sidebottom G	Mahy B	Hemstead DW	Smith RW	Burrows F	Burkinshaw KH	Sloan D	Barton F	Thomas BEB	Ash M	Colquhoun J
R1	Aug 24	Chesterfield	1-2	Barton	5418	1	2	3	4	5	6	7	8	9	10	11

		P	W	D	L	F	A	W	D	L	F	A	Pts
1	Queen's Park Rgs.	46	18	4	1	66	15	8	11	4	37	23	67
2	Middlesbrough	46	16	3	4	51	20	7	6	10	36	44	55
3	Watford	46	15	5	3	39	17	5	9	9	22	29	54
4	Reading	46	13	7	3	45	20	9	2	12	31	37	53
5	Bristol Rovers	46	13	8	2	47	28	7	5	11	29	39	53
6	Shrewsbury Town	46	15	5	3	48	24	5	7	11	29	38	52
7	Torquay United	46	17	3	3	57	20	4	6	13	16	34	51
8	Swindon Town	46	14	5	4	53	21	6	5	12	28	38	50
9	Mansfield Town	46	12	4	7	48	37	8	5	10	36	42	49
10	Oldham Athletic	46	15	4	4	51	16	4	6	13	29	47	48
11	Gillingham	46	11	9	3	36	18	4	7	12	22	44	46
12	Walsall	46	12	8	3	37	16	6	2	15	28	56	46
13	Colchester United	46	14	3	6	52	30	3	7	13	24	43	44
14	Orient	46	10	9	4	36	27	3	9	11	22	41	44
15	Peterborough Utd.	46	12	4	7	40	31	2	11	10	26	40	43
16	Oxford United	46	10	8	5	41	29	5	5	13	20	37	43
17	Grimsby Town	46	13	5	5	46	23	4	4	15	15	45	43
18	SCUNTHORPE UNITED	46	13	6	4	39	26	4	4	15	19	47	42
19	Brighton & Hove A.	46	10	8	5	37	27	3	7	13	24	44	41
20	Bournemouth	46	8	10	5	24	24	4	7	12	15	33	41
21	Swansea Town	46	9	9	4	50	30	5	6	14	35	59	39
22	Darlington	46	8	7	8	26	28	5	4	14	21	53	37
23	Doncaster Rovers	46	11	6	6	40	40	1	2	20	18	77	32
24	Workington	46	9	3	11	35	35	3	4	16	20	54	31

No		Date	Opponent	Score	Scorers	Att	Arblaster BM	Hemstead DW	Barker J	Lindsey B	Burrows F	Burkinshaw KH	Sloan D	Barton F	Hamey D	Colquhoun J	Foley P	Taylor SR	Foxon DN	Horstead JB	Webster AJ	Drake S	Verity DA	Naylor G	Deere SH	Rusling G	Blyth MR	Lavery J	Welbourne D	Foxton DG	Punton WH	Kerr GAM	Heath RT
1	Aug	19	Peterborough United	1-1	Barton	6984	1	2	3	4	5	6	7	8	9	10	11																
2		25	MANSFIELD TOWN	3-3	Sloan, Barton (p), Burrows	6372	1	2	3	4	5	6	7	8	9	10	11	12															
3	Sep	2	Watford	0-4		6670	1	2	3	4	5	6	7	8	9	10	11																
4		4	Bournemouth	0-1		6302	1	2	3	4	5	6	7	8	9	10	12	11															
5		9	SOUTHPORT	1-0	Sloan	4655	1	2	3	4	5	6	7	8	9	10		11															
6		16	Grimsby Town	1-2	Barton	7825	1	2		4	5	6	9	8	12	10	7	3	11														
7		23	Oldham Athletic	4-3	Barton, Sloan 2, Horstead	5263	1	2			4	5	6	7		9	10	3	11	12													
8		26	BOURNEMOUTH	1-1	Barton	4926	1	2		4	5	6	7	8	9	10		3	11		12												
9		30	BRISTOL ROVERS	1-1	Sloan	3848	1	2			5	6	7	8	9	10		3	11			4											
10	Oct	3	Bury	3-4	Hamey, Colquhoun 2	5932	1	2			5	6	7	4	9	10	8	3	11		12												
11		7	WALSALL	2-5	Barton 2 (1 p)	4170		2			5	6	7	8	9	10		3	11			4	1	12									
12		14	Northampton Town	0-1		10097		2			5	6	7	8	9	10		3	11	4			1										
13		21	ORIENT	1-1	Foxon	3431		2			5	6	7	8	9	10		3	11	4			1										
14		24	BURY	3-1	Sloan, Horstead, Barton	3847		2			5	6	7	8	9	10		3	11	4			1										
15		27	Tranmere Rovers	0-2		6697		2			5	6	7	8	9	10		3	11	4			1		12								
16	Nov	3	STOCKPORT COUNTY	0-2		4338		2			5	6	7	8	9	10		3	11	4			1		12								
17		11	Brighton & Hove Albion	1-3	Deere	11251		2			5	6	7	8	11	10		3	12				1	4	9								
18		14	WATFORD	1-1	Rusling	3445		2			5		7	8		9		3	11				1	4	6	10							
19		17	SHREWSBURY TOWN	0-0		3104		2			5		7	8		9		3	11				1	4	10		6						
20		25	Swindon Town	0-2		11944		2			5		7	8		9		3	11				1	4	10		6						
21	Dec	1	READING	1-2	Colquhoun	3541		2			5		7	8		9		3	11				1	4	10	12	6						
22		15	PETERBOROUGH UTD.	2-1	Deere, Barton	3519		2			5	6	7	8		11		3					1	4	9		10						
23		23	Mansfield Town	0-3		4907		2	3		5	6	7	8		11							1	4	9		10						
24		26	OXFORD UNITED	1-1	Sloan	3839		2	3		5	6	7	8		11					12		1	4	9		10						
25		30	Oxford United	3-2	Deere 2, Sloan	6592		2	3		5	6	7	8						11				4	9					1	10		
26	Jan	20	GRIMSBY TOWN	0-3		6881		2	3		5	6	7		8	11									9		10			1	4	12	
27		26	GILLINGHAM	2-1	Blyth 2	3484		2	3	4	5	6		8		9	7										10	1				11	
28	Feb	3	OLDHAM ATHLETIC	2-0	Sloan, Foley	3697		2	3	4	5	6		8		9	7										10	1				11	
29		10	Bristol Rovers	0-4		5666		2	3	4	5	6		8		9	7	3									10	1				11	
30		17	BARROW	2-4	Lindsey, Sloan	3229		2		4	5	6		8		9	7	3									10	1				11	
31		24	Walsall	0-0		8987		2				8	5	6		11			3			4			9		10	1					7
32		26	Colchester United	0-1		3979		2					5	6		11			3			4	8		9		10	1			12		7
33	Mar	2	NORTHAMPTON T	1-1	Kerr	2745		2	3	4	5			8			7								6		1				10	11	9
34		9	COLCHESTER UNITED	5-1	Colquhoun 2, Punton, Heath, Deere	3098		2	3	4	5					7									9		6			1	11	8	10
35		16	Orient	1-2	Heath	5067		2	3	4	5					7									9		6			1	11	8	10
36		22	TRANMERE ROVERS	1-1	Colquhoun	3986		2	3	4	5					7									9		6			1	11	8	10
37		29	Stockport County	1-4	Heath	6779		2	3	4	5					7		12							9		6			1	11	8	10
38	Apr	6	BRIGHTON & HOVE ALB	1-3	Burrows (p)	2845		2	3	4	5			8		7									9		6			1	11		10
39		13	Shrewsbury Town	0-4		5578			3	4	5					7									9		6		2	1	11	8	10
40		15	Gillingham	1-3	Kerr	5031			3	4	5					7		12				1			9		6		2		11	8	10
41		19	SWINDON TOWN	3-1	Heath, Kerr 2	2725			3	4	5					7						1			9		6		2		11	8	10
42		25	Torquay United	1-2	Heath	10362			3	4	5					7						1			9		6		2		11	8	10
43		27	Reading	1-2	Colquhoun	3879			3	4	5					7						1		10	9		6		2		11	8	10
44	May	3	TORQUAY UNITED	2-0	Rusling, Blyth	2700			3	4	5					7	12					1			9	6		2	11	8	10
45		6	Southport	1-1	Colquhoun	3238		2		4	5					11	7					1	12		9		6		3			8	10
46		11	Barrow	1-2	Kerr	3782			3	4	5			7	11	9						1			6				2		8	10
			Apps				10	46	18	27	46	28	30	25	18	45	13	24	20	9	5	21	4	10	19	8	27	15	4	9	16	15	12
			Goals							1	2		10	9	1	8	1		1	2					5	2	3				1	5	5

F.A. Cup

		Date	Opponent	Score	Scorers	Att			Barker J		Burrows F	Burkinshaw KH	Sloan D	Barton F		Colquhoun J			Foxon DN				Verity DA	Naylor G	Deere SH	Rusling G					Punton WH	Kerr GAM	
R1	Dec	9	SKELMERSDALE UNITED	2-0	Colquhoun, Barton (p)	3847		2			5	6	7	8		11			3				1	4	10	9							
R2	Jan	6	Halifax Town	0-1		7804		2	3		5	6	7	8		11								4	9			1	10				

F.L. Cup

		Date	Opponent	Score	Scorers	Att	Arblaster BM	Hemstead DW	Barker J	Lindsey B	Burrows F	Burkinshaw KH	Sloan D	Barton F	Hamey D	Colquhoun J	Foley P	Taylor SR	Foxon DN
R1	Aug	23	Doncaster Rovers	2-1	Barton, Foley	8666	1	2	3	4	5	6	7	8	9	10	11		
R2	Sep	13	NOTTM. FOREST	0-1		13235	1	2	3	4	5	6	9	8	11	10	7	12	

		P	W	D	L	F	A	W	D	L	F	A	Pts
1	Oxford United	46	18	3	2	49	20	4	10	9	20	27	57
2	Bury	46	19	3	1	64	24	5	5	13	27	42	56
3	Shrewsbury Town	46	14	6	3	42	17	6	9	8	19	32	55
4	Torquay United	46	15	6	2	40	17	6	5	12	20	39	53
5	Reading	46	15	5	3	43	17	6	4	13	27	43	51
6	Watford	46	15	3	5	59	20	6	5	12	15	30	50
7	Walsall	46	12	7	4	47	22	7	5	11	27	39	50
8	Barrow	46	14	6	3	43	13	7	2	14	22	41	50
9	Peterborough Utd.	46	14	4	5	46	23	6	6	11	33	44	50
10	Swindon Town	46	13	8	2	51	16	3	9	11	23	35	49
11	Brighton & Hove A.	46	11	8	4	31	14	5	8	10	26	41	48
12	Gillingham	46	13	6	4	35	19	5	6	12	24	44	48
13	Bournemouth	46	13	7	3	39	17	3	8	12	17	34	47
14	Stockport County	46	16	5	2	49	22	3	4	16	21	53	47
15	Southport	46	13	6	4	35	22	4	6	13	30	43	46
16	Bristol Rovers	46	14	3	6	42	25	3	6	14	30	53	43
17	Oldham Athletic	46	11	3	9	37	32	4	7	12	23	33	43
18	Northampton Town	46	10	8	5	40	25	4	5	14	18	47	41
19	Orient	46	10	6	7	27	24	2	11	10	19	38	41
20	Tranmere Rovers	46	10	7	6	39	28	4	5	14	23	46	40
21	Mansfield Town	46	8	7	8	32	31	4	6	13	19	36	37
22	Grimsby Town	46	10	7	6	33	21	4	2	17	19	48	37
23	Colchester United	46	6	8	9	29	40	3	7	13	21	47	33
24	SCUNTHORPE UNITED	46	8	9	6	36	34	2	3	18	20	53	32

1968/69 16th in Division 4

#	Date	Opponent	Score	Scorers	Att	Barnard G	Foxton DG	Hemstead DW	Lindsey B	Holt R	Welbourne D	Colquhoun J	Kerr GAM	Harney D	Heath RT	Punton WH	Deere SH	Barker J	Foley P	Davidson I	Keegan JK	Wilson AP	Taylor SR	Cassidy N	Jackson NA	Rusling G	Currie JT
1	Aug 10	Rochdale	2-3	Kerr, Deere	3253	1	2	3	4	5	6	7	8	9	10	11	12										
2	17	BRENTFORD	1-1	Deere	3685	1	2	3	4	5	6	7	8		10	11	9										
3	23	Doncaster Rovers	3-4	Heath 2, Kerr	10474	1	2	3	4	5	6	7	8		10	11	9	12									
4	26	Colchester United	4-0	Kerr 2, Heath, Deere	3771	1		2	4	5	6	7	8		10	11	9	3									
5	30	CHESTER	2-2	Kerr, Colquhoun	5072	1		2	4	5	6	7	8		10	11	9	3									
6	Sep 6	BRADFORD CITY	1-0	Deere	5997	1	12	2	4	5	6	7	8		10	11	9	3									
7	14	York City	1-2	Colquhoun	5071	1		2	4	5	6	11	8		10			3		7	12						
8	16	Peterborough United	2-3	Foley, Heath	5401	1		2	4	5		11		12	10		9	3	8		6	7					
9	21	EXETER CITY	2-1	Deere, Foley (p)	3534	1		2	4	5	6	11			10		9	3	8		12	7					
10	28	Port Vale	1-4	Heath	3823	1		2		5	6	11			10		9	3	8	4	12	7					
11	Oct 4	HALIFAX TOWN	0-1		3942	1	2	3		5	6			8	10	11				4		7					
12	8	COLCHESTER UNITED	2-3	Kerr, Heath	2849	1	2	3		5	6		8		10	11	9			4		7					
13	12	Workington	1-1	Welbourne	2287	1	2	3		5	6		8		10	11	9			4		7					
14	18	NEWPORT COUNTY	1-0	Heath (p)	3360	1	2	3		5	6	11	8	12	10		9			4		7					
15	26	Aldershot	2-3	Heath, Rafferty (og)	4991	1		2	12	5	6	11	8		10		9	3		4		7					
16	Nov 1	SWANSEA TOWN	3-1	Kerr, Wilson 2	3451	1		2		5	6	11	8		10		9	3		4	12	7					
17	6	GRIMSBY TOWN	1-2	Colquhoun	5368	1		2		5	6	11	8		10		9	3		4	12	7					
18	9	Wrexham	1-0	Kerr	5848	1		2		5	6	4	8	11	10		9	3				7					
19	23	Darlington	1-0	Heath	4903	1		2		5	6		9		10	11		3		4	8	7					
20	30	LINCOLN CITY	0-0		5855	1		2		5			10		11	12	6			4	8	7	3				
21	Dec 6	BRADFORD PARK AVE.	1-0	Deere	3158	1		2		5	6		9			11	10	3		4	8	7					
22	26	Halifax Town	0-2		7092	1		2		5			11				6			4	10	7	3	9			
23	Jan 4	NOTTS COUNTY	2-1	Kerr, Cassidy	3410	1		2		5			8			11	10	6		4	12	7	3	9			
24	11	Swansea Town	0-2		4888	1			5	6			8	12		11	10	2		4	7			9			
25	25	Grimsby Town	1-0	Cassidy	5983	1		2	10	5	6		8			11		3		4	7			9			
26	28	WORKINGTON	0-1		4233	1		2	10	5			8			11	12	6		4	7			9	3		
27	Feb 1	Bradford Park Avenue	2-2	Kerr, Keegan	3050	1		2	10	5	6		8			11	12	3		4	7			9			
28	15	Lincoln City	2-1	Kerr, Cassidy	8186	1		2	10	5	6		8			11	12			4	7			9	3		
29	24	Newport County	1-1	Lindsey	1504	1		2	10	5			8			11	6			4	7			9	3		
30	Mar 1	ROCHDALE	0-0		3102	1		2	10	5			8			11	6			4	7			9			
31	5	Notts County	0-1		3311	1		2			6		8	12		11	5	3		4	10	7		9			
32	8	Brentford	1-2	Heath (p)	5456	1		2			6		8		10	11	5	3		4	7			9			
33	14	DONCASTER ROVERS	0-2		6650	1		2			6		8		10		5	3		4	11	7		9		12	
34	17	Southend United	3-0	Heath, Haydock (og), Cassidy	10113	1		2			6		8		10		5	3		4	7	11		9			
35	22	Chester	2-0	Wilson, Cassidy	5483	1		2			6		8		10		5	3		4	11	7		9			
36	25	WREXHAM	1-0	Wilson	2876	1		2			6		8		10		5			4	7	11		9			
37	29	Bradford City	0-3		6584	1		2			6		8		10		5			4	7	11	3	9			
38	Apr 5	PORT VALE	0-1		2966	1		2			6		8		10	11	5			4	7		3	9			
39	7	PETERBOROUGH UTD.	1-2	Punton	2822	1		2			6		8		10	11	5				7			9	3	4	
40	8	Chesterfield	2-1	Heath, Kerr	3793	1		2		5			8		4	11	6				10	7		9	3		
41	12	Exeter City	1-3	Heath (p)	4566	1		2		5			8		4	11	6				10	7		9	3		
42	15	CHESTERFIELD	0-1		2398	1		2		5			8		4	11	6			12	10	7		9	3		
43	18	YORK CITY	2-1	Kerr, Heath (p)	2300	1		3		5	6		7	12	10	11				4	8			9	2		
44	29	ALDERSHOT	4-1	Rusling, Cassidy, Keegan, Heath	2200	1		2		5			7	11		6	3			4	8			9		10	
45	May 2	DARLINGTON	0-0		2500	1		2		5			7			11	6	3		4	8			9		10	
46	12	SOUTHEND UNITED	4-1	Cassidy 2, Rusling 2	2080	1		2		5	6		7			11	3				8			9		10	4

Players substituted in games 1 and 23 unknown.

	Barnard G	Foxton DG	Hemstead DW	Lindsey B	Holt R	Welbourne D	Colquhoun J	Kerr GAM	Harney D	Heath RT	Punton WH	Deere SH	Barker J	Foley P	Davidson I	Keegan JK	Wilson AP	Taylor SR	Cassidy N	Jackson NA	Rusling G	Currie JT
Apps	46	8	45	16	35	36	15	42	7	33	29	43	30	4	35	33	23	8	25	8	5	1
Goals				1		1	3	13		15	1	6		2		2	4		8		3	

2 own goals

F.A. Cup

	Date	Opponent	Score	Scorers	Att	Barnard G	Hemstead DW	Holt R	Welbourne D	Kerr GAM	Harney D	Heath RT	Foley P	Davidson I	Keegan JK	Wilson AP	Barker J
R1	Nov 16	Workington	0-2		3325	1	2	5	6	8	9	10	4	11	7	3	

F.L. Cup

	Date	Opponent	Score	Scorers	Att	Barnard G	Foxton DG	Hemstead DW	Lindsey B	Holt R	Welbourne D	Colquhoun J	Kerr GAM	Heath RT	Punton WH	Deere SH	Barker J	Foley P	Davidson I	Keegan JK	Wilson AP	Taylor SR
R1	Aug 13	ROTHERHAM UNITED	2-1	Deere 2	4643	1	2	3	4	5	6	7	8	10	11	9						
R2	Sep 3	LINCOLN CITY	2-1	Kerr 2	11098	1		2	4	5	6	7	8	10	11	9	3					
R3	25	ARSENAL	1-6	Simpson (og)	17230	1		2		5	6	11		10		9	3	8	4	7	12	

		P	W	D	L	F	A	W	D	L	F	A	Pts
1	Doncaster Rovers	46	13	8	2	42	16	8	9	6	23	22	59
2	Halifax Town	46	15	5	3	36	18	5	12	6	17	19	57
3	Rochdale	46	14	7	2	47	11	4	13	6	21	24	56
4	Bradford City	46	11	10	2	36	18	7	10	6	29	28	56
5	Darlington	46	11	6	6	40	26	6	12	5	22	19	52
6	Colchester United	46	12	8	3	31	17	8	4	11	26	36	52
7	Southend United	46	15	3	5	51	21	4	10	9	27	40	51
8	Lincoln City	46	13	6	4	38	19	4	11	8	16	33	51
9	Wrexham	46	13	7	3	41	22	5	7	11	20	30	50
10	Swansea Town	46	11	8	4	35	20	8	3	12	23	34	49
11	Brentford	46	12	7	4	40	24	6	5	12	24	41	48
12	Workington	46	8	11	4	24	17	7	6	10	16	26	47
13	Port Vale	46	12	8	3	33	15	4	6	13	13	31	46
14	Chester	46	12	4	7	43	24	4	9	10	33	42	45
15	Aldershot	46	13	3	7	42	23	6	4	13	24	43	45
16	SCUNTHORPE UNITED	46	10	5	8	28	22	8	3	12	33	38	44
17	Exeter City	46	11	8	4	45	24	5	3	15	21	41	43
18	Peterborough Utd.	46	8	9	6	32	23	5	7	11	28	34	42
19	Notts County	46	10	8	5	33	22	2	10	11	15	35	42
20	Chesterfield	46	7	7	9	24	22	6	8	9	19	28	41
21	York City	46	12	8	3	36	25	2	3	18	17	50	39
22	Newport County	46	9	5	9	31	26	2	5	16	18	48	36
23	Grimsby Town	46	5	7	11	25	31	4	8	11	22	38	33
24	Bradford Park Ave.	46	5	8	10	19	34	0	2	21	13	72	20

1969/70   12th in Division 4

						Barnard G	Foxton DG	Barker J	Deere SH	Holt R	Welbourne D	Kerr GAM	Keegan JK	Cassidy N	Heath RT	Rusling G	Davidson AG	Jackson NA	Currie JT	Lindsey B	Atkin JM	Drake S
1	Aug	9	CHESTER	2-3	Rusling, Deere	3480	1	2	3	4	5	6	7	8	9	10	11						
2		15	Southend United	0-3		8967	1	2	3	4	5	6	7	8	9	10	11	12					
3		23	PETERBOROUGH UTD.	2-1	Heath, Deere	2790	1	2	3	4	5	6		8	9	10	11	7	12				
4		26	BRADFORD PARK AVE.	2-0	Rusling, Keegan	3300	1	2	3	4	5	6		8	9	10	11	7					
5		30	Oldham Athletic	3-1	Deere, Keegan, Cassidy	5426	1	2	3	4	5	6		8	9	10	11	7					
6	Sep	6	EXETER CITY	0-0		3990	1	2	3	4	5	6		8	9	10	11	7					
7		13	Grimsby Town	1-1	Heath (p)	7161	1	2	3	4	5	6		8	9	10	11	7					
8		15	Wrexham	1-2	Heath	9891	1	2	3	4	5	6	12	8	9	10	11	7					
9		20	ALDERSHOT	0-0		3400	1	2		4	5	6	3	8	9	10	11	7	12				
10		27	York City	2-3	Keegan 2	4832	1	2		4	5	6	11	8	9	10		7	3				
11		29	Colchester United	2-0	Deere, Heath (p)	6328	1	2		4	5	6	11	8	9	10		7	3				
12	Oct	4	CHESTERFIELD	1-2	Cassidy	4030	1	2		4	5	6	11	8	9	10	12	7	3				
13		7	SOUTHEND UNITED	2-0	Rusling, Cassidy	3120	1	2		4	5	6		8	9	10	11	7	3	12			
14		11	Brentford	0-3		7493	1	2		4	5	6		8	9	10	11	7	3		12		
15		18	Lincoln City	2-1	Cassidy 2	8172	1	2		6				7	8	10	9	11	3		4	5	
16		25	HARTLEPOOL	3-1	Cassidy, Keegan, Rusling	3600	1	2		6				7	8	10	9	11	3		4	5	
17	Nov	1	Crewe Alexandra	2-0	Heath 2	3190	1	2		6				7	8	10	9	11	3		4	5	
18		8	DARLINGTON	2-0	Cassidy, Rusling	3690	1	2		6				7	8	10	9	11	3		4	5	
19		22	Port Vale	2-1	Heath (p), Sproson(og)	5750	1	2	3	6				7	8	10	9	11			4	5	
20		25	WORKINGTON	1-0	Davidson	3872	1		3	6				7	8	10	9	11	2		4	5	
21		29	Notts County	1-3	Ball (og)	3497	1		3	6				7	8	10	9	11	2		4	5	
22	Dec	13	GRIMSBY TOWN	1-1	Cassidy	7340	1	2	3	6			9	7	8	10		11			4	5	
23		20	Exeter City	1-1	Cassidy	3538	1	2	3	6			9	7	8	10		11			4	5	
24		26	Peterborough United	2-2	Barker, Kerr	7796		2	3	5		6	8	7		10	9	11			4		1
25		27	OLDHAM ATHLETIC	2-1	Davidson, Cassidy	5190		2	3	5		6	9	7	8	10		11			4		1
26	Jan	10	Aldershot	1-3	Davidson	5518	1	2	3	4	5	6	9	7	8	10		11					
27		17	YORK CITY	1-1	Davidson	4860	1	2		4		6	9	7	8	10		11	3		5		
28		27	COLCHESTER UNITED	1-1	Cassidy	6530	1	2		4		6	9	7	8	10	12	11	3		5		
29		31	Chesterfield	1-2	Cassidy	11931	1	2	3	10		6	9	7	8		12	11		4	5		
30	Feb	10	BRENTFORD	1-1	Heath	5316	1	2	3	5		6	9	7	8	10		11			4		
31		14	Chester	1-1	Heath	3968	1	2	3	5		6	9	7	8	10		11			4		
32		18	Northampton Town	1-2	Heath (p)	3635	1	2	3	4		6	9	7		10	8	11		12	5		
33		20	Hartlepool	2-1	Heath, Kerr	1555	1	2	3	5		6	9	7	8	10		11			4		
34		28	LINCOLN CITY	2-1	Cassidy 2	7130	1	2	3	5		6	9	7	8	10		11			4		
35	Mar	3	SWANSEA TOWN	1-2	Keegan	5170	1	2	3	5		6	9	7	8	10		11			4		
36		9	Newport County	0-3		1917	1	2	3	5		6	9	7	8	10	12	11			4		
37		14	NOTTS COUNTY	2-3	Kerr, Cassidy	3960	1	2	3	5		6	9	7	8		10	11	12	4			
38		17	NORTHAMPTON T	1-0	Davidson	3090	1	2		5		6	9	7	8	10		11	3	4			
39		21	Swansea Town	1-2	Barker	10228	1	2	4	5		6	9	7	8	10		11	3				
40		23	Port Vale	2-1	Cassidy 2	6394	1	2	4	5			9	7	8	10		11	3		6		
41		28	NEWPORT COUNTY	4-0	Kerr, Cassidy 2, Davidson	3996	1	2		6		4	9	7	8	10		11	3		5		
42		30	Darlington	0-2		1717	1	2		6		4	9	7	8	10		11	3		5		
43		31	CREWE ALEXANDRA	0-1		3855	1	2		4		6		7	8	10	9	11	3		12	5	
44	Apr	4	Bradford Park Avenue	5-0	Kerr 2, Heath, Cassidy, Davidson	2583	1	2		5		6	9	7	8	10		11	3		4		
45		8	Workington	2-2	Heath, Cassidy	2475	1	2		5		6	9	7	8	10		11	3		4		
46		14	WREXHAM	1-3	Davidson	4292	1	2		5		6	9	7	8	10		11	3		4		
			Apps				44	44	27	46	15	36	31	46	44	44	26	45	25	5	22	17	2
			Goals						2	4			6	6	21	13	5	8					

2 own goals

F.A. Cup

							Barnard G	Foxton DG	Barker J	Deere SH	Holt R	Welbourne D	Kerr GAM	Keegan JK	Cassidy N	Heath RT	Rusling G	Davidson AG	Jackson NA	Currie JT	Lindsey B	Atkin JM	Drake S
R1	Nov	15	Macclesfield Town	1-1	Heath	5477	1	2	3	6			7	8	10	9	11			4	5		
rep		18	MACCLESFIELD TOWN	4-2	Keegan 2, Rusling, Cassidy	5350	1	2	3	6		12	7	8	10	9	11			4	5		
R2	Dec	6	Stockport County	0-0		4200	1	2	3	6			7	8	10	9	11			4	5		
rep		9	STOCKPORT COUNTY	4-0	Cassidy, Kerr 2, Keegan	5646	1	2	3	6		9	7	8	10		11			4	5		
R3	Jan	3	MILLWALL	2-1	Deere, Heath	7875	1	2	3	6	5	9	7	8	10		11			4	12		
R4		24	Sheffield Wednesday	2-1	Barker, Cassidy	38047	1	2	3	4		6	9	7	8	10	12	11			5		
R5	Feb	7	Swindon Town	1-3	Cassidy	24612	1	2	3	4		6	9	7	8	10		11			5		

F.L. Cup

						Barnard G	Foxton DG	Barker J	Deere SH	Holt R	Welbourne D	Kerr GAM	Keegan JK	Cassidy N	Heath RT	Rusling G	Davidson AG
R1	Aug	12	HARTLEPOOL	0-2		2403	1	2	3	4	5	6	7	8	9	10	11	12

		P	W	D	L	F	A	W	D	L	F	A	Pts
1	Chesterfield	46	19	1	3	55	12	8	9	6	22	20	64
2	Wrexham	46	17	6	0	56	16	9	3	11	28	33	61
3	Swansea Town	46	14	8	1	43	14	7	10	6	23	31	60
4	Port Vale	46	13	9	1	39	10	7	10	6	22	23	59
5	Brentford	46	14	8	1	36	11	6	8	9	22	28	56
6	Aldershot	46	16	5	2	52	22	4	8	11	26	43	53
7	Notts County	46	14	4	5	44	21	8	4	11	29	41	52
8	Lincoln City	46	11	8	4	38	20	6	8	9	28	32	50
9	Peterborough Utd.	46	13	8	2	51	21	4	6	13	26	48	48
10	Colchester United	46	14	5	4	38	22	3	9	11	26	41	48
11	Chester	46	14	3	6	39	23	7	3	13	19	43	48
12	SCUNTHORPE UNITED	46	11	6	6	34	23	7	4	12	33	42	46
13	York City	46	14	7	2	38	16	2	7	14	17	46	46
14	Northampton Town	46	11	7	5	41	19	5	5	13	23	36	44
15	Crewe Alexandra	46	12	6	5	37	18	4	6	13	14	33	44
16	Grimsby Town	46	9	9	5	33	24	5	6	12	21	34	43
17	Southend United	46	12	8	3	40	28	3	2	18	19	57	40
18	Exeter City	46	13	5	5	48	20	1	6	16	9	39	39
19	Oldham Athletic	46	11	4	8	45	28	2	9	12	15	37	39
20	Workington	46	9	9	5	31	21	3	5	15	15	43	38
21	Newport County	46	12	3	8	39	24	1	8	14	14	50	37
22	Darlington	46	8	7	8	31	27	5	3	15	22	46	36
23	Hartlepool	46	7	7	9	31	30	3	3	17	11	52	30
24	Bradford Park Ave.	46	6	5	12	23	32	0	6	17	18	64	23

54

1970/71   17th in Division 4

Player columns (left→right): Barnard G, Foxton DG, Jackson NA, Barker J, Deere SH, Welbourne D, Keegan JK, Cassidy N, Kerr GAM, Heath RT, Davidson AG, Lindsey B, McDonald CB, Atkin JM, Rusling G, Muldoon T, Kisby CN, Woolmer AJ, Kirk HJ, O'Riley P, Williams MJ

#	Date	Opponent	Score	Scorers	Att.	Bar	Fox	Jac	Brk	Dee	Wel	Kee	Cas	Ker	Hea	Dav	Lin	McD	Atk	Rus	Mul	Kis	Woo	Kir	ORi	Wil
1	Aug 15	Exeter City	1-1	Keegan	5456	1	2	3	4	5	6	7	8	9	10	11	12									
2	22	SOUTHEND UNITED	3-0	Kerr, Foxton, Heath	4030	1	2	3	4	5	6	7	8	9	10	12		11								
3	28	Stockport County	0-2		4164	1	2	3	4	5	6	7	8	9	10	11			12							
4	Sep 1	OLDHAM ATHLETIC	2-3	Lindsey, Heath	4424	1	2		3		6	7	8	9	10		5		4	11						
5	5	CAMBRIDGE UNITED	0-0		4149	1	2		3	6		7	8	9	10	12	5		4	11						
6	11	Aldershot	1-0	Rusling	5963	1	2		3	5		7		9	10	11			4	6		8				
7	19	YORK CITY	0-1		3953	1	2		3	6		7		9	10	11			4	5			12			
8	22	BARROW	1-1	Keegan (p)	3241	1	2		3	6	10	8	12	9		11	5		4	7						
9	26	Workington	0-0		2242	1	2		3	5	6	10		9		11			4	12		7				
10	30	Bournemouth	2-0	Deere, Davidson	8219	1	2		3	5	6	10	8	9		11			4	7			12			
11	Oct 3	GRIMSBY TOWN	1-2	Keegan (p)	7114	1	2		3	5	6	10	8	9	11	7			4							
12	6	Oldham Athletic	1-1	Davidson	8341	1	2		3	5	6	10	8	9	11	7			4							
13	10	Newport County	3-2	Cassidy 2, Davidson	3540	1	2		3	5	6	10	8	9	11	7			4							
14	17	EXETER CITY	3-0	Keegan, Cassidy 2	3810	1	2		3	5	6	10	8	9	11	7			4							
15	20	PETERBOROUGH UTD.	5-2	Keegan, Heath, Cassidy, Barker, Kerr	4015	1	2	12	3	5	6	10	8	9	11	7			4							
16	24	Crewe Alexandra	1-3	Davidson	2385	1	2		3	5	6	10	8	9	11	7			4							
17	31	NOTTS COUNTY	0-1		5801	1	2	3		5	6	10	8		11	7			4				9			
18	Nov 7	Lincoln City	1-4	Cassidy	7469	1	2	3	12	5	6	10	8		11	7			4				9			
19	9	Darlington	0-3		3651	1	2	12	3	5	6	10	8		11	7			4				9			
20	14	CHESTER	0-2		3303	1	2	3		5	6	10	8		11	7			4				9			
21	28	NORTHAMPTON T	2-2	Barker, Woolmer	3463	1	2	3		5	6	10			7				4	9			8	11		
22	Dec 4	Southport	1-5	Keegan	2444	1	2	12	3	5	6	10			7				4	9			8	11		
23	18	Southend United	2-2	Davidson, Kirk	4762	1	2		3	5	6				4	7		10		9			8	11		
24	26	BRENTFORD	1-1	Heath	4960	1	2		3	5		10			4	7				6			9	8	11	
25	Jan 9	BOURNEMOUTH	1-1	Heath	4366	1	2		3	5	6	10			4	7			8				9		11	
26	16	Peterborough United	2-1	Davidson, Kirk	5209	1	2		3	5	6	10			4	7			8				9		11	
27	23	HARTLEPOOL	2-1	McDonald, Kirk	3887	1		3		5	6	10			4	2		8					9	12	11	
28	30	Northampton Town	0-1		4607	1		3		5	6	10			4	2		8					9	7	11	
29	Feb 6	SOUTHPORT	2-0	Deere, Keegan	3430	1		3		5	6	10			4	2		8					9	7	11	
30	13	Hartlepool	1-1	Rusling	1267	1		3		5	6	10			4	2		8					9	7	11	
31	20	DARLINGTON	0-0		3673	1		3		5	6	10			4	2		8					9	7	11	
32	27	Notts County	0-3		10750	1		3		5	6	10			4	2		8	12	9				7	11	
33	Mar 6	CREWE ALEXANDRA	1-1	Woolmer	2804	1		3		5	6	10			4	2		8	11	9			7			
34	8	Barrow	2-1	Davidson, Heath	1604	1		3		5	6	10			4	2		8	11	9			7			
35	13	Chester	0-2		3738	1		3		5	6	10			4	2		8	11	12			7		9	
36	16	COLCHESTER UNITED	2-0	Woolmer, O'Riley	3926	1		3		5	6	10			4	2		8					7	11	9	
37	20	LINCOLN CITY	3-1	O'Riley 2, McDonald	5919	1		3		5	6	10			4	2		8					7	11	9	
38	22	Colchester United	0-2		5592			3		5	6	10			4	2		8					7	11	9	1
39	27	Cambridge United	1-1	Keegan	3857	1		3		5	6	10			4	2		8		12			7	11	9	
40	Apr 3	STOCKPORT COUNTY	1-2	Keegan	2881	1	2	3				10			4	7		5				6	8	11	9	
41	9	Grimsby Town	0-1		7820	1	2	3	6			10			4	8		5					7	11	9	
42	10	Brentford	1-0	Heath	7561	1	2	6	3			10			4	7		5	12				8	11	9	
43	13	ALDERSHOT	2-1	O'Riley, Heath	3214	1	2	6	3			10			4	8		5	11				7		9	
44	17	NEWPORT COUNTY	0-1		3075	1	2	3				10			4	8		12	5	11		6	7		9	
45	24	York City	0-2		5296	1	2	6	3			10			4	7		8	5					9	11	
46	May 1	WORKINGTON	4-0	Jackson, Heath 2, Kirk	2738	1	2	4	3		6	10			8	7			5					11	9	
		Apps				45	33	28	30	38	36	45	19	16	43	44	9	22	25	22	1	9	26	21	11	1
		Goals					1	1	2	2		9	6	2	10	7	1	2		2			3	4	4	

F.A. Cup

Rd	Date	Opponent	Score	Scorers	Att.	Bar	Fox	Jac	Brk	Dee	Wel	Kee	Cas	Ker	Hea	Dav	McD	Atk	Rus	Woo	Kir	ORi
R1	Nov 21	Tranmere Rovers	1-1	Woolmer	3759	1	2		3	5	6	10			11	7		4	9	8		
rep	24	TRANMERE ROVERS	0-0		5431	1	2	12	3	5	6	10			11	7		4	9	8		
rep2	30	Tranmere Rovers	1-0	Rusling	7235	1	2	12	3	5	6	10			11	7		4	9	8		
R2	Dec 12	MANSFIELD TOWN	3-0	Rusling 2, Kirk	7656	1	2		3	5	6	10			4	7			9	8	11	
R3	Jan 2	West Bromwich Alb.	0-0		21960	1	2		3	5	6	10			4	7			9	8	11	
rep	11	WEST BROM ALB.	1-3	Deere	16237	1	2		3	5	6	10			4	7	8		9	12	11	

R1 replay and replay 2 a.e.t. Replay 2 at Goodison Park. R3 replay a.e.t.

F.L. Cup

Rd	Date	Opponent	Score	Scorers	Att.	Bar	Fox	Jac	Brk	Dee	Wel	Kee	Cas	Ker	Hea	Dav	Lin
R1	Aug 18	NORTHAMPTON TOWN	2-3	Keegan (p), Jackson	4470	1	2	3	4	5	6	7	8	9	10	11	12

		P	W	D	L	F	A	W	D	L	F	A	Pts
1	Notts County	46	19	4	0	59	12	11	5	7	30	24	69
2	Bournemouth	46	16	5	2	51	15	8	7	8	30	31	60
3	Oldham Athletic	46	14	6	3	57	29	10	5	8	31	34	59
4	York City	46	16	6	1	45	14	7	4	12	33	40	56
5	Chester	46	17	2	4	42	18	7	5	11	27	37	55
6	Colchester United	46	14	6	3	44	19	7	6	10	26	35	54
7	Northampton Town	46	15	4	4	39	24	4	9	10	24	35	51
8	Southport	46	15	2	6	42	24	6	4	13	21	33	48
9	Exeter City	46	12	7	4	40	23	5	7	11	27	45	48
10	Workington	46	13	7	3	28	13	5	5	13	20	36	48
11	Stockport County	46	12	8	3	28	17	4	6	13	21	48	46
12	Darlington	46	15	3	5	42	22	2	8	13	16	35	45
13	Aldershot	46	8	10	5	32	23	6	7	10	34	49	45
14	Brentford	46	13	3	7	45	27	5	5	13	21	35	44
15	Crewe Alexandra	46	13	1	9	49	35	5	7	11	26	41	44
16	Peterborough Utd.	46	14	3	6	46	23	4	4	15	24	48	43
17	SCUNTHORPE UNITED	46	9	7	7	36	23	6	6	11	20	38	43
18	Southend United	46	8	11	4	32	24	6	4	13	21	42	43
19	Grimsby Town	46	13	4	6	37	26	5	3	15	20	45	43
20	Cambridge United	46	9	9	5	31	27	6	4	13	20	39	43
21	Lincoln City	46	11	4	8	45	33	2	9	12	25	38	39
22	Newport County	46	8	3	12	32	36	2	5	16	23	49	28
23	Hartlepool	46	6	10	7	28	27	2	2	19	6	47	28
24	Barrow	46	5	5	13	25	38	2	3	18	26	52	22

55

1971/72   4th in Division 4: Promoted

#	Date	Opponent	Score	Scorers	Att	Barnard G	Foxton DG	Barker J	Jackson NA	Deere SH	Welbourne D	McDonald CB	Fletcher JR	Woolmer AJ	Heath RT	Kirk HJ	Davidson AG	Kisby CN	Hutchinson DN	Kerr GAM	Atkin JM	Markham P
1	Aug 14	Grimsby Town	1-4	Fletcher	7614	1	2	3	4	5	6	7	8	9	10	11	12					
2	21	LINCOLN CITY	2-1	Heath, Jackson	5155	1	2	3	4	5	6	7	8		9	11	10					
3	28	Crewe Alexandra	2-0	Jackson, Davidson	2800	1	2	3	6	4	5		8		9	11	10	7				
4	30	Southend United	3-2	Davidson 2, Fletcher	6907	1	2	3	6	4	5	7	8		10	11	9					
5	Sep 4	DONCASTER ROVERS	0-0		5234	1	2	3	8	4	5	6	9		7	11	10					
6	11	Peterborough United	1-0	Heath	6397	1	2	3	6	4	5	9	8		10	11	7					
7	17	NORTHAMPTON T	0-0		5440	1	2	3	4	5	6	12	8		10	11	9	7				
8	25	Aldershot	1-1	Heath	4675	1	2	3	4	5	6	9	8		10	11		7	12			
9	28	COLCHESTER UNITED	2-0	Fletcher, Davidson	5312	1	2		3	5	6	4	8		10	11	9	7				
10	Oct 2	DARLINGTON	3-1	Kisby, Davidson, Heath	5487	1	2	3	6	4	5	9	7		10	11		8				
11	9	Bury	1-3	Davidson	2733	1	2	3	6	5	4	9	8		10	11	7		12			
12	16	GRIMSBY TOWN	1-2	Deere	11754	1	2	3	6	4	5	12	9		7	11	10	8				
13	23	Barrow	1-0	Kirk	2190	1	2	3	8	5	6	9	7			11	4		10			
14	30	BRENTFORD	0-0		6121	1	2	3	8	5	6	9				11	4		10	7		
15	Nov 6	Exeter City	0-1		3556	1	2	3		5	6	8				11	7	4	9	10	12	
16	13	WORKINGTON	2-0	Kisby, McDonald	4741	1	2	3		5		7	9			11	10	4		8	6	
17	27	READING	1-1	Fletcher	4577	1	2	3		5	6	9	7			11	10	4		8		
18	Dec 4	Gillingham	1-0	Fletcher	6488	1	3	2		5	6	12	9		7	11	8			10	4	
19	11	CHESTER	2-0	McDonald, Fletcher	4012	1	3	2		5	6	8	9			11	7		12	10	4	
20	18	Doncaster Rovers	2-0	Fletcher, Kerr	5534	1	3	2		5	4	9	8			11	7			10	6	
21	27	HARTLEPOOL	2-2	McDonald, Kerr	7270	1	12	3	2	5		7	8		10	11	4			9	6	
22	Jan 1	Northampton Town	2-0	Jackson, Kerr	3929	1	2	3	8	4		7	9			11	6			10	5	
23	8	CREWE ALEXANDRA	2-0	Kerr 2	5190	1	2	3	4	5		7	9			11	8			10	6	
24	15	Southport	1-1	McDonald	3602	1	2	3	4	5		7	9			11	8			10	6	
25	21	Colchester United	1-1	Fletcher	4867	1	2	3	10	5		7	8			11	4			9	6	
26	29	NEWPORT COUNTY	1-0	Davidson	4717	1	2	3	6	5		8	9			11	7			10	4	
27	Feb 5	Stockport County	0-0		2452	1	2	3	8	5		7	9			11	4			10	6	
28	12	BARROW	2-1	Fletcher 2	5340	1	2	3	8	5		7	9	12		11	4			10	6	
29	19	Brentford	3-0	McDonald, Fletcher 2	11912	1	2	3	8	5		7	10			11	4			9	6	
30	26	EXETER CITY	3-0	Giles(og), Jackson, Fletcher	6438	1	2	3	7	5	6	10	9			11	8				4	
31	Mar 4	Workington	1-2	Fletcher	1981	1	2	3	10	5	4	9				11	7			8	6	
32	11	BURY	3-0	Saile(og), Fletcher 2	5267	1	2	3	8	5	4	9				11	7		12	10	6	
33	14	SOUTHPORT	1-0	Dunleavy (og)	7056	1	2	3	10	5		7	8			11	4			9	6	
34	18	Lincoln City	0-1		16498	1	2	3	10	6		7	8	12		11	4			9	5	
35	25	PETERBOROUGH UTD.	0-0		5767	1	2	3	10	4	6	7	8			11				9	5	
36	31	Darlington	1-0	Fletcher	2960	1	2	3	10	5		7	8	12		11	4			9	6	
37	Apr 1	Hartlepool	0-1		6197	1	2	3	10	5		7	8	9		11	4				6	
38	4	ALDERSHOT	1-0	Kirk	7171	1		3	10	5		7	8			11	4			9	6	2
39	8	STOCKPORT COUNTY	0-2		7461	1		3	10	5		8	12			11	7	4		9	6	2
40	11	CAMBRIDGE UNITED	2-1	Fletcher 2	6145	1		3		5		7	8	10		11	4			9	6	2
41	15	Reading	0-2		4308	1	2	3		5		7	8	10		11	4	12		9	6	2
42	19	Chester	0-0		2347	1		3	10	5		8	7			11	4			9	6	2
43	22	GILLINGHAM	3-3	Kirk, Kerr, McDonald	5752	1	2	3	10	5	4	8	12			11	7			9	6	
44	25	SOUTHEND UNITED	1-1	Kirk	8867	1		3	10	5		7	8			11	4			9	6	2
45	29	Cambridge United	0-2		3927	1		3	10	5		12	8	9		11	4			7	6	2
46	May 1	Newport County	0-1		3691	1		3	10	5		8	7			11	4	12		9	6	2

Player substituted in game 45 not known

						Barnard G	Foxton DG	Barker J	Jackson NA	Deere SH	Welbourne D	McDonald CB	Fletcher JR	Woolmer AJ	Heath RT	Kirk HJ	Davidson AG	Kisby CN	Hutchinson DN	Kerr GAM	Atkin JM	Markham P
Apps						46	35	44	42	46	19	33	46	14	17	46	45	16	9	29	31	7
Goals									4	1		6	19		4	4	7	2		6		

3 own goals

F.A. Cup

	Date	Opponent	Score	Scorers	Att	Barnard G	Foxton DG	Barker J	Jackson NA	Deere SH	Welbourne D	McDonald CB	Fletcher JR	Woolmer AJ	Heath RT	Kirk HJ	Davidson AG	Kisby CN	Hutchinson DN	Kerr GAM	Atkin JM	Markham P
R1	Nov 20	South Shields	3-3	Deere, Kerr 2	2687	1	2	3		5		9	8			11	7	4		10	6	
rep	29	SOUTH SHIELDS	2-3	Fletcher, Kirk	5435	1	2	3		5	6	12	8	9		11	7	4		10		

F.L. Cup

	Date	Opponent	Score	Scorers	Att	Barnard G	Foxton DG	Barker J	Jackson NA	Deere SH	Welbourne D	McDonald CB	Fletcher JR	Woolmer AJ	Heath RT	Kirk HJ	Davidson AG	Kisby CN	Hutchinson DN	Kerr GAM	Atkin JM	Markham P
R1	Aug 18	LINCOLN CITY	0-1		5864	1	2	3	4	5	6		8	9	10	11	7					

		P	W	D	L	F	A	W	D	L	F	A	Pts
1	Grimsby Town	46	18	3	2	61	26	10	4	9	27	30	63
2	Southend United	46	18	2	3	56	26	6	10	7	25	29	60
3	Brentford	46	16	2	5	52	21	8	9	6	24	23	59
4	SCUNTHORPE UNITED	46	13	8	2	34	15	9	5	9	22	22	57
5	Lincoln City	46	17	5	1	46	15	4	9	10	31	44	56
6	Workington	46	12	9	2	34	7	4	10	9	16	27	51
7	Southport	46	15	5	3	48	21	3	9	11	18	25	50
8	Peterborough Utd.	46	14	6	3	51	24	3	10	10	31	40	50
9	Bury	46	16	4	3	55	22	3	8	12	18	37	50
10	Cambridge United	46	11	8	4	38	22	6	6	11	24	38	48
11	Colchester United	46	13	6	4	38	23	6	4	13	32	46	48
12	Doncaster Rovers	46	11	8	4	35	24	5	6	12	21	39	46
13	Gillingham	46	11	5	7	33	24	5	8	10	28	43	45
14	Newport County	46	13	5	5	34	20	5	3	15	26	52	44
15	Exeter City	46	11	5	7	40	30	5	6	12	21	38	43
16	Reading	46	14	3	6	37	26	3	5	15	19	50	42
17	Aldershot	46	5	13	5	27	20	4	9	10	21	34	40
18	Hartlepool	46	14	2	7	39	25	3	4	16	19	44	40
19	Darlington	46	9	9	5	37	24	5	2	16	27	58	39
20	Chester	46	10	11	2	34	16	0	7	16	13	40	38
21	Northampton Town	46	8	9	6	43	27	4	4	15	23	52	37
22	Barrow	46	8	8	7	23	26	5	3	15	17	45	37
23	Stockport County	46	7	10	6	33	32	2	4	17	22	55	32
24	Crewe Alexandra	46	9	4	10	27	25	1	5	17	16	44	29

24th in Division 3: Relegated

#	Date		Opponent	Score	Scorers	Att	Barnard G	Foxton DG	Barker J	Davidson AG	Deere SH	Welbourne D	Kerr GAM	Fletcher JR	Collier GR	Heath RT	Kirk HJ	Jackson NA	McDonald CB	Sargent GS	Atkin JM	Sowden M	Kisby CN	Williams MJ	Markham P	Warnock N	Charnley DL	Krzywicki RL	Keeley NB
1	Aug	12	SWANSEA CITY	1-0	Davidson	5636	1	2	3	4	5	6	7	8	9	10	11												
2		18	Tranmere Rovers	1-2	Kirk (p)	3537	1	2	3		5	6	7	8	9	10	11												
3		26	WREXHAM	1-1	Deere	4308	1	2	3	7	5	6	12	8	9	10	11	4	12										
4		29	WALSALL	2-1	Fletcher, Kirk	4350	1	2	3	7	5	6	9	8		10	11	4											
5	Sep	2	Bournemouth	1-1	Fletcher	10034	1	2	3	4	5	6	10	9		7	11	8											
6		8	HALIFAX TOWN	0-3		5030	1	2	3	7	5	6	9	8		10	11	4											
7		16	Charlton Athletic	0-2		4984	1	2	3	7	5	6	9	8		10	11	4	12										
8		19	ROCHDALE	1-2	McDonald	3710	1	2	3	8	5	6	12	9		10	11	4	7										
9		23	GRIMSBY TOWN	1-2	Deere	10768	1		3		5	6	10	9	8	7	11	2	4										
10		25	Southend United	0-1		6572	1	2	3		5	6		9		10	11	4	7	9									
11		30	Blackburn Rovers	0-3		5764	1	2	3		5	6		9		7	11	4	8	10									
12	Oct	7	BRENTFORD	1-0	Welbourne	3378	1	2			5	6		8			11	3	7	9	4	10							
13		10	PLYMOUTH ARGYLE	1-1	Kirk	3807	1	2			5	6		8	12		11	3	7	9	4	10							
14		14	Bolton Wanderers	0-0		7459	1	2		8	5	6		9			11	3	7	10	4								
15		21	YORK CITY	1-0	Sargent	3708	1	2			7	5	6	8			11	12	3	10	9	4							
16		24	Oldham Athletic	0-3		5269	1		3	10	5	6		8			11	2	7	9	4		12						
17		28	Rotherham United	1-2	McDonald	4544			3	10	5	6		8		9	11		7		4		12	1	2				
18	Nov	4	SOUTHEND UNITED	0-0		3322			3	7	5	6		8		9	11		10		4			12	2				
19		11	Rochdale	2-0	Heath, Kirk	2551			3		5	6		8		9	11		10		4			1	2	7			
20		25	SHREWSBURY TOWN	1-0	Fletcher	2769		2	3		5		8	9		10	11		6		4			1		7			
21	Dec	2	Bristol Rovers	1-5	Fletcher	5750		2			5		7	9	12	8	10		6		4			3	1	11			
22		16	Port Vale	0-2		3833		2	3		5	6		8		9	11		10		4					7			
23		23	NOTTS COUNTY	1-0	Davidson	3983	1	2	3	10	5	6		8		9	11				4					7			
24		26	Grimsby Town	0-1		16807	1	2	3	10	5	6		8		9	11				4		12			7			
25		30	TRANMERE ROVERS	1-5	Fletcher	3543	1	2	3	10	5	4		8	12	9		11					6			7			
26	Jan	6	Wrexham	2-1	Heath, Fletcher	2818	1		3		5	4	10	8		9	11				6				2	7			
27		20	BOURNEMOUTH	1-1	Kirk (p)	3635	1			7	5	4	10	8		9	11				6		3		2				
28		27	Halifax Town	0-1		1769	1		3	7	5	4	10	8		9	11				6				2				
29	Feb	3	Swansea City	1-2	McDonald	1607	1		3	7	5	6	10	8		9	11	12				4			2				
30		6	Plymouth Argyle	0-3		10008			3	4	5	6	10	8		9	11	7					2	1		12			
31		10	CHARLTON ATHLETIC	0-2		2974			3	7	5	4	10	8			11	12		6			2	1		9			
32		24	PORT VALE	0-1		2734			3	2	5	4		8		9	11			6			12	1		7		10	
33	Mar	3	Brentford	0-1		7896			3	2	5			9	4		11			6			8	1		7		10	
34		6	Watford	1-5	Fletcher	4578			3	2	5	6		8	10		11				9	12	4	1		7			
35		10	BOLTON WANDERERS	1-1	Fletcher	4610			3	2	5	6		8	9		11	12	10	4				1		7			
36		13	OLDHAM ATHLETIC	0-0		2842			3		5	6		8			11	4	9	2				1		7			
37		17	York City	1-3	Kirk	3118			3		5	6	12	8	10		11	4	9	2				1		7			
38		20	CHESTERFIELD	0-1		2144			3		5	6	12	8	10		11	4	9	2				1		7			
39		24	ROTHERHAM UNITED	2-1	Kirk (p), Fletcher	2357		12	3		5	4		8	10		11	6	9	2				1		7			
40		30	Shrewsbury Town	2-4	Kirk (p), Collier	2277		2	3		5	6		8	10		11	4	9	12				1		7			
41	Apr	7	BRISTOL ROVERS	0-2		1928		2	3	10	5	4		8	9		11			6				12	1	7			
42		14	Chesterfield	1-2	Warnock	3678			3	4	5	6	9			10	11	8						1	2	7			
43		21	WATFORD	1-0	Fletcher	1687			3	4	5	6	12	9		10	11	8						1	2	7			
44		23	Notts County	0-2		15697		12	3	2	5	6	4	9		10	11	8						1		7			
45		24	BLACKBURN ROVERS	1-1	Garbett (og)	2706		12	3	2	5		4	9	10		11	8					6	1		7			
46		28	Walsall	1-1	Collier	3402			3	2	4		6	10	8		11	7					5	1					9

	Barnard	Foxton	Barker	Davidson	Deere	Welbourne	Kerr	Fletcher	Collier	Heath	Kirk	Jackson	McDonald	Sargent	Atkin	Sowden	Kisby	Williams	Markham	Warnock	Charnley	Krzywicki	Keeley
Apps	24	25	40	30	46	41	24	45	21	27	45	15	31	15	27	3	14	22	9	23	1	2	1
Goals				2	2	1		10	2	2	8		3	1						1			

One own goal

F.A. Cup

	Date		Opponent	Score	Scorers	Att	Barnard	Foxton	Barker	Davidson	Deere	Welbourne	Kerr	Fletcher	Collier	Heath	Kirk	Jackson	McDonald	Sargent	Atkin	Sowden	Kisby	Williams	Markham	Warnock
R1	Nov	18	Hartlepool United	0-0		4588			3	7	5	6		9			10	11		8		4			1	2
rep		21	HARTLEPOOL UNITED	0-0		4478			3		5	6		8	12	9	11		10		4	7			1	2
rep2		27	Hartlepool United	2-1	Dawes (og), Deere	7917		2			5			7	8		9	11	10		4		6	1		3
R2	Dec	9	HALIFAX TOWN	3-2	Heath, Fletcher, Barker	4037	1	2	3		5	6		9			10	11	8		4					7
R3	Jan	13	CARDIFF CITY	2-3	Welbourne, Kirk	6428	1		3	12	5	6	10	8		9	11				4				2	7

R1 replay 2 at Roker Park. R1 replay and replay 2 a.e.t.

F.L. Cup

	Date		Opponent	Score		Att	Barnard	Foxton	Barker	Davidson	Deere	Welbourne	Kerr	Fletcher	Collier	Heath	Kirk	Jackson
R1	Aug	15	CHESTERFIELD	0-0		5619	1	2	3		5	6	7	8	9	10	11	4
rep		23	Chesterfield	0-5		8288	1	2	3		5	6	7	8	9	10	11	4

		P	W	D	L	F	A	W	D	L	F	A	Pts
1	Bolton Wanderers	46	18	4	1	44	9	7	7	9	29	30	61
2	Notts County	46	17	4	2	40	12	6	7	10	27	35	57
3	Blackburn Rovers	46	12	8	3	34	16	8	7	8	23	31	55
4	Oldham Athletic	46	12	7	4	40	18	7	9	7	32	36	54
5	Bristol Rovers	46	17	4	2	55	20	3	9	11	22	36	53
6	Port Vale	46	15	6	2	41	21	6	5	12	15	48	53
7	Bournemouth	46	14	6	3	44	16	3	10	10	22	28	50
8	Plymouth Argyle	46	14	3	6	43	26	6	7	10	31	40	50
9	Grimsby Town	46	16	2	5	45	18	4	6	13	22	43	48
10	Tranmere Rovers	46	12	8	3	38	17	3	8	12	18	35	46
11	Charlton Athletic	46	12	7	4	46	24	5	4	14	23	43	45
12	Wrexham	46	11	9	3	39	23	3	8	12	16	31	45
13	Rochdale	46	8	8	7	22	26	6	9	8	26	28	45
14	Southend United	46	13	6	4	40	14	4	4	15	21	40	44
15	Shrewsbury Town	46	10	10	3	31	21	5	4	14	15	22	44
16	Chesterfield	46	13	4	6	37	22	4	5	14	20	39	43
17	Walsall	46	13	4	6	37	26	4	4	15	19	40	43
18	York City	46	8	10	5	24	14	5	5	13	18	32	41
19	Watford	46	11	8	4	32	23	1	9	13	11	25	41
20	Halifax Town	46	9	8	6	29	23	4	7	12	14	30	41
21	Rotherham United	46	12	4	7	34	25	5	3	15	17	38	41
22	Brentford	46	12	5	6	33	18	3	2	18	18	51	37
23	Swansea City	46	11	5	7	37	29	3	4	16	14	44	37
24	SCUNTHORPE UNITED	46	8	7	8	18	25	2	3	18	15	47	30

1973/74 18th in Division 4

		Date	Opponent	Score	Scorers	Att	Williams MJ	Lynch BJ	Collard JB	Welbourne D	Barker J	Davidson AG	Houghton K	Pilling S	Fletcher JR	Keeley NB	Warnock N	Bernard G	Collier GR	Money R	Goodwin SA	Simpkin CJ	Woods E	Charnley DL	Bennett R	Horsfall TW	Atkin JM	Roberts DE	Andrews LL	Markham P	Norris M
1	Aug	25	Lincoln City	0-1		6327	1	2	3	4	5	6	7	8	9	10	11														
2	Sep	1	BARNSLEY	3-0	Houghton, Barker, Keeley	3612		2	6	5	3	4	7	8	9	10	11	1													
3		8	Peterborough United	0-1		6399		2	5	3	6	4	7	8	9	10	11	1	12												
4		12	Gillingham	2-7	Houghton, Welbourne	4610		2	4	3	5	9	7	8		10	11	1	6												
5		14	CREWE ALEXANDRA	0-0		3580		2	4	3	5	9	7	8		10	11	1	6	12											
6		18	BRADFORD CITY	2-1	Pilling, Fletcher	3143		2	4	3	5	6	7	8	9	10	11	1		12											
7		21	Northampton Town	0-2		5049		4			3	5	2	7	8	9	10	11	1		6										
8		29	HARTLEPOOL	1-1	Houghton	2626		2	4	5	3		7	8	9	10	11	1			6										
9	Oct	3	Bradford City	1-2	Podd(og)	2445		2		3	5		7	9	12	10	11	1	8		6	4									
10		6	Swansea City	2-1	Collier, Money	1743		2		3		6	7	5		10	11	1	9	8		4									
11		13	NEWPORT COUNTY	0-0		2782		2		5	3	6	7	8		10	11	1	9	12		4									
12		19	Colchester United	0-2		4862		2		3	5		7	8		10	11	1		6		4	9	12							
13		23	GILLINGHAM	1-1	Simpkin	2544		2		3	5	12	7	8		10	11	1		6		4	9								
14		27	BRENTFORD	4-1	Woods 2, Simpkin, Keeley	2523		2		5	3	6	7	8		10	11	1				4	9								
15	Nov	2	Stockport County	1-3	Welbourne	2419		2		3	5	6	7	8		10	11	1				4	9		12						
16		10	CHESTER	2-1	Keeley, Collier	2329		2		5	3	9	7	8			11		1	4		6			10						
17		13	READING	1-0	Davidson	2689		2		5	9	6	8			11		1	7			4			10						
18		17	Torquay United	1-1	Davidson	3064		2	11	6	5	9	4	8		10		1	7			3									
19	Dec	8	MANSFIELD TOWN	5-3	Houghton 2, Horsfall 2, Davidson	2575		2		3	5	9	6	8		11		1	7			4				10					
20		22	Hartlepool	0-3		844	1	2	5	3	6	10	7	9		11	12		8			4									
21		26	DONCASTER ROVERS	2-1	Pilling, Barker	5775	1	2		3	5	10	6	8		11			7			4				9					
22		29	PETERBOROUGH UTD.	2-1	Collier, Keeley	5238	1	2		5	3	10	6	8		11			7			4				9					
23	Jan	1	Barnsley	0-5		6158	1	6		7	2	10	3	5		11	12		4			8				9					
24		12	Crewe Alexandra	0-1		1591		2		3	5	11	6	8		10		1	7	12		4				9					
25		19	LINCOLN CITY	1-1	Keeley	5624		2	3	5		10	7	8		11	9	1		4		6									
26	Feb	3	Darlington	0-3		3006		2	5	3		10	6	8		11	9	1	7	12		4									
27		10	NORTHAMPTON T	1-2	Collier	3603		2	12	3		10	6	5		11	9	1	7	8		4									
28		17	Newport County	1-2	Warnock	3051		2	4	3			10	8	5		11	12	1	6	9						7				
29		23	SWANSEA CITY	0-0		2395		2	6	5	3	10	7	9		11	12	1	4	8											
30	Mar	2	Doncaster Rovers	0-1		1587		2		3	5	9	7	8		11		1	6			4					10				
31		9	Brentford	1-2	Roberts	4053		2		5	3	12		10		7		1	6	8		4					11	9			
32		16	COLCHESTER UNITED	1-0	Keeley	2293		2		5	3	12		8		11		1	6	7		4					10	9			
33		19	DARLINGTON	1-0	Roberts	1887		2		3	5	12	8			10		1	6	7		4					10	9			
34		23	Chester	0-2		2158		2		5	3	12	4	8		11		1		7		6					10	9			
35		26	Bury	0-0		5190			6	3	5	11		9			12	1	8	7						4	10		2		
36		30	STOCKPORT COUNTY	2-1	Davidson, Collier	1900			3			10		8			1	6	7	4						5	11	9	2		
37	Apr	6	Reading	0-0		3721		2	4		6	9		8		11		1	7	5						3	10				
38		10	Workington	2-1	Davidson, Keeley	1329		2	8		5	10		9		6		1	7	4						3	11	12			
39		13	TORQUAY UNITED	0-0		2538		2	7		3			8		11	12	1	4	6						5	10	9			
40		15	Rotherham United	1-1	Keeley	2682		2	8		5			9		6	10	1	7	4						3	11				
41		16	ROTHERHAM UNITED	3-0	Warnock 2, Roberts	2772		2	8		5			6		6	10	1	7	4						3	11				
42		20	Mansfield Town	2-2	Roberts, Andrews	2342		2	7		5			9		6	10	1	8	4						3	11	12			
43		22	Exeter City	0-4		2226		2			5		7	9		6	12		8	4						3	11	10		1	
44		27	WORKINGTON	0-1		2054			5	2	11		8			6			7	4			10			3	9			1	
45		30	BURY	1-2	Keeley	2167		12		7	5	6			9	11			8	4						3	10		2	1	

Home game with Exeter City not played. Scunthorpe awarded two points.

	Williams MJ	Lynch BJ	Collard JB	Welbourne D	Barker J	Davidson AG	Houghton K	Pilling S	Fletcher JR	Keeley NB	Warnock N	Bernard G	Collier GR	Money R	Goodwin SA	Simpkin CJ	Woods E	Charnley DL	Bennett R	Horsfall TW	Atkin JM	Roberts DE	Andrews LL	Markham P	Norris M
Apps	5	42	22	37	39	37	33	43	7	43	29	37	24	29	2	34	4	2	3	5	12	16	9	3	3
Goals			2	2	5	5	2	1		9	3		5	1		2	2			2		4	1		

One own goal

F.A. Cup

		Date	Opponent	Score	Scorers	Att	Williams MJ	Lynch BJ	Collard JB	Welbourne D	Barker J	Davidson AG	Houghton K	Pilling S	Fletcher JR	Keeley NB	Warnock N	Bernard G	Collier GR	Money R	Goodwin SA	Simpkin CJ
R1	Nov	24	DARLINGTON	1-0	Houghton	3191		2		5	3	9	7	8		11	12	1	6			4	10
R2	Dec	15	Mansfield Town	1-1	Houghton	4580	1	2	5	3	6	10	7	9		11			8			4
rep		18	MANSFIELD TOWN	1-0	Warnock	2744	1	2	12	3	5	10	6	8		11	9		7			4
R3	Jan	5	Millwall	1-1	Collier	7888		2		5	3	9	6	8		11	9	1	7			4
rep		8	MILLWALL	1-0	Pilling	5084		2		3	5	10	6	8		11	9	1	7			4
R4		26	Newcastle United	1-1	Keeley	38913	3	2	5			11	7	8		10	9	1		6		4
rep		30	NEWCASTLE UNITED	0-3		19028		2	5	3		10	6	8		11	9	1	7	12		4

F.L. Cup

		Date	Opponent	Score	Scorers	Att	Williams MJ	Lynch BJ	Collard JB	Welbourne D	Barker J	Davidson AG	Houghton K	Pilling S	Fletcher JR	Keeley NB	Warnock N	Bernard G	Collier GR	Money R	Goodwin SA	Simpkin CJ
R1	Aug	29	Peterborough United	2-2	Pilling, Keeley	8340		2	4	3	5	6	7	8	9	10	11	1				
rep	Sep	4	PETERBOROUGH UNITED	2-1	Keeley 2	4443		2		3	5	6	7	8	9	10	11	1	4			
R2	Oct	9	BRISTOL CITY	0-0		4418		2		3	5	6	7	8		10	11	1	9		4	
rep		16	Bristol City	1-2	Welbourne	7837		2		3	5		7	8	9	10	11	1		6	4	

		P	W	D	L	F	A	W	D	L	F	A	Pts
1	Peterborough Utd.	46	19	4	0	49	10	8	7	8	26	28	65
2	Gillingham	46	16	5	2	51	16	9	7	7	39	33	62
3	Colchester United	46	16	5	2	46	14	8	7	8	27	22	60
4	Bury	46	18	3	2	51	14	6	8	9	30	35	59
5	Northampton Town	46	14	7	2	39	14	6	6	11	24	34	53
6	Reading	46	11	9	3	37	13	5	10	8	21	24	51
7	Chester	46	13	6	4	31	19	4	9	10	23	36	49
8	Bradford City	46	14	7	2	45	20	3	7	13	13	32	48
9	Newport County	46	13	6	4	39	23	3	8	12	17	42	45
10	Exeter City	45	12	5	6	37	20	6	3	13	21	35	44
11	Hartlepool	46	11	4	8	29	16	5	8	10	19	31	44
12	Lincoln City	46	10	8	5	40	30	6	4	13	23	37	44
13	Barnsley	46	15	5	3	42	16	2	5	16	16	48	44
14	Swansea City	46	11	6	6	28	15	5	5	13	17	31	43
15	Rotherham United	46	10	9	4	33	22	5	4	14	23	36	43
16	Torquay United	46	11	7	5	37	23	2	10	11	15	34	43
17	Mansfield Town	46	13	8	2	47	24	0	9	14	15	45	43
18	SCUNTHORPE UNITED	45	12	7	3	33	17	2	5	16	14	47	42
19	Brentford	46	9	7	7	31	20	3	9	11	17	30	40
20	Darlington	46	9	8	6	29	24	4	5	14	11	38	39
21	Crewe Alexandra	46	11	5	7	28	30	3	5	15	15	41	38
22	Doncaster Rovers	46	10	7	6	32	22	2	4	17	15	58	35
23	Workington	46	10	8	5	33	26	1	5	17	10	48	35
24	Stockport County	46	4	12	7	22	25	3	8	12	22	44	34

#	Date	Opponent	Score	Scorers	Att
1	Aug 17	Workington	1-1	Davidson	1656
2	24	MANSFIELD TOWN	0-1		2918
3	31	Bradford City	0-3		3255
4	Sep 3	Barnsley	2-2	Collier, Roberts	5603
5	7	READING	0-1		2095
6	14	Darlington	1-3	Davidson	1863
7	17	Doncaster Rovers	1-1	Roberts	3116
8	21	HARTLEPOOL	1-1	Roberts	2069
9	24	TORQUAY UNITED	0-2		2066
10	28	Shrewsbury Town	0-5		3281
11	Oct 1	BARNSLEY	1-0	Warnock	2582
12	5	Chester	0-1		3023
13	12	CAMBRIDGE UNITED	2-0	Warnock, Keeley	2167
14	15	SOUTHPORT	3-3	Markham, Roberts, Keeley	2272
15	19	Stockport County	2-3	Welbourne, Keeley	1500
16	26	ROTHERHAM UNITED	0-3		2969
17	Nov 2	CREWE ALEXANDRA	1-1	Roberts	1633
18	9	Exeter City	0-0		3058
19	16	ROCHDALE	2-2	Pilling 2	1787
20	30	SWANSEA CITY	1-2	Roberts	1440
21	Dec 7	Newport County	0-2		3137
22	21	Brentford	0-2		4364
23	26	DARLINGTON	1-1	Davidson	2266
24	28	Lincoln City	0-1		7883
25	Jan 4	DONCASTER ROVERS	0-0		2472
26	11	NEWPORT COUNTY	4-1	Roberts 3, Collier	1659
27	18	Swansea City	0-1		1428
28	Feb 1	EXETER CITY	2-1	Collier, Roberts	2003
29	8	Crewe Alexandra	1-1	Davidson	1986
30	11	Northampton Town	0-3		3079
31	15	NORTHAMPTON T	2-1	Roberts, Pilling	1975
32	22	Rochdale	2-4	Collier, Roberts	1430
33	Mar 1	BRADFORD CITY	1-2	Charnley	2118
34	8	Torquay United	1-1	Warnock	1822
35	15	SHREWSBURY TOWN	1-0	Davidson	1793
36	18	WORKINGTON	2-1	Davidson, Collier	2044
37	22	Reading	1-1	Davidson	4639
38	28	Hartlepool	0-1		2471
39	Apr 1	LINCOLN CITY	1-1	Davidson	6044
40	5	Rotherham United	2-3	Keeley, Roberts	6520
41	8	Southport	0-1		924
42	12	CHESTER	1-3	Earl	2014
43	15	BRENTFORD	1-2	Pilling	1556
44	19	Cambridge United	0-2		3278
45	21	Mansfield Town	0-7		11020
46	26	STOCKPORT COUNTY	0-0		1565

Appearances and Goals

	Barnard G	Markham P	Atkin JM	Simpkin CJ	Peacock JC	Keeley NB	Money R	Collier GR	Sproates A	Roberts DE	Davidson AG	Warnock N	Lavery J	Taylor EK	Welbourne D	Earl S	Barker J	Charnley DL	Anderson TK	Lynch BJ	Marshall B	Mountford RW	Pilling S	Oates RA	Norris M
Apps	14	42	10	27	19	34	43	40	24	39	34	20	11	7	33	7	13	8	10	22	3	3	31	14	12
Goals		1				4		5		13	8	3		1	1		1						4		

F.A. Cup

	Date	Opponent	Score	Scorers	Att
R1	Nov 23	ALTRINCHAM	1-1	Keeley	2627
rep	25	Altrincham	1-3	Collier	4176

F.L. Cup

	Date	Opponent	Score	Scorers	Att
R1	Aug 20	SHEFFIELD WEDNESDAY	1-0	Davidson	5214
R2	Sep 10	Manchester City	0-6		14790

League table

		P	W	D	L	F	A	W	D	L	F	A	Pts
1	Mansfield Town	46	17	6	0	55	15	11	6	6	35	25	68
2	Shrewsbury Town	46	16	3	4	46	18	10	7	6	34	25	62
3	Rotherham United	46	13	7	3	40	19	9	8	6	31	22	59
4	Chester	46	17	5	1	48	9	6	6	11	16	29	57
5	Lincoln City	46	14	8	1	47	14	7	7	9	32	34	57
6	Cambridge United	46	15	5	3	43	16	5	9	9	19	28	54
7	Reading	46	13	6	4	38	20	8	4	11	25	27	52
8	Brentford	46	15	6	2	38	14	3	7	13	15	31	49
9	Exeter City	46	14	3	6	33	24	5	8	10	27	39	49
10	Bradford City	46	10	5	8	32	21	7	8	8	24	30	47
11	Southport	46	13	7	3	36	19	2	10	11	20	37	47
12	Newport County	46	13	5	5	43	30	6	4	13	25	45	47
13	Hartlepool	46	13	6	4	40	24	5	4	15	12	38	43
14	Torquay United	46	10	7	6	30	25	4	7	12	16	36	42
15	Barnsley	46	10	7	6	34	24	4	4	14	28	41	41
16	Northampton Town	46	12	6	5	43	22	3	5	15	24	51	41
17	Doncaster Rovers	46	10	9	4	41	29	4	3	16	24	50	40
18	Crewe Alexandra	46	9	9	5	22	16	2	9	12	12	31	40
19	Rochdale	46	9	9	5	35	22	4	4	15	24	53	39
20	Stockport County	46	10	8	5	26	27	2	6	15	17	43	38
21	Darlington	46	11	4	8	38	27	2	6	15	16	40	36
22	Swansea City	46	9	4	10	25	31	6	2	15	21	42	36
23	Workington	46	7	5	11	23	29	6	4	13	13	37	31
24	SCUNTHORPE UNITED	46	7	8	8	27	29	0	7	16	14	49	29

1975/76 — 19th in Division 4

#	Date	Opponent	Score	Scorers	Att.	Norris M	Markham P	Peacock JC	Irvine A	Wiggington CA	Money R	Charnley DL	Robinson A	Keeley NB	Pilling S	Davidson AG	Oates RA	Collier GR	Roberts DE	O'Connor D	Hemmerman JL	Woodward J	Welbourne D	Green R	O'Meara AM	Farrell KM	Bond LA	Ferguson RC	Dale AG
1	Aug 16	Darlington	0-2		1920	1	2	3	4	5	6	7	8	9	10	11	12												
2	23	EXETER CITY	0-1		1783	1	2	3	6	5	4	11		8	9			7	10										
3	30	Newport County	0-0		2749	1	2	3		5	4	11		10	8	9	6	7											
4	Sep 6	HUDDERSFIELD T	0-1		2232	1	2	3	6	5		10		11	8	9	4	7				12							
5	13	Hartlepool	2-1	Hemmerman, Collier	1972	1	2		4	6	5			9	3	8		7			10	11							
6	20	TORQUAY UNITED	3-1	Collier, Woodward 2	2134	1	2		6	5	4	12		11	3	9		8			10	7							
7	22	Tranmere Rovers	1-2	Money	2308	1	2		6	5	4	9		8		3		7			10	11	12						
8	27	Swansea City	0-2		3098	1	2		12	6	3			8		4		7			10	11	5	9					
9	Oct 4	READING	2-1	Keeley, Collier	2321	1	2	3	4	6	5			10		11	8	7						9					
10	11	ROCHDALE	1-3	Green	2671	1	2	3	4	6	5			10		11	8	7			12			9					
11	18	Crewe Alexandra	0-1		1939		2		4	5	6			11	3			7				9	10	8			1		
12	21	Watford	0-1		3581		2		6	5	3	12		8		9		7				11	4	10			1		
13	25	NORTHAMPTON T	0-2		2112		2		6	5	3			12		8		7	9			11	4	10			1		
14	Nov 1	Brentford	2-5	Charnley, Green	4227		2		6	5	3	9				8		7	11				4	10			1		
15	4	CAMBRIDGE UNITED	0-1		1673		2		6		5	8		10	3			7	9	12			4	11			1		
16	8	WORKINGTON	3-0	Keeley, Green 2	1633		2	3		5	10			7	9			6		11			4	8			1	12	
17	15	Bournemouth	0-1		4333		2	3		5	7			10	12	8		6		11			4	9			1		
18	28	Lincoln City	0-3		8494		2	3		5	10	12		8				6	9	7			4	11			1		
19	Dec 6	SOUTHPORT	1-2	Collier	1962		2	3		5	4	11		8				6		7		10		9	1				
20	13	Reading	0-1		5763		2	3		5	6			8		4	12	7		9				11	1		10		
21	20	STOCKPORT COUNTY	0-0		1730		2			5	4	3		8		6	12	7		9				11	1		10		
22	26	Bradford City	0-0		3465		2			5	4			8		3	9	6		7				10	1		11		
23	27	DONCASTER ROVERS	2-1	Davidson, Woodward	5969					5	4	2		10		3	7	8	6			9		11	1				
24	Jan 3	Barnsley	0-1		2947					5	4	2		10		3	7	8	6			9		11	1				
25	10	NEWPORT COUNTY	1-2	Money	1879					5	4	2		10		3	7	8	6	12		9		11	1				
26	17	Torquay United	0-1		2934		2	8		5	4			10	3			7		6		11		9	1			12	
27	Feb 7	Cambridge United	2-2	Keeley, Davidson	1777		2	3	6	5	4	12		8		9				7				10	1				
28	10	WATFORD	0-1		2345		2	3	6	5	4	12		8		9				7				10	1				
29	14	Workington	3-2	Green 2, Davidson	1273		2	3	7	5	4			8		9		6		11				10	1				
30	21	BOURNEMOUTH	2-0	Money, Charnley	2209		2	3	6	5	4	12		8		9				7		11		10	1				
31	24	TRANMERE ROVERS	2-2	Wiggington (pen), O'Connor	3202		2	3	6	5	4	12		8		9				7		11		10	1				
32	27	Northampton Town	1-2	O'Connor	6804		2	3	6	5	4			8		9				7		11		10	1				
33	Mar 2	HARTLEPOOL	5-1	Collier 2, Green 2, Oates	3098		2	3		5	4			8		9	12	6		7		11		10	1				
34	6	BRENTFORD	2-1	Green, O'Connor	3377		2	3		5	4			8		9		6		7		11		10	1				
35	12	Rochdale	1-1	Green	1430		2	3	4	5				8		9		7		6		11	12	10	1				
36	16	CREWE ALEXANDRA	1-0	Green	3272		2	3		5	6			8		9	4			7		11		10	1				
37	20	LINCOLN CITY	0-2		10322		2	3		5	4	12		8		9	6			7		11		10	1				
38	26	Southport	1-1	Collier	1805		2	3		5	4			8		9	6	7				11		10	1				
39	29	Stockport County	0-0		2078		2	3		5	6			8		9	4			7		11		10	1				
40	Apr 3	DARLINGTON	2-1	Irvine, Davidson	2651		2	3	11	5	6			8		9	4			7				10	1				
41	6	SWANSEA CITY	1-1		3167		2	3	11	5	6			8		9	4			7				10	1				
42	10	Huddersfield Town	1-1	Davidson	6502		2	3	11	5	6	12		8		9	4			7				10	1				
43	17	BRADFORD CITY	2-0	Green, O'Connor	3408			3		5	6	2		8		9	4	7				11		10	1				
44	19	Doncaster Rovers	1-0	Green	4097		2	3		5	6			8		9	4	7				11		10	1				
45	20	BARNSLEY	1-0	O'Connor	4940		2	3		5		8		6		9	4	7				11	12	10	1				
46	23	Exeter City	4-5	Green, Woodward 2, Wiggington	1863		2	3		5	6	8					4	7				9		10	1				11
Apps						10	42	31	23	42	45	27	1	43	12	45	25	45	4	21	5	19	10	39	28	2	8	3	1
Goals									1	2	3	2		3		5	1	7		5	1	5		15					

F.A. Cup

Round	Date	Opponent	Score	Scorers	Att.	Norris M	Markham P	Peacock JC	Irvine A	Wiggington CA	Money R	Charnley DL	Robinson A	Keeley NB	Pilling S	Davidson AG	Oates RA	Collier GR	Roberts DE	O'Connor D	Hemmerman JL	Woodward J	Welbourne D	Green R	O'Meara AM	Farrell KM	Bond LA	Ferguson RC	Dale AG
R1	Nov 22	Preston North End	1-2	Green	8119		2	3	6	8				10				7		4		11		5	9		1		

F.L. Cup

Round	Date	Opponent	Score		Att.	Norris M	Markham P	Peacock JC	Irvine A	Wiggington CA	Money R	Charnley DL	Robinson A	Keeley NB	Pilling S	Davidson AG	Oates RA	Collier GR	Roberts DE	O'Connor D	Hemmerman JL	Woodward J	Welbourne D	Green R	O'Meara AM	Farrell KM	Bond LA	Ferguson RC	Dale AG
R1/1	Aug 20	Mansfield Town	0-4		4810	1	2	3	6	5	4	10		9	7	11	12	8											
R1/2	26	MANSFIELD TOWN	0-2		2412	1	2	3		5	4	11		8	9	6		7	10										

Division 4 — Final Table

		P	W	D	L	F	A	W	D	L	F	A	Pts
1	Lincoln City	46	21	2	0	71	15	11	8	4	40	24	74
2	Northampton Town	46	18	5	0	62	20	11	5	7	25	20	68
3	Reading	46	19	3	1	42	9	5	9	9	28	42	60
4	Tranmere Rovers	46	18	3	2	61	16	6	7	10	28	39	58
5	Huddersfield Town	46	11	6	6	28	17	10	8	5	28	24	56
6	Bournemouth	46	15	5	3	39	16	5	7	11	18	32	52
7	Exeter City	46	13	7	3	37	17	5	7	11	19	30	50
8	Watford	46	16	4	3	38	18	6	2	15	24	44	50
9	Torquay United	46	12	6	5	31	24	6	8	9	24	39	50
10	Doncaster Rovers	46	10	6	7	42	31	9	5	9	33	38	49
11	Swansea City	46	14	8	1	51	21	2	7	14	15	36	47
12	Barnsley	46	12	8	3	34	16	2	8	13	18	32	44
13	Cambridge United	46	7	10	6	36	28	7	5	11	22	34	43
14	Hartlepool	46	10	6	7	37	29	6	4	13	25	49	42
15	Rochdale	46	7	11	5	27	23	5	7	11	13	31	42
16	Crewe Alexandra	46	10	7	6	36	21	3	8	12	22	36	41
17	Bradford City	46	9	7	7	35	26	3	10	10	28	39	41
18	Brentford	46	12	7	4	37	18	2	6	15	19	42	41
19	SCUNTHORPE UNITED	46	11	3	9	31	24	3	7	13	19	35	38
20	Darlington	46	11	7	5	30	14	3	3	17	18	43	38
21	Stockport County	46	8	7	8	23	23	5	5	13	20	53	38
22	Newport County	46	8	7	8	35	33	5	2	16	22	57	35
23	Southport	46	6	6	11	27	31	2	4	17	14	46	26
24	Workington	46	5	4	14	19	43	2	3	18	11	44	21

1976/77   20th in Division 4

#	Date		Opponent	Result	Scorers	Att	Letheran G	Czuczman M	Peacock JC	Oates RA	Wiggington CA	Money R	Wadsworth M	Collier GR	Keeley NB	Green R	Pilling S	Davidson AG	O'Connor D	Markham P	O'Meara AM	Bridges B	Dale AG	Lee R	Kilmore K	Lumby JA	Walton IJ	Barnard G
1	Aug	21	ROCHDALE	0-1		3536	1	2	3	4	5	6	7	8	9	10	11	12										
2		28	Watford	1-2	Wadsworth	5001	1	4	3	6	5		8	7		10	9		2									
3	Sep	3	CREWE ALEXANDRA	4-0	Wiggington 2(1p), Keeley, O'Connor	3432	1	6	3	4	5		7		9	10		8	11	2								
4		11	Bournemouth	2-2	Green 2	4297	1	2	3	4	5	6	6	7	8	10	9		12	11								
5		18	WORKINGTON	3-1	Wiggington (p), Keeley, Peacock	3598	1		3	4	5	6		7	8	10		9	11	2								
6		24	Southend United	1-1	Keeley	5381	1		3	6	4	5		7	8	10		9	11	2								
7		29	Exeter City	0-2		2934	1		3	4	5	6		8	9	10	12	7	11	2								
8	Oct	2	HARTLEPOOL	2-0	Keeley, Davidson	3514	1		3	4	5	6		7	10	11	8	9		2								
9		9	Halifax Town	1-0	Wiggington	1854	1		3	4	5	6		7	10	11	8	9		2								
10		15	Cambridge United	0-1		3413	1		3	4	5	6	12	7	10	11	8	9		2								
11		23	COLCHESTER UNITED	2-0	Keeley, Pilling	3278	1		3	4	5	6	12	7	11	10	8	9		2								
12		30	DARLINGTON	3-0	Davidson, Green, Wadsworth	4044	1		3	4	5	6	12	7	10	11	8	9		2								
13	Nov	2	SOUTHPORT	1-1	Davidson	4900	1		3	4	5	6	12	8	9	10	11	7		2								
14		6	Barnsley	1-5	Pilling	4595	1		3		5	6	7	4	10	11	8	9		2								
15		13	ALDERSHOT	1-3	Keeley	3716	1		3	4	5	6		7	8	10	11		9	2								
16		27	Torquay United	3-1	O'Connor 3	2087	1		3	4	5	6		7	10	9		8	11	2								
17	Dec	11	Swansea City	0-2		2392	1	12	3	4	5	6		7	10	9		8	11	2								
18		17	Stockport County	0-1		2827	1	7	3	4	5	6		8	9	10		12	11	2								
19		27	DONCASTER ROVERS	1-1	Green	7128	1	7	3	4	5	6	12	8	9	10		11		2								
20		28	Huddersfield Town	0-1		7028	1	7	3	4	5	6	11	8	9	10		12		2								
21	Jan	8	BRADFORD CITY	2-1	Wiggington, Keeley	4354	1	4	3	12	5	6	11	7	8	9		10		2								
22		22	Rochdale	0-5		1640	1	6	3	12	5	4	11	7	10	9		8		2								
23		25	BRENTFORD	2-1	Wadsworth, Keeley	2867			2	4	5		11	8	9	10	3	7			1	6	12					
24		28	Newport County	0-0		1581		6	2	4	5		11	8	9	10	3	7			1							
25	Feb	5	WATFORD	0-0		3325	1	6	2	4	5		11	7	10	9	3	8						12				
26		8	BARNSLEY	1-2	Pilling	4698		6	2	4	5		11	8	9	10	3	7			1			12				
27		12	Crewe Alexandra	1-2	Keeley	2189	1	6	2	4	5		11	12	9	10	3	7						8				
28		19	BOURNEMOUTH	0-0		2836	1	6	2	4	5		11	7	10		3	9						8	12			
29		26	Workington	0-1		1063	1	6	2	4	5	7	12		10		3	9						8	11			
30	Mar	5	SOUTHEND UNITED	1-0	Lumby	2869	1	7	2	4	5	6			11		3							8	9	10		
31		7	Darlington	2-5	Kilmore, Keeley	2134		6	2	4	5	7			9		3							12	11	8	10	
32		12	Hartlepool	0-3		1698		7	2	4	5	6		8	9		3		11		1				10			
33		15	EXETER CITY	4-1	Lumby 2, Czuczman, Hore(og)	2257		7	2	4	5	6			9		3				1			11	8	10		
34		19	HALIFAX TOWN	2-1	Lumby, Keeley	3031		7	2	4	5	6			9		3				1			11	8	10		
35		26	CAMBRIDGE UNITED	0-2		3729		7	2	4	5	6			9		3	12			1			11	8	10		
36	Apr	2	Colchester United	1-1	Lumby	3799		7	2	4	5	6			9		3	12			1			11	8	10		
37		9	HUDDERSFIELD T	0-4		4347		4	2		5	6	12		9		3	7			1			11	8	10		
38		11	Doncaster Rovers	0-3		4876			2	4	5	6	12		9		3	7			1			11	8	10		
39		12	Southport	1-2	Lumby	964		7	2	4	5	6			9		3	8			1			12	10	11		
40		16	SWANSEA CITY	0-3		2199			2	4	5	6	8	7	9		3	11			1			12	10			
41		19	NEWPORT COUNTY	1-0	Keeley	1988		2		4	5	6	7		9		3	11						8	10			1
42		23	Aldershot	1-1	Kilmore	2392		2	12	4	5	6	9		8		3	7						11	10			1
43		30	TORQUAY UNITED	0-0		2223		2		4	5	6	9		11		3	7						8	10			1
44	May	4	Bradford City	0-4		5982		2		4	5	6			12	9	3	7						11	8	10		1
45		7	Brentford	2-4	Kilmore, Lumby	5298		2		4	5	6			12	9	3	7						11	8	10		1
46		14	STOCKPORT COUNTY	2-2	Lumby, Oates	2244		2		4	5	6			9		3	7						11	8	10		1
			Apps				27	31	41	44	46	38	28	31	46	27	33	41	10	19	13	1	2	16	19	16	1	6
			Goals					1	1	1	5		3		12	4	3	3	4						3	8		

One own goal

F.A. Cup

	Date		Opponent	Result	Scorers	Att			Peacock	Oates	Wiggington	Money		Collier	Keeley	Green		Davidson	O'Connor	Markham								
R1	Nov	20	CHESTERFIELD	1-2	Keeley	5426			3	4	5	6		7	10	9		8	11	2	1							

F.L. Cup

	Date		Opponent	Result	Scorers	Att	Letheran	Czuczman	Peacock	Oates	Wiggington	Money	Wadsworth	Collier	Keeley	Green	Pilling	Davidson	O'Connor	Markham								
R1/1	Aug	14	Mansfield Town	0-2		5224	1	2	3	4	5	6		8	9	10	11	7										
R1/2		17	MANSFIELD TOWN	2-0	Keeley, Wiggington	3200	1	2	3	4	5	6	7	8	9	10	11											
rep		24	MANSFIELD TOWN	2-1	O'Connor, Wadsworth	4338	1	2	3	4	5	6	7	8	9	10		12	11									
R2		31	NOTTS COUNTY	0-2		6255	1	6	3	4	5		7	8	9	10		2	11									

		P	W	D	L	F	A	W	D	L	F	A	Pts
1	Cambridge United	46	16	5	2	57	18	10	8	5	30	22	65
2	Exeter City	46	17	5	1	40	13	8	7	8	30	33	62
3	Colchester United	46	19	2	2	51	14	6	7	10	26	29	59
4	Bradford City	46	16	7	0	51	18	7	6	10	27	33	59
5	Swansea City	46	18	3	2	60	30	7	5	11	32	38	58
6	Barnsley	46	16	5	2	45	18	7	4	12	17	21	55
7	Watford	46	15	7	1	46	13	3	8	12	21	37	51
8	Doncaster Rovers	46	16	2	5	47	25	5	7	11	24	40	51
9	Huddersfield Town	46	15	5	3	36	15	4	7	12	24	34	50
10	Southend United	46	11	9	3	35	19	4	10	9	17	26	49
11	Darlington	46	13	5	5	37	25	5	8	10	22	39	49
12	Crewe Alexandra	46	16	6	1	36	15	3	5	15	11	45	49
13	Bournemouth	46	13	8	2	39	13	2	10	11	15	31	48
14	Stockport County	46	10	10	3	29	19	3	9	11	24	38	45
15	Brentford	46	14	3	6	49	27	4	4	15	20	40	43
16	Torquay United	46	12	5	6	33	22	5	4	14	26	45	43
17	Aldershot	46	10	8	5	29	19	6	3	14	20	40	43
18	Rochdale	46	8	7	8	32	25	5	5	13	18	34	38
19	Newport County	46	11	6	6	33	21	3	4	16	9	37	38
20	SCUNTHORPE UNITED	46	11	6	6	32	24	2	5	16	17	49	37
21	Halifax Town	46	11	6	6	36	18	0	8	15	11	40	36
22	Hartlepool	46	8	9	6	30	20	2	3	18	17	53	32
23	Southport	46	3	12	8	17	28	0	7	16	16	49	25
24	Workington	46	3	7	13	23	42	1	4	18	18	60	19

#	Date		Opponent	Res	Scorers	Att	Crawford PG	Czuczman M	Peacock JC	Pilling S	Money R	Bridges B	Oates RA	Kilmore K	Keeley NB	Lumby JA	Heron B	Kavanagh EA	Farrell KM	Wigg RG	Cooper T	Davy SJ	Lee R	O'Donnell JD	Grimes V	Holyoak P	Deere SH	Couch GR
1	Aug	20	Southport	1-1	Lumby (p)	2069	1	2	3	4	5	6	7	8	9	10	11											
2		23	CREWE ALEXANDRA	3-0	Keeley, Kilmore, Lumby	3443	1	2	3	4	5	6	7	8	9	10	11											
3		26	BOURNEMOUTH	0-0		4255	1	2	3	4	5	6	7	8	9	10	11											
4	Sep	3	Hartlepool United	0-1		1960	1	2	3	4	5	6	7	8	9	10	11	12										
5		10	SOUTHEND UNITED	1-2	Lumby	2896	1	2	3	4	5	6	7	8	9	10	11											
6		13	Barnsley	0-3		5888	1	2	3	4	5	6	7	8	9	10	11	12										
7		17	WIMBLEDON	3-0	Lumby 2, Oates	2739	1	2	3	12	5	6	7	10	9	8	11	4										
8		24	Brentford	0-2		6115	1	2	3	12	5	6	7	8	9	10	11	4										
9		27	SWANSEA CITY	1-0	Kilmore	2787	1	2	3		5	6	7	8	9	10	11	4										
10	Oct	1	NORTHAMPTON T	2-2	Heron, Lumby (p)	2711	1	2	3	12	5	6	7	8	9	10	11	4										
11		4	Newport County	1-3	Farrell	3263	1	2	3	8	5	6	7		9	10	11	4	12									
12		8	Grimsby Town	0-0		5489	1	2	3	8	5		6		9	10	11	4	7									
13		15	READING	0-1		2699	1	2	3	7	5		6	12	9	10	11	4	8									
14		22	Torquay United	2-4	Lumby (p), Wigg	2521	1	2	3		5	6	7	8	9	10		4		11								
15		29	HALIFAX TOWN	2-0	Lumby (p), Keeley	2548	1	2	3		5	6	7	8	9	10		4		11								
16	Nov	5	HUDDERSFIELD T	1-1	Lumby	3211	1	2	3		5	6	7	8	9	10	11	4										
17		12	Watford	1-4	Lumby	10565	1	2	3	12	5		7	8	9	10		4		11	6							
18		19	ROCHDALE	1-0	Kilmore	2204	1	2	3	12	5		7	8	9		11	4		10	6							
19	Dec	3	Aldershot	0-4		3070	1	5	3	8			4		9	10	12			11		2	7					
20		10	DARLINGTON	3-0	Lumby, Keeley, Oates	1959	1	5	3				4	8	9	10	12			11		2	7					
21		26	Doncaster Rovers	1-1	Wigg	5097	1	5	3	12		6	4	8	9	10				11		2	7	4				
22		27	YORK CITY	2-1	Lumby 2	3381	1	5	3			6	4		9	10		7		11		2		8				
23		31	Huddersfield Town	1-4	Lumby (p)	5104	1	5	3			6	4	12	9	10		7		11		2		8				
24	Jan	2	STOCKPORT COUNTY	3-0	Oates, Lumby 2	3385	1	5	3			6	4		9	10		7		11		2		8				
25		7	Crewe Alexandra	1-1	Lumby	1926	1	5	3			6	4	12	9	10		7		11		2		8				
26		14	SOUTHPORT	0-2		2699	1	5	3	12		6	4		9	10		7		11		2		8				
27		21	Bournemouth	1-1	Keeley	2869	1	5	3			6	4	8	9	10		7		11	12	2						
28	Feb	3	Southend United	0-2		7139	1	5	3			6	4		9	10		7		11	12	2		8				
29		11	Wimbledon	0-0		1603	1	5		3			4		9	10		11		12		2		8	7	6		
30		25	Northampton Town	2-1	Lumby, Deere	2952	1	6		3			4		9	10				11		2		8	7		5	
31	Mar	3	GRIMSBY TOWN	2-1	Lumby 2 (1p)	7771	1	6	3				4		9	10				11		2		8	7		5	
32		7	BARNSLEY	1-0	Keeley	4987	1	6	3				4		9	10				11		2		8	7		5	
33		11	Reading	0-1		3628	1	6	3	12			4		9	10				11		2		8	7		5	
34		14	BRENTFORD	1-1	Wigg	3053	1	6	3				4	12	9	10				11		2		8	7		5	
35		18	TORQUAY UNITED	0-1		2292	1	6		3			4		9	10				11		2		8	7		5	
36		24	York City	2-0	Grimes, Kilmore	2639	1	6		3			4	8	9	10				11					7		5	
37		27	DONCASTER ROVERS	0-0		3724	1	6		3			4		9	10				11					7		5	
38		28	Halifax Town	2-2	Lumby (p), Grimes	2215	1	6		3			4		9	10				11					7		5	
39		31	Stockport County	1-1	Keeley	2774	1	6					4	8	9	10				11		2			7		5	
40	Apr	4	NEWPORT COUNTY	2-0	Kilmore 2	2577	1	6					4	8	9	10				11		2			7		5	
41		8	WATFORD	0-1		5134	1	6		3			4	8	9			12		11		2			7		5	10
42		15	Rochdale	1-1	O'Donnell	857	1	6		3			4		9	8				11		12		2	7		5	10
43		18	HARTLEPOOL UNITED	2-0	Kilmore 2	2317	1	6		3			4		9	8				11				2	7		5	10
44		22	ALDERSHOT	1-1		2686	1	6		3			4		9	8				11				2	7		5	10
45		25	Swansea City	1-3	Oates	13228	1	6		3			4	8	9					11		12		2	7		5	10
46		29	Darlington	1-1	Wigg	1302	1	6		3			4	8	9			12		11				2	7		5	10
			Apps				46	46	31	30	18	22	46	32	46	39	25	15	5	32	4	24	3	23	18	1	17	6
			Goals										5	8	6	21	1		1	4				1	2		1	

F.A. Cup

	Date		Opponent	Res		Att	Craw	Czu	Pea	Pil	Mon	Bri	Oat	Kil	Kee	Lum	Her	Kav	Far	Wig	Coo	Dav	Lee	ODo	Gri	Hol	Dee	Cou
R1	Nov	26	Stockport County	0-3		4512	1	6	3		5			8	9	10		4	12	11		2	7					

F.L. Cup

	Date		Opponent	Res	Scorers	Att	Craw	Czu	Pea	Pil	Mon	Bri	Oat	Kil	Kee	Lum	Her	Kav	Far	Wig	Coo	Dav	Lee	ODo	Gri	Hol	Dee	Cou
R1/1	Aug	13	Darlington	0-0		2173	1	2	3		5	6	7	8	9	10	11							4				
R1/2		16	DARLINGTON	3-1	Lumby, Kilmore, Oates	2971	1	2	3	12	5	6	7	8	9	10	11							4				
R2		30	Peterborough United	1-1	Pilling	3697	1	2	3	4	5	6	7	8	9	10	11	12										
rep	Sep	6	PETERBOROUGH UTD.	0-1		4564	1	2	3	4		6	7	8	9	10	11	5										

		P	W	D	L	F	A	W	D	L	F	A	Pts
1	Watford	46	18	4	1	44	14	12	7	4	41	24	71
2	Southend United	46	15	5	3	46	18	10	5	8	20	21	60
3	Swansea City	46	16	5	2	54	17	7	5	11	33	30	56
4	Brentford	46	15	6	2	50	17	6	8	9	36	37	56
5	Aldershot	46	15	8	0	45	16	4	8	11	22	31	54
6	Grimsby Town	46	14	6	3	30	15	7	5	11	27	36	53
7	Barnsley	46	15	4	4	44	20	3	10	10	17	29	50
8	Reading	46	12	7	4	33	23	6	7	10	22	29	50
9	Torquay United	46	12	6	5	43	25	4	9	10	14	31	47
10	Northampton Town	46	9	8	6	32	30	8	5	10	31	38	47
11	Huddersfield Town	46	13	5	5	41	21	2	10	11	22	34	45
12	Doncaster Rovers	46	11	8	4	37	28	3	9	11	15	39	45
13	Wimbledon	46	8	11	4	39	26	6	5	12	27	41	44
14	SCUNTHORPE UNITED	46	12	6	5	31	14	2	10	11	19	41	44
15	Crewe Alexandra	46	11	8	4	34	25	4	6	13	16	44	44
16	Newport County	46	14	6	3	43	22	2	5	16	22	51	43
17	Bournemouth	46	12	6	5	28	20	2	9	12	13	31	43
18	Stockport County	46	14	4	5	41	19	2	6	15	15	37	42
19	Darlington	46	10	8	5	31	22	4	5	14	21	37	41
20	Halifax Town	46	7	10	6	28	23	3	11	9	24	39	41
21	Hartlepool United	46	12	4	7	34	29	3	3	17	17	55	37
22	York City	46	8	7	8	27	31	4	5	14	23	38	36
23	Southport	46	5	13	5	30	32	1	6	16	22	44	31
24	Rochdale	46	8	6	9	29	28	0	2	21	14	57	24

1978/79 — 12th in Division 4

#	Date	Opponent	Score	Scorers	Att	Crawford PG	Davy SJ	Peacock JC	Oates RA	Deere SH	Czuczman M	Grimes V	Wigg RG	Keeley NB	Pilling S	Kilmore K	Bloomer BMc	O'Donnell JD	Gibson D	Kavanagh EA	Couch GR	Armstrong KT	Earl S	Hall DA
1	Aug 19	Port Vale	2-2	Wigg, Pilling	3027	1	2	3	4	5	6	7	8	9	10	11	12							
2	22	BOURNEMOUTH	1-0	Pilling	2573	1		3	4	5	6	7		9	10	11	8	12	2					
3	25	HUDDERSFIELD T	3-1	Pilling, Grimes, Kilmore	3200	1		3	4	5	6	7		9	10	11	8	12	2	4				
4	Sep 1	Doncaster Rovers	0-0		4687	1		3	4	5	6	7		9	10	11	8	12	2					
5	9	BARNSLEY	0-1		7767	1		3	4	5	6	7		9		11	8	12	2	10				
6	12	Portsmouth	0-0		10965	1		3	4	5	6	7		9		11	8		2	10	12			
7	15	Northampton Town	0-1		3859	1		3	4	5	6	7		9		11	8		2	10	12			
8	23	STOCKPORT COUNTY	1-0	Wigg	3084	1		3	4	5	6	7	9			12	8		2	10	11			
9	26	ALDERSHOT	2-0	Kilmore 2	2700	1		3	4	5	6	7	9			11	8		2		10			
10	30	Wigan Athletic	0-1		4459	1		3	4	5	6	7	9			11	8		2	12	10			
11	Oct 7	NEWPORT COUNTY	2-3	Deere, Oates	2568	1		3	4	5	6		9				8	10	2	7	11			
12	14	Wimbledon	1-3	Wigg	3808	1		3	4	5	6	7	9		10		8		2		11			
13	17	Hartlepool United	1-1	Kilmore	2981	1	2		4	5	6	7	9		3	8				10	11	12		
14	21	BRADFORD CITY	3-2	Couch, Kilmore 2 (1 p)	2908	1	2		4	5	6	7		9	3	8				10	11			
15	28	York City	0-1		1970	1	2		4	5		7	6	9	3	8				10	11			
16	Nov 4	READING	0-3		2541	1	2		4	5	6	7	11	9	3	8				10	12			
17	11	DONCASTER ROVERS	0-0		3403	1	2		4		6	7	9	11	3	8		5			10			
18	18	Huddersfield Town	2-3	Oates, Keeley	3375	1	2		4	5	6	7	9	11	3	8		10			12			
19	Dec 9	Torquay United	1-0	Kilmore (p)	2744	1			4	5	6	7			10	3	8		2		11		9	
20	16	HEREFORD UNITED	4-2	Kilmore 2, Pilling, Earl	1794	1			4	5	6	7			10	3	8		2		11		9	
21	23	Darlington	2-2	Kilmore 2	1512	1			4	5	6	7			10	3	8		2		11		9	
22	26	GRIMSBY TOWN	2-1	Kilmore (p), Grimes	8165	1			4	5	6	7			11	3	8		2		10		9	
23	30	ROCHDALE	0-4		2714	1			4	5	6	7	12		10	3	8		2		11		9	
24	Feb 3	Aldershot	0-2		3869	1			4	5	6	7			11	3	8		2	12	10		9	
25	26	Stockport County	2-0	Kavanagh, Earl	2676	1			4	5	6	7			11	3	8		2	12	10		9	
26	Mar 3	Bradford City	1-1	Pilling	4938	1	12		4	5	6	7			11	3	8		2		10		9	
27	10	YORK CITY	2-3	Kilmore 2 (2p)	2366	1			4	5	6	7			11	3	8		2		10		9	
28	13	Barnsley	1-4	Grimes	9309	1			4	5	6	7			11	3	8		2		10		9	
29	16	Reading	1-0	Keeley	5390	1			4	5	6	7			11	3	12		2	8	10		9	
30	20	NORTHAMPTON T	0-3		1868	1			4	5	6	7			11	3	12		2	8	10		9	
31	24	Bournemouth	0-0		3028	1		3	4	5	6	7			11		8		2		10		9	
32	27	PORT VALE	2-0	Grimes, Earl	1580	1		3	4	5	6	7			11		8		2		10		9	
33	31	CREWE ALEXANDRA	0-1		1985	1		3	4	5	6	7					8		2		10	11	9	6
34	Apr 3	PORTSMOUTH	2-2	Couch, Bloomer	1649	1	12	3	4	5		7					8	9	2		10	11		6
35	7	Hereford United	1-3	Kilmore (p)	2859	1	12	3	4	5	6	7					8	9	2		10		11	
36	10	DARLINGTON	1-0	Craig (og)	1491	1	12		4	5		7	9				8		3		10	11		6
37	14	Grimsby Town	1-1	Kavanagh	10464	1		3	4	5	6	7					8		2	12	10	11	9	
38	16	HALIFAX TOWN	1-0	Earl	1739	1		3	4	5	2	7					8			11	10	12	9	6
39	18	Newport County	0-2		2600	1		3	4	5	2	7					8			11	10		9	6
40	21	Rochdale	0-1		1224	1	2	3	4	5		7					8			11	10	12	9	6
41	24	HARTLEPOOL UNITED	3-1	Oates, Earl 2	1339	1	2		4	5	3	7					8				10		9	6
42	28	TORQUAY UNITED	2-2	Kilmore (p), Earl	1543	1		2	4	5	3	7					8				10	9	11	6
43	May 1	WIGAN ATHLETIC	0-1		1701	1		3	4	5	2	7					8			11	10	9	6	12
44	5	Crewe Alexandra	2-0	Couch 2	1121	1	2	3	4	5		7	11				8				10	9	6	
45	8	WIMBLEDON	2-0	Kilmore (p), Earl	1907	1	2	3	4	5		7	6				8				10	9	11	
46	18	Halifax Town	3-2	Couch, Grimes, Gibson	1037	1	2	3	4	5		7					8		11		10	9		6
Apps						46	14	28	45	45	39	45	18	25	30	46	7	32	18	39	18	1	23	11
Goals									3	1		5	3	2	5	17	1		1	2	5		8	

One own goal

F.A. Cup

R	Date	Opponent	Score	Scorers	Att	Crawford PG	Davy SJ	Peacock JC	Oates RA	Deere SH	Czuczman M	Grimes V	Wigg RG	Keeley NB	Pilling S	Kilmore K	Bloomer BMc	O'Donnell JD	Gibson D	Kavanagh EA	Couch GR	Armstrong KT	Earl S	Hall DA
R1	Nov 25	SHEFFIELD WEDNESDAY	1-1	Pilling	8697	1			4	5	6	7		9	11	3	8		2		10			
rep	28	Sheffield Wednesday	0-1		9780	1			4	5	6	7		9	11	3	8		2		10			

F.L. Cup

R	Date	Opponent	Score	Scorers	Att	Crawford PG	Davy SJ	Peacock JC	Oates RA	Deere SH	Czuczman M	Grimes V	Wigg RG	Keeley NB	Pilling S	Kilmore K	Bloomer BMc	O'Donnell JD	Gibson D	Kavanagh EA	Couch GR	Armstrong KT	Earl S	Hall DA
R1/1	Aug 12	NOTTS COUNTY	0-1		2389	1		3	4	5	6	7		9	10	11	12		2	8				
R1/2	15	Notts County	0-3		5064	1		3	4	5	6	7		9	10	11	12		2	8				

		P	W	D	L	F	A	W	D	L	F	A	Pts
1	Reading	46	19	3	1	49	8	7	10	6	27	27	65
2	Grimsby Town	46	15	5	3	51	23	11	4	8	31	26	61
3	Wimbledon	46	18	3	2	50	20	7	8	8	28	26	61
4	Barnsley	46	15	5	3	47	23	9	8	6	26	19	61
5	Aldershot	46	16	5	2	38	14	4	12	7	25	33	57
6	Wigan Athletic	46	14	5	4	40	24	7	8	8	23	24	55
7	Portsmouth	46	13	7	3	35	12	7	5	11	27	36	52
8	Newport County	46	12	5	6	39	28	9	5	9	27	27	52
9	Huddersfield Town	46	13	8	2	32	15	5	3	15	25	38	47
10	York City	46	11	6	6	33	24	7	5	11	18	31	47
11	Torquay United	46	14	4	5	38	24	5	4	14	20	41	46
12	SCUNTHORPE UNITED	46	12	3	8	33	30	5	8	10	21	30	45
13	Hartlepool United	46	7	12	4	35	28	6	6	11	22	38	44
14	Hereford United	46	12	8	3	35	18	3	5	15	18	35	43
15	Bradford City	46	11	5	7	38	20	0	4	13	24	42	43
16	Port Vale	46	8	10	5	29	28	6	4	13	28	42	42
17	Stockport County	46	11	5	7	33	21	3	7	13	25	39	40
18	Bournemouth	46	11	6	6	34	19	3	5	15	13	29	39
19	Northampton Town	46	12	4	7	40	30	3	5	15	24	46	39
20	Rochdale	46	11	4	8	25	26	4	5	14	22	38	39
21	Darlington	46	8	8	7	25	21	3	7	13	24	45	37
22	Doncaster Rovers	46	8	8	7	25	22	5	3	15	25	51	37
23	Halifax Town	46	7	5	11	24	32	3	8	18	15	40	26
24	Crewe Alexandra	46	3	7	13	24	41	3	7	13	19	49	26

Match Details (League)

No		Date	Opponent	Score	Scorers	Att
1	Aug	18	Torquay United	0-3		3177
2		21	HARTLEPOOL UNITED	1-3	Kavanagh	1822
3		25	Portsmouth	1-6	Pilling	12234
4	Sep	1	BOURNEMOUTH	2-1	Green, Earl	1586
5		8	Aldershot	0-2		2709
6		14	HUDDERSFIELD T	1-1	Green	2679
7		18	YORK CITY	6-1	Green 2, Partridge 3(1p), Cammack	2485
8		22	Bradford City	0-2		6248
9		28	DONCASTER ROVERS	0-0		4640
10	Oct	2	York City	0-2		2397
11		6	WALSALL	2-2	Green, O'Berg	2617
12		9	Hartlepool United	2-3	Partridge (p), Green	2803
13		13	Lincoln City	0-4		5011
14		20	NEWPORT COUNTY	1-3	Keeley	1995
15		23	DARLINGTON	3-0	O'Berg, Cammack, Green	1667
16		26	Tranmere Rovers	2-1	Green, Pilling	1876
17	Nov	3	TORQUAY UNITED	1-1	Cammack	1989
18		6	Darlington	1-3	Cammack	1306
19		10	STOCKPORT COUNTY	1-1	Cammack	1967
20		17	Wigan Athletic	1-4	Partridge	4618
21		30	ROCHDALE	2-0	Oates 2	1887
22	Dec	8	Northampton Town	0-0		2120
23		15	Newport County	1-2	Stewart	4158
24		21	HALIFAX TOWN	1-0	Cammack	1587
25		26	Port Vale	0-1		3433
26		29	HEREFORD UNITED	1-0	Green	1880
27	Jan	5	Peterborough United	1-3	Davy	3014
28		26	PORTSMOUTH	1-0	Partridge	2742
29	Feb	9	BRADFORD CITY	3-3	Pilling, Partridge 2	2969
30		16	Doncaster Rovers	0-5		3304
31		23	LINCOLN CITY	1-0	Pilling	3838
32	Mar	4	CREWE ALEXANDRA	1-1	O'Berg	2038
33		8	TRANMERE ROVERS	2-2	Pilling, Cammack	1911
34		15	Walsall	1-1	Partridge	5078
35		21	Stockport County	2-1	Stewart, Partridge	2215
36		25	Bournemouth	3-3	Pilling 2, Stewart	2675
37		29	WIGAN ATHLETIC	1-3	Cammack	2278
38	Apr	5	PORT VALE	1-0	Pilling	1981
39		7	Crewe Alexandra	1-1	Cammack	2596
40		8	Halifax Town	2-2	Oates, Cammack	1660
41		12	PETERBOROUGH UTD.	1-0	Stewart	2046
42		15	Huddersfield Town	1-2	Partridge	10900
43		18	Rochdale	1-0	Partridge	993
44		22	ALDERSHOT	1-1	Partridge	1702
45		25	NORTHAMPTON T	3-0	Stewart, Cammack 2	1810
46	May	3	Hereford United	1-1	Pilling	2099

Appearance Grid (League)

Column headers: Crawford PG, Davy SJ, Peacock JC, Kavanagh EA, Deere SH, Oates RA, O'Berg PJ, Kilmore K, Earl S, Partridge M, Keeley NB, Pilling S, Green R, Cammack SR, Gibson D, Couch GR, Cowling C, Gordon JS, Grimes V, Dall DG, Hall DA, Stewart CD, Pugh JG, Skipper PD, Botham IT, O'Donnell JD, Neenan JP

No	Cra	Dav	Pea	Kav	Dee	Oat	O'B	Kil	Ear	Par	Kee	Pil	Gre	Cam	Gib	Cou	Cow	Gor	Gri	Dal	Hal	Ste	Pug	Ski	Bot	O'D	Nee
1	1	2	3	4	5	6	7	8	9	10	11	12															
2	1	2	3	4	5	6	7	8	9	10	11																
3	1	2	3	4		6	7	8	9	5	11	10															
4	1		2	4	5	6		8	9	7	11	3	10														
5	1		2	4	5	6	12	8	9	7	11	3	10														
6	1	2	3	4	5	6	7			10	11		9	8	12												
7	1	2	3	4	5	6	7			10	11		9	8													
8	1	2	3	4	5	6			7	10	11		9	8													
9	1	2	3		5	6			7	10	11		9			4	8	12									
10	1	2	3	4	5	6	7			10	11		9				8	12									
11	1	2	3		5	6	7			10	11	4	9	8													
12	1	2	3		5	6	7	12		10	11	4	9	8													
13		2	3		5	6	7	12		10		11	9	8	1	4											
14		2	3	4		6	7			10	11	12	9	8	1					5							
15		2	3	4		6	7			10	11	12	9	8	1					5							
16		2	3	4		6				10	11	7	9	8		12		1		5							
17		2	3			6	7			10	11	12	9	8				1		5							
18		2	3			6	7				11	10	9	8				1		5							
19		2	3	4		6				10	11		9	8		12	7	1		5							
20		2		4		6				10	11	3	9	8			7	1		5							
21		2	3	12		6	4			10	9			8			7	1		5		11					
22		2	3	4		6				10	9			8			7	1		5		11					
23		2	3	12		6	4			10	9			8			7	1		5		11					
24		2	3		5	6				10	9	7		8			12	1		4		11					
25		2	3	4		6				10	9	7		8			12	1		5		11					
26		2	3	4		6				10	9	7		8				1		5		11					
27		2	3	12		6	4			10			9	8				1		5		11	7				
28		2	3	4		6				10			9	8				1		5		11	7				
29		2	3	4		6				10			9	8				1		5		11	7				
30		2		4		6				10			9	8				1		5	3	11	7			12	
31		2	3	4	5	6	11			10			9	8				1					7				
32		2	3	4	5	6	11			10			9	8			12	1					7				
33		2	3	4	6		7			10		11	9	8				1		5		12					
34		2	3	12		6	4			10		11	9	8				1		5			7				
35		2	3	4		6				10			9	8				1		5		11	7			12	
36		2	3	4		6				10			9	8				1		5		11	7			12	
37		2	3	4	5	6				10			9				7	1				11				12	
38			3	4	5	6				10			9	8				1				11	7			2	
39			2	10		6				9				3				8		5		11	7				
40			3		5	6				10			9	8			12	1		6		11	7				
41			3			6				10		9	12	8				1		5		11	7			2	
42				4		6	9			10		3	12	8				1		5		11	7			2	
43						6	4			10		3	12	8				1		5	9	11	7			2	
44		2				6	4			10		9		8				1		5	3	11	7				
45		2				6	4			10		9		8						5	3	11	7				1
46			2			6	4			10		9		8			12			5	3	11	7				1
Apps	12	37	40	23	43	44	18	5	9	44	21	39	26	38	3	2	15	32	1	27	6	23	17	1	2	5	2
Goals		1		1		3	3		1	13	1	9	9	12								5					

F.A. Cup

R		Date	Opponent	Score	Scorers	Att	Appearances
R1	Nov	24	Rochdale	1-2	Pilling	1985	Davy 2, Peacock 3, Kavanagh 4, Deere 5, Oates 6, Partridge 10, Keeley 9, Pilling 11, Green 12, Cammack 8, Cowling 7, Gordon 1

F.L. Cup

R		Date	Opponent	Score	Scorers	Att	Appearances
R1/1	Aug	11	Grimsby Town	0-2		5083	1,2,3,4,5,6,7,8,9,10,11; Cammack 12
R1/2		14	GRIMSBY TOWN	0-0		3908	1,2,3,4,5,6,7,8,9,10,11; Cammack 12

League Table

		P	W	D	L	F	A	W	D	L	F	A	Pts
1	Huddersfield Town	46	16	5	2	61	18	11	7	5	40	30	66
2	Walsall	46	12	9	2	43	23	11	9	3	32	24	64
3	Newport County	46	16	5	2	47	22	11	2	10	36	28	61
4	Portsmouth	46	15	5	3	62	23	9	7	7	29	26	60
5	Bradford City	46	14	6	3	44	14	10	6	7	33	36	60
6	Wigan Athletic	46	13	5	5	42	26	8	8	7	34	35	55
7	Lincoln City	46	14	8	1	43	12	4	9	10	21	30	53
8	Peterborough Utd.	46	14	3	6	39	22	7	7	9	19	25	52
9	Torquay United	46	13	7	3	47	25	2	10	11	23	44	47
10	Aldershot	46	10	7	6	35	23	6	6	11	27	30	45
11	Bournemouth	46	8	9	6	32	25	5	9	9	20	26	44
12	Doncaster Rovers	46	11	6	6	37	27	4	8	11	25	36	44
13	Northampton Town	46	14	5	4	33	16	2	7	14	18	50	44
14	SCUNTHORPE UNITED	46	11	9	3	37	23	3	6	14	21	52	43
15	Tranmere Rovers	46	10	4	9	32	24	4	9	10	18	32	41
16	Stockport County	46	9	7	7	30	31	5	5	13	18	41	40
17	York City	46	9	6	8	35	34	5	5	13	30	48	39
18	Halifax Town	46	11	9	3	29	20	2	4	17	17	52	39
19	Hartlepool United	46	10	7	6	34	28	4	3	16	23	36	38
20	Port Vale	46	8	6	9	34	24	4	6	13	22	46	36
21	Hereford United	46	8	7	8	22	23	3	7	13	16	31	36
22	Darlington	46	7	11	5	33	26	2	6	15	17	48	35
23	Crewe Alexandra	46	10	6	7	25	27	1	7	15	10	41	35
24	Rochdale	46	6	7	10	20	28	1	6	16	13	51	27

1980/81 16th in Division 4

#		Date	Opponent	Score	Scorers	Att	Neenan JP	Davy SJ	Jarvis NC	Grimes V	Dall DG	Oates RA	Pugh JG	Cammack SR	Lambert AJ	Partridge M	O'Berg PJ	Ashworth PA	Pilling S	Boxall AR	Stewart CD	Gordon JS	Cowling C	Wood HS	Green R	Duffy VG
1	Aug	16	ALDERSHOT	2-2	Grimes, Cammack	2022	1	2	3	4	5	6	7	8	9	10	11									
2		19	Rochdale	0-4		2427	1	2	3	4	5	6	7	8	9	10	11	12								
3		23	Bradford City	0-0		3177	1			4		6	7	8	9	10			3	5	11					
4		30	WIMBLEDON	1-2	O'Berg	1712				4	2	6	7	8	9	10		12	3	5	11	1				
5	Sep	6	CREWE ALEXANDRA	1-1	Partridge	1498				4	5	6	2	8	9	10		12	3		11	1	7			
6		13	Halifax Town	0-1		1228	1			4	5	6	2	8	9	10	12	7	3		11					
7		16	Darlington	1-0	Cammack	2633	1	2		4	5	6	7	8	9	12	11	10	3							
8		19	STOCKPORT COUNTY	2-0	Cammack, O'Berg	2005	1	2		4	5	6	7	8	9		11	10	3							
9		27	Lincoln City	2-2	Ashworth, Lambert	4336	1	2		4	5	6	7	8	9	12	11	10	3							
10		30	DARLINGTON	3-0	Cammack 2, Partridge (p)	2328	1			4	5	6	7	8	9	2	11	10	3							
11	Oct	4	Bournemouth	2-2	Lambert, O'Berg	3079	1			4	5	6	7	8	9	2	11	10	3		12					
12		7	HARTLEPOOL UNITED	3-3	Cammack, Ashworth 2	2900	1			4	5	6	7	8	9	2	11	10	3		12					
13		11	NORTHAMPTON T	0-2		2650	1			4	5	6	7	8	9	2	11	10	3		12					
14		17	Southend United	0-2		5537	1		3	4	5	6	7	8		2	11	10			9				12	
15		22	Peterborough United	2-0	Lambert, Partridge (p)	4262	1		3	4	5	6	7	8	9	2	11								10	
16		25	TORQUAY UNITED	0-2		2262	1		3	4	5	6	7	8	9	2	11				12				10	
17		28	DONCASTER ROVERS	1-1	Cammack	4058	1		3	4	5	6	7	8	9	2	11				12				10	
18	Nov	1	York City	0-1		1959	1		3	4	5	6	7	8	9	2	11				12				10	
19		4	Hartlepool United	0-2		4400	1		3	4	5	6	7	8	9	2	11	10							12	
20		8	HEREFORD UNITED	3-1	Stewart 2, Cammack	1534	1	2	3	4		6		8	12	7		11		5	9				10	
21		11	ROCHDALE	1-1	Stewart	2030	1	2	3	4		6		8		7		11		5	9				10	
22		15	Aldershot	0-0		2512	1	2	3	4		6		8		7		11		5	9				10	
23	Dec	6	Wigan Athletic	1-1	Partridge (p)	3790	1	2	3	4		6	12	8		7		11		5	9				10	
24		20	TRANMERE ROVERS	2-0	Lambert, Stewart	1667	1	2	3	4		6	10	8		7	9			5	12				11	
25		26	Mansfield Town	0-1		4261	1	2	3	4		6	10	8		7	9	12		5	11					
26		27	BURY	2-2	Boxall, Cammack	2368	1	2	3	4		6	10	8		7	9	12		5	11					
27	Jan	10	PETERBOROUGH UTD.	1-1	Green	2072	1	2	3	4		6	10	8		7				5	11				9	
28		19	Wimbledon	2-2	Green, O'Berg	2112	1	2	3	4	5	6	10	8	12	7					11				9	
29		31	BRADFORD CITY	1-0	Cammack	2628	1	2	3			6	10	8	4	7					11				9	
30	Feb	4	Torquay United	1-2	Green	1687	1	2	3	4	5	6	10	8		11	7				12				9	
31		7	HALIFAX TOWN	2-2	Stewart, Grimes	2163	1	2		4		6	10	8		7				5	11				9	
32		14	Crewe Alexandra	0-1		2231	1	2		4		6	10	8		7			3	5	11				9	
33		21	LINCOLN CITY	2-2	O'Berg, Pilling	5032	1			4		6	10	8	2	7		12	3	5	11				9	
34		24	PORT VALE	1-1	Cammack (p)	1878	1			4		6	10	8	2	7			3	5	11				9	12
35		27	Stockport County	0-2		1675	1	2		4		6	10	8	9	7		12	3	5	11					
36	Mar	3	Port Vale	2-2	Partridge (p), Cammack	2277	1	2		4		6	10	8	9	7		12	3	5	11					
37		6	BOURNEMOUTH	1-1	Partridge (p)	2519	1	2		4		6		8	9	7		10	3	5	11				12	
38		13	Northampton Town	3-3	Grimes, O'Berg, Green	2046	1	2		4		6		8	10	7			3	5	11				9	
39		22	SOUTHEND UNITED	2-1	Pilling, Green	3614	1	2		4		6		8		7			3	5	11				10	
40		27	Doncaster Rovers	0-1		8001	1	2		4		6		8		7			3	5	11				10	
41	Apr	4	YORK CITY	3-2	Green 2, Stewart	1694	1	2		4		6		8	9	7			3	5	11				10	
42		11	Hereford United	1-2	O'Berg	2009	1	2		4	6			8	9	7			3	5	11				10	
43		18	Bury	1-6	Stewart	2357	1	2		4	6			8	9	7			3	5	11				10	
44		20	MANSFIELD TOWN	2-0	O'Berg, Cammack	1875	1	2	3	4			10	8	12			5	7	6	11				9	
45		24	Tranmere Rovers	2-1	Pilling, Stewart	1073	1	2		4			10	8				5	7	6	3				11	
46	May	2	WIGAN ATHLETIC	4-4	O'Berg 2, Cammack 2	1704	1	2		4				8	10	5	7	6	3		11				9	
			Apps				44	31	21	45	22	40	38	46	24	40	43	23	26	24	34	2	2	1	27	1
			Goals							3				15	4	6	10	3	3	1	8				7	

F.A. Cup

	Date	Opponent	Score	Scorers	Att	Neenan	Davy	Jarvis	Grimes	Dall	Oates	Pugh	Cammack	Lambert	Partridge	O'Berg	Ashworth	Pilling	Boxall	Stewart	Gordon	Cowling	Wood	Green	Duffy
R1	Nov 22	HARTLEPOOL UNITED	3-1	Grimes, Green, Partridge (p)	5162	1	2	3	4		6		8		7	11			5	9				10	
R2	Dec 13	ALTRINCHAM	0-0		3762	1	2	3	4		6	12	8		7	11			5	9				10	
rep	15	Altrincham	0-1		5176	1	2	3	4		6	7	8	11				12	5	9				10	

F.L. Cup

	Date	Opponent	Score	Scorers	Att	Neenan	Davy	Jarvis	Grimes	Dall	Oates	Pugh	Cammack	Lambert	Partridge	O'Berg	Ashworth	Pilling	Boxall	Stewart	Gordon	Cowling	Wood	Green	Duffy
R1/1	Aug 9	BARNSLEY	0-1		4550	1	2	3	4	5	6	7	8	9	10	12				11					
R1/2	12	Barnsley	1-2	Cammack	8430	1	2	3	4	5	6	7	8	9	10	12				11					

1981/82   23rd in Division 4

#	Date		Opponent	Score	Scorers	Att	Neenan JP	Davy SJ	Partridge M	Keeley AJ	Dall DG	Oates RA	Grimes V	Hughes DT	Green R	O'Berg PJ	Stewart CD	Pilling S	Duffy VG	Lambert AJ	Cowling C	Moss PM	DeVries RS	Arins AF	Telfer GA	Pointon NG	Johnson NG	Duncan JP	Botham IT	Boyd G	Thompson WA	Hamill SP	Goodlass R	Cammack SR	Walker D
1	Aug	29	Northampton Town	1-1	Green	2064	1	2	3	4	5	6	7	8	9	10	11	12																	
2	Sep	5	BLACKPOOL	1-1	Oates	2223	1	2	12	4	5	6	7	8	9		11	3	10																
3		12	Torquay United	0-1		2156	1	2	8	4	5	6	7		9		11		10	3	12														
4		19	TRANMERE ROVERS	2-1	Cowling, Moss	1623	1	2		4	5	6	7	3	9		11				8	10													
5		22	HARTLEPOOL UNITED	2-1	Oates, Moss	2060	1	2		4	5	6	7	3	9	12	11				8	10													
6		26	Sheffield United	0-1		11687	1	2		4	5	6	7	3	9		11			12	8	10													
7		29	Bury	0-4		2684	1	2	12	4	5	6	7	3	9		11				8	10													
8	Oct	3	BRADFORD CITY	1-3	Grimes	3239	1	2	12	4	5	6	7	3s	9		11				8	10													
9		10	Crewe Alexandra	0-3		1586	1	8	2	4	5	6	7		9		11				12	10	3												
10		17	HEREFORD UNITED	2-2	Grimes, Moss	1498	1		2	4		6	7		9	8	11				5	10	3												
11		20	HULL CITY	4-4	Stewart, Partridge 2(2p), Green	3575	1	12	2	4		6	7		9	8	11				5	10	3												
12		24	Wigan Athletic	1-2	DeVries	4553	1	2	8	4		6	7	5	9		11			12		10	3												
13		31	PETERBOROUGH UTD.	0-1		2104	1		8	4		6	7	2	9		11			12	5	10	3												
14	Nov	3	Bournemouth	0-2		5032	1		8	4		6	7	2	9		11	10	12		5		3												
15		7	YORK CITY	0-3		1626	1	3	8	4		6	7	5		9	11					2													
16		13	Colchester United	1-2	Stewart	3838	1		6	4	5		7		9	8	11	3			12	2													
17		28	Halifax Town	2-1	Cowling, Moss	1396	1	2		4		6	7			8	11	3			9	10		5											
18	Dec	5	PORT VALE	0-0		2021	1	2		4		6				8	11	3	7		9	10		5	12										
19	Jan	9	Blackpool	0-2		4136	1	2		4	5	6		12			11	3	8		9	10			7										
20		23	NORTHAMPTON T	2-1	Stewart, Telfer	1439	1			4	5	6	8	2			11	3			9	10			7										
21		30	Tranmere Rovers	1-0	Green	1582	1	12		4	5	6		2	9		11	3	8			10			7										
22	Feb	2	MANSFIELD TOWN	1-0	Dall	2172	1			4	5	6		2	9		11	3	8			10			7										
23		6	TORQUAY UNITED	0-2		1804	1			4	5	6		12	9		11					10			7	2	8	3							
24		10	Hartlepool United	3-3	Telfer, Stewart, Moss (p)	2001	1			4	5	6	9	12			11	3				10			7	2	8								
25		14	Bradford City	0-0		5103		2		4	5	6	9				11	3				10			7		8	1							
26		17	Darlington	1-4	Stewart	1633		2		4		6	9	12			11	3				10		5	7		8	1							
27		20	SHEFFIELD UNITED	2-1	Moss, Telfer	8105	1	2			5	6	9	7			11	3				10		4	8										
28		28	CREWE ALEXANDRA	0-1		2798	1	2		4	5	6	9				11	3				10		7	8				12						
29	Mar	6	Hereford United	1-2	Dall	2159	1			4	5	6	9				11	3		2		10		7	8										
30		9	Hull City	0-2		6121	1	2		4	5	6					11	3	12	9		10		7	8										
31		12	WIGAN ATHLETIC	2-7	Telfer 2	2599	1	12		4	5	6						3		2		10		7	8	11				9					
32		16	BOURNEMOUTH	0-2		1441	1	3		4	5	6					11			2		10		7	8					9					
33		20	Peterborough United	1-2	Stewart	4785	1	2		4	5	6	11				12			3		10		7	8					9					
34		23	ALDERSHOT	1-1	Telfer	1658	1	2			5	6	3				11					10		7	8					9	4				
35		26	York City	1-1	Arins	2189	1			3	5	9										10		2	8					4	6	7	11		
36		30	STOCKPORT COUNTY	0-0		1815	1			3		6										10		2	8					4	5	7	11	9	
37	Apr	2	COLCHESTER UNITED	2-1	Moss, Telfer	1762	1			3		6	2									10		7	8					4	5		11	9	
38		10	ROCHDALE	1-0	Keeley (p)	1742	1			3	5		2				7				12	10			8					4	6		11	9	
39		13	Mansfield Town	1-1	Cowling	2204	1			3	5		2				7				9	10		4	8						6		11	12	
40		17	Port Vale	1-2	Cammack	2507	1				5		2				3					10		4	8				12		6	7	11	9	
41		20	Rochdale	1-1	Telfer	1129	1			6			2				12	3				10		4	8						5	7	11	9	
42		24	HALIFAX TOWN	0-0		1643	1			6			2				7	3				10			8				12	4	5		11	9	
43	May	1	Aldershot	0-4		1304	1	2		6			7								9	10			8				12	4	5		11		3
44		4	Bury	2-2	Telfer, Cammack	1106	1	2		6			7			12	11				5	10			8	3				4				9	
45		8	DARLINGTON	1-1	Cammack	1274	1			6			7			12	11				2	10			8	3				4	5			9	
46		14	Stockport County	1-1	Cowling	1945	1	2					7				12				5	10	11		8	3				4	6			9	
			Apps				44	28	13	42	28	37	34	20	18	10	40	18	7	15	26	42	6	20	29	5	2	3	4	11	11	4	9	10	1
			Goals						2	1	2	2	2		3		6				4	7	1	1	9									3	

F.A. Cup

	Date		Opponent	Score	Scorers	Att	Neenan JP	Davy SJ	Partridge M	Keeley AJ	Dall DG	Oates RA	Grimes V	Hughes DT	Green R	O'Berg PJ	Stewart CD	Pilling S	Duffy VG	Lambert AJ	Cowling C	Moss PM	DeVries RS	Arins AF	Telfer GA
R1	Nov	21	BRADFORD CITY	1-0	Cowling	3339	1	2		4	5	6	7			8	11	3		12	9	10			
R2	Jan	2	Crewe Alexandra	3-1	Cowling, Telfer, O'Berg	2729	1	2		4	5	6				8	11	3		12	9	10			7
R3		6	HEREFORD UNITED	1-1	Stewart	3781	1	2		4	5	6				8	11	3			9	10			7
rep		20	Hereford United	1-4	Grimes	4025	1			4	5	6	3	2		8	11	12			9	10			7

F.L. Cup (Milk Cup)

	Date		Opponent	Score		Att	Neenan JP	Davy SJ	Partridge M	Keeley AJ	Dall DG	Oates RA	Grimes V	Hughes DT	Green R	Stewart CD	Pilling S	Duffy VG	Lambert AJ
R1/1	Sep	1	MANSFIELD TOWN	0-0		2249	1	2	12	4	5	6	7	8	9	11	3	10	
R1/2		14	Mansfield Town	0-2		2258	1	2	12	4	5	6	7		9	11	3	10	8

1982/83 4th in Division 4: Promoted

#	Date	Opponent	Score	Scorers	Att	Neenan JP	Keeley AJ	Pointon NG	Fowler M	Boxall AR	Hunter L	Cammack SR	Parkinson ND	Cowling C	Telfer GA	Leman D	O'Berg PJ	Oates RA	Duncan JP	Baines SJ	Gilbert DJ	Angus MA	Cartwright P	Mann JA	Reid AJ	Graham T	Lester MJ	Webster IA	Snow SG
1	Aug 28	Hartlepool United	0-0		1009	1	2	3	4	5	6	7	8	9	10	11	12												
2	Sep 4	ALDERSHOT	1-1	Hunter	1309	1	2	11	4	5	6	7	8	9	10		12	3											
3	7	STOCKPORT COUNTY	3-0	Telfer 2, Cowling	1335	1		3	4	5	6		8	9	10	11	7	2	12										
4	11	Wimbledon	2-2	O'Berg 2	1611	1	2	3	4	5	6		8		10	11	7		9	12									
5	19	YORK CITY	0-0		2436	1	2	3	4	5	6		8		10	11	9		12		7								
6	25	Bristol City	2-0	O'Berg, Parkinson	4025	1	2	3	4	5	6		12		10	11	9		8			7							
7	28	Darlington	1-0	Hunter	1574	1	2	3	4	5	6	7	10	9		11			12			8							
8	Oct 2	COLCHESTER UNITED	2-1	O'Berg, Angus	2616	1	2	3	4	5	6		8	9			7					10							
9	9	Peterborough United	1-0	Angus	3075	1	2	3	4		6		8	9			7					10							
10	15	HULL CITY	0-1		7483	1	2	3		12	6	8	4	9			7				5	10							
11	18	Mansfield Town	2-0	Hunter, Cowling	2647	1	2	3			6	4		9		11	7				5	10							
12	23	TRANMERE ROVERS	2-1	Baines, Cowling	3052	1	2	3			6	8	4	9		11	7				5	10							
13	30	Torquay United	1-1	Cammack	3120	1	2	3	12		6	8	4	9		11	7				5	10							
14	Nov 2	PORT VALE	1-0	Cammack	3766	1	2	3			6	8	4	9		11	7				5	10							
15	6	NORTHAMPTON T	5-1	O'Berg 2, Cammack 3	3412	1	2	3			6	8	4	9		11	7				5	10							
16	12	Crewe Alexandra	1-0	O'Berg	2195	1	2	3	12		6	8	4	9		11	7				5	10							
17	27	BURY	0-1		6335	1	2	3	12		6	8	4	9		11	7				5	10							
18	Dec 4	Hereford United	2-0	Cammack, Cartwright	2103	1	2	3			6	8		9		11	7				5	10	4						
19	18	Blackpool	1-3	Cammack	2860	1	2	3			6	8		9		11	7	12			5	10	4						
20	27	ROCHDALE	1-1	Cammack	4989	1	2	3	4		6	8	11	9			7				5	10	12						
21	28	Halifax Town	1-3	Parkinson (p)	2270	1		3	4		6	8	11	9			7	10			5		2						
22	Jan 1	CHESTER	2-0	Cammack 2	3639	1		3	4		6	8	11	9			7	2			5	10	12						
23	3	Swindon Town	2-2	Parkinson, Cammack	6912	1		3	4		6	8	11	9			7	2			5	10							
24	16	HARTLEPOOL UNITED	3-0	Hunter, Cowling, Parkinson	4261	1		3	4	5	6	8	11	9	12		7	2				10							
25	23	York City	1-2	Cowling	7097	1		3		12	6	9	11	8		10		2		5		4			7				
26	29	WIMBLEDON	0-0		3846	1		3		5	6	8	10	9		11	7	2		4									
27	Feb 5	BRISTOL CITY	1-1	Parkinson	3624	1		3		4	6	8	10	9		11	7	2		5				9					
28	12	Stockport County	1-1	Cammack	2232	1		3	4	12	6	8	10	9		11	7	2		5									
29	26	Hull City	1-1	Leman	11933	1	2	3			6	8	10	9		11	7			5					4				
30	Mar 1	MANSFIELD TOWN	2-2	Cammack 2	3562	1	2	3		12	6	8	10	9		11		7		5					4				
31	5	Tranmere Rovers	4-0	Leman, Cammack 2, Parkinson	1647	1	2	3			6	8	10	9		11	7			5					4				
32	12	TORQUAY UNITED	2-0	Hunter 2	3342	1	2	3			6	8	10	9		11	7			5					4	12			
33	15	Aldershot	1-1	O'Berg	1422	1	2	3			6	8	10	9		11	7			5					4				
34	20	Northampton Town	1-2	Cowling	2634	1	2	3			6	8	10	9		11	7	12		5					4				
35	25	CREWE ALEXANDRA	2-0	Hunter 2	2938	1	2	3			6	8	10	9		11				5						7	4		
36	Apr 1	HALIFAX TOWN	2-0	Lester, Cammack	3775	1	2	3	4		6	8		9		11				5			12			7	10		
37	4	Rochdale	1-0	Graham	2056	1	2	3	4		6	8		9		11				5						7	10		
38	8	HEREFORD UNITED	1-2	Cammack (p)	3785	1	2	3	4		6	8		9		11				5						7	10		
39	15	Colchester United	1-5	Cammack	3155	1	2	3	4		6	8		9		11				5						7	10		
40	23	BLACKPOOL	4-3	Cowling 2, Cammack 2 (1p)	2771	1	2	3	4		6	8		9		11		12		5						7	10		
41	26	PETERBOROUGH UTD.	3-0	Lester, Cammack, Pointon	3211	1	2	3	4		6	8		9		11				5						7	10		
42	30	Bury	0-1		4739	1	12	3	4		6	8		9		11		2		5						7	10		
43	May 2	SWINDON TOWN	2-0	Cammack, Lester	3546	1		3		4	6	8		9			11	2		5						7	10		
44	7	DARLINGTON	2-2	Cammack 2	3305	1		3		4	6	8		9			11	2		5						7	10		
45	9	Port Vale	1-0	Cowling	6212	1	12	3		4	6	8		9			11	2		5						7	10		
46	14	Chester	2-1	Graham 2	2764	1	11	3		4	6	8		9				2		5						7		10	12
		Apps				46	35	46	18	26	48	41	31	42	7	36	34	20	6	38	1	20	4	2	6	13	11	1	1
		Goals						1			8	25	6	9	2	2	8			1		2	1			3	3		

F.A. Cup

Rd	Date	Opponent	Score	Scorers	Att	Neenan JP	Keeley AJ	Pointon NG	Fowler M	Boxall AR	Hunter L	Cammack SR	Parkinson ND	Cowling C	Telfer GA	Leman D	O'Berg PJ	Oates RA	Duncan JP	Baines SJ	Gilbert DJ	Angus MA	Cartwright P
R1	Nov 20	Darlington	1-0	Cammack	2540	1	2	3	12		6	8	4	9		11	7			5		10	
R2	Dec 11	NORTHWICH VICTORIA	2-1	Cowling, O'Berg	5457	1	2	3	4		6	8		9		11	7			5		10	
R3	Jan 8	GRIMSBY TOWN	0-0		11010	1		3	4		6	8	11	9			7	2		5		10	
rep	11	Grimsby Town	0-2		9509	1		3	4		6	8	11	9	12		7	2		5		10	

F.L. Cup (Milk Cup)

Rd	Date	Opponent	Score	Scorers	Att	Neenan JP	Keeley AJ	Pointon NG	Fowler M	Boxall AR	Hunter L	Cammack SR	Parkinson ND	Cowling C	Telfer GA	Leman D	O'Berg PJ	Oates RA	Duncan JP	Baines SJ	Gilbert DJ
R1/1	Aug 31	GRIMSBY TOWN	1-2	Cowling	2620	1	2		4	5	6	7	8	9	10	11	12	3			
R1/2	Sep 14	Grimsby Town	0-0		3347	1	2	3	4	5	6		8		10	11	9		12		7

F.L. Trophy

Gp	Date	Opponent	Score	Scorers	Att	Neenan JP	Keeley AJ	Pointon NG	Fowler M	Boxall AR	Hunter L	Cammack SR	Parkinson ND	Cowling C	Telfer GA	Leman D	O'Berg PJ	Angus MA	Reid AJ
Gp	Aug 14	LINCOLN CITY	1-1	Hunter	1022	1	2	3	4	5	6	7	8	12	10	11	9		
Gp	17	SHEFFIELD UNITED	0-0		1874		2	3	4	5	6		8	9	10	11	7	12	14
Gp	21	Grimsby Town	0-2		2334	1	12	3	4	5	6		8			11	7	10	14

P Johnson played v. Lincoln (at 13) and Sheff. U (at 1).
Tutty played v. Grmisby (at 2, substituted).
(Two substitutes allowed in this competition).

Player columns (left to right):
Neenan JP · Longden DP · Pointon NG · Brolly MJ · Boxall AR · Hunter L · Graham T · Cammack SR · Cowling C · Dey G · Broddle JR · Webster IA · Green JR · Lester MJ · Holden R · O'Berg PJ · Richardson R · Snow SG · Hill DM · Wilson DJ · Leman D · Botham IT · Matthews M · Whitehead A · Bell DM · Pratley RG · Parkinson ND · Steele SP

#		Date	Opponent	Score	Scorers	Att	Nee	Lon	Poi	Bro	Box	Hun	Gra	Cam	Cow	Dey	Brd	Web	Grn	Les	Hol	O'B	Ric	Sno	Hil	Wil	Lem	Bot	Mat	Whi	Bel	Pra	Par	Ste
1	Aug	27	Port Vale	0-0		4565	1	2	3	4	5	6	7	8	9	10	11	12																
2	Sep	3	EXETER CITY	3-1	Lester, Cammack, Graham	2900	1	2	3	4		6	7	8	9	11			5	10														
3		7	OXFORD UNITED	0-0		3516	1	2	3	4		6	7	8	9	11			5	10														
4		9	Orient	0-1		2823	1	2	3	4		6	7	8	9	11		12	5	13														
5		16	BOLTON WANDERERS	1-0	Cowling	4406	1	2	3	4	7	6		8	9	11			5	10	12													
6		24	Newport County	1-1	Green	2699	1	2	3	4	7	6			9	11			5	10	8	12												
7		27	Plymouth Argyle	0-4		3821	1	2	3	4	7	6			9	11			5	10	8	12												
8		30	SOUTHEND UNITED	1-6	Holden (p)	3335	1		3	4		6							5	10	8	7	2	9	11									
9	Oct	8	Bradford City	2-2	Leman, Lester	2555	1	2	3	7		6			9				5	10	8	12				4	11							
10		15	ROTHERHAM UNITED	1-2	Lester	3139	1	2	3	7		6		12	9				5	10	8					4	11							
11		18	WIGAN ATHLETIC	0-0		2345	1	2	3	7		6			9				5	10	8	11				4								
12		22	Bristol Rovers	1-4	Pointon	5324	1	2	3	7		6			9	12			5	10	8	11				4								
13		29	WIMBLEDON	5-1	Peters (og), Wilson 2, Cammack 2	2347	1	2	3	7				8	6	9			5	10		11				4								
14	Nov	1	Sheffield United	3-5	Dey, Broddle, Wilson	10502	1	2	3					8	6	7	9		5	10		11				4								
15		5	WALSALL	0-0		2932	1	2	3	7				8	6	4	9		5	10		11												
16		12	Lincoln City	1-2	O'Berg	4657	1	2	3	7				8	6	4	9		5	10		11												
17		26	Millwall	1-2	Cammack	3776	1	2	3	7			4	8			9	6	5	10		11												
18	Dec	3	BOURNEMOUTH	1-2	Cammack	2344	1	2	3	7			4	8			9	6	5	10		11				12								
19		17	GILLINGHAM	2-0	Cammack (p), Cowling	2127	1	2	3	4				8	7			6	5	10		11							9					
20		26	Hull City	0-1		15461	1	2	3	4				8	7				5	10		11							9	6				
21		27	PRESTON NORTH END	1-5	Cammack	3986	1	2	3	12	4			8	7				5	10		11							9	6				
22		31	Burnley	0-5		7668	1	2	3	7		6	9	8					5	10		11							4					
23	Jan	2	BRENTFORD	4-4	Graham, Cammack 2, O'Berg	2239	1		3	7		6	9	8					5	10		11	2						4					
24		21	Bolton Wanderers	0-0		5379	1	2	3	7			9	8					5	10		11							4	6				
25	Feb	3	Southend United	0-0		2290	1	2	3	7			9	8	10	12	6		5										4			11		
26		10	NEWPORT COUNTY	3-3	Brolly 2, Cammack	2879	1	2	3	7				8			11	6	5	10									4		9			
27		18	Wimbledon	1-1	Cammack (p)	3117	1	2	3	7				8	11			6	5	10									4		9			
28		25	BRISTOL ROVERS	2-2	Cammack (p), O'Berg	2737	1	2	3	7				8				6	5	10		11							4		9			
29	Mar	3	Wigan Athletic	0-2		3092	1	2	3	7			11	8					5	10									4		9	6		
30		6	Walsall	1-1	Bell	4735	1	2	3	7			11	8					5	10									4		9	6		
31		10	LINCOLN CITY	0-0		3889	1	2	3	7			11	8					5	10									4		9	6		
32		17	BRADFORD CITY	2-1	Cammack, Matthews	3274	1	2	3	7			11	8					5	10									4		9	6		
33		27	SHEFFIELD UNITED	1-1	Bell	6750	1	2	3	7				8					5										4	10	9	6	11	
34		31	Oxford United	0-1		6955	1	2	3	7			12	8					5										4	10	9	6	11	
35	Apr	7	PLYMOUTH ARGYLE	3-0	Bell, Brolly, Cammack	2780	1	2	3	7			11	8					5										4	10	9	6		
36		11	Exeter City	1-1	Brolly	2003	1	2	3	7			11	8					5										4	10	9	6		
37		14	Bournemouth	1-1	Cammack	3501	1			7			11	8			3	2	5	4										10	9	6	12	
38		17	PORT VALE	1-1	Bell	2952	1	2	3	7			11	8					5	4										10	9	6		
39		21	HULL CITY	2-0	Bell (p), Cammack	8286	1	2	3	7			11	8					5										4	10	9	6		
40		24	Preston North End	0-1		3413	1	2	3	7			11	8					5										4	10	9	6		
41		27	MILLWALL	0-1		2867	1	2	3	7			11	8					5										4	10	9	6		
42	May	1	ORIENT	3-1	Graham, Parkinson	2284		2	3				11	8					5			7							4	10	9	6	1	
43		5	Brentford	0-3		4561		2	3				11	8	12				5			7							4	10	9	6	1	
44		7	BURNLEY	4-0	Cammack 2, Cowling, Green	2720		2	3				11	8	9				5			7							4	10		6	1	
45		12	Gillingham	1-1	Cowling	2914		2	3					8	9		5	11				7							4	10		6	1	
46		15	Rotherham United	0-3		4298		2	3	6			11	8	9			12	5			7							4	10			1	
			Apps				41	43	45	41	4	15	27	39	22	12	13	9	45	33	7	25	2	1	2	6	2	3	25	15	19	10	10	5
			Goals						1	4			4	18	4	1	1		2	3	1	3				3	1		1		5		1	

One own goal

F.A. Cup

		Date	Opponent	Score	Scorers	Att	Nee	Lon	Poi	Bro	Box	Hun	Gra	Cam	Cow	Dey	Brd	Web	Grn	Les	Hol	O'B	Ric	Whi
R1	Nov	19	PRESTON NORTH END	1-0	Cammack (p)	3484	1	2	3	7			12	8	6	4	9		5	10		11		
R2	Dec	10	BURY	2-0	Coleman (og), Cammack	3246	1	2	3	4				8			7	6	5	10		11		9
R3	Jan	7	Leeds United	1-1	Cammack	17130	1		3	7			9	8			4	6	5	10		11	2	
rep		10	LEEDS UNITED	1-1	Dey	13129	1	2	3	7			9	8			4	6	5	10		11		
rep2		16	LEEDS UNITED	4-2	Brolly, Cammack, Lester, Graham	13302	1	2	3	7			9	8			4	6	5	10		11		
R4	Feb	1	West Bromwich Albion	0-1		18235	1	2	3	7			9	8	10			6	5			11		4

R3 replay a.e.t.

F.L. Cup (Milk Cup)

		Date	Opponent	Score	Scorers	Att	Nee	Lon	Poi	Bro	Box	Hun	Gra	Cam	Cow	Dey	Grn	Les	Web
R1/1	Aug	30	DONCASTER ROVERS	1-1	Cammack	4295	1	2	3	4	5	6	7	8	9	11		10	
R1/2	Sep	13	Doncaster Rovers	0-3		4377	1	2	3	4		6	7	8	9	11	5	10	12

Associate Members Cup

		Date	Opponent	Score	Scorers	Att	Nee	Lon	Poi	Bro	Gra	Cam	Cow	Brd	Web	Grn	Les	O'B	Mat	Bel	Pra	Par
R1	Feb	21	CHESTERFIELD	2-1	Cammack, Brolly	2507	1	2	3	7		8	11	6		5	10		4	9		
R2	Mar	13	CREWE ALEXANDRA	4-4	Bell 3 (1 pen), Matthews	1524	1	2	3	7	11	8				5		10	4	9	6	12
R3		20	SHEFFIELD UNITED	2-3	Matthews, Cammack	2720	1	2		7	11	8	12			5	10	3	4	9	6	

R2 won on penalties, a.e.t. R3 a.e.t.

#		Date	Opponent	Score	Scorers	Att	Neenan JP	Longden DP	Pointon NG	Matthews M	Green JR	Whitehead A	Brolly MJ	Dey G	Bell DM	Lester MJ	Cowling C	Webster IA	Cammack SR	Broddle JR	Hill DM	Graham T	Lees T	Gregory PG	Botham IT	Shutt SJ	O'Berg PJ	Finney SB	Ferry W	Atkins MN	Stobart SA
1	Aug	25	Chester City	1-1	Whitehead	2180	1	2	3	4	5	6	7	8	9	10	11	12													
2		31	COLCHESTER UNITED	2-2	Cammack, Cowling	1818	1	2	3	4	5	6	7			10	11		8	9											
3	Sep	8	Exeter City	1-2	Lester	2658	1	2	3	4	5	6	7	8		10	11			9											
4		15	CHESTERFIELD	2-4	Broddle, Cowling	2853	1	2	3	4	6	5	7	8		10	11			9											
5		18	CREWE ALEXANDRA	2-3	Scott(og), Cowling	1619	1	2	3	4	6	5	7	8		10	11			9											
6		22	Darlington	1-2	Bell	1762	1		3	4	2	5			8	10	11	6		9		7									
7		28	HALIFAX TOWN	4-0	Broddle, Cowling, Brolly, Matthews	1929	1	2	3	4		6	7			10	11	5		9		8	12								
8	Oct	3	Peterborough United	1-3	Brolly	3620	1	2	3	4	6	5	7			10	11			9		8									
9		6	Northampton Town	2-0	Matthews, Cowling	1813	1		3	4	6	5	7			10	11			9		8	2								
10		13	BLACKPOOL	1-1	Bell (pen)	2408	1		3	4	6	5	7		9	10	11			12		8	2								
11		19	Southend United	1-1	Cowling	2408			3	4	6	5	7			10	11	9	12			8	2	1							
12		23	TORQUAY UNITED	2-0	Broddle 2	2046			3	4	6	5				10	11		9	7		8	2	1							
13		27	Bury	1-0	Lester	3324			3	4	6	5				10	11		8	7		9	2	1							
14	Nov	3	ALDERSHOT	2-1	Cowling, Cammack	2253			3	4	6	5				10	11		8	7		9	2	1							
15		6	Swindon Town	0-0		3063			3	4	6	5				10	11		8	7		9	2	1							
16		9	HEREFORD UNITED	1-1	Graham	2902			3	4	6	5				10	11		8	7		9	2	1							
17		24	Hartlepool United	2-3	Cowling 2	3292	1		3	4	6	5				10	11		8	7		9	2								
18		30	WREXHAM	5-2	Cammack 3 (1 p), Matthews, Whitehead	2180	1		3	4	6	5				10	11		8	7		9	2								
19	Dec	22	Port Vale	1-1	Graham	2521			3	4	6	5	12				11		8	7	10	9	2	1							
20		26	STOCKPORT COUNTY	1-0	Cammack	2881		2	3	4	6	5					11		8	7	9	10		1							
21	Jan	1	Tranmere Rovers	0-2		1953	1		3	4	6	5				10			8	7	11	9	2		12						
22		26	Chesterfield	0-1		3698			3		6	5	7			10	11		8	12	4	9	2	1							
23	Feb	1	Halifax Town	2-1	Whitehead, Broddle	1317			3	4	6	5				10	11		7	8	4	9	2	1							
24		8	DARLINGTON	0-1		1762			3		6	5	4			10	11		7	8	4	9	2	1							
25		12	PETERBOROUGH UTD.	2-1	Broddle, Brolly	1219			3		6	5	7			10			8	11	4	9	2	1	12						
26		16	Crewe Alexandra	1-1	Shutt	1782			3		6	5	11			10				7	4	9	2	1		8					
27		23	Aldershot	2-1	Graham, Broddle	1926			3		6	5	11			10			8	7	4	9	2	1							
28		26	ROCHDALE	4-2	Cammack 2, Brolly 2	1694			3		6	5	11			10			8	7	4	9	2	1							
29	Mar	2	BURY	2-2	Graham, Cammack	2710			3		6	5	7			10			8	11	4	9	2	1							
30		5	Torquay United	0-0		989			3		6	5	7			10			8	11	4	9	2	1							
31		8	SOUTHEND UNITED	2-1	Cammack, Graham	1952		2	3		6	5	7			10			8	11	4	9		1							
32		12	CHESTER CITY	2-1	Cammack 2 (1 p)	1875		2	3		6	5	7			10			8	11	4	9		1							
33		16	Blackpool	0-1		3937			3		6	5	7			10	12		8	11	4	9		1							
34		19	EXETER CITY	7-1	*See below	1566			3		6	5	7			10	12		8	11	4	9		2	1						
35		22	NORTHAMPTON T	2-1	Hill, Broddle	2024			3		6	5	7			10			8	11	4	9		2	1			12			
36		29	SWINDON TOWN	6-2	Cammack, Broddle, Brolly, Hill, Graham, Green	2042			3		6	5	7			10			8	11	4	9		2	1						
37	Apr	2	Colchester United	1-1	Broddle	2509			3		6	5	7			10	12		8	11	4	9		2	1						
38		6	Stockport County	0-2		1285			3		6	5	7			10	12		8	11	4	9		2	1						
39		9	TRANMERE ROVERS	5-2	Brolly 2, Cammack 2, Broddle	2260			3		6	5	7			10			8	11	4	9		2	1			12			
40		13	Hereford United	0-1		3257			3		6	5	7			10			8	11	4	9		2	1						
41		19	HARTLEPOOL UNITED	2-0	Broddle, Lester	2037		2	3		6	5	7			10			8	11	4			1		9		12			
42		24	Mansfield Town	1-0	Cammack	1964		2	3		6	5	7			10			8	11	4			1			9	12			
43		27	Wrexham	1-2	Cammack	1352		2	3		6	5	7			10			8	11	4	9		1					12		
44	May	4	MANSFIELD TOWN	2-2	Cammack 2	1705			3		6	5	7			10			8	11	4	9		1					2		
45		6	Rochdale	3-3	Cammack 2 (2p), Stobart	1482		2	3		6	5	7			10			8	11	4	9		1							12
46		10	PORT VALE	3-3	Graham, Broddle, Cammack	1867	1		3		6	5	7			10			8	11	4	9	2								12

Scorers in game 34: Broddle, Whitehead, Cammack 2 (1p), Graham 2, Brolly

	Neenan JP	Longden DP	Pointon NG	Matthews M	Green JR	Whitehead A	Brolly MJ	Dey G	Bell DM	Lester MJ	Cowling C	Webster IA	Cammack SR	Broddle JR	Hill DM	Graham T	Lees T	Gregory PG	Botham IT	Shutt SJ	O'Berg PJ	Finney SB	Ferry W	Atkins MN	Stobart SA
Apps	14	14	46	22	46	45	34	5	3	44	27	3	34	45	29	38	31	32	2	2	2	2	1	2	2
Goals			3	1	4	9			2	3	9		24	14	2	9				1					1

One own goal

F.A. Cup

		Date	Opponent	Score	Scorers	Att	Neenan	Longden	Pointon	Matthews	Green	Whitehead	Brolly			Lester	Cowling		Cammack	Broddle		Graham		Gregory							
R1	Nov	17	Nuneaton Borough	1-1	Cowling	4287	1		3	4	6	5				10	11		8	7				2							
rep		20	NUNEATON BOROUGH	2-1	Lester, Cammack	3376	1		3	4	6	5	12			10	11		8	7				2							
R2	Dec	7	Port Vale	1-4	Ridley (og)	4268	1	12	3	4	6	5	10				11		8	7	9			2							

R1 replay a.e.t.   P Stanley played in R1 (at 9) and R1 replay (at 9, substituted).

F.L. Cup (Milk Cup)

		Date	Opponent	Score	Scorers	Att	Neenan	Longden	Pointon	Matthews	Green	Whitehead	Brolly	Dey	Bell	Lester	Cowling	Webster	Cammack	Broddle		Graham	Lees								
R1/1	Aug	28	MANSFIELD TOWN	0-1		2106	1	2	3	4	5	6	7	9		10	11		8	12											
R1/2	Sep	5	Mansfield Town	2-1	Brolly, Cowling	3107	1	2	3	4	5	6	7	8		10	11	12	9												
R2/1		24	ASTON VILLA	2-3	Lester, Whitehead	6212	1	2	3	4	5	6	7			12	10	11		9		8									
R2/2	Oct	10	Aston Villa	1-3	Pointon	11421	1		3	4	6	5	7				10	11		9		8	2								

R1 won on away goals rule

Associate Members Cup (Freight Rover Trophy)

		Date	Opponent	Score	Scorers	Att		Longden	Pointon	Matthews	Green	Whitehead	Brolly			Lester	Cowling	Webster	Cammack	Broddle		Graham	Lees	Gregory		Shutt					
R1/1	Jan	22	BRADFORD CITY	1-4	Graham	1380			3	4	6	5	7			10	11		8			12	9	2	1	14					
R1/2	Feb	6	Bradford City	1-2	Brolly	2388		2	3	4	6	5	7					12		11	8	9		1	10		14				

#		Date	Opponent	Score	Scorers	Att	Gregory PG	Russell WM	Pointon NG	Lister SH	Whitehead A	Green JR	Brolly MJ	Cammack SR	Broddle JR	Graham T	Hill DM	Lester MJ	Hawley JE	Matthews M	Smith MC	Longden DP	Money R	Ferry W	Matthews N	Barnes DO	Dixon KL	Webster IA	Stevenson AJ	Travis DA	Johnson P	Hunter L	Houchen KM
1	Aug	17	TORQUAY UNITED	4-0	Graham, Broddle, Cammack, Green	1929	1	2	3	4	5	6	7	8	9	10	11																
2		23	Halifax Town	1-2	Cammack (p)	1094	1	2	3	4	5	6	7	8	9	10	11																
3		26	WREXHAM	1-1	Broddle	2097	1	2	3	4	5	6	7	8	9	10	11																
4		31	Peterborough United	0-1		2928	1	2	3	4	5	6		8	9	10	11	7	12														
5	Sep	6	TRANMERE ROVERS	0-1		2058	1	2	3	4	5	6	7	8	9		11		10	12													
6		14	Southend United	1-2	Cammack (p)	2985	1	2	3	4	5	6	7	8	9		11		10	12													
7		18	Exeter City	0-2		1723	1	2	3	4	5			8	9	12	7	11	10														
8		21	MANSFIELD TOWN	0-3		1780	1	2	3	4	5	6	7	8			11	10	9	12													
9		28	Aldershot	1-2	Graham	1056	1	2	3	4	5			8	9	7	11	10				6	12										
10	Oct	1	CREWE ALEXANDRA	3-1	Graham, Holland(og), Hill	1443	1		3		5	6	7	8	9	4	11	10					2										
11		5	Orient	0-3		2847	1	12	3	6	5		7	8	9	4	11	10					2										
12		11	CAMBRIDGE UNITED	0-0		1496	1		3	6	5		7	8		4	11	10	9				2										
13		18	Colchester United	1-1	Broddle	3462	1	2	3	4	5		7	8	9		11	10					6										
14		22	PORT VALE	0-0		1888	1	2	3	4	5		7	8	9		11	10					6										
15		25	HEREFORD UNITED	2-1	Whitehead, Cammack	1564	1	2	3	4	5		7	8	9	12	11	10					6										
16	Nov	2	Northampton Town	2-2	Brolly, Lister	2343	1	2	3	4	5		7	8	9		11	10					6										
17		5	Preston North End	1-0	Cammack	2007	1	2	3	4	5		7	8	9			10					6	11									
18		9	SWINDON TOWN	0-2		1920	1	2		4	5		7	8		12		10				3	6	11	9								
19		23	Rochdale	0-1		1586	1	2		4	5		7	8	9		11	10				3	6										
20		30	BURNLEY	1-1	Hawley	2001	1	2		4	5				9	10	11		8			3	6					7					
21	Dec	14	Chester City	1-1	Hawley	2675	1	2			5				9		11	10	8	4		3	6					7					
22		22	HALIFAX TOWN	3-3	Hawley 3 (1 p)	2285	1	2		12	5				9		11	10	8	4		3	6					7					
23		26	HARTLEPOOL UNITED	1-0	Matthews M	2495	1	2		11	5				9			10	8	4		3	6					7					
24	Jan	1	Stockport County	0-0		3505	1	2		10	5				9		11		8	4		3	6					7					
25		11	PETERBOROUGH UTD.	2-0	Broddle, Whitehead	1832	1	2		4	5				9	10	11		8	12		3	6						7				
26		18	Torquay United	0-1		947	1	2			5				9	10	11		8	4		3	6						7				
27		24	SOUTHEND UNITED	2-0	Hill, Broddle	1473	1	2			5				9	10	11		8	4		3	6							7	12		
28		31	Tranmere Rovers	1-2	Hawley	1417	1	2		4	5				9	10	11		8			3	6							7			
29	Feb	3	Port Vale	1-3	Graham	2977	1	2		4	5				9	10	11		8			3	6						12	7			
30	Mar	1	ALDERSHOT	1-0	Hawley	1270	1	2		4	5				9	10	11		8	7		3				6							
31		4	Crewe Alexandra	0-4		1072	1	2		4	5				9	10	11		8	7		3				6							
32		8	ORIENT	2-2	Whitehead, Cammack	1478	1	2		4	5		12	9			11		8			3				6	10			7			
33		15	Cambridge United	1-0	Cammack	1785	1	2		4	5			10	12		11		8			3				6	9			7			
34		18	NORTHAMPTON T	1-0	Broddle	1355	1	2			5			9	12	4	11		8			3				6	10			7			
35		22	Hereford United	1-1	Graham	2367		2			5			8	9	4	11					3					10			7	1	6	
36		25	Mansfield Town	1-1	Travis	3923		2			5			9	8	4	11					3					10			7	1	6	
37		28	STOCKPORT COUNTY	2-3	Dixon, Cammack	2025		2		4	5			9	8	12	11					3					10			7	1	6	
38	Apr	1	Hartlepool United	1-0	Cammack	2575					5			8		4	11					2	3				10			7	1	6	9
39		4	PRESTON NORTH END	1-3	Cammack	2261				12	5			8		4	11					2	3				10			7	1	6	9
40		12	Swindon Town	1-1	Hunter	6775		2		4	5			8			11					3					10			7	1	6	9
41		15	COLCHESTER UNITED	1-1	Dixon	1238		2		4	5			8	12		11					3					10			7	1	6	9
42		18	ROCHDALE	3-1	Broddle, Houchen, Lister	1406		2		4			7	8	12		11					3	5				10				1	6	9
43		22	EXETER CITY	1-0	Cammack	1343		2					7	8	4	10	11					3	5								1	6	9
44		26	Burnley	2-1	Houchen 2	2542		2					12	8	4	7	11					3	5								1	6	9
45		29	Wrexham	0-1		1042		2		4	5			8	7		11					3	10								1	6	9
46	May	3	CHESTER CITY	2-0	Brolly, Cammack	2256		2		4			7	8		10	11					3	5							12	1	6	9
					Apps		34	42	17	37	41	9	20	33	41	31	42	18	21	11	1	31	25	2	1	6	14	5	2	12	12	12	9
					Goals					2	3	1	2	12	7	5	2		7	1										1		1	3

One own goal

F.A. Cup

	Date	Opponent	Score	Scorers	Att	Gregory PG	Russell WM	Pointon NG	Lister SH	Whitehead A	Green JR	Brolly MJ	Cammack SR	Broddle JR	Graham T	Hill DM	Lester MJ	Hawley JE	Matthews M	Smith MC	Longden DP	Money R
R1	Nov 16	Halifax Town	3-1	Hill, Broddle, Lister	1501	1	2		4	5		7	8	9	12	11	10				3	6
R2	Dec 7	ROCHDALE	2-2	Graham, Hill	2868	1	2		7	5				9	10	11	8	4			3	6
rep	10	Rochdale	1-2	Broddle	5066	1	2		4	5				9	7	11	10	8			3	6

F.L. Cup (Milk Cup)

	Date	Opponent	Score	Scorers	Att	Gregory PG	Russell WM	Pointon NG	Lister SH	Whitehead A	Green JR	Brolly MJ	Cammack SR	Broddle JR	Graham T	Hill DM	Lester MJ
R1/1	Aug 20	Darlington	2-3	Lister, Cammack	2159	1	2	3	4	5	6	7	8	9	10	11	12
R1/2	Sep 10	DARLINGTON	0-0		1504	1	2	3	4	5	6	7	8	9		11	10

Associate Members Cup (Freight Rover Trophy)

	Date	Opponent	Score	Scorers	Att	Gregory PG	Russell WM	Lister SH	Whitehead A	Green JR	Broddle JR	Graham T	Hill DM	Lester MJ	Hawley JE	Matthews M	Longden DP	Money R	Stevenson AJ	Travis DA
R1	Jan 15	Lincoln City	3-1	Money, Hawley, Whitehead	1235	1	2		5		9	10	11	8	4		3	6	7	
R1	21	HALIFAX TOWN	3-2	Matthews M, Hawley 2	1244	1	2	4	5		9	10	11	8	7		3	6	12	14
QF	Mar 10	PORT VALE	1-1	Hawley	1415	1	2	4	5	9		12	11	8	7		3	6		10

QF lost on penalties a.e.t.

1986/87   8th in Division 4

#	Date	Opponent	Score	Scorers	Att	Green RR	Russell WM	Longden DP	Money R	Lister SH	Hunter L	Birch A	Cammack SR	Johnson SA	McLean DJ	Stevenson AJ	Hill DM	Broddle JR	Whitehead A	Travis DA	Atkins MN	Nicol PJ	Ferry W	Richardson IP	Harle D	Gregory PG	Reeves D	De Mange KJP	North MV	Smith B	Flounders AJ
1	Aug 23	NORTHAMPTON T	2-2	Cammack, Hunter	2302	1	2	3	4	5	6	7	8	9	10	11															
2	30	Burnley	0-1		3008	1	2	3	4	5	6	7	8	9	10		11	12													
3	Sep 7	CREWE ALEXANDRA	2-1	Johnson, Hunter	2098	1	2	3	4	5	6	7	8	9			11	10	12												
4	13	Orient	1-3	Birch	1857	1					6	7	8	9		5	11	10	12												
5	16	Aldershot	1-2	McLean	1696	1	2	3	4	5		7		9	8		11	10			6										
6	19	PRESTON NORTH END	4-0	Lister 2, Broddle, Russell	2689	1	2	3	4	5		7		9	8		11	10			6										
7	30	CAMBRIDGE UNITED	1-1	Broddle	1694	1	2	3	4	5		7		9	8	12	11	10			6										
8	Oct 5	WOLVERHAMPTON W.	0-2		3296	1	2	3	4	5		7		9			11	10		6	8	12									
9	11	Swansea City	2-1	Whitehead, Broddle	5412	1		3	2	5		7		8			11	10	9		6	4	12								
10	17	TORQUAY UNITED	2-0	McLean, Johnson	1703	1		3	2	5		7		9	8		11	10			6	4									
11	21	Tranmere Rovers	0-1		1469	1	12	3	2	5		7		9	8		11	10			6	4									
12	25	Cardiff City	1-1	Johnson	2145	1		3	2	5	6	7		9	8		11	10			4	12									
13	Nov 1	WREXHAM	3-3	Richardson, Johnson, Broddle	1948	1		3	4	5	6			9	8		11	10			2			7							
14	4	Southend United	1-3	Johnson	2792	1	12	3	4	5	6			9	8		11	10			2			7							
15	9	HALIFAX TOWN	2-1	Johnson, Lister	2059	1	12	3	4	5	6			9	8		11	10			2			7							
16	21	COLCHESTER UNITED	5-2	Lister, Broddle, Johnson 2, McLean(p)	1725	1	7	3	4	5	6			9	8		11	10			2										
17	29	Hereford United	2-2	Rodgerson (og), Hill	2003	1	7	3		5	6			9			11	10			2	12			4						
18	Dec 13	Rochdale	1-1	Lister	1244		8	3		5	6			9			11	10			2	12		7	4	1					
19	19	EXETER CITY	3-1	Reeves 2, Hill	1545		7	3	2	5	6						11	10						8	4	1	9				
20	26	Peterborough United	1-1	Russell	4267	1	7	3		5	6						11	10			2			8	4		9				
21	27	LINCOLN CITY	2-1	Harle, Lister	4299	1	7	3	2	5	6			9			11	10						8	4						
22	Jan 1	HARTLEPOOL UNITED	1-2	Richardson	2726	1	7	3	2	5	6			9			11	10						8	4			12			
23	3	Colchester United	0-1		2100	1	7	3	2	5	6			9			11	10			12			8	4						
24	24	Crewe Alexandra	2-2	De Mange, Broddle	1430	1	4	3	11	5	6				8			10			2							7	9		
25	31	TRANMERE ROVERS	6-0	*See below	1611	1	4			5	6			9			11	10			3							7	8		
26	Feb 7	ALDERSHOT	2-0	North 2	1991	1	4	3	2	5	6			9			11	10			7								8		
27	10	ORIENT	0-2		2087	1	4	3	2		6			9			11	10			7	12		5					8		
28	14	Preston North End	1-2	Birch	7969	1	4	3	2		6	7		9	12		11	10			5			8							
29	21	STOCKPORT COUNTY	1-2	Hunter	1752	1		3	2	5	6			9	8		11	10			7				4				12		
30	28	Cambridge United	0-1		2136	1	7	3	2	5	6	12		9	8		11	10							4						
31	Mar 3	Wrexham	1-1	Lister	1330	1	2	3		5	6	7		9	8		11	10							4						
32	7	CARDIFF CITY	1-3	Smith	1936	1	2	3	11		6	7		9	8			10							4					5	
33	11	Northampton Town	0-1		5352	1	2	3	8	11	5	7		9				10							4					6	
34	14	Torquay United	2-2	Johnson, Flounders	1465	1	2	3	7	5	8			9			11								4					6	10
35	21	SWANSEA CITY	3-2	Johnson, Flounders, Lister	1590	1	2	3		5	8			9			11		12		7				4					6	10
36	28	Wolverhampton Wan.	0-1		7348	1	2	3		5	8			9			11		12		7				4					6	10
37	Apr 3	Halifax Town	1-1	Lister (p)	1232	1	2		7	5	8			9			11				3				4					6	10
38	11	SOUTHEND UNITED	3-0	Broddle, Johnson 2	1602	1	2	3	4		8			9			11	7			6			5							10
39	13	Stockport County	0-1		1773	1	2	3	4		8			9			11	7			6		12								10
40	17	Hartlepool United	2-0	Harle, Flounders	1805	1	2	3	4	5	8			9			11	7							6						10
41	20	PETERBOROUGH UTD.	2-0	Hill, Gage (og)	2470	1	2	3	4	5	8			9			11	7							6						10
42	25	Exeter City	0-0		1525	1	2	3	4	5	8	12		9			11	7							6						10
43	28	BURNLEY	2-1	Johnson 2	1770	1	2	3	4	5	7			9		8	11								6						10
44	May 1	HEREFORD UNITED	3-1	Johnson, Broddle, Russell	1660	1	2	3	4	5	8			9		11	12	7							6						10
45	4	Lincoln City	2-1	Flounders 2	2567	1	2	3	4	5	8			9		12	11	7							6						10
46	9	ROCHDALE	2-0	Lister, Flounders	2347	1	2	3	4	5	8			9			11	7			12				6						10

Scorers in game 25: Hunter, Lister, De Mange, Johnson, Broddle 2

| | | | | | Apps | 43 | 41 | 42 | 42 | 40 | 37 | 21 | 4 | 40 | 20 | 7 | 41 | 38 | 7 | 1 | 26 | 9 | 2 | 8 | 26 | 3 | 4 | 3 | 5 | 6 | 15 |
| | | | | | Goals | | 3 | | | 11 | 4 | 2 | 1 | 16 | 3 | | 3 | 10 | 1 | | | | | 2 | 2 | | 2 | 2 | 2 | 1 | 6 |

Two own goals

F.A. Cup

Rnd	Date	Opponent	Score	Scorers	Att	Green RR	Russell WM	Longden DP	Money R	Lister SH	Hunter L	Birch A	Cammack SR	Johnson SA	McLean DJ	Stevenson AJ	Hill DM	Broddle JR	Whitehead A	Travis DA	Atkins MN	Nicol PJ	Ferry W	Richardson IP	Harle D	Gregory PG	Reeves D	De Mange KJP	North MV	Smith B	Flounders AJ
R1	Nov 15	SOUTHPORT	2-0	Hill, Broddle	2601	1	14	3	4	5	6			9	8		11	10			2	12		7							
R2	Dec 6	RUNCORN	1-0	Broddle	3006	1	7	3		5	6			9			11	10	12		2	4		8							
R3	Jan 10	Tottenham Hotspur	2-3	Johnson S, De Mange	19339	1	7	3	2	5	12			9	8		11	10			6							4			

Played in R2: J Talbot (at 14).

F.L. Cup (Littlewoods Challenge Cup)

Rnd	Date	Opponent	Score	Scorers	Att	Green RR	Russell WM	Longden DP	Money R	Lister SH	Hunter L	Birch A	Cammack SR	Johnson SA	McLean DJ	Stevenson AJ	Hill DM	Broddle JR	Whitehead A	Travis DA	Atkins MN	Nicol PJ	Ferry W	Richardson IP	Harle D	Gregory PG	Reeves D	De Mange KJP	North MV	Smith B	Flounders AJ
R1/1	Aug 26	DARLINGTON	2-0	Lister, Johnson S	1350	1	2	3	4	5	6	7	8	9	10		11					12									
R1/2	Sep 2	Darlington	2-1	Lister 2	1469	1	2	3	4	5	6	7	8	9			11	10													
R2/1	23	IPSWICH TOWN	1-2	Broddle	3919	1	2	3	4	5		7		9			11	10		6	12										
R2/2	Oct 7	Ipswich Town	0-2		6587	1	2	3	9	5		7					11	10		6	8	4	12								

Associate Members Cup (Freight Rover Trophy)

Rnd	Date	Opponent	Score	Scorers	Att	Green RR	Russell WM	Longden DP	Money R	Lister SH	Hunter L	Birch A	Cammack SR	Johnson SA	McLean DJ	Stevenson AJ	Hill DM	Broddle JR	Whitehead A	Travis DA	Atkins MN	Nicol PJ	Ferry W	Richardson IP	Harle D	Gregory PG	Reeves D	De Mange KJP	North MV	Smith B	Flounders AJ
PR	Nov 25	Lincoln City	0-1		1003	1	7	3		5	6			9	8		11	10			2	4									
PR	Dec 2	HARTLEPOOL UNITED	1-0	Broddle	972	1	7	3		5	6			9			11	10			2	8						4	1		
R1	Jan 27	WREXHAM	1-2	Hunter	1227	1	4	3		5	6		12		8			10			2	14		11					7	9	

Played v. Lincoln: J Talbot (at 12).

#	Date	Opponent	Score	Scorers	Att	Green RR	Russell WM	Longden DP	McLean DJ	Brown AJ	Nicol PJ	Dixon KL	Harle D	Daws A	Flounders AJ	Hill DM	Atkins MN	Johnson SA	Broddle JR	Stevenson AJ	Lister SH	Heyes D	Money R	Birch A	Taylor K	Reeves D	Cowling DR	Taylor MJ	Shearer DJ	Richardson IP
1	Aug 15	TRANMERE ROVERS	3-0	Russell, Flounders 2	2277	1	2	3	4	5	6	7	8	9	10	11														
2	22	Carlisle United	1-3	Johnson	2074	1	2	3	4		6	7	8		10	11	5	9	12											
3	29	COLCHESTER UNITED	2-2	Johnson, Flounders	2003	1	2	3	4	5	6	7	8		10	11		9	12											
4	31	Wolverhampton Wan.	1-4	Flounders	6832	1	2	3	4	5	6	7	8		10			9	11	12										
5	Sep 5	ROCHDALE	1-0	Dixon	1959	1	2	3		5		7	8		10	11	6	9	4											
6	12	Cambridge United	3-3	Flounders 2, Harle	1830	1	2	3		5		7	8		10		6	9	11		4									
7	15	BOLTON WANDERERS	1-1	Russell (p)	2501		2	3		5		7	8		10		6	9	11		4	1								
8	19	NEWPORT COUNTY	3-1	Flounders 2, Atkins	2004		2	3		5		7	8		10		6	9	11		4	1								
9	26	Darlington	4-1	Russell, Dixon, Lister, Flounders	1638	1	2	3			5	7	8		10		6	9			4		11							
10	29	STOCKPORT COUNTY	0-0		2191	1	2	3			5	7	8		10		6	9			4		11	12						
11	Oct 3	Peterborough United	1-1	Dixon	3616	1	2	3			5	7	8		10		6	9			4		11	12						
12	10	HALIFAX TOWN	1-0	Johnson	2105	1	2					7	8		10	11	3	9			5		6		4					
13	17	Hereford United	3-2	Reeves 3	2092	1	2	11				7	8		10		3				5		6		4	9				
14	20	Burnley	1-1	Flounders	6353	1	2	11				7	8		10		3			12	5		6		4	9				
15	24	CARDIFF CITY	2-1	Ford(og), Taylor	2872	1	2	11				7	8		10		3			12	5		6		4	9				
16	31	Hartlepool United	0-1		2532	1	2	11			6	7	8		10		3		12		5				4	9				
17	Nov 3	WREXHAM	3-1	Reeves, Flounders 2	2348	1	2	11			5	7	8		10		3						6		4	9				
18	7	SCARBOROUGH	0-1		4506	1	2	3				7	8				14	12			5		6		4	9	11			
19	21	Crewe Alexandra	2-2	Atkins, Flounders	2045	1	2	3				7	8		10	11	9				5		6		4					
20	28	SWANSEA CITY	1-2	Flounders	2309	1	2	3				7	8	12	10	11	9				5		6		4					
21	Dec 12	Exeter City	1-1	Johnson	1831		2	3				7	8	12	10	11	9			14	5	1	6		4					
22	18	TORQUAY UNITED	2-3	Impey(og), Russell	2261		7	3						12	8	11	10	2	9	14	5		6		4			1		
23	26	DARLINGTON	1-0	Flounders	3140		2	3			6	7	8	11	10			9			5				4			1		
24	28	Leyton Orient	1-1	Harle	5542		2	3			9	7	8	11	10						5		6		4			1		
25	Jan 1	Colchester United	3-0	Daws 2, Lister	2287		2	3			9	7	8	11	10						5		6		4			1		
26	2	CAMBRIDGE UNITED	3-2	Hill, Taylor K, Daws	3253		2	3	12	6		7	8	9	10	11					5				4			1		
27	16	Newport County	1-1	Taylor K	1760			3		6		7		9	10	11			12	8	5		2		4			1		
28	30	WOLVERHAMPTON W.	0-1		5476		2	3		6		7	8		10	11		9			5				4			1		
29	Feb 6	Rochdale	1-2	Flounders	1455		2	3		6		7	8		10	11		12			5		9		4			1		
30	13	LEYTON ORIENT	3-2	Harle 2, Shearer	2951	1	2	3		6			8		10	11		12			5		7		4				9	
31	20	Tranmere Rovers	3-1	Flounders 2, Lister	2835	1	2	3		6			8		10	11		12			5		7		4				9	
32	27	PETERBOROUGH UTD.	5-0	Shearer, Flounders 3, Gunn(og)	3378	1	2	3		6			8		10	11					5		7		4				9	
33	Mar 1	Stockport County	1-1	Shearer	1834	1	2	3			6	14	8		10	11		12			5		7		4				9	
34	5	HEREFORD UNITED	3-0	Hill, Shearer, Lister	3313	1	2	3			6	12	8		10	11					5		7		4				9	
35	12	Halifax Town	2-2	Harle, Lister	1807	1		3	12		6	7	8		10	11		9			5		2		4					
36	19	HARTLEPOOL UNITED	3-0	Flounders, Dixon, Hill	3783	1		3			6	7	8		10	11		12			5		2		4				9	
37	26	Cardiff City	1-0	Shearer	4527	1		3			12	7	8		10	11	2	14			5				4				9	
38	Apr 2	Scarborough	0-0		4710	1		3			6	7	8		10	11					5		2		4				9	
39	4	CREWE ALEXANDRA	2-1	Flounders, Taylor K	4136	1		3			6	7	8		10	11		12			5		2		4				9	
40	9	Wrexham	1-2	Shearer	2589	1		3			12	7	8			11	10			14	5		2		4				9	
41	12	CARLISLE UNITED	1-0	Shearer	3514	1		3			6	7	8		10	11					5		2		4				9	
42	19	Bolton Wanderers	0-0		6669	1					6	7	8		10	11	3				5		2		4				9	
43	23	BURNLEY	1-1	Harle (p)	5347	1		3		5	6	7	8		10	11	2	12							4				9	
44	30	Swansea City	1-1	Lister	3482	1	7	3		12	6	7	8	14	10	11					5		2		4				9	
45	May 2	EXETER CITY	1-1	Shearer	6736	1		3			7	6	8		10	11		12			5		2		4				9	
46	7	Torquay United	2-1	Flounders, Richardson	4989	1		3			6		8	9		11		14		12	5		2		4					7
		Apps				35	34	44	4	22	25	41	45	10	45	26	22	32	7	8	39	3	32	2	35	6	1	8	15	1
		Goals					4					4	6	3	24	3	2	4			6				4	4			8	1

Three own goals

Play Offs

	Date	Opponent	Score	Scorers	Att	Green RR	Russell WM	Longden DP	McLean DJ	Brown AJ	Nicol PJ	Dixon KL	Harle D	Daws A	Flounders AJ	Hill DM	Atkins MN	Johnson SA	Broddle JR	Stevenson AJ	Lister SH	Heyes D	Money R	Birch A	Taylor K	Reeves D	Cowling DR	Taylor MJ	Shearer DJ	Richardson IP
SF1	May 15	Torquay United	1-2	Flounders	4062	1		3	8		6			9	10	11					5		2		4				12	7
SF2	18	TORQUAY UNITED	1-1	Lister (p)	6483	1		3	6			12		9	10	11	14				5		2		4				8	7

F.A. Cup

	Date	Opponent	Score	Scorers	Att	Green RR	Russell WM	Longden DP	McLean DJ	Brown AJ	Nicol PJ	Dixon KL	Harle D	Daws A	Flounders AJ	Hill DM	Atkins MN	Johnson SA	Broddle JR	Stevenson AJ	Lister SH	Heyes D	Money R	Birch A	Taylor K	Reeves D	Cowling DR	Taylor MJ	Shearer DJ	Richardson IP
R1	Nov 14	BURY	3-1	Russell 3 (1 p)	3151	1	2	3				7	8		10		11	9			5		6		4					
R2	Dec 5	SUNDERLAND	2-1	Taylor, Harle	7178	1	2	3				7	8		10		11	9			5		6		4					
R3	Jan 9	BLACKPOOL	0-0		6217		2	3			6	7	8	9	10	11					5				4					
rep	12	Blackpool	0-1		6127		2	3			6	7	8	9	10	11		14			5		12		4					

Played in R3 and R3 replay: P Johnson (at 1)

F.L. Cup (Littlewoods Challenge Cup)

	Date	Opponent	Score	Scorers	Att	Green RR	Russell WM	Longden DP	McLean DJ	Brown AJ	Nicol PJ	Dixon KL	Harle D	Daws A	Flounders AJ	Hill DM	Atkins MN	Johnson SA	Broddle JR	Stevenson AJ	Lister SH	Heyes D	Money R	Birch A	Taylor K	Reeves D	Cowling DR	Taylor MJ	Shearer DJ	Richardson IP
R1/1	Aug 18	HARTLEPOOL UNITED	3-1	Hill, Nicol, Russell (p)	1613	1	2	3	4	5	6	7	8		10	11		9												
R1/2	26	Hartlepool United	1-0	Johnson	872	1	2	3	4	5	6	7	8		10	11		9												
R2/1	Sep 23	Leicester City	1-2	Flounders	7718	1	2	3		5		7	8		10		6	9			4	1	11	12						
R2/2	Oct 6	LEICESTER CITY	1-2	Johnson	4031	1	2	12		5		7	8		10		6	9			4		3	11						

Ascoiate Members Cup (Freight Rover Trophy)

	Date	Opponent	Score	Scorers	Att	Green RR	Russell WM	Longden DP	McLean DJ	Brown AJ	Nicol PJ	Dixon KL	Harle D	Daws A	Flounders AJ	Hill DM	Atkins MN	Johnson SA	Broddle JR	Stevenson AJ	Lister SH	Heyes D	Money R	Birch A	Taylor K	Reeves D	Cowling DR	Taylor MJ	Shearer DJ	Richardson IP
PR	Oct 13	GRIMSBY TOWN	2-0	Dixon, Stevenson	1710		2	11				7	8		10		3	9		12	5	1	6		4					
PR	Nov 24	Halifax Town	0-3		686		2	3		6	4	7	8	9	10		11	12			5	1								
Po	Dec 15	Grimsby Town	2-1	Harle, Flounders	970			3		5		7	8	11	10			9		2			1	6	4					
R2	Jan 19	Mansfield Town	0-1		3637			3				7	8	9	10	12	6	14		11	5		2		4					

Played in R2: P Johnson (at 1)

No.	Date	Opponent	Score	Scorers	Att.	Musselwhite PS	Longden DP	Rumble P	Taylor K	Lister SH	Brown AJ	Hodkinson AJ	Winter J	Shearer DJ	Flounders AJ	Cowling DR	Daws A	Stevenson AJ	Richardson IP	Money R	Smalley PT	Harle D	Hamilton IR	Brown DJ	Nicol PJ	Cork D	Cotton P
1	Aug 27	HEREFORD UNITED	3-1	Cowling, Daws, Taylor	3663	1	2	3	4	5	6	7	8	9	10	11	12										
2	Sep 3	Crewe Alexandra	2-3	Flounders, Lister (p)	1514	1	2		4	5	6	7	8		10	11	9	3	12								
3	10	GRIMSBY TOWN	1-1	Lister	6037	1	2	3	4	5	6	7	8		10	11	9										
4	17	York City	2-1	Daws 2	2735	1	2	3	4	5		7	8		10	11	9	6									
5	20	CARLISLE UNITED	1-1	Flounders	3113	1	2	3	4	5	6	7			10	11	9	8	12	14							
6	24	Exeter City	2-2	Daws, Rumble	1876	1	2	3	4	5	6	7			10	11	9	8	12								
7	Oct 1	SCARBOROUGH	0-3		4167	1		3	4	5	6	7			10		9		11		2	8					
8	5	Lincoln City	0-1		5443	1		3	4	5	12	7			10		9	6	11		2	8					
9	8	Colchester United	2-1	Flounders, Richardson	1299	1	12	3	4	5	11	7			10		9	6	14		2	8					
10	15	CAMBRIDGE UNITED	1-0	Taylor	3514	1	3		4	5	11	7			10		9	6			2	8					
11	22	Rochdale	0-1		2250	1	3		4	5	6	7			10	11	9				2	8					
12	25	WREXHAM	3-1	Daws, Hodkinson, Flounders	2999	1	3		4	5		7			10	11	9	6			2	8					
13	29	Peterborough United	2-1	Hodkinson, Harle (p)	3532	1	3			5		7			10	11	9	6		4	2	8					
14	Nov 5	BURNLEY	2-1	Flounders, Lister	6358	1	3			5		7			10	11	9	6		4	2	8					
15	8	Rotherham United	3-3	Flounders, Lister, Hodkinson	5923	1	3			5		7			10	11	9	6		4	2	8					
16	12	LEYTON ORIENT	2-2	Daws 2	4239	1	3		12	5		7			10	11	9	6	14	4	2	8					
17	26	TORQUAY UNITED	1-0	Daws	3359	1	3		4	5	12	7			10	11	9	6			2	8					
18	Dec 3	Darlington	3-3	Smalley, Daws, Lister	1745	1	3		4	5	11	7			10		9	6			2	8					
19	17	Doncaster Rovers	2-2	Hodkinson, Flounders	3381	1	3		4	5	6	7			10	11	9	2	12			8					
20	26	HARTLEPOOL UNITED	1-1	Harle (p)	4595	1	3		4	5	6	7			10	11	9	12			2	8	14				
21	31	TRANMERE ROVERS	0-1		4154	1	3		4	5	6	7			10	11	9	14			2	8	12				
22	Jan 2	Halifax Town	1-5	Hamilton	2650	1	3		4	5	6	7			12		9	11			2	8	10				
23	7	Stockport County	2-1	Flounders, Daws	2656		3		4	5		7			10	14	9	6			2	8	11	1	12		
24	14	CREWE ALEXANDRA	2-2	Daws 2	4034		12		4	5	14	7			10	3	9	6			2	8	11	1			
25	21	Hereford United	2-1	Hodkinson, Daws	2024		3		4		6	7			10	8	9				2		11	1	5		
26	28	YORK CITY	4-2	Smith(og), Brown A, Daws 2	4196		3		4		6	7			10	8	9				2		11	1	5		
27	Feb 4	Carlisle United	3-0	Lister, Taylor (p), Flounders	2647		3		4	7	6				10	8	9				2		11	1	5		
28	11	EXETER CITY	2-0	Lister, Cowling	4102	1			4	7	6				10	8	9	3			2		11		5		
29	18	COLCHESTER UNITED	2-3	Lister, Nicol	4286	1			4	7	6	12			10	8	9	3			2		11		5	14	
30	25	Cambridge United	3-0	Taylor, Flounders, Daws	2563	1			4	7	6	3			10	8	9				2		11		5		
31	28	Wrexham	0-2		2609	1	3		4	7	6	5			10	8	9				2		11		12		
32	Mar 4	ROCHDALE	4-0	Daws 2, Brown A, Hodkinson	4098	1	3		4	7	6	5			10	8	9				2		11		14	12	
33	11	Burnley	1-0	Lister	6813	1	3			7	6				10	8	9				2		11		5	4	
34	14	PETERBOROUGH UTD.	3-0	Flounders 3	3983	1	3			7	6				10	8	9				2		11		5	4	
35	18	Grimsby Town	1-1	Flounders	9796	1	3		12	7	6				10	8	9				2		11		5	4	
36	25	HALIFAX TOWN	0-0		4591	1	3		4	7	6	12			10	8	9				2		11		5		
37	27	Hartlepool United	2-0	Flounders, Daws	1895	1	3		4		6	7			10	8	9				2		11		5	12	
38	Apr 1	DONCASTER ROVERS	2-1	Taylor (p), Hodkinson	5334	1	3		4		6	7			10	8	9				2		11		5	12	
39	4	STOCKPORT COUNTY	1-1	Taylor (p)	3958	1	3		4			7			10	8	9	6			2		11		5	12	14
40	7	Tranmere Rovers	1-2	Daws	10468	1	3		4			12			10	8	9	6		7	2		11		5	14	
41	15	Scarborough	0-1		4456	1	3		4		6	7			10	8	9				2		11		5	12	
42	22	LINCOLN CITY	0-0		5739	1	3		4			7			10	8	9				2		11		5	6	
43	28	Torquay United	2-0	Daws, Hodkinson	2544	1	3		4			7			10	8	9	12			2		11		5	6	
44	May 1	ROTHERHAM UNITED	0-0		8775	1	3		4			7			10		9	8	12		2		11		5	6	
45	6	DARLINGTON	5-1	Daws 3, Taylor, Flounders	5296	1	3		4			7			10	8	9				2		11		5	6	
46	13	Leyton Orient	1-4	Taylor	6266	1	3		4			7			10	8	9				2		11		5	6	
		Apps				41	41	8	41	34	32	41	4	1	46	39	46	26	9	6	39	18	27	5	23	15	1
		Goals						1	8	9	2	8			16	2	24		1		1	2	1		1		

One own goal

Play Offs

No.	Date	Opponent	Score	Scorers	Att.	Musselwhite PS	Longden DP	Rumble P	Taylor K	Lister SH	Brown AJ	Hodkinson AJ	Winter J	Shearer DJ	Flounders AJ	Cowling DR	Daws A	Stevenson AJ	Richardson IP	Money R	Smalley PT	Harle D	Hamilton IR	Brown DJ	Nicol PJ	Cork D	Cotton P
SF1	May 21	Wrexham	1-3	Cowling	5449	1	3		4			7			10	8	9				2		11		5	6	12
SF2	26	WREXHAM	0-2		5516	1	3		4			7			10	8	9		14	12	2		11		5	6	

F.A. Cup

Rnd	Date	Opponent	Score	Scorers	Att.	Musselwhite PS	Longden DP	Rumble P	Taylor K	Lister SH	Brown AJ	Hodkinson AJ	Winter J	Shearer DJ	Flounders AJ	Cowling DR	Daws A	Stevenson AJ	Richardson IP	Money R	Smalley PT	Harle D	Hamilton IR	Brown DJ	Nicol PJ	Cork D	Cotton P
R1	Nov 19	Blackpool	1-2	Harle (p)	3976	1	3		4	5	14	7			10	11	9	6	12		2	8					

F.L. Cup (Littlewoods Challenge Cup)

Rnd	Date	Opponent	Score	Scorers	Att.	Musselwhite PS	Longden DP	Rumble P	Taylor K	Lister SH	Brown AJ	Hodkinson AJ	Winter J	Shearer DJ	Flounders AJ	Cowling DR	Daws A	Stevenson AJ	Richardson IP	Money R	Smalley PT	Harle D	Hamilton IR	Brown DJ	Nicol PJ	Cork D	Cotton P
R1/1	Aug 30	HUDDERSFIELD TOWN	3-2	Flounders, Lister, Hodkinson	3820	1	2		4	5	6	7			10	11	9	3	12	8							
R1/2	Sep 6	Huddersfield Town	2-2	Flounders 2	4237	1	2		4	5	6	7			10	11	9	3		8							
R2/1	27	CHELSEA	4-1	Daws 2, Stevenson, Taylor	5061	1		3	4	5	6	7			10		9	2	11			8					
R2/2	Oct 12	Chelsea	2-2	Harle (p), Flounders	5814	1	3		4	5	11	7			10		9	6	12		2	8					
R3	Nov 2	Bradford City	1-1	Daws	8011	1	3			5		7			10	11	9	6		4	2	8					
rep	22	BRADFORD CITY	0-1		5793	1	3		4	5	12	7			10	11	9	6			2	8					

R1/2 a.e.t.

Associate Members Cup (Sherpa Van Trophy)

Rnd	Date	Opponent	Score	Scorers	Att.	Musselwhite PS	Longden DP	Rumble P	Taylor K	Lister SH	Brown AJ	Hodkinson AJ	Winter J	Shearer DJ	Flounders AJ	Cowling DR	Daws A	Stevenson AJ	Richardson IP	Money R	Smalley PT	Harle D	Hamilton IR	Brown DJ	Nicol PJ	Cork D	Cotton P
PR	Dec 6	HALIFAX TOWN	1-2	Harle (p)	1547	1	3		4	5	11	7			10		9	6			2	8					
PR	13	Huddersfield Town	0-1		2216	1	3			5	4	7	12		10		9	6	11		2	8					

Played v. Halifax: G Alexander (at 12)

1989/90 11th in Division 4

#	Date		Opponent	Score	Scorers	Att	Litchfield P	Smalley PT	Longden DP	Taylor K	Knight LJ	Tucker G	Hodkinson AJ	Cowling DR	Cotton P	Flounders AJ	Marshall G	Nicol PJ	Money R	Butler MC	Daws A	Hamilton IR	Musselwhite PS	Stevenson AJ	Lillis MA	Lister SH	Ward PT	Hall RA	Bramhall J
1	Aug	19	Lincoln City	0-1		4504	1	2	3	4	5	6	7	8		9	10	11	12										
2		26	ROCHDALE	0-1		2808	1	2	12	4	3	6		8			10	11	5	7	9								
3	Sep	2	Gillingham	3-0	Taylor (p), Flounders 2	3462		2	3	4		6	7	8		9	10	11	5			12	1						
4		9	SCARBOROUGH	0-1		3370		2	3	4		6	7	8		9	10	11	5			9	1						
5		16	Peterborough United	1-1	Taylor	4350		2	3	4		6	7	8		9	10	11	5			8	1	12					
6		23	EXETER CITY	5-4	Lillis 2, Hamilton 2, Taylor	2935		2	3	4		6	7	12			10	11	5			8	1		9				
7		26	TORQUAY UNITED	2-0	Flounders, Lillis	3242		2	3	4		6	7				10	11	5			8	1		9				
8		30	Aldershot	2-4	Lillis, Tucker	1892		2	3	4		6	7	14			10	11	5		12	8	1		9				
9	Oct	7	Hartlepool United	2-3	Lillis, Daws	1815	1	2	3	4		6	7	12		14	11	5			10	8			9				
10		14	MAIDSTONE UNITED	1-0	Lister (p)	3165	1	2	3	4				7		12	11				10	8		6	9	5			
11		17	Carlisle	1-0	Lillis	4825	1	2	3	4			12	7		14	11				10	8		6	9	5			
12		21	COLCHESTER UNITED	4-0	Stevenson, Daws, Hamilton, Taylor	3254	1	2	3	4				7			11				10	8		6	9	5			
13		28	Cambridge United	3-5	Marshall, Daws, Hamilton	2395	1	2	3	4				7		14	11				10	8		6	9	5	12		
14		31	YORK CITY	1-1	Flounders	3800	1	2	3				5	7		10	11				9	8		6			4		
15	Nov	4	Doncaster Rovers	2-1	Daws, Flounders	3274	1		3					2		10	11	5			9	8		6	7		4		
16		11	BURNLEY	3-0	Marshall, Ward (p), Hamilton	4745	1		3				9	2		10	11	5				8		6	7		4		
17		25	Stockport County	2-4	Ward, Flounders	3259	1	12	3				9	2		10	11	5				8		6	7		4		
18	Dec	2	SOUTHEND UNITED	1-1	Ward	3714	1	2	3	8			9		14	10	11	5						6	7	12	4		
19		16	Hereford United	2-1	Nicol, Lillis	1924	1	2	3	8			4		14	12	11	6			9	10			7	5			
20		26	GRIMSBY TOWN	2-2	Daws, Marshall	8384	1	2	3	8			4			12	11	6			9	10			7			5	
21		30	CHESTERFIELD	0-1		5006		2	3	8			4			9	11	5			12	10	1	6	7				
22	Jan	1	Wrexham	0-0		1887		2	3	4			7	11		10			6		9	8	1	5					
23		6	HALIFAX TOWN	1-1	Taylor	3051		2	3	4				11	6	10	7				12	8	1	5	9				
24		13	Rochdale	0-3		1781		2	3	4				8	6	10	7				9	11	1	5					
25		20	LINCOLN CITY	1-1	Lillis	3830		2	3	14				8	6	10	7				9	11	1		12		4		5
26		27	Scarborough	0-0		2329		2	3	6				8			7				9	11	1		10		4		5
27	Feb	10	PETERBOROUGH UTD.	0-0		3188		2	3	6				8		12	7				9	11	1		10		4		5
28		13	GILLINGHAM	0-0		2226		2	3	6				8		9	7				12	11	1		10		4		5
29		16	Southend United	0-0		3154		2	3	6				8		10					9	11	1	12	7		4		5
30		24	STOCKPORT COUNTY	5-0	Lillis 2, Daws 2, Ward	3280		2	3	6				8		10					9	11	1	12	7		4		5
31	Mar	3	Halifax Town	1-0	Daws	1793		2	3				7	8		10					9	11	1	6			4		5
32		6	ALDERSHOT	3-2	Lillis, Hamilton, Flounders	3202		2	3					8		10	12				9	11	1	6	7		4		5
33		10	Torquay United	3-0	Daws, Flounders, Lillis	1935		2	3				6	8		10					9	11	1	12	7		4		5
34		17	HARTLEPOOL UNITED	0-1		3868		2	3	14			6	8		10	12	5			9	11	1		7		4		
35		21	Maidstone United	1-1	Flounders	1299		2	3	6				8		10	7				9	11	1				4		5
36		24	CARLISLE UNITED	2-3	Flounders, Lillis (p)	3406		2	3	6				8	9	10	7					11	1		12		4		5
37		28	Exeter City	0-1		5805		2	3	6				8	9	10						11	1		7		4		5
38		31	Colchester United	0-1		2920		2	3	6				8	9	10	14				12	11	1		7		4		5
39	Apr	7	CAMBRIDGE UNITED	1-1	Taylor	2486		2	3	6					12	10					9	11	1	8	7		4		5
40		10	York City	1-0	Taylor	2232		2	3	6			7		9	10						11	1	8			4		5
41		14	WREXHAM	3-1	Flounders 2 (1 p), Taylor	2820		2	3	6			7		9	10	4					11	1	8					5
42		17	Grimsby Town	1-2	Flounders	11894		2	3	6			7		9	10	4					11	1	8					5
43		21	HEREFORD UNITED	3-3	Flounders 2 (1 p), Pejic (og)	2247		2	3	6			7	4	9	10					8	11	1	12					5
44		28	Burnley	1-0	Cotton	4098	1	2	3	6				7	9	10					8	11					4		5
45	May	1	Chesterfield	1-1	Daws	3469	1	2	3	6			7		9	10					8	11					4		5
46		5	DONCASTER ROVERS	4-1	Flounders 3, Daws	3020	1	2	3	6			7		9	10					8	11					4		5
	Apps						17	44	46	39	2	15	21	32	17	44	34	18	1	2	33	43	29	24	29	6	25	1	21
	Goals								8	1					1	18	3	1			11	6		1	13	1	4		

One own goal

F.A. Cup

	Date		Opponent	Score	Scorers	Att	Litchfield P	Smalley PT	Longden DP	Taylor K	Knight LJ	Tucker G	Hodkinson AJ	Cowling DR	Cotton P	Flounders AJ	Marshall G	Nicol PJ	Money R	Butler MC	Daws A	Hamilton IR	Musselwhite PS	Stevenson AJ	Lillis MA	Lister SH	Ward PT	Hall RA	Bramhall J
R1	Nov	18	MATLOCK TOWN	4-1	Lillis 3, Hodkinson	4307	1	12	3				9	2		10	11	5				8		6	7		4		
R2	Dec	9	BURNLEY	2-2	Taylor 2	5968	1	12	3	8			9	2		10	11							6	7	5	4		
rep		12	Burnley	1-1	Daws	7682	1	2	3	10			12			14	11				9	8		6	7	5	4		
rep2		18	Burnley	0-5		7429	1	2	3	8			4			12	14	11	6		9	10			7	5			

R2 replay a.e.t.

F.L. Cup (Littlewoods Challenge Cup)

	Date		Opponent	Score	Scorers	Att	Litchfield P	Smalley PT	Longden DP	Taylor K	Knight LJ	Tucker G	Hodkinson AJ	Cowling DR	Cotton P	Flounders AJ	Marshall G	Nicol PJ	Money R	Butler MC	Daws A	Hamilton IR	Musselwhite PS	Stevenson AJ	Lillis MA	Lister SH	Ward PT	Hall RA	Bramhall J
R1/1	Aug	23	Scarborough	0-2		2259	1	2	3	4		6		8	9	10	11	5	7						12				
R1/2		29	SCARBOROUGH	1-1	Flounders	1853		2	3	4		6	7	8		10	11	5		9			1						

Associate Members Cup (Leyland DAF Trophy)

	Date		Opponent	Score	Scorers	Att	Litchfield P	Smalley PT	Longden DP	Taylor K	Knight LJ	Tucker G	Hodkinson AJ	Cowling DR	Cotton P	Flounders AJ	Marshall G	Nicol PJ	Money R	Butler MC	Daws A	Hamilton IR	Musselwhite PS	Stevenson AJ	Lillis MA	Lister SH	Ward PT	Hall RA	Bramhall J
PR	Nov	7	SCARBOROUGH	1-0	Flounders	1496	1		3				9	2		10	11	5				8		6	7		4		
PR	Dec	22	Carlisle United	1-1	Taylor	1942		2	3	8				7		10					9	11	1	6				5	
R1	Jan	9	Tranmere Rovers	1-2	Cotton	2766		2	3	4			14	11	6	10	7	12			9	8	1	5					

Played v. Carlisle Utd.: G Alexander (at 4), NJ Cox (at 12).

#	Date	Opponent	Score	Scorers	Att	Litchfield P	Longden DP	Cowling DR	Ward PT	Hicks SJ	Hall RA	Taylor K	Hamilton IR	Lillis MA	Flounders AJ	Marshall G	Miller I	Daws A	Smalley PT	Cotton P	Musselwhite PS	Cox NJ	Bramhall J	Powell G	Stevenson AJ	Joyce JP	Humphries G	Hill DM	Hine M	Lister SH	Alexander G
1	Aug 25	BLACKPOOL	2-0	Flounders, Hamilton	3024	1	2	3	4	5	6	7	8	9	10	11															
2	Sep 1	Aldershot	2-3	Flounders (p), Daws	2001	1	2	3	4	5	6	7	12		10	11	8	9	14												
3	8	PETERBOROUGH UTD.	1-1	Flounders	3028	1	2	3	4	5			8	9	10	11	7			6											
4	15	Maidstone United	1-6	Lillis	1778	1	2	3	4	5			11	8	9	10	7			6											
5	18	Torquay United	1-1	Lillis	2811	1	2	3	4	5	6	12	8	9	10	11	7			14											
6	22	LINCOLN CITY	2-1	Lillis, Hall	2844	1	2	3	4	5	6	12	8	9	10	11	7														
7	29	CARDIFF CITY	0-2		2573	1	2	3	4	5	6	12	8	9	10	11	7	14													
8	Oct 2	Walsall	0-3		3676	1	2	3	4	5	6		8		10	11	7	9													
9	6	Halifax Town	0-0		1441		2	3	4	5	6	8			12			9		10	1	7	11								
10	13	GILLINGHAM	1-0	Hall	2357		2		4	5	6	8		3	10			9			1	7	11								
11	20	SCARBOROUGH	3-0	Daws 2, Taylor	2786		2		4	5	6	8		3	10		14	9		12	1	7	11								
12	23	Chesterfield	0-1		3371		2		4	5	6	8		3	10			9			1	7	11								
13	27	Darlington	0-0		3854		2		4	5	6	8		3	10			9			1	7	11								
14	Nov 3	STOCKPORT COUNTY	3-0	Lillis, Flounders (p), Daws	2826		2		4	5	6	8		3	10			9			1	7	11								
15	10	ROCHDALE	2-1	Flounders, Cotton	3070		2			5	6	8		3	10		12	9		4	1	7	11								
16	24	Wrexham	0-1		1333		2			5	6	8		3	10					4	1	7	11	9	12						
17	Dec 1	York City	2-2	Hall, Powell	2495		2	10		5	6	8		3	12				14	4	1	7	11	9							
18	15	DONCASTER ROVERS	1-1	Flounders	3963		2	11	4	5	6	14		3	10			9		8	1	7				12					
19	22	Hereford United	0-2		2218		2	11		5	6	4	12	3	10					8	1	7				9					
20	29	CARLISLE UNITED	2-0	Flounders (p), Lillis	2971		2	11		5	6	4	9	3	10					8	1	7	6								
21	Jan 1	Burnley	1-1	Lillis	8559		2	11	12	5		4	9	3	10		14			8	1	7	6								
22	12	ALDERSHOT	6-2	Cowling, Flounders 3(1p), Hamilton, Lillis	2727		2	11	8	5	6	4	9	3	10					12	1	7									
23	19	Blackpool	1-3	Cowling	2494		2	11	8	5	6	4	9		10			12		3	1	7									
24	26	MAIDSTONE UNITED	2-2	Ward, Daws	2703		2	11	8	5	6	4	9		10					8	1	7									
25	Feb 2	TORQUAY UNITED	3-0	Cowling, Cox, Flounders	2502		2	11	3	5	6	8			10			9		4	1	7					12				
26	23	Rochdale	1-2	Daws	1832		2	11	4	5		8		3	10			9			1					6	7				
27	26	HARTLEPOOL UNITED	2-1	Taylor, Lillis	2220		2		4	5		11	8	3	10			9			1					6	7				
28	Mar 2	YORK CITY	2-1	Ward, Daws	2860		2		4	5		11	8	3	10			9			1					6	7				
29	5	NORTHAMPTON T	3-0	Daws, Chard(og), Lillis	2852		2		4	5		11	8	3	10			9			1					6	7				
30	8	Doncaster Rovers	3-2	Flounders 2, Daws	4244		2		4	5		11	8	3	10			9			1					7	6				
31	12	WALSALL	1-0	Daws	3352		2		4	5		11	8	3	10			9			1					7	6				
32	16	Cardiff City	0-1		2873		2		4	5		11	8	3	10			9			1					7	6				
33	19	Gillingham	1-1	Flounders	2319		2		4	5		11	8	3	10			9			1					7	6				
34	23	HALIFAX TOWN	4-4	Flounders (p), Taylor, Humphries, Lillis	3134		2		4	5		11	8	3	10			9		12	1					7	6				
35	30	Northampton Town	1-2	Taylor	3728		2			5		11	8	12	10			9			1					7	6	3	4		
36	Apr 1	HEREFORD UNITED	3-0	Flounders 2, Daws	3001		2			5		11	8	12	10			9			1					7	6	3	4		
37	6	Carlisle United	3-0	Hill, Hine, Dalziel(og)	1909		2			5		11	8		10			9			1					7	6	3	4		
38	9	Hartlepool United	0-2		3040		2			5		11	8	12	10			9			1					7	6	3	4		
39	13	BURNLEY	1-3	Hine	4449		2			5		11	8	12	10			9		14	1					7	6	3	4		
40	17	Lincoln City	2-1	Flounders 2	3212		2			5			8		10			9			1				12	7		3	4	6	
41	20	Scarborough	1-3	Flounders (p)	2026		2			5		11	12	8	10			9			1				14	7		3	4	6	
42	23	Peterborough United	0-0		5774		2			5		11		8	10			9			1					7		3	4	6	
43	27	CHESTERFIELD	3-0	Daws, Flounders 2	3046		2			5		11	8		10			9			1					7			4	6	12
44	May 4	DARLINGTON	2-1	Flounders, Daws	5769		2			5		11	8	3	10			9			1					7			4	6	
45	7	WREXHAM	2-0	Daws, Lillis	3572		2			5		11	8	3	10			9			1					7			4	6	
46	11	Stockport County	0-5		6212		2			5		11	8	3	10			9			1				12	7		14	4	6	
		Apps				8	46	18	30	46	21	42	34	39	46	7	12	34	3	15	38	17	11	4	9	21	10	9	12	7	1
		Goals						3	2		3	4	2	11	23			14		1		1	1	1			1	1	2		

Two own goals

Play Offs

	Date	Opponent	Score	Scorers	Att	Longden DP	Hicks SJ	Taylor K	Hamilton IR	Lillis MA	Flounders AJ	Daws A	Musselwhite PS	Joyce JP	Humphries G	Hill DM	Hine M	Lister SH
SF1	May 19	BLACKPOOL	1-1	Lillis	6536	2	5	11	12	3	10	9	1	7		8	4	6
SF2	22	Blackpool	1-2	Hill	7596	2	5	11	4	3	10	9	1		6	7	8	12

F.A. Cup

	Date	Opponent	Score	Scorers	Att	Longden DP	Cowling DR	Ward PT	Hicks SJ	Hall RA	Taylor K	Hamilton IR	Lillis MA	Flounders AJ	Miller I	Daws A	Cotton P	Musselwhite PS	Cox NJ	Bramhall J	Powell G
R1	Nov 17	Rochdale	1-1	Hicks	3259	2			5	6	8		3	10		9	4	1	7	11	
rep		ROCHDALE	2-1	Flounders, Lillis	3761	2			5	6	8		3	10		9	4	1	7	11	12
R2	Dec 8	TRANMERE ROVERS	3-2	Ward, Lillis, Flounders	3576	2	11	4	5	6		12	3	10		9	8	1	7		
R3	Jan 5	Brighton & Hove Albion	2-3	Flounders (p), Bramhall	7785	2	11	12	5		4	9	3	10	14		8	1	7	6	

R1 replay a.e.t.   Played in R1: G Tucker (at 12).

F.L. Cup (Rumbelows Cup)

	Date	Opponent	Score	Scorers	Att	Litchfield P	Longden DP	Cowling DR	Ward PT	Hicks SJ	Hall RA	Taylor K	Hamilton IR	Lillis MA	Flounders AJ	Marshall G	Miller I	Daws A
R1/1	Aug 28	Carlisle United	0-1		2531	1	2	3	4	5	6	7	8		10	11		9
R1/2	Sep 4	CARLISLE UNITED	1-1	Lillis	2130	1	2	3	4	5	6		8	9	10	11	7	12

Associate Members Cup (Leyland DAF Trophy)

	Date	Opponent	Score	Scorers	Att	Longden DP	Cowling DR	Ward PT	Hicks SJ	Hall RA	Taylor K	Hamilton IR	Lillis MA	Flounders AJ	Miller I	Daws A	Cotton P	Musselwhite PS	Cox NJ	Powell G	Stevenson AJ
PR	Nov 27	Doncaster Rovers	0-1		1394	2	12		5	6	8		3	10			4	1	7	9	11
PR	Dec 18	CHESTERFIELD	3-1	Lillis 2, Taylor	859	2	11		5	6	4		3	10	9		8	1	7		12
R1	Jan 15	Doncaster Rovers	0-0		1635	2	11	8	5	6	4	9		10		12	3	1	7		
R2	29	PRESTON NORTH END	1-4	Flounders	2155	2	11	3	5		4	9		10		8	12	1	7		

R1 won on penalties a.e.t.   Played in R2: G Tucker (at 6).

1991/92   5th in Division 4

No	Date		Opponent	Score	Scorers	Att	Musselwhite PS	Batch N	Joyce JP	Longden DP	Hine M	Hicks SJ	Humphries G	Alexander G	Hamilton IR	Daws A	Buckley JW	Helliwell I	Martin DS	Lister SH	Hyde GS	Hill DM	White JG	Stevenson AJ	Whitehead PM	Marples C	Samways M	Elliott MS
1	Aug	17	Gillingham	0-4		3463		1	2	3	4	5	6	7	8	9	10	11	12									
2		24	DONCASTER ROVERS	3-2	Helliwell, Alexander, Daws	3505	1		2	3	4	5	6	7	8	9	10	11										
3		31	Blackpool	1-2	Buckley	3273	1		2	3			6	7	8	9	10	11	4	12	14							
4	Sep	3	SCARBOROUGH	1-1	Joyce	3185	1		2	3	4	5	6	7	8	9	10	11										
5		7	MAIDSTONE UNITED	2-0	Hill, Daws	2738	1		2	3	4	5	6	7	8	9		11			12	14	10					
6		14	Chesterfield	1-0	Humphries	3338	1		2	3		5	6	7	8	9		11	4		12		10					
7		17	Barnet	2-3	Humphries, White	3094	1		2	3			6	7	8	9		11	4	5		10	12					
8		21	CREWE ALEXANDRA	1-0	Hamilton	3021	1		2	3			6	7	8	9			4	5	12	10	11					
9		28	Wrexham	0-4		1635	1		2	3	14		6	7	8	9	12	11	4	5		10						
10	Oct	5	HEREFORD UNITED	1-1	Daws (p)	2384	1		2	3	8		6	14		9	7	11	4	5		10		12				
11		12	Carlisle United	0-0		1988	1		2	3			6	12	8	9	7	11	4	5		10						
12		19	Northampton Town	1-0	Helliwell	2583	1		2	3			6		8	9	7	11	4	5		10						
13		26	MANSFIELD TOWN	1-4	Daws	3610	1		2	3		5			8	9	7	11	4			10			6			
14	Nov	2	Cardiff City	2-2	Hill, Own goal (Pike)	2356	1		2	3		5		7	8	9	12	11	4	6		10						
15		5	ROCHDALE	6-2	*see below	2331	1		2	3		5		7	8	9		11	4	6		10						
16		9	ROTHERHAM UNITED	1-0	Daws	4175	1		2	3		5		7	8	9		11	4	6		10						
17		23	Lincoln City	2-4	Martin, Alexander	3078	1			3		5		2	8	9	7	11	4	6		10						
18		30	YORK CITY	1-0	Hamilton	2887			2	3		5		7	8	9		11	4	6		10			1			
19	Dec	14	Burnley	1-1	Own goal (Pender)	8422			2	3		5		7	8	9		11	4		6	10	12		1			
20		20	Doncaster Rovers	2-1	Humphries, Alexander	1825			2	3		5		7	8	9		11	4	12		10	14		1			
21		26	GILLINGHAM	2-0	White, Martin	3883			2	3		5	6	7	8	9			4			10	11		1			
22		28	BLACKPOOL	2-1	White 2	4271			2	3		5	6	7	8	9			4		12	10	11		1			
23	Jan	1	Scarborough	1-4	White	2237			2	3		5	6	7	8	9		12	4		14	10	11		1			
24		18	Halifax Town	4-1	White 3, Hamilton	1219			2			5	6	7	8	9		11	4		3	10			1			
25		25	WALSALL	1-1	White	3165			2	3		5	6	7	8			11	4			10	9		1			
26	Feb	8	Mansfield Town	3-1	Alexander, Hamilton (p), White	3496	1		2	3			6	7	8		5	11	4			10	9					
27		11	York City	0-3		2255	1		2	3	14	5		7	8		6	11	4		12	10	9					
28		15	BURNLEY	2-2	Helliwell, White	5303			2	3	12	5		7	8	14	6	11	4			10	9			1		
29	Mar	3	HALIFAX TOWN	1-0	Buckley	2448	1		2	3		5		7	8	12	10	11	4	6			9					
30		7	Walsall	1-2	Buckley	2722	1		2	3		5		7	8	12	10	11	4	6		14	9					
31		10	Rochdale	0-2		2036	1		2	3	7				8	9	10	11	4	6		5	12					
32		14	CARDIFF CITY	1-0	Buckley	2766	1		2	3	7			12	8	9	10	11	4	6		5	14					
33		21	Rotherham United	0-5		4504	1		2	3		5		14	8	9	10	11	4	6		7	12					
34		28	LINCOLN CITY	0-2		3296	1		2	14		5	6	7	8	9	10	11				3	12					
35		31	CHESTERFIELD	2-0	Helliwell, Hamilton (p)	2224				2			6	7	8		10	11	4			3	9				1	5
36	Apr	4	Maidstone United	1-0	Hamilton	1237			2	3			6	7	8		10	11				4	9				1	5
37		11	BARNET	1-1	Hamilton (p)	3361			2	3			6	7	8	12	10	11				4	9				1	5
38		14	NORTHAMPTON T	3-0	Hill, Buckley, Daws	2286			2	3			6	12	8	9	10	11	7			4					1	5
39		18	Crewe Alexandra	1-1	Helliwell	3313			2	3			6		8	9	10	11	7			4					1	5
40		20	WREXHAM	3-1	Joyce, Hamilton (p), Buckley	2900			2	3			6		8		10	11	7			4	9				1	5
41		25	Hereford United	2-1	Helliwell 2	1587			2	3			6		8	12	10	11	7			4					1	5
42	May	2	CARLISLE UNITED	4-0	Elliott, Daws, Hill, Helliwell	3853			2	3			6		8	9	10	11	7			4					1	5

Scorers in game 15: Hamilton, A Brown (og), Lister, Helliwell, Alexander, Hill

| | | | | | | Apps | 24 | 1 | 40 | 41 | 10 | 21 | 32 | 36 | 41 | 36 | 28 | 39 | 37 | 19 | 8 | 37 | 22 | 2 | 8 | 1 | 8 | 8 |
| | | | | | | Goals | | | 2 | | | | 3 | 5 | 9 | 7 | 6 | 9 | 2 | 1 | | 5 | 11 | | | | | 1 |

Three own goals

Play Offs

	Date		Opponent	Score	Scorers	Att	Musselwhite PS	Batch N	Joyce JP	Longden DP	Hine M	Hicks SJ	Humphries G	Alexander G	Hamilton IR	Daws A	Buckley JW	Helliwell I	Martin DS	Lister SH	Hyde GS	Hill DM	White JG	Stevenson AJ	Whitehead PM	Marples C	Samways M	Elliott MS
SF1	May	10	Crewe Alexandra	2-2	Helliwell 2	6083			2	3			6	12	8	9	10	11	7			4					1	5
SF2		13	CREWE ALEXANDRA	2-0	Martin, Hamilton	7938			2	3			6		8	9	10	11	7			4					1	5

F.A. Cup

	Date		Opponent	Score	Scorers	Att	Musselwhite PS	Batch N	Joyce JP	Longden DP	Hine M	Hicks SJ	Humphries G	Alexander G	Hamilton IR	Daws A	Buckley JW	Helliwell I	Martin DS	Lister SH	Hyde GS	Hill DM	White JG	Stevenson AJ	Whitehead PM	Marples C	Samways M	Elliott MS
R1	Nov	16	ROTHERHAM UNITED	1-1	Helliwell	4511	1			3		5		2	8	9	7	11	4	6	12	10	14					
rep		26	Rotherham United	3-3	Helliwell, Daws, White	4829	1			3	12	5		2	8	9	7	11	4	6		10	14					

Lost on penalties a.e.t.

F.L. Cup (Rumbelows Cup)

	Date		Opponent	Score	Scorers	Att	Musselwhite PS	Batch N	Joyce JP	Longden DP	Hine M	Hicks SJ	Humphries G	Alexander G	Hamilton IR	Daws A	Buckley JW	Helliwell I	Martin DS	Lister SH	Hyde GS	Hill DM	White JG	Stevenson AJ	Whitehead PM	Marples C	Samways M	Elliott MS
R1/1	Aug	20	Wrexham	0-1		1621	1		2	3	4	5	6	7	8	9	10	11		12								
R1/2		27	WREXHAM	3-0	Humphries, Alexander, Helliwell	2125	1		2	3	4	5	6	7	8	9	10	11			12							
R2/1	Sep	24	LEEDS UNITED	0-0		8392	1		2	3			6	7	8	9		11	4	5		10						
R2/2	Oct	8	Leeds United	0-3		14558	1		2	3	14			12	8	9	7	11	4	5		10			6			

Associate Members Cup (Autoglass Trophy)

	Date		Opponent	Score	Scorers	Att	Musselwhite PS	Batch N	Joyce JP	Longden DP	Hine M	Hicks SJ	Humphries G	Alexander G	Hamilton IR	Daws A	Buckley JW	Helliwell I	Martin DS	Lister SH	Hyde GS	Hill DM	White JG	Stevenson AJ	Whitehead PM	Marples C	Samways M	Elliott MS
PR	Oct	22	BURY	1-3	Hamilton	1122	1		2	3			6	14	8	9	7	11	4	5	12	10						
PR	Jan	7	Halifax Town	2-0	White, Alexander	646			2	3		5		7	8	9			4	6		10	11		1			
R1		21	Hartlepool United	1-2	Hamilton	1351				2		5	6	7	8		12	11	4		9	3	10		1			

76

1992/93   14th in the new Football League Division 3

#	Date		Opponent	Res	Scorers	Att	Samways M	Stevenson AJ	Longden DP	Hill DM	Elliott MS	Humphries G	Martin DS	Alexander G	Daws A	Buckley JW	Helliwell I	White JG	Whitehead PM	Goodacre SD	Greaves SR	Broddle JR	McCullagh PA	Joyce JP	Charles S	Farrell D	Duffy DG	Constable S	Crisp RI	Platnauer NR	Foy DL	Thompstone IP	Wilmott R	Maxwell J
1	Aug	22	Halifax Town	0-0		1793	1	2	3	4	5	6	7	8	9	10	11	12																
2		29	SHREWSBURY TOWN	1-1	Alexander	3438	1	2	3	4	5	6	7	8	9	10	11																	
3	Sep	1	WALSALL	2-0	Elliott, Helliwell	2828	1	2	3	4	5	6	7	8	9		11	10																
4		5	Lincoln City	0-1		3764		2	3	4	5	6	7	8	9		11	10	1															
5		12	Northampton Town	0-1		1961		2	3	4	5	6	7	8	9		11	10	1	12	14												
6		19	CREWE ALEXANDRA	3-3	Goodacre, Humphries, Daws (p)	2995		2	3		5	6	7	8	9		11	12	1	10	14	4												
7		26	Carlisle United	2-0	Helliwell 2	4472		2	3		5		7	8			11	9	1	10		4	6											
8	Oct	3	Chesterfield	2-1	Goodacre, White	3552		2	3		5			8	12		11	9	1	10	7	4	6											
9		10	YORK CITY	1-2	White	4114		2	3		5			8	12	14	11	9	1	10	7	4	6											
10		17	Barnet	0-3		2924		2	3		5		7	8	12	14	11	9	1	10			4											
11		24	COLCHESTER UNITED	3-1	Daws, Martin, Helliwell	2473		6	3		5		4	8	7	10	11	9	1					2										
12		31	Cardiff City	0-3		6027	1	6	3		5		4	8	7	10	11	9		14	12			2										
13	Nov	3	Wrexham	2-0	Stevenson, Buckley	2759	1	6	3		5		4	8	9	10	11				7			2										
14		7	DONCASTER ROVERS	0-1		4451	1	6	3		5		4	8	9	10	11	12		14	7			2										
15		21	Torquay United	1-0	Helliwell	1860	1		3		5	6		4	9		11	10			7			2	8									
16		28	SCARBOROUGH	1-2	McCullagh	2807	1				5	6	8	4	9		11	10			7			2	8									
17	Dec	12	HEREFORD UNITED	3-1	Alexander, Elliott 2	1970	1		3		5	6		4	9		11			10	7			2	8									
18		19	Darlington	2-2	White 2	1801	1	6	3		5		7	4	9		11	10						2	8									
19		26	Rochdale	0-2		3043	1	6	3		5	8	7	4	9		11	10						2										
20		28	GILLINGHAM	2-2	Daws 2 (1 p)	2835	1	6	3		5	12	7	4	9	10	11	8						2										
21	Jan	16	CARLISLE UNITED	0-0		2570	1		3		5	6	4	10	11	7	9	8		12				2										
22		26	Shrewsbury Town	1-2	Helliwell	2190	1		3		5	6	4	10	8	7	9	14		12				2		11								
23		30	HALIFAX TOWN	4-1	Helliwell 2, Martin, Buckley	2480	1		3		5	6	4	10	8	7	9	14		12				2		11								
24	Feb	13	LINCOLN CITY	1-1	Stevenson	3748	1		3			6	4	10		7	9	8						2		11			5	12				
25		20	Walsall	2-3	Stevenson, Helliwell	2935	1		3			6	4	10		7	9	8						2		11			5	12				
26		27	York City	1-5	Farrell	2990	1		3		5	6		4		7	9	8		14				2					12	10	11			
27	Mar	6	CHESTERFIELD	0-1		2725	1		3		5	6		4	7	11	9	8		12				2						10				
28		9	BURY	2-0	Alexander, Platnauer	2589	1		11		5	6	4	7	9		8			12				2					10	3				
29		13	Doncaster Rovers	1-0	Elliott	2760	1		11		5	6	4	7	9		8			12				2					10	3				
30		20	WREXHAM	0-0		3282	1		11		5	6	4		9		8							2					10	3	7			
31		23	Scarborough	2-1	White, Alexander	2007	1		11		5	6	4	7	9		8							2					10	3				
32		27	TORQUAY UNITED	2-2	Alexander, Elliott	2588	1	3	11		5	6	4	7	9		8			14				2					10			12		
33		30	NORTHAMPTON T	5-0	Elliott, Goodacre 2, Helliwell, Thompstone	2307	1		11		5	6	4	7	9		8							2					12	3		10		1
34	Apr	3	Bury	0-0		2509	1		11		5	6	4	7	9		8							2					12	3		10		1
35		6	Hereford United	2-2	Helliwell, Goodacre	1740	1		11		5	6		7	9		12			8				2		4	14		3	10				1
36		10	ROCHDALE	5-1	Helliwell, Goodacre 2, Platnauer, Martin	2926	1		11		5	6	4	7	9		12			8				2			14		3	10				
37		12	Gillingham	1-1	Thompstone	3763	1		11		5	6	4	7	9		12			8				2					3			10		
38		17	DARLINGTON	1-3	Goodacre	2774	1		11		5	6	4	7	9		12			8				2						3	14	10		
39		20	Crewe Alexandra	0-1		3006	1		11		5	6	4	7			12	9		8				2						3		10		
40		24	BARNET	2-0	Goodacre, Helliwell	2810	1		11			6	4	7	9		6			8	5			2				12				10		
41	May	1	Colchester United	0-1		3421	1				5		4	7	9		8			6				2		11			3	12	10			14
42		8	CARDIFF CITY	0-3		7407	1		11		5	6	4	7	9		8							2					3			10		12
			Apps				31	25	20	19	39	30	38	41	24	15	41	37	8	21	15	5	5	30	4	5	4	7	8	14	3	11	3	2
			Goals					3			6	1	3	5	4	2	13	5		9			1			1				2		2		

Played in game 10: TJ Ryan (at 6).

F.A. Cup

Rd	Date		Opponent	Res	Scorers	Att	Samways M	Stevenson AJ	Longden DP	Hill DM	Elliott MS	Humphries G	Martin DS	Alexander G	Daws A	Buckley JW	Helliwell I	White JG	Whitehead PM	Goodacre SD	Greaves SR	Broddle JR	McCullagh PA	Joyce JP	Charles S	Farrell D
R1	Nov	14	HUDDERSFIELD TOWN	0-0		4312	1	6	3		5	12	4		9	10	11	8			7			2		
ep		25	Huddersfield Town	1-2	Buckley	4841	1		3		5	6	8	4	9	12	11	10			7			2		

Replay a.e.t.

F.L. Cup (Coca Cola Cup)

Rd	Date		Opponent	Res	Scorers	Att	Samways M	Stevenson AJ	Longden DP	Hill DM	Elliott MS	Humphries G	Martin DS	Alexander G	Daws A	Buckley JW	Helliwell I	White JG	Whitehead PM	Goodacre SD	Greaves SR	Broddle JR	McCullagh PA	Joyce JP
1/1	Aug	18	Darlington	1-1	Helliwell	1489	1		3	4	5	6	7	8	9	10	11							2
1/2		25	DARLINGTON	2-0	Daws, Alexander	2299	1	2	3	4	5	6	7	8	9	10	11							
2/1	Sep	22	Leeds United	1-4	Helliwell	10113		2	3		5		7	8	9		11		1	10		4	6	
2/2	Oct	27	LEEDS UNITED	2-2	Helliwell 2	7419		6	3		5			8	7	10	11	9	1	12		4		2

Associate Members Cup (Autoglass Trophy)

Rd	Date		Opponent	Res	Scorers	Att	Samways M	Stevenson AJ	Longden DP	Hill DM	Elliott MS	Humphries G	Martin DS	Alexander G	Daws A	Buckley JW	Helliwell I	White JG	Whitehead PM	Goodacre SD	Greaves SR	Broddle JR	McCullagh PA	Joyce JP	Charles S	Farrell D	Duffy DG	Constable S	Crisp RI
R1	Dec	8	Rotherham United	1-3	Goodacre	1634	1		3		5	6		4	9		11	12		10	7			2	8				
R1		14	LINCOLN CITY	2-2	Clarke (og), Alexander	1263	1	12	3		5	6		4	9		11	10			7			2	8				
R2	Feb	2	Rochdale	2-1	Daws 2	1312	1		3		5	6	4	10	8	7	9							2		11			
QF		9	Wigan Athletic	1-2	Humphries (p)	1516	1		3		5	6	4	10	9	7	8			12	14			2		11			

1993/94   11th in Division 3

No	Date	Opponents	Score	Scorers	Att	Samways M	Thompstone IP	Mudd PA	Carmichael M	Elliott MS	Bradley R	Alexander G	Martin DS	Trebble ND	Thorber SJ	Smith MC	Hope CJ	Goodacre SD	Juryeff IM	Toman JA	Watson JI	White JG	Knill AR	Henderson DR	Sansam C	Bullimore WA	Danzey MJ	Ryan TJ	Heath M
1	Aug 14	Wigan Athletic	2-0	Mudd, Smith	2353	1	2	3	4	5	6	7	8	9		10	11	12	14										
2	21	BURY	1-1	Thompstone	3375	1	7	3	2	5		14	4	12		11	6	8	9	10									
3	28	Mansfield Town	1-0	Toman	2751	1	7	3	8	5		2	4			11	6	12	9	10									
4	31	Walsall	0-0		2519	1	7	3	8	5		2	4	12	11		6		9	10									
5	Sep 4	HEREFORD UNITED	1-2	Thompstone	3091	1	7	3	8	5		2	4	14	12	11	6		9	10									
6	11	Chester City	2-0	Toman, Juryeff	2195	1	7	3	11	5	6	2	8	12			4		9	10									
7	18	CARLISLE UNITED	2-1	Carmichael 2	3361	1	7	3	11	5	6	2	8				12	4	9	10	14								
8	25	Gillingham	0-1		2872	1	2	3	11	5	6	7	8	14	10	12			9										
9	Oct 2	SCARBOROUGH	1-1	Thompstone	2910	1	7	3	4	5	6	2	8	11			12		9	10									
10	9	Colchester United	1-2	Carmichael	3405	1	7	3	4	5	6	2	8	14		9	10		11			12							
11	16	NORTHAMPTON T	7-0	Carmichael 3, Thompstone, Smith 2, Elliott	2814	1	7	3	9	5	6	2	8			11	4		14	10		12							
12	23	Torquay United	1-1	Toman	3241	1	7	3	9	5	6	2	8		11		4			10	12	14							
13	30	DARLINGTON	3-0	Carmichael (p), Alexander, Trebble	3025	1	7	3	9	5	6	2		11	8		4			10	12	14							
14	Nov 1	Doncaster Rovers	1-3	Trebble	4439	1	7	3	9	5	6	2		11	8		4			10	14	12							
15	6	WYCOMBE WANDERERS	0-0		3604	1	7	3	9		6	2	8		14		4			10	11	12	5						
16	20	Shrewsbury Town	0-0		2436	1	7	3	9		6	2				11	4	12		10			5						
17	27	ROCHDALE	2-1	Toman, Thompstone	3106	1	7	3	9		6	2				11	4	12		10			5	14					
18	Dec 11	Bury	0-1		2389	1	7	3	9		6	2				11	4						5	10					
19	18	WIGAN ATHLETIC	1-0	Carmichael	2873	1		3	9		6	2				11	4	12	14				5	10	7				
20	27	Lincoln City	0-2		6030	1		3	9		6	2				10	7	4	11				5	12					
21	28	CHESTERFIELD	2-2	Carmichael (p), Mudd	3266	1		3	9		6	2					4	12					5	11	7	10			
22	Jan 1	Preston North End	2-2	Knill, Carmichael	7669	1		12	9		6	2	8	3			4						5	10	7	14			
23	3	WALSALL	5-0	Martin, Smith, Bullimore, Carmichael, Henderson	3417	1		12	9		6		8	7		11	4					3	5	10	14	2			
24	22	COLCHESTER UNITED	1-1	Carmichael	2854	1	7	3	9		6	2				11	4						5	8	12	10			
25	29	Darlington	1-2	Carmichael	2142	1	7	3	9		6	2					4						5	11		10			
26	Feb 5	TORQUAY UNITED	1-3	Carmichael	2755	1		3	9		6	2	8				4						5	7	12	10	11		
27	12	Crewe Alexandra	3-3	Martin, Carmichael, Danzey	3507	1		3	9		6	2	8	12		11	4						5	7			10		
28	19	MANSFIELD TOWN	2-3	Carmichael 2	3089	1		3	9		6	2	8	12									5	7			10		
29	Mar 5	CHESTER CITY	1-1	Mudd	2669	1	7	3	9		6	2	8	11	10	12	4		14				5						
30	8	Northampton Town	0-4		3192	1	2	10	6			7	8		3		4						5	9		11			
31	12	Carlisle United	1-3	Goodacre	4076	1		3	6			2			10	11	4		7			9	5	14	12	8			
32	15	CREWE ALEXANDRA	2-1	Alexander, Thomber	2122	1		3	6			2	8		11		4		7			9	5	14	12	10			
33	19	GILLINGHAM	1-1	Juryeff	2386	1		3	6			2	8		11		4		7			9	5	14	12	10			
34	26	Scarborough	1-0	Smith	1571	1	3		6	5		2			10	11	4		7			9				8			
35	29	Hereford United	2-1	Carmichael, Juryeff	1429	1	3		6	5		2			10	11	4		7			9				8	12		
36	Apr 2	LINCOLN CITY	2-0	Alexander, Goodacre	3571	1	3		6	5		2			10	11	4		7			9				8			
37	4	Chesterfield	1-1	Alexander	3629	1	3		6	5		2			10		4		7			9	11	14		8			12
38	9	PRESTON NORTH END	3-1	Smith, Bradley, Bullimore	3790	1	3		6	5		2	8		11		4		7			9				10			
39	16	DONCASTER ROVERS	1-3	Goodacre	4151	1	3		6	5		2			10	11	9	12					4		7	8			
40	23	Wycombe Wanderers	2-2	Smith, Bullimore (p)	5755				6	5		2			10	11	3	12	9				4		7	8		1	
41	30	SHREWSBURY TOWN	1-4	Juryeff	4587	1			6	5		2			10	11	3	12	9				4		7	8			
42	May 7	Rochdale	3-2	Thomber, Juryeff 2	3118	1	3		6	5		2			10	11	12		7			9	4			8			
	Apps					41	30	33	42	14	34	41	26	14	24	30	41	18	23	15	5	9	25	20	10	18	3	1	2
	Goals						5	3	18	1	1	4	2	2	2	7		3	6	4			1	1		3	1		

F.A. Cup

R	Date	Opponents	Score	Scorers	Att	Samways M	Thompstone IP	Mudd PA	Carmichael M	Elliott MS	Bradley R	Alexander G	Martin DS	Trebble ND	Thorber SJ	Smith MC	Hope CJ	Goodacre SD	Juryeff IM	Toman JA	Watson JI	White JG	Knill AR	Henderson DR	Sansam C	Bullimore WA
R1	Nov 13	Accrington Stanley	3-2	Toman, Goodacre 2	5858	1	7	3	6			2	8			11	4	12		10		9	5			
R2	Dec 4	Walsall	1-1	Carmichael	4962	1	7	3	9		6	2	8			11	4			10		12	5			
rep	14	WALSALL	0-0		3300	1	7	3	9		6	2	8	14	12	4		10	11				5			
R3	Jan 8	Wimbledon	0-3		4944	1		3	9		6	2	8	7		11	4					12	5		10	

R2 replay won on penalties a.e.t.

F.L. Cup (Coca Cola Cup)

R	Date	Opponents	Score	Scorers	Att	Samways M	Thompstone IP	Mudd PA	Carmichael M	Elliott MS	Bradley R	Alexander G	Martin DS	Trebble ND	Thorber SJ	Smith MC	Hope CJ	Goodacre SD	Juryeff IM	Toman JA	Watson JI	White JG
R1/1	Aug 17	Shrewsbury Town	0-1		1939	1	2	3	4	5		7	8			10	11	6	12		14	9
R1/2	24	SHREWSBURY TOWN	1-1	Martin	2320	1	7	3		5		2	4	12		11	6	8		10		9

Associate Members Cup (Autoglass Trophy)

R	Date	Opponents	Score	Scorers	Att	Samways M	Thompstone IP	Mudd PA	Carmichael M	Elliott MS	Bradley R	Alexander G	Martin DS	Trebble ND	Thorber SJ	Smith MC	Hope CJ	Goodacre SD	Juryeff IM	Toman JA	Watson JI	White JG	Knill AR	Henderson DR	Sansam C
R1	Sep 27	Scarborough	2-2	Carmichael 2 (1 p)	412	1		3	7	5	6	2	8	10			4			9					12
R1	Oct 19	HULL CITY	1-1	Carmichael	2366	1		3	9	5	6	2	8				4			7	10	12	14		
R2	Dec 1	Scarborough	2-0	Carmichael 2	679	1	7	3	9		6	2			10	11	4					12	5		
QF	Jan 11	Stockport County	0-2		4404	1		3	9		6	2		12		11	4			7			5		10

Played in R2: KA Jobling (at 8).

1994/95   7th in Division 3

#	Date	Opponent	Score	Scorers	Att	Samways M	Ford T	Mudd PA	Thornber SJ	Knill AR	Bradley R	Alexander G	Bullimore WA	Juryeff IM	Henderson DR	Smith MC	Carmichael M	Goodacre SD	Hope CJ	Martin DS	Thompstone IP	Sansam C	Nicholson M	Eyre JR	Young SR	Eli R	Turnbull LM	Gregory NR	Kiwomya AD	Housham SJ	Walsh MS
1	Aug 13	Barnet	2-1	Henderson, Juryeff	2221	1	2	3	4	5	6	7	8	9	10	11															
2	20	FULHAM	1-2	Juryeff	3165	1	2	3	4	5	6	7	8	9	10	11	12	14													
3	27	NORTHAMPTON T	1-1	Bradley	2499	1	2	3	4		6	7	8	9	10	11	12		5	14											
4	30	GILLINGHAM	3-0	Thornber, Henderson, Smith	2098	1	2	3	4	5	6	7	8		10	11			9	12											
5	Sep 3	CARLISLE UNITED	2-3	Juryeff, Thornber	3217	1	2	3	4	5	6	7	8	9	10	11			12	14											
6	10	Bury	0-2		2540	1	4	3		5	6	7	8	9	10	11	2														
7	13	Darlington	3-1	Bullimore, Ford, Alexander	2181	1	4	3		5	6	7	8	9	10	11	2			12											
8	17	BARNET	1-0	Juryeff	2481	1	2	3	4	5	6	7	8	9	10	11															
9	24	WIGAN ATHLETIC	3-1	Thornber, Alexander, Bullimore (p)	2602	1	2	3	4	5	6	7	8	9	10	11															
10	Oct 1	Hereford United	1-2	Bradley	2234	1	2	3	4	5	6	7	8	9	10	11			14	12											
11	8	Preston North End	1-0	Alexander	6895	1	2	3	4	5	6	7	8	9	10						11										
12	15	WALSALL	0-1		3609	1	2	3	4	5	6	7	8	9	10		12				11		14								
13	22	Exeter City	2-2	Henderson, Juryeff	2511	1	2	3	4	5	6	7		9	10	11		14	8		12										
14	29	HARTLEPOOL UNITED	0-0		2624	1	2	3	4	5	6	7		9	10	11	12	14	8												
15	Nov 5	Torquay United	1-1	Juryeff	3036	1	2	3	4	5	6	7		9	10	11	12		8												
16	19	MANSFIELD TOWN	3-4	Bullimore, Nicholson, Juryeff	2975	1	4	3		5	6	7	8	9					2				10		11						
17	26	Colchester United	2-4	Thornber, Knill	2904	1	2	3	4	5		7	8	9			6		12				14	10	11						
18	Dec 10	Fulham	0-1		3358	1	2	3	4	5	6	7	8	9	10	11	12				14										
19	16	Northampton Town	1-0	Knill	3841	1	2	3	4	5	6	7	8	9		11	14				12				10						
20	26	LINCOLN CITY	2-0	Juryeff, Eyre	4785	1	2	3	4	5	6	7	8	9		11	14				12			10							
21	27	Doncaster Rovers	1-1	Carmichael	3852	1	2	3	4	5	6	7	8	9		11	14				12			10							
22	31	ROCHDALE	4-1	Mudd, Bullimore (p), Eyre, Thompstone	2653	1	2	3	4		6	7	8			11	5		12					10	9						
23	Jan 7	EXETER CITY	3-0	Eyre 2, Alexander	2463	1	2	3	4		6	7	8			11	5							10	9						
24	14	Chesterfield	1-3	Bullimore (p)	3245	1	2	3	4	5	6	7	8			11	14		12					10	9						
25	21	TORQUAY UNITED	3-2	Smith, Eyre, Carmichael	2229	1	2	3	4	5	6	7	8			11	12							10	9						
26	28	Hartlepool United	4-1	Knill, Young, Thornber, Eyre	1660	1	2	3	4	5		7	8			11	6		12				14	10	9						
27	Feb 4	COLCHESTER UNITED	3-4	Ford, Bullimore, Eyre	2748	1	2	3	4	5		7	8				6		12				14	11	10						
28	18	CHESTERFIELD	0-1		3566	1	2		4	5		7	10				6	3	8						11		12				
29	21	Mansfield Town	0-1		3079	1	2		4	5		7	12				6	3	8				10		11	14			9		
30	25	HEREFORD UNITED	1-0	Nicholson	2193	1	2	3	4	5		7	8				12		6				10		11				9		
31	28	Scarborough	0-3		1179	1	2	3	4	5		7			14	11	12		6				9		10		8				
32	Mar 11	BURY	3-2	Gregory 2, Hughes(og)	2767	1	2	3	4	5							12		6		7			9	11		8	10			
33	18	Gillingham	2-2	Young, Turnbull	2501	1	2	3	4	5		7			14		12		6					9	11		8	10			
34	25	Carlisle United	1-2	Kiwomya	6704	1	2	3	4	5		7					6								9		8	10	11		
35	Apr 1	DARLINGTON	2-1	Gregory 2	2449	1	2	3	4	5		7					6		12						9		8	10	11		
36	4	Wigan Athletic	0-0		1307	1		3	4	5		7					6		2						9		8	10	11		
37	8	Rochdale	2-1	Turnbull, Kiwomya	1720	1		3	4	5		7					6		2					9		14	8	10	11		
38	15	DONCASTER ROVERS	0-5		4366	1			4	5	12	7	9				6	3					2			14	8	10	11		
39	17	Lincoln City	3-3	Turnbull, Gregory, Nicholson	3330	1			5		7	4					6	3							9		8	10	11	2	
40	22	SCARBOROUGH	3-1	Gregory, Kiwomya, Nicholson	2079	1	7		4	5			8				6						14		9			10	11	2	3
41	29	Walsall	1-2	Gregory	4539	1	7		4	5			8				6				12		14		9			10	11	2	3
42	May 6	PRESTON NORTH END	2-1	Ford, Knill	3691	1	7		4	5			8				6				12		14	10	9				11	2	3
		Apps				42	38	35	37	39	25	40	35	21	17	32	20	5	24	5	19	6	15	9	14	2	10	10	9	4	3
		Goals					2	1	5	4	2	4	6	8	3	2	2				1		4	8	2		3	7	3		

One own goal

F.A. Cup

Rd	Date	Opponent	Score	Scorers	Att	Samways M	Ford T	Mudd PA	Thornber SJ	Knill AR	Bradley R	Alexander G	Bullimore WA	Juryeff IM	Henderson DR	Smith MC	Carmichael M	Goodacre SD	Hope CJ	Martin DS	Thompstone IP	Sansam C	Nicholson M
R1	Nov 12	Bradford City	1-1	Hope	5468	1	8	3		5	6	7	4	9		11			2		10		
rep	22	BRADFORD CITY	3-2	Carmichael, Alexander, Thompstone	4514	1	4	3	11	5	6	7	8	9			12		2		14		10
R2	Dec 2	Birmingham City	0-0		13832	1	2	3	4	5	6	7	8	9	10	11	12				14		
rep	14	BIRMINGHAM CITY	1-2	Bullimore	6280	1	2	3	4	5	6	7	8	9		11	12				10	14	

R1 replay a.e.t.

F.L. Cup (Coca Cola Cup)

Rd	Date	Opponent	Score	Scorers	Att	Samways M	Ford T	Mudd PA	Thornber SJ	Knill AR	Bradley R	Alexander G	Bullimore WA	Juryeff IM	Henderson DR	Smith MC	Carmichael M	Goodacre SD	Hope CJ	Martin DS
R1/1	Aug 16	HUDDERSFIELD TOWN	2-1	Henderson, Bullimore	2841	1	2	3	4	5	6	7	8	9	10	11				
R1/2	23	Huddersfield Town	0-3		6455	1	2	3		5	6	7	8	9	10	11	12	14	4	

Associate Members Cup (Auto Windscreen Trophy)

Rd	Date	Opponent	Score	Scorers	Att	Samways M	Ford T	Mudd PA	Thornber SJ	Knill AR	Bradley R	Alexander G	Bullimore WA	Juryeff IM	Henderson DR	Smith MC	Carmichael M	Goodacre SD	Hope CJ	Martin DS	Thompstone IP	Sansam C	Nicholson M	Housham SJ
R1	Sep 27	ROTHERHAM UNITED	1-3	Alexander	1404	1	2	3	4	5	6	7	8		10	11			9		12		14	
R1	Nov 8	Chesterfield	1-1	Bullimore (pen)	1424	1			6	5	3	7	8			11	9	10	2		4	14		12

1995/96 12th in Division 3

Player columns (left to right): Samways M, Walsh MS, Wilson PA, Thomber SJ, Knill AR, Bradley R, Ford T, Turnbull LM, McFarlane AA, Eyre JR, Nicholson M, Hope CJ, Bullimore WA, Young SR, Housham SJ, Graham DWT, Sansam C, Murfin AJ, Varadi I, Paterson JR, Clarkson PI, D'Auria DA, Jones RA, Butler LS, Germaine GP, O'Halloran KJ

#	Date	Opponent	Score	Scorers	Att	Sam	Wal	Wil	Tho	Kni	Bra	For	Tur	McF	Eyr	Nic	Hop	Bul	You	Hou	Gra	San	Mur	Var	Pat	Cla	DAu	Jon	But	Ger	OHa
1	Aug 12	CAMBRIDGE UNITED	1-2	Eyre	2561	1	2	3	4	5	6	7	8	9	10	11															
2	19	Wigan Athletic	1-2	Turnbull	3153	1	2	3	4		6	7	8	9	10	11	5		12	14	13										
3	26	BARNET	2-0	Thomas (og), McFarlane	1970	1		3	4	7	6			9	10	11	5		8		2										
4	28	Lincoln City	2-2	Graham, Eyre	2674	1		3	4	7	6			9	10	11	5		8		2	12									
5	Sep 2	Exeter City	0-1		2893	1	3		4	5				9	10			6	8	12		2	7	11							
6	9	GILLINGHAM	1-1	Hope	2423	1		3	4	5	6	12		9	10	11	7		8	13	2										
7	12	CHESTER CITY	0-2		1875	1		3	4	5	6	12		9	10	11	7		8	14	2	13									
8	16	Preston North End	2-2	Bullimore (p), Sansam	7397	1	2	3		5	14	4	12	10	11	6	8	9	7			13									
9	23	Mansfield Town	1-1	McFarlane	2478	1	2	3		5	14	4	12	10	11	6	8	9	7			13									
10	30	COLCHESTER UNITED	1-0	Eyre	2051	1		3	8	5	6	4	14	10	13		2	9	7			11			12						
11	Oct 7	NORTHAMPTON T	0-0		2455	1		3	8	5	6	4	13	10	12		2	9	7			11			14						
12	14	Hartlepool United	0-2		2603	1		3	8	5	6	4	13	10		2	12	9	7			14			11						
13	21	LEYTON ORIENT	2-0	Paterson, Hope	2315	1		3	6	5		4		9	10	13	2	8	12	7					11						
14	28	Torquay United	8-1	McFarlane 4, Eyre 2, Knill, Ford	2137	1	12	3	7	5		4		9	10	14	6	8	13		2				11						
15	31	Cardiff City	1-0	McFarlane	2159	1	12	3	7	5	6	4		9	10	13					2				11	8					
16	Nov 4	ROCHDALE	1-3	Ford	3003	1		3	7	5	6	4		9	10				12		2				11	8					
17	18	Darlington	0-0		2078	1	2	3	12	5	6	4		9	10				8						11	7					
18	25	SCARBOROUGH	3-3	Ford, Clarkson, Bullimore	2231	1	2	3		5	6	4		9	10	13	12	8							11	7					
19	Dec 9	MANSFIELD TOWN	1-1	McFarlane	2552	1	2	3			6	4	12	9	10		7	5	13						11		8				
20	16	Colchester United	1-2	Young	2138	1	2	3			6	4	7	9			12	5	10						11		8				
21	19	Hereford United	0-3		2588	1	2	3	13		6	4	7	9			12	5	10						11		8				
22	Jan 13	WIGAN ATHLETIC	3-1	Jones, D'Auria, McFarlane	2288	1	2	3			6	4	13	9	10		12	5							11		8	7			
23	20	Cambridge United	2-1	McFarlane, Wilson (p)	2413	1	2	3			6	4	13	9	10	12	5								11		8	7			
24	23	Plymouth Argyle	3-1	Hope, Turnbull, McFarlane	4712	1	2	3			6	4	10	9			11	5		12							8	7			
25	30	Fulham	3-1	D'Auria, Jones, Paterson	2176	1	2	3		5		4	10	9			12	6		13					11		8	7			
26	Feb 3	Barnet	0-1		1674	1	2	3		6			4	10	9		12	8	5			13			11			7			
27	10	PLYMOUTH ARGYLE	1-1	McFarlane	2789		2	3		5	6	12		9	10										11	4	8	7	1		
28	17	Chester City	0-3		2401		2	3			6	4		9			12	5							11	10	8	7	1		
29	24	PRESTON NORTH END	1-2	Jones	3638	1	2			5	6	4		9	13	14	3			12					11	10	8	7			
30	27	Gillingham	0-0		5547	1				5	6	4		9	10		2			3					11	7	8				
31	Mar 2	Bury	0-3		3035	1	13			5	6	4	14	9	10	12	2			3					11	8	7				
32	5	LINCOLN CITY	2-3	Eyre, Clarkson	2411	1	2	3		5	6	4	13	9	10	12									11	8	7				
33	9	HEREFORD UNITED	0-1		1903		2	3		5	6	4	13	9	10	12	14								11	8	7		1		
34	16	Doncaster Rovers	0-2		1920		2	3		5	6	4	12	9	10	11	7								13	8			1		
35	23	FULHAM	3-1	Knill, Ford, D'Auria	1919		3			5	6	4	7	9	10		2			12					11	8			1		
36	26	EXETER CITY	4-0	Eyre 2, Ford, McFarlane	1615			3		5	6	4	7	9	10		2								12	8					11
37	30	Northampton Town	2-1	Clarkson, McFarlane	4290			3		5	6	4	7	9	10		2								11	8			1		
38	Apr 2	HARTLEPOOL UNITED	2-1	Ford, Bradley	2100			3		5	6	4		9	10		2								11	8			1		7
39	6	TORQUAY UNITED	1-0	Ford	2247			3		5	6		4	9	10	13	2			6					12	11	8		1		7
40	8	Leyton Orient	0-0		2814			3		5				7	9	10	12			6					4	11	8		1		
41	13	CARDIFF CITY	1-1	Knill	2044			3		5		4	7	9	10	13	2								12	11	8		1		6
42	16	BURY	1-2	Nicholson	2132			3		5	6	4	7	9		13	2								11	12	8		1		10
43	20	Rochdale	1-1	Clarkson	1654			3		5	6		7	9		12	2			13					10	11	8		1		4
44	23	DONCASTER ROVERS	2-2	Turnbull, Clarkson	2614	1				5	6		7	9	10	12	2			3					4	11	8				13
45	27	Scarborough	4-1	McFarlane, Clarkson, D'Auria 2	1738	1		3		5	6		7	9	12	10	2			4					13	11	8		1		
46	May 4	DARLINGTON	3-3	Eyre 2, McFarlane	4847			3		5	6			9	10	12	2			4					7	11	8		1		
		Apps				33	25	40	16	38	38	38	23	46	39	36	40	14	14	28	3	5	1	2	26	24	27	11	2	11	7
		Goals					1		3	1	7	3	16	10	1	3	2	1				1	1		2	6	5	3			

One own goal

F.A. Cup

	Date	Opponent	Score	Scorers	Att	Sam	Wal	Wil	Tho	Kni	Bra	For	Tur	McF	Eyr	Nic	Hop	Bul	You	Hou	Gra	San	Mur	Var	Pat	Cla	DAu	Jon	But	Ger	OHa
R1	Nov 11	Northwich Victoria	3-1	Ford, McFarlane 2	2685	1		3	7	5	6	4		9	10	12			8		2				11						
R2	Dec 2	SHREWSBURY TOWN	1-1	Eyre	2718	1	2	3			6	4	7	9	10	8	5								11						
rep	12	Shrewsbury Town	1-2	Paterson	3313	1	2	3			6	4	7		10	12	5	8	9						11						

F.L. Cup (Coca Cola Cup)

	Date	Opponent	Score	Scorers	Att	Sam	Wal	Wil	Tho	Kni	Bra	For	Tur	McF	Eyr	Nic	Hop	Bul	You	Hou	Gra	San	Mur	Var	Pat	Cla	DAu	Jon	But	Ger	OHa
R1/1	Aug 15	ROTHERHAM UNITED	4-1	Eyre 2, McFarlane, Ford	2110	1	2	3	4	5	6	7	8	9	10	11	12	13	14												
R1/2	22	Rotherham United	0-5		2206	1	2	3	4		6	7	8	9	10	11	5	13	12												

R1/2 a.e.t.

Associate Members Cup (Auto Windscreens Shield)

	Date	Opponent	Score	Scorers	Att	Sam	Wal	Wil	Tho	Kni	Bra	For	Tur	McF	Eyr	Nic	Hop	Bul	You	Hou	Gra	San	Mur	Var	Pat	Cla	DAu	Jon	But	Ger	OHa
R1	Sep 26	Wigan Athletic	1-1	Housham	1064	1		3	8	5	6	4		9			12	2		10	7			11							
R1	Oct 17	BURY	4-0	McFarlane 2, Matthewson (og), Eyre	877	1		3	5	6	4		9	10	12	2	8	13	7				14		11						
R2	Nov 28	York City	0-3		1734	1	2	3			6	4	7	9	10	12	5	8	13						11						

1980/81 Division 4

1	Southend United	46	19	4	0	47	6	11	3	9	32	25	67
2	Lincoln City	46	15	7	1	44	11	10	8	5	22	14	65
3	Doncaster Rovers	46	15	4	4	36	20	7	8	8	23	29	56
4	Wimbledon	46	15	4	4	42	17	8	5	10	22	29	55
5	Peterborough Utd.	46	11	8	4	37	21	6	10	7	31	33	52
6	Aldershot	46	12	9	2	28	11	6	5	12	15	30	50
7	Mansfield Town	46	13	5	5	36	15	7	4	12	22	29	49
8	Darlington	46	13	6	4	43	23	6	5	12	22	36	49
9	Hartlepool United	46	14	3	6	42	22	6	6	11	22	39	49
10	Northampton Town	46	11	7	5	42	26	7	6	10	23	41	49
11	Wigan Athletic	46	13	4	6	29	16	5	7	11	22	39	47
12	Bury	46	10	8	5	38	21	7	3	13	32	41	45
13	Bournemouth	46	9	8	6	30	21	7	5	11	17	27	45
14	Bradford City	46	9	9	5	30	24	5	7	11	23	36	44
15	Rochdale	46	11	6	6	33	25	3	9	11	27	45	43
16	SCUNTHORPE UNITED	46	8	12	3	40	31	3	8	12	20	38	42
17	Torquay United	46	13	2	8	38	26	5	3	15	17	37	41
18	Crewe Alexandra	46	10	7	6	28	20	3	7	13	20	41	40
19	Port Vale	46	10	8	5	40	23	2	7	14	17	47	39
20	Stockport County	46	10	5	8	29	25	6	2	15	15	32	39
21	Tranmere Rovers	46	12	5	6	41	24	1	5	17	18	49	36
22	Hereford United	46	8	8	7	29	20	3	5	15	9	42	35
23	Halifax Town	46	9	3	11	28	32	2	9	12	16	39	34
24	York City	46	10	2	11	31	23	2	7	14	16	43	33

1981/82 Division 4

1	Sheffield United	46	15	8	0	53	15	12	7	4	41	26	96
2	Bradford City	46	14	7	2	52	23	12	6	5	36	22	91
3	Wigan Athletic	46	17	5	1	47	18	9	8	6	33	28	91
4	Bournemouth	46	12	10	1	37	15	11	9	3	25	15	88
5	Peterborough Utd.	46	16	3	4	46	22	8	7	8	25	35	82
6	Colchester United	46	12	6	5	47	23	8	6	9	35	34	72
7	Port Vale	46	9	12	2	26	17	9	4	10	30	32	70
8	Hull City	46	14	3	6	36	23	5	9	9	34	38	69
9	Bury	46	13	7	3	53	26	4	10	9	27	33	68
10	Hereford United	46	10	9	4	36	25	6	10	7	28	33	67
11	Tranmere Rovers	46	7	9	7	27	25	7	9	7	24	31	60
12	Blackpool	46	11	5	7	40	26	4	8	11	26	34	58
13	Darlington	46	10	5	8	36	28	5	8	10	25	34	58
14	Hartlepool United	46	9	8	6	39	34	4	8	11	34	50	55
15	Torquay United	46	9	8	6	30	25	5	5	13	17	34	55
16	Aldershot	46	8	7	8	34	29	5	8	10	23	39	54
17	York City	46	9	5	9	45	37	5	3	15	24	54	50
18	Stockport County	46	10	5	8	34	28	2	8	13	14	39	49
19	Halifax Town	46	6	11	6	28	30	3	11	9	23	42	49
20	Mansfield Town	46	8	6	9	39	39	5	4	14	24	42	47
21	Rochdale	46	7	9	7	26	22	3	7	13	24	40	46
22	Northampton Town	46	9	5	9	32	27	2	4	17	25	57	42
23	SCUNTHORPE UNITED	46	7	9	7	26	35	2	6	15	17	44	42
24	Crewe Alexandra	46	3	6	14	19	32	3	3	17	10	52	27

1982/83 Division 4

1	Wimbledon	46	17	4	2	57	23	12	7	4	39	22	98
2	Hull City	46	14	8	1	48	14	11	7	5	27	20	90
3	Port Vale	46	15	4	4	37	16	11	6	6	30	18	88
4	SCUNTHORPE UNITED	46	13	7	3	41	17	10	7	6	30	25	83
5	Bury	46	15	4	4	43	20	8	8	7	31	26	81
6	Colchester United	46	17	5	1	51	19	7	4	12	24	36	81
7	York City	46	18	4	1	59	19	4	9	10	29	39	79
8	Swindon Town	46	14	3	6	45	27	5	8	10	16	27	68
9	Peterborough Utd.	46	13	6	4	38	23	4	7	12	20	29	64
10	Mansfield Town	46	11	6	6	32	26	5	7	11	29	44	61
11	Halifax Town	46	9	8	6	31	23	7	4	12	28	43	60
12	Torquay United	46	12	3	8	38	30	5	4	14	18	35	58
13	Chester	46	8	6	9	28	24	7	5	11	27	36	56
14	Bristol City	46	10	8	5	32	25	3	9	11	27	45	56
15	Northampton Town	46	10	8	5	43	29	4	4	15	22	46	54
16	Stockport County	46	11	8	4	41	31	3	4	16	19	48	54
17	Darlington	46	8	5	10	27	30	5	8	10	34	41	52
18	Aldershot	46	11	5	7	40	35	1	10	12	21	47	51
19	Tranmere Rovers	46	8	8	7	30	29	5	3	15	19	42	50
20	Rochdale	46	11	8	4	38	25	0	8	15	17	48	49
21	Blackpool	46	10	8	5	32	23	3	4	16	23	51	49
22	Hartlepool United	46	11	5	7	30	24	2	4	17	16	52	48
23	Crewe Alexandra	46	9	5	9	35	32	2	3	18	18	39	41
24	Hereford United	46	8	6	9	19	23	3	2	18	23	56	41

1983/84 Division 3

1	Oxford United	46	17	5	1	58	22	11	6	6	33	28	95
2	Wimbledon	46	15	5	3	58	35	11	4	8	39	41	87
3	Sheffield United	46	14	7	2	56	18	10	4	9	30	35	83
4	Hull City	46	16	5	2	42	11	7	9	7	29	27	83
5	Bristol Rovers	46	16	5	2	47	21	6	8	9	21	33	79
6	Walsall	46	14	4	5	44	22	8	5	10	24	39	75
7	Bradford City	46	11	9	3	46	30	9	2	12	27	35	71
8	Gillingham	46	13	4	6	50	29	7	6	10	24	40	70
9	Millwall	46	16	4	3	42	18	2	9	12	29	47	67
10	Bolton Wanderers	46	13	4	6	36	17	5	6	12	20	43	64
11	Orient	46	13	5	5	40	27	5	4	14	31	54	63
12	Burnley	46	12	5	6	52	25	4	9	10	24	36	62
13	Newport County	46	11	9	3	35	27	5	5	13	23	48	62
14	Lincoln City	46	11	4	8	42	29	6	6	11	17	33	61
15	Wigan Athletic	46	11	5	7	26	18	5	8	10	20	38	61
16	Preston North End	46	12	5	6	42	27	3	6	14	24	39	56
17	Bournemouth	46	11	5	7	38	27	5	2	16	25	46	55
18	Rotherham United	46	10	5	8	29	17	5	4	14	28	47	54
19	Plymouth Argyle	46	11	8	4	38	17	2	4	17	18	45	51
20	Brentford	46	8	9	6	41	30	3	7	13	28	49	49
21	SCUNTHORPE UNITED	46	9	9	5	40	31	0	10	13	14	42	46
22	Southend United	46	8	9	6	34	24	2	5	16	21	52	44
23	Port Vale	46	10	4	9	33	29	1	6	16	18	54	43
24	Exeter City	46	4	8	11	27	39	2	7	14	23	45	33

1984/85 Division 4

1	Chesterfield	46	16	6	1	40	13	10	7	6	24	22	91
2	Blackpool	46	15	7	1	42	15	9	7	7	31	24	86
3	Darlington	46	16	4	3	41	22	8	9	6	25	27	85
4	Bury	46	15	6	2	46	20	9	6	8	30	30	84
5	Hereford United	46	16	2	5	38	21	6	9	8	27	26	77
6	Tranmere Rovers	46	17	1	5	50	21	7	2	14	33	45	75
7	Colchester United	46	13	7	3	49	29	7	7	9	38	36	74
8	Swindon Town	46	16	4	3	42	21	5	5	13	20	37	72
9	SCUNTHORPE UNITED	46	14	6	3	61	33	5	8	10	22	29	71
10	Crewe Alexandra	46	10	7	6	32	28	8	5	10	33	41	66
11	Peterborough Utd.	46	11	7	5	29	21	5	7	11	25	32	62
12	Port Vale	46	11	8	4	39	24	3	10	10	22	35	60
13	Aldershot	46	11	6	6	33	20	6	2	15	23	43	59
14	Mansfield Town	46	10	8	5	25	15	3	10	10	16	23	57
15	Wrexham	46	10	6	7	39	27	5	3	15	28	43	54
16	Chester City	46	11	3	9	35	30	4	6	13	25	42	54
17	Rochdale	46	8	7	8	33	30	5	7	11	22	39	53
18	Exeter City	46	9	7	7	30	27	4	7	12	27	52	53
19	Hartlepool United	46	10	6	7	34	29	4	4	15	20	38	52
20	Southend United	46	8	8	7	30	34	5	3	15	28	49	50
21	Halifax Town	46	9	3	11	26	32	6	2	15	16	37	50
22	Stockport County	46	11	5	7	40	26	2	3	18	18	53	47
23	Northampton Town	46	10	1	12	32	32	4	4	15	21	42	47
24	Torquay United	46	5	11	7	18	24	4	3	16	20	39	41

1985/86 Division 4

1	Swindon Town	46	20	2	1	52	19	12	4	7	30	24	##
2	Chester City	46	15	5	3	44	16	8	10	5	39	34	84
3	Mansfield Town	46	13	8	2	43	17	10	4	9	31	30	81
4	Port Vale	46	13	9	1	42	11	8	7	8	25	26	79
5	Orient	46	11	6	6	39	21	9	6	8	40	43	72
6	Colchester United	46	12	6	5	51	22	7	7	9	37	41	70
7	Hartlepool United	46	15	6	2	41	20	5	4	14	27	47	70
8	Northampton Town	46	9	7	7	44	29	9	3	11	35	29	64
9	Southend United	46	13	4	6	43	27	5	6	12	26	40	64
10	Hereford United	46	15	6	2	55	30	3	4	16	19	43	64
11	Stockport County	46	9	9	5	35	28	8	4	11	28	43	64
12	Crewe Alexandra	46	10	6	7	35	26	8	3	12	19	35	63
13	Wrexham	46	11	5	7	34	24	6	4	13	34	56	60
14	Burnley	46	11	3	9	35	30	5	8	10	25	35	59
15	SCUNTHORPE UNITED	46	11	7	5	33	23	4	7	12	17	32	59
16	Aldershot	46	12	5	6	45	25	5	2	16	21	49	58
17	Peterborough Utd.	46	9	11	3	31	19	4	6	13	21	45	56
18	Rochdale	46	12	7	4	41	29	2	6	15	16	48	55
19	Tranmere Rovers	46	9	1	13	46	41	6	8	9	28	32	54
20	Halifax Town	46	10	8	5	35	27	4	4	15	25	44	54
21	Exeter City	46	10	4	9	26	25	3	11	9	21	34	54
22	Cambridge United	46	12	2	9	45	38	3	7	13	20	42	54
23	Preston North End	46	7	4	12	32	41	4	6	13	22	48	43
24	Torquay United	46	8	5	10	29	32	1	5	17	14	56	37

1986/87 Division 4

1	Northampton Town	46	20	2	1	56	20	10	7	6	47	33	99
2	Preston North End	46	16	4	3	36	18	10	8	5	36	29	90
3	Southend United	46	14	4	5	43	27	11	1	11	25	28	80
4	Wolverhampton Wan.	46	12	3	8	36	24	12	4	7	33	26	79
5	Colchester United	46	15	3	5	41	20	6	4	13	23	36	70
6	Aldershot	46	13	5	5	40	22	7	5	11	24	35	70
7	Orient	46	15	2	6	40	25	5	7	11	24	36	69
8	SCUNTHORPE UNITED	46	15	3	5	52	27	3	9	11	21	30	66
9	Wrexham	46	8	13	2	38	24	7	7	9	32	27	65
10	Peterborough Utd.	46	10	7	6	29	21	7	7	9	28	29	65
11	Cambridge United	46	12	6	5	37	23	5	5	13	23	39	62
12	Swansea City	46	13	3	7	31	21	4	8	11	25	40	62
13	Cardiff City	46	6	12	5	24	18	9	4	10	24	32	61
14	Exeter City	46	11	10	2	37	17	0	13	10	16	32	56
15	Halifax Town	46	10	5	8	32	32	5	5	13	27	42	55
16	Hereford United	46	10	6	7	33	23	4	5	14	27	38	53
17	Crewe Alexandra	46	8	9	6	38	35	5	5	13	32	37	53
18	Hartlepool United	46	6	11	6	24	30	5	7	11	20	35	51
19	Stockport County	46	9	6	8	25	27	4	6	13	15	42	51
20	Tranmere Rovers	46	6	10	7	32	37	5	7	11	22	35	50
21	Rochdale	46	8	8	7	31	30	3	9	11	23	43	50
22	Burnley	46	9	7	7	31	35	3	6	14	22	39	49
23	Torquay United	46	8	8	7	28	29	2	10	11	28	43	48
24	Lincoln City	46	8	7	8	30	27	4	5	14	15	38	48

1987/88 Division 4

1	Wolverhampton Wan.	46	15	3	5	47	19	12	6	5	35	24	90
2	Cardiff City	46	15	6	2	39	14	9	7	7	27	27	85
3	Bolton Wanderers	46	15	6	2	42	12	7	6	10	24	30	78
4	SCUNTHORPE UNITED	46	14	5	4	42	20	6	12	5	34	31	77
5	Torquay United	46	10	7	6	34	16	11	7	5	32	25	77
6	Swansea City	46	9	7	7	35	28	11	3	9	27	28	70
7	Peterborough Utd.	46	10	5	8	28	26	10	5	8	24	27	70
8	Leyton Orient	46	13	4	6	55	27	6	8	9	30	36	69
9	Colchester United	46	10	5	8	23	22	9	5	9	24	29	67
10	Burnley	46	12	5	6	31	22	8	2	13	26	40	67
11	Wrexham	46	13	3	7	46	26	7	3	13	23	32	66
12	Scarborough	46	12	8	3	38	19	5	6	12	18	29	65
13	Darlington	46	13	6	4	39	25	5	5	13	32	44	65
14	Tranmere Rovers	46	14	2	7	43	20	5	7	11	18	33	64
15	Cambridge United	46	10	6	7	32	24	6	7	10	18	28	61
16	Hartlepool United	46	9	7	7	25	25	6	7	10	25	32	59
17	Crewe Alexandra	46	7	11	5	25	19	6	8	9	32	34	58
18	Halifax Town	46	11	7	5	37	25	3	7	13	17	34	55
19	Hereford United	46	8	7	8	25	27	6	5	12	16	32	54
20	Stockport County	46	7	7	9	26	26	5	8	10	18	32	51
21	Rochdale	46	5	9	9	28	34	6	6	11	19	42	48
22	Exeter City	46	8	6	9	33	29	3	7	13	20	39	46
23	Carlisle United	46	9	5	9	38	33	3	3	17	19	53	44
24	Newport County	46	4	5	14	19	36	2	2	19	16	69	25

1988/89 Division 4

1	Rotherham United	46	13	6	4	44	18	9	10	4	32	17	82
2	Tranmere Rovers	46	15	6	2	34	13	6	11	6	28	30	80
3	Crewe Alexandra	46	13	7	3	42	24	8	8	7	25	24	78
4	SCUNTHORPE UNITED	46	11	9	3	40	22	10	5	8	37	35	77
5	Scarborough	46	12	7	4	33	23	9	7	7	34	29	77
6	Leyton Orient	46	16	2	5	61	19	5	10	8	25	31	75
7	Wrexham	46	12	7	4	44	28	7	7	9	33	35	71
8	Cambridge United	46	13	7	3	45	25	5	7	11	26	37	68
9	Grimsby Town	46	11	9	3	33	18	6	6	11	32	41	66
10	Lincoln City	46	12	6	5	39	26	6	4	13	25	34	64
11	York City	46	10	8	5	43	27	7	5	11	19	36	64
12	Carlisle United	46	9	6	8	26	25	6	9	8	27	27	60
13	Exeter City	46	14	4	5	46	23	4	2	17	19	45	60
14	Torquay United	46	15	2	6	32	23	2	6	15	13	37	59
15	Hereford United	46	11	8	4	40	27	3	8	12	26	45	58
16	Burnley	46	12	6	5	35	20	2	7	14	17	41	55
17	Peterborough Utd.	46	10	3	10	29	32	4	9	10	23	42	54
18	Rochdale	46	10	10	3	32	26	3	4	16	24	56	53
19	Hartlepool United	46	10	6	7	33	33	4	4	15	17	45	52
20	Stockport County	46	8	10	5	31	20	2	11	10	23	32	51
21	Halifax Town	46	10	7	6	42	27	3	4	16	27	48	50
22	Colchester United	46	8	7	8	35	30	4	7	12	25	48	50
23	Doncaster Rovers	46	9	6	8	32	32	4	4	15	17	46	49
24	Darlington	46	3	12	8	28	38	5	6	12	25	38	42

1989/90 Division 4

1	Exeter City	46	20	3	0	50	14	8	2	13	33	34	89
2	Grimsby Town	46	14	4	5	41	20	8	9	6	29	27	79
3	Southend United	46	15	3	5	35	14	7	6	10	26	34	75
4	Stockport County	46	13	6	4	45	27	8	5	10	23	35	74
5	Maidstone United	46	14	4	5	49	21	8	3	12	28	40	73
6	Cambridge United	46	14	3	6	45	30	7	7	9	31	36	73
7	Chesterfield	46	12	9	2	41	19	7	5	11	22	31	71
8	Carlisle United	46	15	4	4	38	20	6	4	13	23	40	71
9	Peterborough Utd.	46	10	8	5	35	23	7	9	7	24	23	68
10	Lincoln City	46	11	6	6	30	27	7	8	8	18	21	68
11	SCUNTHORPE UNITED	46	9	9	5	42	25	8	6	9	27	29	66
12	Rochdale	46	11	4	8	28	23	9	2	12	24	32	66
13	York City	46	10	5	8	29	24	6	11	6	26	29	64
14	Gillingham	46	9	8	6	28	21	8	3	12	18	27	62
15	Torquay United	46	12	2	9	33	29	3	10	10	20	37	57
16	Burnley	46	6	10	7	19	18	8	4	11	26	37	56
17	Hereford United	46	7	4	12	31	32	8	6	9	25	30	55
18	Scarborough	46	10	5	8	35	28	5	5	13	25	45	55
19	Hartlepool United	46	12	4	7	45	33	3	6	14	21	55	55
20	Doncaster Rovers	46	7	7	9	29	29	7	2	14	24	31	51
21	Wrexham	46	8	8	7	28	28	5	4	14	23	39	51
22	Aldershot	46	8	7	8	28	26	4	7	12	21	43	50
23	Halifax Town	46	5	9	9	31	29	7	4	12	26	36	49
24	Colchester United	46	9	3	11	26	25	2	7	14	22	50	43

1990/91 Division 4

1	Darlington	46	13	8	2	36	14	9	9	5	32	24	83
2	Stockport County	46	16	6	1	54	19	7	7	9	30	28	82
3	Hartlepool United	46	15	5	3	35	15	9	5	9	32	33	82
4	Peterborough Utd.	46	13	9	1	38	15	8	8	7	29	30	80
5	Blackpool	46	17	3	3	55	17	6	7	10	23	30	79
6	Burnley	46	17	5	1	46	16	6	5	12	24	35	79
7	Torquay United	46	14	7	2	37	13	4	11	8	27	34	72
8	SCUNTHORPE UNITED	46	17	4	2	51	20	3	7	13	20	42	71
9	Scarborough	46	13	5	5	36	21	6	7	10	23	35	69
10	Northampton Town	46	14	5	4	34	21	4	8	11	23	37	67
11	Doncaster Rovers	46	12	5	6	36	22	5	9	9	20	24	65
12	Rochdale	46	10	9	4	29	22	5	8	10	21	31	62
13	Cardiff City	46	10	6	7	26	23	5	9	9	17	31	60
14	Lincoln City	46	10	7	6	32	27	4	10	9	18	34	59
15	Gillingham	46	9	9	5	35	27	3	9	11	22	33	54
16	Walsall	46	7	12	4	25	17	5	5	13	23	34	53
17	Hereford United	46	9	10	4	32	19	4	4	15	21	39	53
18	Chesterfield	46	8	12	3	33	26	5	2	16	14	36	53
19	Maidstone United	46	9	5	9	42	34	4	7	12	24	37	51
20	Carlisle United	46	12	3	8	30	30	1	6	16	17	59	48
21	York City	46	8	6	9	21	23	3	7	13	24	34	46
22	Halifax Town	46	9	6	8	34	29	3	4	16	25	50	46
23	Aldershot	46	8	7	8	38	43	2	4	17	23	58	41
24	Wrexham	46	8	7	8	33	34	2	3	18	15	40	40

1991/92 Division 4

1	Burnley	42	14	4	3	42	16	11	4	6	37	27	83
2	Rotherham United	42	12	6	3	38	16	10	5	6	32	21	77
3	Mansfield Town	42	13	4	4	43	26	10	4	7	32	27	77
4	Blackpool	42	17	3	1	48	13	5	7	9	23	32	76
5	SCUNTHORPE UNITED	42	14	5	2	39	18	7	4	10	25	41	72
6	Crewe Alexandra	42	12	6	3	33	20	8	4	9	33	31	70
7	Barnet	42	16	1	4	48	23	5	5	11	33	38	69
8	Rochdale	42	12	6	3	34	22	6	7	8	23	31	67
9	Cardiff City	42	13	3	5	42	26	4	12	5	24	27	66
10	Lincoln City	42	9	5	7	21	24	8	6	7	29	20	62
11	Gillingham	42	12	5	4	41	19	3	7	11	22	34	57
12	Scarborough	42	12	5	4	39	28	3	7	11	25	40	57
13	Chesterfield	42	6	7	8	26	28	8	4	9	23	33	53
14	Wrexham	42	11	4	6	31	26	3	5	13	21	47	51
15	Walsall	42	5	10	6	28	26	7	3	11	20	32	49
16	Northampton Town	42	5	9	7	25	23	6	4	11	21	34	46
17	Hereford United	42	9	4	8	31	24	3	4	14	13	33	44
18	Maidstone United	42	6	9	6	24	22	2	9	10	21	34	42
19	York City	42	6	9	6	26	23	2	7	12	16	35	40
20	Halifax Town	42	7	5	9	23	35	3	3	15	11	40	38
21	Doncaster Rovers	42	6	2	13	21	35	3	6	12	19	30	35
22	Carlisle United	42	5	9	7	24	27	2	4	15	17	40	34

1992/93 Division 3 (of the "new" Football League)

1	Cardiff City	42	13	7	1	42	20	12	1	8	35	27	83
2	Wrexham	42	14	3	4	48	26	9	8	4	27	26	80
3	Barnet	42	16	4	1	45	19	7	6	8	21	29	79
4	York City	42	13	6	2	41	15	8	6	7	31	30	75
5	Walsall	42	11	6	4	42	31	11	1	9	34	30	73
6	Crewe Alexandra	42	13	3	5	47	23	8	4	9	28	33	70
7	Bury	42	10	7	4	36	19	8	2	11	27	36	63
8	Lincoln City	42	10	6	5	31	20	8	3	10	26	33	63
9	Shrewsbury Town	42	11	3	7	36	30	6	8	7	21	22	62
10	Colchester United	42	13	3	5	38	26	5	2	14	29	50	59
11	Rochdale	42	10	3	8	38	29	6	7	8	32	41	58
12	Chesterfield	42	11	3	7	32	28	4	8	9	27	35	56
13	Scarborough	42	7	7	7	32	30	8	2	11	34	41	54
14	SCUNTHORPE UNITED	42	8	7	6	38	25	6	5	10	19	29	54
15	Darlington	42	5	6	10	23	31	7	8	6	25	22	50
16	Doncaster Rovers	42	6	5	10	22	28	5	9	7	20	29	47
17	Hereford United	42	7	9	5	31	27	3	6	12	16	33	45
18	Carlisle United	42	7	5	9	29	27	4	6	11	22	38	44
19	Torquay United	42	6	4	11	18	26	6	3	12	27	41	43
20	Northampton Town	42	6	5	10	19	28	5	3	13	29	46	41
21	Gillingham	42	9	4	8	32	28	0	9	12	16	36	40
22	Halifax Town	42	3	5	13	20	35	6	4	11	25	33	36

1993/94 Division 3

1	Shrewsbury Town	42	10	8	3	28	17	12	5	4	35	22	79
2	Chester City	42	13	5	3	35	18	8	6	7	34	28	74
3	Crewe Alexandra	42	12	4	5	45	30	9	6	6	35	31	73
4	Wycombe Wanderers	42	11	6	4	34	21	8	7	6	33	32	70
5	Preston North End	42	13	5	3	46	23	5	8	8	33	37	67
6	Torquay United	42	8	10	3	30	24	9	6	6	34	32	67
7	Carlisle United	42	10	4	7	35	23	8	6	7	22	19	64
8	Chesterfield	42	8	8	5	32	22	8	6	7	23	26	62
9	Rochdale	42	10	5	6	38	22	6	7	8	25	29	60
10	Walsall	42	7	5	9	28	26	10	4	7	20	27	60
11	SCUNTHORPE UNITED	42	9	7	5	40	26	6	7	8	24	30	59
12	Mansfield Town	42	9	3	9	28	30	6	7	8	25	32	55
13	Bury	42	9	6	6	33	22	5	5	11	22	34	53
14	Scarborough	42	8	4	9	29	28	7	4	10	26	33	53
15	Doncaster Rovers	42	8	6	7	24	26	6	4	11	20	31	52
16	Gillingham	42	8	8	5	27	23	4	7	10	17	28	51
17	Colchester United	42	8	4	9	31	33	5	6	10	25	38	49
18	Lincoln City	42	7	4	10	26	29	5	7	9	26	34	47
19	Wigan Athletic	42	6	7	8	33	33	5	5	11	18	37	45
20	Hereford United	42	6	4	11	34	33	6	2	13	26	46	42
21	Darlington	42	7	5	9	24	28	3	6	12	18	36	41
22	Northampton Town	42	6	7	8	25	23	3	4	14	19	43	38

1994/95 Division 3

1	Carlisle United	42	14	5	2	34	14	13	5	3	33	17	91
2	Walsall	42	15	3	3	42	18	9	8	4	33	22	83
3	Chesterfield	42	11	7	3	26	10	12	5	4	36	27	81
4	Bury	42	13	7	1	39	13	10	4	7	34	23	80
5	Preston North End	42	13	3	5	37	17	6	7	8	21	24	67
6	Mansfield Town	42	10	5	6	45	27	8	6	7	39	32	65
7	SCUNTHORPE UNITED	42	12	2	7	40	30	6	6	9	28	33	62
8	Fulham	42	11	5	5	39	22	5	9	7	21	32	62
9	Doncaster Rovers	42	9	5	7	28	20	8	5	8	30	23	61
10	Colchester United	42	8	5	8	29	30	8	5	8	27	34	58
11	Barnet	42	8	7	6	37	27	7	4	10	19	36	56
12	Lincoln City	42	10	7	4	34	22	5	4	12	20	33	56
13	Torquay United	42	10	8	3	35	25	4	5	12	19	32	55
14	Wigan Athletic	42	7	6	8	28	30	7	4	10	25	30	52
15	Rochdale	42	8	6	7	25	23	4	8	9	19	44	50
16	Hereford United	42	9	6	6	22	19	3	7	11	23	43	49
17	Northampton Town	42	8	5	8	25	29	2	9	10	20	38	44
18	Hartlepool United	42	9	5	7	33	32	2	5	14	10	37	43
19	Gillingham	42	8	7	6	31	25	2	4	15	15	39	41
20	Darlington	42	7	5	9	25	24	4	3	14	18	33	41
21	Scarborough	42	4	7	10	26	31	4	3	14	23	39	34
22	Exeter City	42	5	5	11	25	36	3	5	13	11	34	34

1995/96 Division 3

1	Preston North End	46	11	8	4	44	22	12	9	2	34	16	86
2	Gillingham	46	16	6	1	33	6	6	11	6	16	14	83
3	Bury	46	11	6	6	33	21	11	7	5	33	27	79
4	Plymouth Argyle	46	14	5	4	41	20	8	7	8	27	29	78
5	Darlington	46	10	6	7	30	21	10	12	1	30	21	78
6	Hereford United	46	13	5	5	40	22	7	9	7	25	25	74
7	Colchester United	46	13	7	3	37	22	5	11	7	24	29	72
8	Chester City	46	11	9	3	45	22	7	7	9	27	31	70
9	Barnet	46	13	6	4	40	19	5	10	8	25	26	70
10	Wigan Athletic	46	15	3	5	36	21	5	7	11	26	35	70
11	Northampton Town	46	9	10	4	32	22	9	3	11	19	22	67
12	SCUNTHORPE UNITED	46	8	8	7	36	30	7	7	9	31	31	60
13	Doncaster Rovers	46	11	6	6	25	19	5	5	13	24	41	59
14	Exeter City	46	9	9	5	25	22	4	9	10	21	31	57
15	Rochdale	46	7	8	8	32	33	7	5	11	25	28	55
16	Cambridge United	46	8	8	7	34	30	6	4	13	27	41	54
17	Fulham	46	10	9	4	39	26	2	8	13	18	37	53
18	Lincoln City	46	8	7	8	32	26	5	7	11	25	47	53
19	Mansfield Town	46	6	10	7	25	29	5	10	8	29	35	53
20	Hartlepool United	46	8	9	6	30	24	4	4	15	17	43	49
21	Leyton Orient	46	11	4	8	29	22	1	7	15	15	41	47
22	Cardiff City	46	8	6	9	24	22	3	6	14	17	42	45
23	Scarborough	46	5	11	7	22	28	3	5	15	17	41	40
24	Torquay United	46	4	9	10	17	36	1	5	17	13	48	29

LEAGUE MEETINGS WITH OTHER CLUBS

		Home:					Away:					Totals:		
	P	W	D	L	F	A	W	D	L	F	A	F	A	% won
Accrington Stanley	16	5	0	3	21	11	2	2	4	7	10	28	21	43.75
Aldershot	32	9	6	1	30	16	2	4	10	15	33	45	49	34.38
Aston Villa	2	0	0	1	1	2	0	0	1	0	5	1	7	0.00
Barnet	8	3	1	0	6	1	1	0	3	4	8	10	9	50.00
Barnsley	20	7	0	3	17	6	2	1	7	6	23	23	29	45.00
Barrow	22	6	3	2	17	11	6	1	4	16	13	33	24	54.55
Blackburn Rovers	2	0	1	0	1	1	0	0	1	0	3	1	4	0.00
Blackpool	10	3	2	0	10	6	0	0	5	3	11	13	17	30.00
Bolton Wan.	6	1	2	0	3	2	0	3	0	0	0	3	2	16.67
Bournemouth	28	5	6	3	16	11	2	8	4	15	17	31	28	25.00
Bradford City	36	12	3	3	29	17	3	6	9	18	32	47	49	41.67
Bradford PA	20	5	4	1	22	11	3	6	1	18	13	40	24	40.00
Brentford	26	6	6	1	23	15	3	0	10	11	28	34	43	34.62
Brighton & Hove A.	14	0	3	4	11	16	3	2	2	10	8	21	24	21.43
Bristol City	8	1	3	0	10	7	3	1	0	7	2	17	9	50.00
Bristol Rovers	20	4	4	2	17	13	0	3	7	8	28	25	41	20.00
Burnley	16	4	3	1	16	9	3	3	2	7	10	23	19	43.75
Bury	30	6	5	4	23	17	2	2	11	12	33	35	50	26.67
Cambridge U	22	4	4	3	11	10	3	3	5	15	18	26	28	31.82
Cardiff City	20	3	2	5	10	16	3	2	5	10	18	20	34	30.00
Carlisle Utd.	34	7	5	5	28	18	7	2	8	23	35	51	53	41.18
Charlton Ath.	14	2	4	1	13	8	2	2	3	10	14	23	22	28.57
Chelsea	2	1	0	0	3	0	0	0	1	0	3	3	3	50.00
Chester City	38	10	5	4	30	21	6	7	6	25	28	55	49	42.11
Chesterfield	34	7	3	7	24	18	3	4	10	12	24	36	42	29.41
Colchester Utd.	42	12	6	3	46	24	5	4	12	23	30	69	54	40.48
Crewe Alexandra	58	15	10	4	52	27	6	11	12	32	42	84	69	36.21
Darlington	62	20	7	4	61	22	8	8	15	36	54	97	76	45.16
Derby County	16	4	1	3	14	15	1	3	4	14	24	28	39	31.25
Doncaster Rov.	38	6	9	4	21	23	6	5	8	20	31	41	54	31.58
Exeter City	37	14	3	1	45	13	1	7	11	17	37	62	50	40.54
Fulham	6	1	0	2	5	5	1	1	1	4	3	9	8	33.33
Gateshead	16	2	4	2	8	9	2	3	3	5	6	13	15	25.00
Gillingham	28	5	6	3	21	15	4	6	4	14	20	35	35	32.14
Grimsby Town	42	5	7	9	24	32	5	5	11	20	35	44	67	23.81
Halifax Town	52	14	10	2	48	27	9	7	10	36	37	84	64	44.23
Hartlepool Utd.	60	17	9	4	57	25	8	6	16	36	49	93	74	41.67
Hereford Utd.	34	10	4	3	35	19	6	4	7	23	27	58	46	47.06
Huddersfield T	22	2	3	6	9	19	3	1	7	12	20	21	39	22.73
Hull City	16	3	3	2	15	11	2	2	4	9	12	24	23	31.25
Ipswich Town	6	1	2	0	7	3	0	0	3	1	6	8	9	16.67
Leeds United	8	2	0	2	5	6	1	1	2	6	5	11	11	37.50
Leyton Orient	26	5	6	2	21	17	1	4	8	11	24	32	41	23.08
Lincoln City	48	11	9	4	37	24	5	4	15	27	47	64	71	33.33
Liverpool	8	0	2	2	5	7	0	0	4	3	10	8	17	0.00
Luton Town	8	4	0	0	13	1	1	2	1	3	3	16	4	62.50
Maidstone U	6	2	1	0	5	2	1	1	1	3	7	8	9	50.00
Manchester City	2	0	0	1	2	4	0	0	1	1	8	3	12	0.00
Mansfield T	46	7	7	9	38	37	5	7	11	29	43	67	80	26.09
Middlesbrough	14	2	4	1	8	9	2	0	5	11	19	19	28	28.57
Millwall	4	0	1	1	4	5	0	1	1	3	4	7	9	0.00
New Brighton	2	1	0	0	6	0	1	0	0	2	1	8	1	100.00

Newcastle Utd.	6	3	0	0	7	3	0	1	2	3	6	10	9	50.00
Newport County	26	7	2	4	23	14	1	5	7	9	20	32	34	30.77
Northampton T	46	11	7	5	44	23	6	4	13	20	32	64	55	36.96
Norwich City	8	3	1	0	9	4	1	2	1	7	7	16	11	50.00
Notts County	8	2	0	2	5	5	0	0	4	1	9	6	14	25.00
Oldham Ath.	28	5	8	1	22	13	5	3	6	21	24	43	37	35.71
Oxford United	8	0	3	1	4	5	2	0	2	7	5	11	10	25.00
Peterborough U	40	12	5	3	36	15	5	7	8	22	27	58	42	42.50
Plymouth Argyle	16	5	3	0	17	5	2	0	6	9	23	26	28	43.75
Port Vale	28	4	6	4	12	12	3	5	6	12	22	24	34	25.00
Portsmouth	12	3	2	1	11	6	2	2	2	9	16	20	22	41.67
Preston North End	18	6	0	3	19	14	2	2	5	9	15	28	29	44.44
QPR	6	1	0	2	3	5	0	0	3	2	8	5	13	16.67
Reading	20	3	2	5	8	12	1	2	7	3	15	11	27	20.00
Rochdale	62	18	6	7	62	34	7	8	16	34	56	96	90	40.32
Rotherham U	26	8	3	2	22	13	1	3	9	11	30	33	43	34.62
Scarborough	18	2	3	4	12	13	3	2	4	9	13	21	26	27.78
Sheffield Utd.	10	1	3	1	6	7	0	0	5	5	14	11	21	10.00
Sheffield Wed.	2	0	0	1	1	4	0	0	1	0	2	1	6	0.00
Shrewsbury T	18	4	3	2	10	11	1	1	7	13	26	23	37	27.78
Southampton	8	3	0	1	10	4	0	1	3	9	18	19	22	37.50
Southend U	30	9	4	2	25	14	4	5	6	14	19	39	33	43.33
Southport	30	7	5	3	18	11	2	8	5	22	31	40	42	30.00
Stockport County	56	12	9	7	46	27	5	10	13	29	47	75	74	30.36
Stoke City	10	0	5	0	5	5	2	0	3	9	10	14	15	20.00
Sunderland	12	3	3	0	14	9	0	1	5	1	11	15	20	25.00
Swansea City	36	9	4	5	29	23	4	2	12	18	35	47	58	36.11
Swindon Town	14	5	0	2	17	8	0	4	3	4	10	21	18	35.71
Torquay Utd.	46	12	5	6	36	22	7	9	7	33	26	69	48	41.30
Tranmere Rovers	40	11	4	5	39	25	8	1	11	28	29	67	54	47.50
Walsall	28	9	3	2	29	13	1	6	7	11	24	40	37	35.71
Watford	16	2	3	3	4	6	1	0	7	5	23	9	29	18.75
Wigan Ath.	16	3	2	3	14	17	1	2	5	6	12	20	29	25.00
Wimbledon	10	3	1	1	11	3	0	4	1	6	8	17	11	30.00
Wolves	4	0	0	2	0	3	0	0	2	1	5	1	8	0.00
Workington	36	13	3	2	41	15	6	7	5	25	22	66	37	52.78
Wrexham	40	12	6	2	39	21	7	3	10	19	27	58	48	47.50
Wycombe Wan.	2	0	1	0	0	0	0	1	0	2	2	2	2	0.00
York City	48	12	5	7	41	28	8	4	12	25	35	66	63	41.67

OVERALL RECORD

	Home:						Away:					Totals:		
	P	W	D	L	F	A	W	D	L	F	A	F	A	Pts
	2075	499	309	229	1755	1136	241	270	527	1126	1785	2881	2921	2315

Made up of:

	P	W	D	L	F	A	W	D	L	F	A	F	A	Pts
Division 2	252	59	40	27	226	157	27	23	76	150	274	376	431	235
Division 3(old)	276	56	45	37	219	177	25	27	86	127	267	346	444	243
Division 3(new), 4(old)	1179	289	168	132	977	626	133	170	287	605	942	1582	1568	1429
Division 3(North)	368	95	56	33	333	176	56	50	78	244	302	577	478	408

F.A. CUP RECORD IN NON-LEAGUE SEASONS

Players appearances and goals are included in the A-Z section only if they also made a League appearance.

1909/10

Rnd	Date	Opponent	Res	1	2	3	4	5	6	7	8	9	10	11	Scorers
P	Sep 18	WITHERNSEA	8-0	Wogin	Parrott	Barrick	Garrett	Fewster	Foster	Hollin	Clapham	Carr	Cox	Harrison	Cox 2, Hollin 2, Clapham 2, Harrison, Carr
Q1	Oct 2	York City	0-4	Wogin	Parrott	Barrick	Garrett	Fewster	Foster	Hollin	Clapham	Fisher	Cox	Harrison	

1910/11

Rnd	Date	Opponent	Res	1-11
P	Sep 17	Denaby Utd.	0-6	Not known

1911/12

Rnd	Date	Opponent	Res	1	2	3	4	5	6	7	8	9	10	11	Scorers
P	Sep 14	York City	2-1	Wogin	Parrott	Long	Holland	Tune	Brown	Hollin	Blanchard	Cox	Silvester	Knight	Blanchard 2
Q1	30	Mexborough Town	2-3	Wogin	Parrott	Long	Holland	Tune	Brown	Hollin	Blanchard	Cox	Silvester	Knight	Ibbotson 2 (?)

1912/13

Rnd	Date	Opponent	Res	1	2	3	4	5	6	7	8	9	10	11	Scorers
P	Sep 28	Brodsworth Colliery	3-0	Wogin	Drury	Burkhill	Henderson	Hill	Brown	Damms	Spelvins	Walden	Bell	Pearce	Pearce 2 (1 pen), Walden
Q1	Oct 12	GOOLE TOWN	2-1	Wogin	Burkhill	Long	Hill	Henderson	Brown	Damms	Watkins	Walden	Barrick	Bell	Walden 2
Q2	Nov 2	YORK CITY	2-2	Hurst	Burton	Burkhill	Hill	Henderson	Watkins	James	Spelvins	Walden	Bell	Pearce	Bell, Walden
rep	6	York City	4-5	Hurst	Burkhill	Long	Hill	Watkins	Brown	James	Rusling	Walden	Hollin	Pearce	Walden 2, Hill, Pearce

1913/14

Rnd	Date	Opponent	Res	1	2	3	4	5	6	7	8	9	10	11	Scorers
P	Sep 27	Mexborough Town	2-2	Wogin	Roberts A	Burkhill	Hill	Morris	Fulljames	Roberts HP	Mulholland	Bradbury	Walden	Root	Mulholland, Bradbury
rep	Oct 4	MEXBOROUGH TOWN	3-0	Wogin	Roberts A	Burkhill	Hill	Morris	Fulljames	Roberts HP	Mulholland	Bradbury	Walden	Root	Morris, Bradbury, Walden
Q1	11	York City	1-2	Wogin	Roberts A	Burkhill	Hill	Morris	Clark	Roberts HP	Mulholland	Walden	Thompson	Root	Walden

1914/15

Rnd	Date	Opponent	Res	1	2	3	4	5	6	7	8	9	10	11	Scorers
P	Sep 26	HULL OLD BOYS *	5-1	Taylor	Cowley	Burkhill	Hill	Pinch	Jacques	Monaghan	Robinson	Armitage	Clark	Platts	Robinson, Armitage, Clark 3
Q1	Oct 10	GRIMSBY ROVERS	4-0	Taylor	Cowley	Clark	Hill	Pinch	Jacques	Monaghan	Robinson	Armitage	Ibbotson	Platts	Robinson, Clark 2, Ibbotson
Q2	24	DONCASTER ROVERS	1-0	Taylor	Cowley	Burkhill	Hill	Pinch	Jacques	Monaghan	Robinson	Armitage	Clark	Platts	Robinson
Q3	Nov 14	GOOLE TOWN	1-1	Taylor	Cowley	Robinson	Hill	Pinch	Jacques	Monaghan	Robinson	Armitage	Clark	Platts	Robinson
rep	19	Goole Town	1-5	Taylor	Cowley	Clark	Hill	Pinch	Jacques	Monaghan	Robinson	Armitage	Hollin	Platts	Platts

* Played at Scunthorpe to guarantee gate receipts.

1919/20

Rnd	Date	Opponent	Res	1	2	3	4	5	6	7	8	9	10	11	Scorers
P	Sep 27	GOOLE TOWN	7-0	Hanna	Bullivant	Robinson	Hill	Robson	Hobson	Butler	Spavin	Mahon	Millington	Clark	Butler, Spavin 3, Mahon 2, Millington
Q1	Oct 11	BRODSWORTH M.	2-1	Hanna	Patterson	Bullivant	Maw	Hill	Robinson	Butler	Spavin	Brown	Mahon	Booth	Butler, Brown
Q2	25	CLEETHORPES	0-1	Hanna	Patterson	Bullivant	Hill	Robson	Wield	Butler	Spavin	Brown	Lemon	Booth	

1920/21

Rnd	Date	Opponent	Res	1	2	3	4	5	6	7	8	9	10	11	Scorers
P	Sep 25	HULL BRUNSWICK INST.	6-0	Hanna	Ackroyd	Betts	Robson	Duffus R	Simpson	Bell	Lloyd	Duffus J	Lemon	Tunstall	J.Duffus 2, Lemon, Tunstall, Ackroyd, Bell
Q1	Oct 9	BENTLEY COLLIERY	3-0	Hanna	Ackroyd	Betts	Robson	Duffus R	Lloyd	Bell	Simpson	Duffus J	Lemon	Tunstall	J.Duffus, Simpson, Ackroyd
Q2	23	Grimsby Charltons	4-1	Hanna	Ackroyd	Betts	Robson	Duffus R	Lloyd	Harvey	Simpson	Duffus J	Lemon	Tunstall	Simpson, Lemon 2, Harvey
Q3	Nov 6	BRODSWORTH MAIN	1-1	Hanna	Ackroyd	Betts	Lloyd	Duffus R	Robson	Harvey	Simpson	Duffus J	Lemon	Tunstall	J.Duffus
rep	?	Brodsworth Main	0-0	Hanna	Ackroyd	Betts	Roebuck	Duffus R	Lloyd	Duffus J	Simpson	Sylvester	Lemon	Tunstall	
r2	15	Brodsworth Main*	3-1	Hanna	Ackroyd	Betts	Roebuck	Duffus R	Robson	Harvey	Hinton	Simpson	Lemon	Moore	Harvey, Simpson, Moore
Q4	20	Mansfield Town	0-1	Hanna	Ackroyd	Betts	Roebuck	Duffus R	Lloyd	Harvey	Simpson	Lemon	Moore	Tunstall	

* Played at Bramall Lane, Sheffield

85

1921/22

Rd	Mo	Dy	Opponent	Score	Scorers											
P	Sep	24	Retford Town	2-1	Calthorpe 2	Bates	Ackroyd	Betts	Richards	Brandon	Lloyd	Meredith	Gibson	Calthorpe	Whitham	Maycock
Q1	Oct	8	HULL HOLDERNESS	10-0	Calthorpe 4, Witham 3, Richards 2, Meredith	Bates	Ackroyd	Betts	Richards	Brandon	Lloyd	Meredith	Gibson	Calthorpe	Whitham	Maycock
Q2	Oct	22	BRODSWORTH MAIN	4-1	Witham 2, Lloyd, Meredith	Bates	Ackroyd	Betts	Richards	Lloyd	Broadhead	Meredith	Gibson	Reed	Whitham	Maycock
Q3	Nov	5	Gainsborough Trinity	0-2		Bates	Ackroyd	Betts	Richards	Lloyd	Broadhead	Meredith	Gibson	Reed	Whitham	Maycock

1922/23

Rd	Mo	Dy	Opponent	Score	Scorers											
Q1	Oct	7	GRIMSBY CHARLTONS	3-0	Gittos, Rushby 2	Reynolds	Smith T	Betts	Hill	Crooks	Lloyd	Meredith	Whitham	Gittos	Rushby	Maycock
Q2	Oct	21	Gainsborough Trinity	2-1	Rushby, Moore	Wogin	Smith T	Betts	Hill	Hargreaves	Lloyd	Meredith	Rushby	Gittos	Maycock	Moore
Q3	Nov	4	Boston United	1-0	Maycock	Wogin	Smith T	Betts	Hill	Hargreaves	Lloyd	Meredith	Rushby	Gittos	Maycock	Moore
Q4	Nov	18	Worksop Town	2-4	Meredith, Gittos	Wogin	Smith T	Betts	Hill	Hargreaves	Lloyd	Meredith	Rushby	Gittos	Redford	Maycock

1923/24

Rd	Mo	Dy	Opponent	Score	Scorers											
P	Sep	22	GRIMSBY ROVERS	5-1	Burkinshaw 2, Meredith, Raby, Kitchen	Reynolds	Bradbury	Hargreaves	Skull	Forbes	Blenko	Meredith	Burkinshaw	Kitchen	Raby	Foster
Q1	Oct	6	CLEETHORPES	5-0	Kitchen 3, Raby, Thorpe	Reynolds	Bradbury	Hargreaves	Skull	Crooks	Blenko	Thorpe	Burkinshaw	Raby	Kitchen	Foster
Q2	Oct	20	GAINSBOROUGH TRINITY	2-0	Kitchen, Skull	Reynolds	Bradbury	Hargreaves	Skull	Ashmore	Millson	Lawton	Kitchen	Burkinshaw	Burkinshaw	Raby
Q3	Nov	3	BOSTON UNITED	2-0	White 2	Reynolds	Bradbury	Hargreaves	Skull	Ashmore	Millson	Lawton	Burkinshaw	White	Kitchen	Thorpe
Q4	Nov	17	ROTHERHAM TOWN	0-0		Reynolds	Bradbury	Hargreaves	Skull	Ashmore	Millson	Lawton	Gregson	Kitchen	Raby	Foster
rep		22	Rotherham Town	1-0	Kitchen	Reynolds	Bradbury	Hargreaves	Skull	Ashmore	Millson	Lawton	Burkinshaw	Kitchen	Raby	Foster
R1	Dec	1	ROTHERHAM COUNTY	1-1	Kitchen	Reynolds	Bradbury	Hargreaves	Skull	Ashmore	Millson	Lawton	Burkinshaw	Wilson	Kitchen	Foster
rep		6	Rotherham County	0-2		Reynolds	Bradbury	Crooks	Skull	Ashmore	Millson	Cook	Skull	Burkinshaw	Kitchen	Foster

1924/25

Rd	Mo	Dy	Opponent	Score	Scorers											
P	Sep	20	BARTON TOWN	2-1	Fenwick 2	Reynolds	Bradbury	Greaves	Skull	Millson	Price	Cammack	Fenwick	Shaw	Needham	Clarkson
Q1	Oct	4	BOSTON UNITED	0-0		Reynolds	Bradbury	Greaves	Skull	Burnham	Millson	Cammack	Price	Shaw	Fenwick	Clarkson
rep		9	Boston United	0-3		Reynolds	Bradbury	Greaves	Millson	Burnham	Skull	Maughan	Price	Shaw	Fenwick	Cammack

1925/26

Rd	Mo	Dy	Opponent	Score	Scorers											
P	Sep	19	Cleethorpes	4-0	Vowles 3, Cawley	Reynolds	Glennie	Liversidge	Skull	Hooper	Evans	Lawrie	Whitham	Vowles	Cawley	Clarkson
Q1	Oct	3	GRIMSBY HAYCROFT ROVERS	5-1	Vowles 2, Cawley 4	Reynolds	Glennie	Liversidge	Skull	Wilson	Evans	Lawrie	Whitham	Vowles	Cawley	Clarkson
Q2	Oct	17	GAINSBOROUGH TRINITY	2-2	Vowles, Cawley	Reynolds	Glennie	Liversidge	Skull	Wilson	Evans	Lawrie	Whitham	Vowles	Cawley	Clarkson
Q2		22	Gainsborough Trinity	0-1		Reynolds	Glennie	Liversidge	Evans	Wilson	Hill	Lawrie	Whitham	Vowles	Cawley	Clarkson

1926/27

Rd	Mo	Dy	Opponent	Score	Scorers											
P	Sep	18	HULL HOLDERNESS	10-0	Skull, Johnson 3, Simms 3, Allen 2, Alford	Reynolds	Cook	Thomas	Skull	Smith	Hunter	Thompson	Simms	Johnson	Allen	Alford
Q1	Oct	2	GRIMSBY HAYCROFT ROVERS	7-2	Johnson 2, Simms 2, Allen 2, Smith	Reynolds	McKenzie	Holland	Skull	Smith	Hunter	Thompson	Simms	Johnson	Allen	Alford
Q2	Oct	16	Selby Olympia CO	0-0		Reynolds	McKenzie	Holland	Skull	Smith	Hunter	Thompson	Simms	Johnson	Allen	Alford
rep		21	SELBY OLYMPIA CO	1-0	Allen	Reynolds	McKenzie	Holland	Skull	Smith	Hunter	Thompson	Johnson	Simms	Allen	Alford
Q3		30	Gainsborough Trinity	3-3	Johnson 2, Alford	Reynolds	McKenzie	Holland	Skull	Smith	Hunter	Thompson	Johnson	Simms	Allen	Alford
rep	Nov	4	GAINSBOROUGH TRINITY	1-0	Simms	Reynolds	McKenie	Holland	Skull	Smith	Hunter	Thompson	Johnson	Simms	Allen	Alford
Q4		13	KETTERING	1-2	Johnson	Reynolds	McKenie	Hunter	Skull	Hunter	Moore	Thompson	Johnson	Simms	Allen	Alford

1927/28

Rd	Mo	Dy	Opponent	Score	Scorers											
P	Sep	17	CLEETHORPES	5-2	Simms 4, Hunter	Watts	Hollinsworth	Holland	Skull	Millson	Hunter	Wainwright	Brookes	Simms	Allen	Foster
Q1	Oct	1	Gainsborough Trinity	0-3		Watts	Severn	Hollinsworth	Skull	Murphy	Hunter	Wainwright	Brookes	Simms	Allen	Foster

1928/29

Rd	Date	Opponent	Score	Scorers	1	2	3	4	5	6	7	8	9	10	11
P	Sep 15	Barton Town	3-2	Webb, King, Pearson	Lloyd	Severn	Hesselgrove	Skull	Mooney	Gregson	Brandon	Maw	King	Pearson	Webb
Q1	Sep 29	Spalding United	3-0	Haywood 2, Maw	Lloyd	Severn	Purcell	Skull	Mooney	Bailey	Wadsworth	Maw	Haywood	Allen	Webb
Q2	Oct 13	CLEETHORPES	4-3	Reid 3, Maw	Watson	Severn	Hill	Skull	Mooney	Bailey	Wadsworth	Maw	Reid	Allen	Webb
Q3	Oct 27	Boston United	1-0	Wadsworth	Watson	Severn	Hill	Skull	Mooney	Bailey	Brandon	Maw	Wadsworth	Allen	Webb
Q4	Nov 10	Grantham	1-2	Maw	Watson	Severn	Hill	Skull	Mooney	Bailey	Brandon	Maw	Wadsworth	Allen	Webb

1929/30

Rd	Date	Opponent	Score	Scorers	1	2	3	4	5	6	7	8	9	10	11
P	Sep 21	Selby Town	3-1	Smalley, Bailey, Cooke	Bromage	Severn	Baynham	Skull	Cooke	Bailey	Simmons	Stringfellow	Smalley	Calladine	Beynon
Q1	Oct 5	SELBY OLYMPIA CO	1-0	Simmons	Bromage	Severn	Kennedy	Skull	Cooke	Bailey	Simmons	Stringfellow	Smalley	Calladine	Beynon
Q2	Oct 19	GOOLE TOWN	2-1	Simmons 2	Bromage	Severn	Baynham	Skull	Cooke	Bailey	Hackett	Stringfellow	Simmons	Calladine	Beynon
Q3	Nov 2	BROUGHTON RANGERS	7-0	Kennedy 4, Smalley 2, Simmons	Bromage	Severn	Baynham	Skull	Cooke	Bailey	Simmons	Stringfellow	Kennedy	Smalley	Beynon
Q4	Nov 16	South Kirkby Colliery	6-1	Smalley 2, Simmons 2, Stringfellow, 2	Bromage	Severn	Baynham	Skull	Cooke	Bailey	Simmons	Stringfellow	Smalley	Calladine	Beynon
R1	Nov 30	HARTLEPOOLS UNITED	1-0	Smalley	Bromage	Severn	Baynham	Skull	Cooke	Bailey	Simmons	Stringfellow	Smalley	Calladine	Beynon
R2	Dec 14	ROTHERHAM UNITED	3-3	Smalley, Calladine 2	Bromage	Severn	Baynham	Skull	Cooke	Bailey	Simmons	Stringfellow	Smalley	Calladine	Beynon
rep		Rotherham United	4-5	Beynon 2, Smalley, Calladine	Bromage	Severn	Baynham	Skull	Cooke	Bailey	Simmons	Stringfellow	Smalley	Calladine	Beynon

1930/31

Rd	Date	Opponent	Score	Scorers	1	2	3	4	5	6	7	8	9	10	11
Q4	Nov 15	WORCESTER CITY	3-0	Pattison 2, Beynon	Bromage	Webster	Baynham	Foster	Ross	Bailey	Oakton	Stringfellow	Pattison	Green	Beynon
R1	Nov 29	Gainsborough Trinity	0-1		Bromage	Webster	Baynham	Foster	Ross	Bailey	Oakton	Stringfellow	Pattison	Green	Beynon

1931/32

Rd	Date	Opponent	Score	Scorers	1	2	3	4	5	6	7	8	9	10	11
Q4	Nov 14	SUTTON JUNCTION	7-1	Hubbard 3, Methven 2, Grainger, Dawson	Bromage	Cross	Baynham	Wilson	Grainger	Stimpson	Davs	Hubbard	Methven	Dawson	Reed
R1	Nov 28	ROCHDALE	2-1	Hubbard, Methven	Bromage	Cross	Baynham	Staniland	Wilson	Stimpson	Davs	Hubbard	Methven	Dawson	Reed
R2	Dec 12	QUEENS PARK RANGERS	1-4	Baynham (pen)	Bromage	?	Baynham	Staniland	Wilson	Stimpson	Davs	Hubbard	Methven	Dawson	Reed

1932/33

Rd	Date	Opponent	Score	Scorers	1	2	3	4	5	6	7	8	9	10	11
R1	Nov 12	BURTON TOWN	4-1	Murfin 3, Hubbard	Young	Cross	Baynham	Staniland	Milson	Sharman	Tucker	Hubbard	Price	Chapman J	Murfin
R2	Nov 26	Workington	1-5	Tucker	Young	Cross	Baynham	Staniland	Robinson	Sharman	Tucker	Hubbard	Price	Chapman J	Murfin

1933/34

Rd	Date	Opponent	Score	Scorers	1	2	3	4	5	6	7	8	9	10	11
Q1	Sep 30	SELBY TOWN	4-1	Sumpter, Cross, Barry, Fenwick	Young	Cross	Hill	Davidson	Nicholson	Staniland	Sumpter	Fenwick	Smalley	Allen	Barry
Q2	Oct 14	HUMBER UNITED	5-0	Mills, Smalley, Allen, Reed, Nicholson	Young	Cross	Hill	Davidson	Nicholson	Staniland	Barry	Smalley	Mills	Allen	Reed
Q3	Oct	LOUTH TOWN	4-1	Nicholson, Oates, Mills, Smalley	Young	Cross	Hill	Mills	Nicholson	Staniland	Barry	Smalley	Oates	Allen	Reed
Q4	Nov 1	HEANOR TOWN	4-2	Pattison 2, Sumpter, Cross	Young	Cross	Hill	Mills	Nicholson	Staniland	Sumpter	Smalley	Pattison	Allen	Reed
R1	Nov 25	ACCRINGTON STANLEY	1-1	Sumpter	Young	Cross	Hill	Mills	Nicholson	Staniland	Sumpter	Oates	Pattison	Allen	Reed
rep		Accrington Stanley	0-3		Young	Cross	Hill	Mills	Nicholson	Staniland	Sumpter	Smalley	Pattison	Allen	Reed

1934/35

Rd	Date	Opponent	Score	Scorers	1	2	3	4	5	6	7	8	9	10	11
Q4	Nov 10	KETTERING TOWN	2-2	Allen, Lax	Young	Cross	Nicholson	Mills	Skull	Staniland	Barkley	Lynch	Pattison	Allen	Lax
rep	Nov 15	Kettering Town	3-1	Lax 2, Barley	Young	Cross	Nicholson	Mills	Skull	Staniland	Barley	Fenwick	Pattison	Allen	Lax
R1	2-	Coventry City	0-7		Young	Cross	Nicholson	Mills	Skull	Staniland	Barley	Fenwick	Pattison	Allen	Lax

1935/36

Rd	Date	Opponent	Score	Scorers	1	2	3	4	5	6	7	8	9	10	11
Q4	Nov 16	DENABY UNITED	4-1	Snaith 2, Lewis 2	Young	Cross	Crilley	Davies	Millington	Barker	Kilsby	Lewis	Snaith	Roberts	Allen
R1	Nov 30	Coventry City	1-1	Snaith	Young	Cross	Crilley	Davies	Millington	Barker	Kilsby	Lewis	Snaith	Roberts	Allen
rep	Dec	COVENTRY CITY	4-2	Davies, Roberts, Lewis, Kilsby	Young	Cross	Crilley	Davies	Millington	Barker	Kilsby	Lewis	Snaith	Roberts	Allen
R2	Dec 14	Tranmere Rovers	2-6	Lewis, Allen	Young	Cross	Crilley	Davies	Millington	Barker	Kilsby	Lewis	Snaith	Roberts	Allen

Season	Rd	Date	Opponent	Score	Scorers	Eamshaw	Cross	Jones	Moore	Millington	Stocks	Pattison	Norris	Smithson	Beckett	Allen
1936/37	Q4	Nov 14	Gainsborough Trinity	1-0	Norris	Eamshaw	Cross	Jones	Moore	Millington	Stocks	Pattison	Norris	Smithson	Beckett	Allen
	R1	28	Walsall	0-3		Eamshaw	Cross	Jones	Moore	Millington	Stocks	Pattison	Norris	Smithson	Beckett	Allen
1937/38	Q4	Nov 13	GRANTHAM	4-2	Johnson, Wilkinson 3	Eamshaw	Cross	Jones	Stocks	Millington	Allen	Baldry	Bett	Johnson	Lewis	Wilkinson
	R1	27	Hull City	0-4		Eamshaw	Proctor F	Jones	Stocks	Millington	Allen	Baldry	Bett	Johnson	Lewis	Wilkinson
1938/39	Q1	Oct 1	BARTON TOWN	9-1	Johnson 5, Fleetwood 2, Norris 2	Poxton	Dunn	Jones T	Stocks	Millington	Allen	Norris	Fleetwood	Johnson	Nightingale	Wilkinson
	Q2	15	APPLEBY FRODINGHAM	4-1	Johnson 3, Stocks	Poxton	Dunn	Jones T	Stocks	Millington	Allen	Norris	Fleetwood	Johnson	Nightingale	Robertshaw
	Q3	29	LYSAGHTS SPORTS	11-3	Johnson 5, Nightingale 4, Norris, Fleetwood	Poxton	Dunn	Jones T	Stocks	Millington	Allen	Norris	Fleetwood	Johnson	Nightingale	Wilkinson
	Q4	Nov 12	BOSTON UNITED	2-1	Nightingale, Johnson	Poxton	Jones T	Staniland	Staniland	Millington	Allen	Oxley	Fleetwood	Johnson	Nightingale	Wilkinson
	R1	26	LANCASTER CITY	4-2	Nightingale, Fleetwood 2, Johnson	Poxton	Jones T	Staniland	Staniland	Millington	Allen	Norris	Fleetwood	Johnson	Nightingale	Wilkinson
	R2	Dec 10	WATFORD	1-2	Jones (pen)	Poxton	Jones T	Staniland	Staniland	Millington	Allen	Norris	Fleetwood	Johnson	Nightingale	Oxley
1945/46	Q3	Oct 20	LYSAGHTS SPORTS	4-1	Johnson 2, Allen, Marriott	Poxton	Staniland	Pickering	Burnip	Millington	Allen	Marriott	Fleetwood	Johnson	Leeman	Readhead
	Q4	Nov 3	YORKSHIRE AMATEURS	1-2	Fleetwood	Poxton	Staniland	Betts	Burnip	Millington	Allen	Marriott	Fleetwood	Carver	Leeman	Readhead
1946/47	P	Sep 21	NORTON WOODSEATS	5-2	Bowers 3, Fleetwood, Wallace	Poxton	Staniland	Reed	Burnip	Millington	Leeman	Marriott	Fleetwood	Bowers	Wallace	Robertshaw
	Q1	Oct 5	HAWORTH COLLIERY	5-2	Bowers 2, Robertshaw, Wallace 2	Middleton	Reed	Catlin	Staniland	Millington	Harper	Marriott	Lindeman	Bowers	Wallace	Robertshaw
	Q2	19	Rawmarsh Welfare	3-0	Robertshaw, Marriott, Wallace	Poxton	Cooke	Reed	Staniland	Millington	Harper	Marriott	Bowers	Wynn	Wallace	Robertshaw
	Q3	Nov 2	Wombwell Athletic	5-2	Bowers, Wynn 3, Marriott	Poxton	Cooke	Reed	Staniland	Millington	Harper	Marriott	Bowers	Wynn	Wallace	Robertshaw
	Q3	16	BOSTON UNITED	4-1	Bowers 2, Robertshaw, Wallace	Poxton	Cooke	Reed	Staniland	Millington	Harper	Marriott	Bowers	Wynn	Wallace	Robertshaw
	R1	Dec 4	York City	1-0	Marriott	Poxton	Marriott	Reed	Staniland	Millington	Harper	Marriott	Bowers	Wynn	Wallace	Robertshaw
	R2	14	Rotherham United	1-4	Bowers	Poxton	Cooke	Reedd	Staniland	Millington	Harper	Marriott	Bowers	wynn	Wallace	Robertshaw
1947/48	P	Sep 20	THE SHEFFIELD CLUB	5-1	Bowers 2, Rowney, Robertshaw, Norris	Poxton	Watford	Brownsword	Staniland	Millington	Harper	Norris	Rowney	Bowers	Wallace	Robertshaw
	Q1	Oct 4	RAWMARSH WELFARE	8-0	Bowers 5, Wallace 2, Turner	Poxton	Watford	Brownsword	Staniland	Millington	Harper	Turner	Rowney	Bowers	Wallace	Crack
	Q2	18	DENABY UNITED	1-0	Rowney	Rymer	Watford	Brownsword	Staniland	Millington	Harper	Norris	Rowney	Bowers	Wallace	Crack
	Q3	Nov 1	NORTON WOODSEATS	2-1	Pinchbeck 2	Rymer	Watford	Brownsword	Staniland	Millington	Harper	Norris	Hydes	Pinchbeck	Wallace	Bowers
	Q4	15	GAINSBOROUGH TRINITY	4-2	Pinchbeck, Rowney, Robertshaw, Bowers	Rymer	Watford	Brownsword	Staniland	Millington	Harper	Bowers	Rowney	Pinchbeck	Wallace	Robertshaw
	R1	29	Runcorn	2-4	Bowers, Rowney	Poxton	Watford	Brownsword	Staniland	Millington	Harper	Bowers	Rowney	Pinchbeck	Wallace	Robertshaw
1948/49	Q4	Nov 13	SELBY TOWN	2-1	Murphy 2	Rymer	Waford	Brownsword	Davies	Taylor RE	Barker	Little	Rowney	Murphy	Wallace	Whitehead
	R1	Dec 4	Halifax Town	0-0		Rymer	Watford	Brownsword	Little	Taylor RE	Barker	Taylor J	Rowney	Murphy	Wallace	Whitehead
	rep	6	HALIFAX TOWN	1-0	Barker	Rymer	Watford	Brownsword	Littel	Taylor RE	Barker	Bowers	Rowney	Murphy	Taylor J	Whitehead
	R2	11	STOCKPORT COUNTY	0-1		Rymer	Watford	Brownsword	Little	Taylor RE	Barker	Rowney	Davies	Murphy	Wallace	Whitehead
1949/50	Q4	Nov 12	GOOLE TOWN	0-0		Thompson	Barker	Brownsword	Conroy	Taylor RE	Pigdon	Wilson	Barkas	Whitfield	Wallace	Malcolm
	rep	22	Goole Town	1-3	Barkas	Thompson	Dixon	Brownsword	Conroy	Taylor RE	Barker	Bowers	Barkas	Whitfield	Wallace	Malcolm

SCUNTHORPE'S MANAGERS SINCE 1950

Leslie Jones	1950-51	
Bill Corkhill	1951-56	
Ron Suart	1956-58	
Tony MacShane	1958-59	
Bill Lambton	1959	(3 days)
Frank Soo	1959-60	
Dick Duckworth	1960-64	
Freddie Goodwin	1964-67	
Ron Ashman	1967-73	
Ron Bradley	1973-74	
Dickie Rooks	1974-76	
Ron Ashman	1976-81	
John Duncan	1981-83	
Allan Clarke	1983-84	
Frank Barlow	1984-87	
Mick Buxton	1987-91	
Bill Green	1991-93	
Richard Money	1993-95	
Dave Moore	1995-96	
Mick Buxton	1996 on	

Bill Lambton holds the record as the Football League manager with the shortest spell at a club. He received an offer to coach Grimsby Town the day after he took over as manager and decided that this was a better job than the one he already had.

Manager Ron Suart and the 1957/58 squad. Back: Sharpe, Hubbard, Hardwick, Whitnall, Gleadall, Strong (masseur). Middle: Suart, Marshall, Horstead, Minton, Heward, Bushby, Brownsword. Front: Davies, Marriott, Waldock, Davis, Fletcher, Haigh, Jones.

Player			D.O.B	Place of Birth	Died	First Lge Season	Last Lge Season	Previous Club	Next Club	Appearances				Goals			
										League	FAC	FLC	Other	League	FAC	FLC	Oth.
Agnew	DY	David	04/08/39	Kilwinning		1961		Leicester City	Notts County	1	0	0	0	0	0	0	0
Alexander	G	Graham	10/10/71	Coventry		1988	1994	YTS	Luton Town	159	12	12	16	18	1	2	3
Allen	W	Bill	22/10/17	Newburn		1950	1951	York City		64	2	0	0	1	0	0	0
Anderson	AA	Alan	21/12/39	Edinburgh		1962		Millwall	Hearts	6	0	4	0	0	0	0	0
Anderson	TK	Terry	11/03/44	Woking	1980	1974		Colchester Utd.	Crewe Alexandra	10	0	0	0	0	0	0	0
Andrews	LL	Les	29/10/53	Dudley		1973		Wolves (loan)		9	0	0	0	1	0	0	0
Angus	MA	Mike	28/10/60	Middlesbrough		1982		Middlesbrough (loan)		20	4	0	0	2	0	0	0
Arblaster	BM	Brian	06/06/43	Kensington		1967		Chesterfield	Barnsley	10	0	2	0	0	0	0	0
Arins	AF	Tony	26/10/58	Chesterfield		1981		Leeds United		20	0	0	0	1	0	0	0
Armstrong	KT	Keith	11/10/57	Corbridge		1978		Sunderland (loan)		1	0	0	0	0	0	0	0
Ash	M	Micky	04/09/43	Sheffield		1965	1966	Sheffield Utd.	New York Generals	49	2	1	0	7	0	0	0
Ashworth	PA	Phil	04/04/53	Burnley		1980		Portsmouth	Cambridge City	23	1	0	0	3	0	0	0
Atkin	JM	Mick	14/02/48	Scunthorpe		1969	1974	Local	Gainsborough Tr.	122	16	2	0	0	0	0	0
Atkins	MN	Mark	14/08/68	Doncaster		1984	1987	Jnrs.	Blackburn Rovers	50	5	4	7	2	0	0	0
Babes	J	John	20/11/29	Lurgan		1950	1951	Arsenal		9	0	0	0	0	0	0	0
Baines	SJ	Steve	23/06/54	Newark		1982		Walsall	Chesterfield	38	4	0	0	1	0	0	0
Bakes	MS	Martin	08/02/37	Bradford		1959	1962	Bradford City	Retired	77	3	3	0	5	2	0	0
Bannister	J	Jack	26/01/42	Chesterfield		1964		West Bromwich A.	Crystal Palace	9	0	6	0	0	0	0	0
Barker	J	Jeff	16/10/15	Scunthorpe	1985	1950	1951	Huddersfield T	Retired	73	14	0	0	1	1	0	0
Barker	J	John	04/07/48	Huddersfield		1965	1974	App.	Scarborough	263	28	13	0	6	2	0	0
Barley	PJ	Peter	25/04/36	Scunthorpe		1953		Leeds United		5	0	0	0	0	0	0	0
Barnard	G	Geoff	23/03/46	Southend-on-Sea		1968	1974	Norwich City	Scarborough	262	25	13	0	0	0	0	0
						1976		Scarborough	Retired								
Barnes	DO	David 'Bobby'	17/12/62	Kingston		1985		West Ham Utd. (loan)		6	0	0	0	0	0	0	0
Barrett	J	John	26/03/31	Birmingham		1954	1955	Aston Villa		17	1	0	0	0	0	0	0
Barton	F	Frank	22/10/47	Barton-on-Humber		1964	1967	App.	Carlisle Utd.	93	4	3	0	26	2	2	0
Batch	NA	Nigel	09/09/57	Huddersfield		1991		Stockport Co.	Retired	1	0	0	0	0	0	0	0
Bedford	NB	Brian	24/12/33	Ferndale		1965	1966	QPR	Brentford	37	1	0	0	23	0	0	0
Bell	DM	Derek	30/10/56	Wyberton		1983	1984	Chesterfield	Boston Utd.	22	0	1	3	7	0	0	3
Bennett	R	Bobby	29/12/51	Harrow		1973		Southend U (loan)		3	1	0	0	0	0	0	0
Benson	JR	Joe	07/01/33	Misterton		1955				2	0	0	0	0	0	0	0
Betts	JB	Barry	18/09/32	Barnsley		1964		Manchester City	Lancaster City	7	0	2	0	0	0	0	0
Birch	A	Alan	12/08/56	West Bromwich		1986	1987	Rotherham Utd.	Stockport Co.	23	1	6	1	2	0	0	0
Bloomer	BMc	Brian	03/05/52	Cleethorpes		1978		Brigg Town	Brigg Town	7	0	0	0	1	0	0	0
Blyth	MR	Mel	28/07/44	Norwich		1967		Gt. Yarmouth	Crystal Palace	27	0	0	0	3	0	0	0
Bond	LA	Len	12/02/54	Ilminster		1975		Bristol City (loan)		8	0	0	0	0	0	0	0
Bonson	J	Joe	19/06/36	Barnsley		1960	1961	Cardiff City	Doncaster Rovers	52	2	2	0	11	3	1	0
Botham	IT	Ian	24/11/55	Heswall		1979	1984		Yeovil Town	11	1	0	2	0	0	0	0
Bowen	D	Danny	16/11/21	Ynysybwl		1950		Treharris	Hastings Utd.	5	0	0	0	0	0	0	0
Boxall	AR	Alan	11/05/53	Woolwich		1980	1983	Barton Town	Chesterfield	54	3	3	3	1	0	0	0
Boyd	G	Gordon	27/03/58	Glasgow		1981		Barnsley	Goole Town	11	0	0	0	0	0	0	0
Boyes	WE	Wally	05/01/13	Killamarsh	1960	1950		Notts County	Retford T (p/m)	13	0	0	0	2	0	0	0
Bradley	R	Russell	28/03/66	Birmingham		1993	1995	Halifax Town		97	10	4	9	4	0	0	0
Bramhall	J	John	20/11/56	Warrington		1989	1990	Halifax Town	Hyde United	32	3	0	0	0	1	0	0
Bramley	JS	Stuart	19/04/46	Scunthorpe		1964	1966	App.	Plymouth Argyle	35	0	0	0	3	0	0	0
Bridges	B	Bernard	28/02/59	Doncaster		1976	1977	Jnrs.	Barton Town	23	0	4	0	0	0	0	0
Broadley	L	Les	10/08/30	Goole		1952		Goole Town		5	0	0	0	2	0	0	0
Broddle	JR	Julian	01/11/64	Laughton		1983	1992	Sheffield Utd.	Barnsley	149	11	11	6	32	4	1	1
Brolly	MJ	Mike	06/10/54	Galston		1983	1985	Derby County	Scarborough	95	9	8	5	15	1	1	2
Brown	AJ	Tony	17/09/58	Bradford		1987	1988	Doncaster Rovers	Rocdale	54	3	8	3	2	0	0	0
Brown	DJ	David	28/01/57	Hartlepool		1988		Preston NE (loan)		5	0	0	0	0	0	0	0
Brown	GA	Gordon	30/06/33	Ellesmere Port		1952	1958	Wolves	Derby County	164	11	0	0	68	7	0	0
Brown	MR	Monty	07/09/43	Grimsby		1964	1965	Jnrs.	Corby Town	19	0	1	0	6	0	0	0
Brownsword	NJ	Jack	15/05/23	Campsall		1950	1964	Hull City	(Trainer)	597	56	10	0	50	3	0	0
Buckley	JW	John	10/05/62	Glasgow		1991	1992	Partick Thistle	Rotherham Utd.	43	4	6	6	8	1	0	0
Bullimore	WA	Wayne	12/09/70	Sutton-in-Ashfield		1993	1995	Stockport Co.	Bradford City	67	7	4	5	11	1	1	1
Burkinshaw	KH	Keith	23/06/35	Barnsley		1965	1967	Workington	Newcastle U(coach)	108	4	4	0	3	0	0	0
Burrows	F	Frank	30/01/44	Larkhall		1965	1967	Raith Rovers	Swindon Town	106	4	3	0	4	1	0	0
Bushby	A	Alan	15/01/32	Doncaster	1967	1952	1958	Local	Rochdale	218	23	0	0	10	2	0	0
Butler	LS		30/05/66	Sheffield		1995		Barnsley (loan)		2	0	0	0	0	0	0	0
Butler	MC	Martin	03/03/66	Hull		1989		Carlisle Utd.	Mcclesfield Town	2	0	1	0	0	0	0	0
Callaghan	R	Robert	05/10/31	Glasgow		1955		Duntocher H.	Barrow	19	1	0	0	6	0	0	0
Cammack	SR	Steve	20/03/54	Sheffield		1979	1980	Chesterfield	Lincoln City	245	18	10	6	110	6	3	2
						1981	1986	Lincoln City	Scarborough								
Carmichael	M	Matt	13/05/64	Singapore		1993	1994	Lincoln City	Preston NE	62	7	2	5	20	2	0	5
Cartwright	P	Peter	23/08/57	Newcastle		1982		Newcastle U (loan)		4	0	0	0	1	0	0	0
Cassidy	N	Nigel	07/12/45	Sudbury		1968	1970	Norwich City	Oxford Utd.	88	7	2	0	35	4	0	0
Charles	S	Steve	10/05/60	Sheffield		1992		Mansfield Town (loan)		4	0	0	2	0	0	0	0
Charlesworth	T	Terry	13/07/33	Scunthorpe		1952	1956	Local		19	2	0	0	0	0	0	0
Charnley	DL	Derek	07/05/54	Doncaster		1972	1975	Jnrs.	Bridlington Trin.	38	0	1	0	3	0	0	0
Clarkson	PI	Phil	13/11/68	Hambleton		1995		Crewe Alexandra (loan)		24	0	0	0	6	0	0	0
Clelland	D	David	18/03/24	Netherburn		1950		Weymouth	Met. Police	16	0	0	0	8	0	0	0
Clemence	RN	Ray	05/08/48	Skegness		1965	1966	Notts County	Liverpool	48	3	0	0	0	0	0	0
Coatsworth	FW	Fred	05/07/48	Lincoln		1965	1966	Jnrs.	Rugby Town	15	0	0	0	2	0	0	0
Collard	JB	Bruce	21/08/53	Hetton-le-Hole		1973		West Bromwich A.	Dunstable Town	22	4	1	0	0	0	0	0
Collier	GR	Graham	12/09/51	Nottingham		1972	1976	Nottm. Forest	Barnsley	161	11	11	0	19	2	0	0
Colquhoun	J	John	03/06/40	Stirling		1965	1968	Oldham Athletic	Oldham Athletic	149	5	7	0	23	1	0	0
Comley	LG	Len	25/01/22	Swansea		1950		Newport County	Llanelly	12	0	0	0	5	0	0	0

Player			D.O.B	Place of Birth	Died	First Lge Season	Last Lge Season	Previous Club	Next Club	Appearances				Goals			
										League	FAC	FLC	Other	League	FAC	FLC	Oth.
Conde	JP	Jim	19/07/44	Creswell		1963		Wolves	Bangor City	4	1	0	0	1	0	0	0
Conroy	RM	Maurice	26/04/19	Bradford		1950		Accrington Stanley	(trainer)	1	0	0	0	0	0	0	0
Constable	S	Shaun	21/03/68	Maidstone		1992			Halifax Town	7	0	0	0	0	0	0	0
Cooper	T	Terry	11/03/50	Croesyceiliog		1977		Lincoln City (loan)		4	0	0	0	0	0	0	0
Cork	D	David	28/10/62	Doncaster		1988		West Bromwich A.	Darlington	15	0	0	2	0	0	0	0
Cotton	P	Perry	11/11/65	Chislehurst		1988	1990	Nelson U (NZ)	Kettering Town	33	5	1	7	2	0	0	1
Couch	GR	Geoff	03/04/53	Crowle		1977	1979	Crowle		26	0	2	0	5	0	0	0
Cowling	C	Chris	19/09/62	Scunthorpe		1979	1984	App.		134	13	9	4	26	4	2	0
Cowling	DR	David	27/11/58	Doncaster		1987	1990	Huddersfield T (loan)		90	5	8	7	5	0	0	1
Cox	NJ	Neil	08/10/71	Scunthorpe		1989	1990	Trainee	Aston Villa	17	4	0	5	1	0	0	0
Cox	S	Sam	30/10/20	Mexborough		1952		Accrington Stanley	Retired	3	0	0	0	0	0	0	0
Crawford	I	Ian	14/07/34	Edinburgh		1962	1963	West Ham Utd.	Peterborough U	35	1	3	0	2	0	1	0
Crawford	PG	Graeme	07/08/47	Falkirk		1977	1979	York City	York City	104	3	8	0	0	0	0	0
Crisp	RI	Richard	23/05/72	Wordsley		1992		Aston Villa (loan)		8	0	0	0	0	0	0	0
Cumner	RH	Horace	31/03/18	Cwmaman		1950	1952	Watford	Bradford City	102	4	0	0	21	0	0	0
Currie	JT	Jim	06/08/48	Stirling		1968	1969		Ashby Town	6	0	0	0	0	0	0	0
Czuczman	M	Mike	27/05/53	Carlisle		1976	1978	Grimsby Town	Stockport County	116	3	10	0	1	0	0	0
D'Auria	DA	David	26/03/70	Swansea		1995		Scarborough		27	0	0	0	5	0	0	0
Dale	AG	Alan	20/09/58	Thorne		1975	1976	App.		3	0	0	0	0	0	0	0
Daley	AJ	Alan 'Digger'	11/10/27	Mansfield	1975	1952		Boston United	Corby Town	35	4	0	0	8	1	0	0
Dall	DG	David	10/10/57	St Andrews		1979	1981	Grantham	East Fife	77	4	4	0	2	0	0	0
Danzey	MJ	Mike	08/02/71	Widnes		1993		Cambridge U (loan)		3	0	0	0	1	0	0	0
Davidson	AG	Angus	02/10/48	Dundee		1969	1976	Grimsby Town		321	28	13	0	45	0	1	0
Davidson	I	Ian	31/01/47	Goole		1968		Hull City (loan)		35	1	1	0	0	0	0	0
Davies	JR	John	26/09/33	Portsmouth		1955	1957	Portsmouth	Walsall	67	9	0	0	10	7	0	0
Davis	EWC	Eric	26/02/32	Stonehouse, Devon		1957	1958	Plymouth Argyle	Chester	40	2	0	0	20	2	0	0
Davy	SJ	Steve	09/04/55	Norwich		1977	1981	West Ham Utd.	App. Frodingham	134	8	6	0	1	0	0	0
Daws	A	Tony	10/09/66	Sheffield		1987	1992	Sheffield Utd.	Grimsby Town	183	9	16	23	63	2	4	2
Deere	SH	Steve	31/03/48	Burnham Market		1967	1972	Norwich City	Hull City	343	26	12	0	22	4	2	0
						1977	1979	Scarborough									
De Mange	KJP	Ken	03/09/64	Dublin		1986		Liverpool (loan)		3	1	0	1	2	1	0	0
DeVries	RS	Roger	25/10/50	Hull		1981		Blackburn Rovers		6	0	0	0	1	0	0	0
Dey	G	Geoff	11/01/64	Chesterfield		1983	1984	Sheffield Utd.		17	5	4	2	1	1	0	0
Dixon	KL	Kevin	27/07/60	Blackhill		1985	1987	Hartlepool Utd.	Hartlepool Utd.	55	4	4	6	6	0	0	1
Donnelly	P	Peter	22/09/36	Hull		1958	1959	Doncaster Rovers	Cardiff City	39	2	0	0	19	0	0	0
Drake	S	Steve	27/08/48	Goole		1967	1969	Huddersfield T	Goole Town	23	1	0	0	0	0	0	0
Duffy	DG	Darrell	18/01/71	Birmingham		1992		Aston Villa	Tamworth	4	0	0	0	0	0	0	0
Duffy	VG	Vince	21/09/62	Nottingham		1980	1981	Nottm. Forest	Heanor Town	8	0	1	0	0	0	0	0
Duncan	JP	John	22/02/49	Dundee		1981	1982	Derby County	(manager)	9	0	1	2	0	0	0	0
Earl	S	Steve	31/08/56	Scunthorpe		1974	1979	App. Frodingham	App. Frodingham	39	0	2	0	10	0	0	0
Eli	R	Roger	11/09/65	Bradford		1994		Burnley	Partick Thistle	2	0	0	0	0	0	0	0
Elliott	MS	Matthew	01/11/68	Wandsworth		1991	1993	Torquay United (loan)		61	2	6	7	8	0	0	0
Ellis	KD	Keith	06/11/35	Sheffield		1963		Sheffield Wed.	Cardiff City	10	0	0	0	5	0	0	0
Eyre	JR	John	09/10/74	Humberside		1994	1995	Oldham Athletic (loan)		48	3	2	2	18	1	2	1
Farrell	D	David	11/11/71	Birmingham		1992		Aston Villa (loan)		5	0	0	2	1	0	0	0
Farrell	KM	Mick	13/03/59	Ilkley		1975	1977	App.		9	1	0	0	1	0	0	0
Fawcett	B	Brian	14/02/32	Doncaster		1954		Bentley Colliery	Bradford	1	0	0	0	0	0	0	0
Ferguson	RC	Ron	09/02/57	Accrington		1975		Sheffield Wed. (loan)		3	0	0	0	0	0	0	0
Ferry	W	Willie	21/11/66	Sunderland		1984	1986	Trainee	Barnsley	5	1	2	0	0	0	0	0
Finney	SB	Shaun	05/10/66	Dinnington		1984		Nottm. Forest	Gainsborough Trin.	2	0	0	1	0	0	0	0
Fletcher	D	Doug	17/09/30	Sheffield		1956	1957	Bury	Darlington	54	6	0	0	26	1	0	0
Fletcher	JR	Rod	23/09/45	Preston		1971	1973	Lincoln City	Grimsby Town	98	7	6	0	30	2	0	0
Flounders	AJ	Andy	13/12/63	Hull		1986	1990	Hull City	Rochdale	196	13	14	19	87	3	6	4
Foley	P	Peter	28/06/44	Glasgow		1967	1968	Workington	Chesterfield	17	0	3	0	3	0	1	0
Ford	T	Tony	14/05/59	Grimsby		1994	1995	Grimsby Town		76	7	4	4	9	1	1	0
Fowler	M	Martin	17/01/57	York		1982		Stockport Co.		18	4	2	3	0	0	0	0
Foxon	DN	Neil	10/07/48	Nottingham		1966	1967	Notts County	Wisbech Town	22	1	1	0	1	1	0	0
Foxton	DG	Graham	02/10/49	Harrogate		1987	1972	Jnrs.	Brigg Town	154	17	6	0	1	0	0	0
Foy	DL	David	20/10/72	Coventry		1992		Birmingham City	Stafford Rangers	3	0	0	0	0	0	0	0
Gannon	MJ	Mick	02/02/43	Liverpool		1962	1963	Everton	Crewe Alexandra	15	0	1	0	0	0	0	0
Germaine	GP	Gary	02/08/76	Birmingham		1995		West Brom. (loan)		11	0	0	0	0	0	0	0
Gibson	A	Archie	30/12/33	Girvan		1960	1963	Leeds United	Barnsley	138	6	10	0	5	0	1	0
Gibson	D	David	14/02/58	Seaham		1978	1979	Hull City		21	0	2	0	1	0	0	0
Gilbert	DJ	David	22/06/63	Lincoln		1982		Lincoln City	Boston United	1	0	1	2	0	0	0	0
Gleadall	E	Eddie	21/08/31	Sheffield		1956	1957	Bury	Weymouth	6	0	0	0	2	0	0	0
Godfrey	BC	Brian	01/05/40	Flint		1960	1963	Everton	Preston NE	87	5	7	0	24	1	2	0
Goodacre	SD	Sam	01/12/70	Sheffield		1992	1994	Sheffield Wed.	Stalybridge Celtic	44	2	5	3	12	2	0	1
Goodlass	R	Ronnie	06/09/53	Liverpool		1981		Fulham	Tranmere Rovers	9	0	0	0	0	0	0	0
Goodwin	F	Freddie	28/06/33	Heywood		1965		Leeds United	New York Generals	6	1	0	0	1	0	0	0
Goodwin	SA	Steve	23/02/54	Chadderton		1973		Norwich City (loan)		2	0	0	0	0	0	0	0
Gordon	JS	Jimmy	03/10/55	Stretford		1979	1980	Reading	Boston United	34	1	0	0	0	0	0	0
Gorin	ER	Ted	02/02/24	Cardiff		1950		Cardiff City	Shrewsbury Town	26	1	0	0	12	0	0	0
Graham	DWT	Deiniol	04/10/69	Cannock		1995		Stockport Co.		3	0	0	0	1	0	0	0
Graham	T	Tommy	31/03/58	Glasgow		1982	1985	Doncaster Rovers	Scarborough	109	8	5	7	21	2	0	1
Grant	J	Jim	10/06/40	Chapelhall		1958		Larkhall Thistle		1	0	0	0	0	0	0	0
Gray	G	George	06/10/29	Glasgow		1951		Sligo Rovers	Kettering Town	9	0	0	0	3	0	0	0
Greaves	SR	Steve	17/01/70	Chelsea		1992		Ipswich Town	Dagenham&Redbdge	15	2	1	3	0	0	0	0
Green	JR	John	07/08/58	Rotherham		1983	1985	Rotherham Utd.	Darlington	100	9	6	5	4	0	0	0

Player			D.O.B	Place of Birth	Died	First Lge Season	Last Lge Season	Previous Club	Next Club	Appearances				Goals			
										League	FAC	FLC	Other	Leagu	FAC	FLC	Oth.
Green	R	Rick	23/11/52	Scunthorpe		1975	1976	App. Frodingham	Chesterfield	137	6	6	0	38	2	0	0
						1979	1981	Notts County	Brigg Town								
Green	RR	Ron	03/10/56	Birmingham		1986	1987	Bristol Rovers	Wimbledon	78	5	7	4	0	0	0	0
Gregory	JE	John	24/09/26	Shoreditch		1953	1956	West Ham Utd.	Aldershot	147	18	0	0	63	6	0	0
Gregory	NR	Neil	07/10/72	Zambia		1994		Ipswich Town (loan)		10	0	0	0	7	0	0	0
Gregory	PG	Paul	26/07/61	Sheffield		1984	1986	Doncaster Rovers	Goole Town	69	3	2	6	0	0	0	0
Grimes	V	Vince	13/05/54	Scunthorpe		1977	1981	Hull City		143	7	6	0	12	2	0	0
Haigh	J	Jack	10/09/28	Rotherham		1952	1959	Liverpool	Doncaster Rovers	329	31	0	0	66	5	0	0
Hall	A	Arthur	23/11/25	Sheffield		1951		Goole Town	Grantham	15	1	0	0	5	0	0	0
Hall	DA	David	26/09/60	Doncaster		1978	1979	App.	Frickley Athletic	17	0	0	0	0	0	0	0
Hall	RA	Richard	14/03/72	Ipswich		1989	1990	Trainee	Southampton	22	3	2	4	3	0	0	0
Hamill	SP	Stewart	22/01/60	Glasgow		1981		Leicester City (loan)		4	0	0	0	0	0	0	0
Hamilton	IR	Ian	14/12/67	Stevenage		1988	1991	Cambridge Utd.	West Bromwich A.	145	7	6	14	18	0	0	3
Harbum	PAP	Peter	18/06/31	Shoreditch		1958	1959	Everton	Workington	20	0	0	0	8	0	0	0
Hardwick	K	Ken	06/01/24	West Auckland		1956	1959	Doncaster Rovers	Barrow	96	6	0	0	0	0	0	0
Harle	D	David	15/08/63	Denaby		1986	1988	Bristol City	Peterborough U	89	5	8	8	10	2	1	2
Harney	D	David	02/03/47	Jarrow		1967	1968	Grimsby Town	Brentford	25	0	2	0	1	0	0	0
Harper	IT	Ian	23/11/44	Scunthorpe		1963	1964	Jnrs.	Gainsborough Trin.	21	0	0	0	0	0	0	0
Hawley	JE	John	08/05/54	Patrington		1985		Bradford City	Retired	21	2	2	3	7	0	0	4
Heath	M	Michael	07/02/74	Hull		1993		Tottenham H	N Ferriby Utd.	2	0	0	0	0	0	0	0
Heath	RT	Terry	17/11/43	Leicester		1967	1972	Hull City	Lincoln City	176	20	8	0	49	3	0	0
Helliwell	I	Ian	07/11/62	Rotherham		1991	1992	York City	Rotherham Utd.	80	4	8	8	22	2	5	2
Hemmerman	JL	Jeff	25/02/55	Hull		1975		Hull City (loan)		5	0	0	0	1	0	0	0
Hemstead	DW	Derek	22/05/43	Scunthorpe		1960	1968	Jnrs.	Carlisle Utd.	248	11	11	0	2	0	0	0
Henderson	DR	Damian	12/05/73	Leeds		1993	1994	Scarborough	Hartlepool U	37	1	2	1	4	0	1	0
Heron	B	Brian	19/06/48	Dumbarton		1977		Oxford United	Retired	25	0	4	0	1	0	0	0
Heward	B	Brian	17/07/35	Lincoln		1953	1960	Jnrs.	Lincoln City	137	12	2	0	0	0	0	0
Heyes	D	Darren	11/01/67	Swansea		1987		Nottm. Forest	Shepshed Chart.	3	0	1	3	0	0	0	0
Hicks	SJ	Stuart	30/05/67	Peterborough		1990	1991	Colchester Utd.	Doncaster Rovers	67	4	4	8	0	1	0	0
Hill	DM	David	06/06/66	Nottingham		1983	1987	Trainee	Ipswich Town	205	11	12	16	16	3	1	1
						1990	1992	Ipswich Town	Lincoln City								
Hine	M	Mark	18/05/64	Middlesbrough		1990	1991	Peterborough Utd.	Gateshead	22	1	3	2	2	0	0	0
Hodgson	K	Ken	19/01/42	Newcastle		1961	1963	Newcastle United	Bournemouth	88	4	2	0	30	0	0	0
Hodkinson	AJ	Andy	04/11/65	Ashton-under-Lyne		1988	1989	Stockport Co.	Hyde United	62	5	7	6	8	1	1	0
Holden	R	Robbie	28/10/65	Sunderland		1983		Sunderland		7	0	1	0	1	0	0	0
Holt	R	Ray	29/10/39	Thorne		1968	1969	Halifax Town	Worksop Town	50	1	4	0	0	0	0	0
Holyoak	P	Phil	22/05/50	Sunderland		1977		Tottenham H (loan)		1	0	0	0	0	0	0	0
Hope	CJ	Chris	14/11/72	Sheffield		1993	1995	Nottm. Forest		105	8	4	8	3	1	0	0
Horsfall	TW	Tommy	07/01/51	Hamilton		1973		Southend Utd. (loan)		5	0	0	0	2	0	0	0
Horstead	JB	Barry	08/05/35	Brigg		1956	1967	Jnrs.		320	21	13	0	3	0	1	0
Houchen	KM	Keith	25/07/60	Middlesbrough		1985		York City	Coventry City	9	0	0	0	3	0	0	0
Houghton	K	Ken	18/10/39	Rotherham		1973		Hull City	Scarborough	33	7	4	0	5	2	0	0
Housham	SJ	Steven	24/02/76	Gainsborough		1994	1995	Trainee		32	1	0	3	0	0	0	1
Howells	R	Ron	03/08/35	Ferndale		1961	1962	Portsmouth	Walsall	69	3	1	0	4	0	0	0
Hubbard	J	Jack	24/03/25	Wath-on-Dearne		1950	1959	Scarborough		359	31	0	0	12	2	0	0
Hughes	DT	David	19/03/58	Birmingham		1981		Lincoln City	Lincoln City	20	1	1	0	0	0	0	0
Humphries	G	Glenn	11/08/64	Hull		1990	1992	Bristol City	Frickley Athletic	72	4	5	6	5	0	1	1
Hunter	L	Les	15/01/58	Middlesbrough		1982	1983	Chesterfield	Chesterfield	110	6	6	6	13	0	0	2
						1985	1986	Chesterfield	Lincoln City								
Hussey	FM	Malcolm	11/09/33	Darfield		1956	1957	Rotherham Utd.	Rochdale	23	0	0	0	0	0	0	0
Hutchinson	DN	David	25/09/41	Grimsby		1971		Brigg Town	Gainsborough Trin.	9	0	0	0	0	0	0	0
Hutton	J	Jack	23/04/44	Bellshill		1963	1965	Hamilton Acad.	St. Mirren	54	7	0	0	7	0	0	0
Hyde	GS	Gary	28/12/69	Wolverhampton		1991		Leicester City	Whitby Town	8	1	1	3	0	0	0	0
Irvine	A	Archie	25/06/46	Coatbridge		1975		Doncaster Rovers		23	0	1	0	1	0	0	0
Jackson	NA	Nigel	27/06/50	Pudsey		1968	1972	App.	Bridlington Trin.	118	2	5	0	5	0	1	0
Jarvis	NC	Nick	19/09/55	Mansfield		1980		Grantham	Grantham	21	3	2	0	0	0	0	0
John	DCJ	Dennis	27/01/35	Swansea		1959	1961	Swansea Town	Millwall	88	4	2	0	0	0	0	0
Johnson	P	Paul	10/05/63	Scunthorpe		1981	1987	App.		14	2	0	3	0	0	0	0
Johnson	SA	Steve	23/06/57	Liverpool		1986	1987	Bristol City	Chester City	72	6	7	6	20	1	3	0
Jones	JM	Merfyn	30/04/31	Bangor		1953	1958	Liverpool	Crewe Alexandra	240	23	0	0	27	6	0	0
Jones	K	Ken	02/01/36	Aberdare		1958	1963	Cardiff City	Charlton Ath.	168	9	9	0	0	0	0	0
Jones	RA	Ryan	23/07/73	Sheffield		1995		Sheffield Wed. (loan)		11	0	0	0	3	0	0	0
Jones	RJ	Ron	27/02/26	Rhondda		1950		Swansea Town		3	0	0	0	0	0	0	0
Joyce	JP	Joe	18/03/61	Consett		1990	1992	Barnsley	Carlisle United	91	0	5	10	2	0	0	0
Juryeff	IM	Ian	24/11/62	Gosport		1993	1994	Darlington	Farnborough Town	44	5	2	3	14	0	0	0
Kavanagh	EA	Eamonn	05/01/54	Manchester		1977	1979	Workington		77	4	4	0	3	0	0	0
Kaye	J	John	03/03/40	Goole		1960	1962	Goole Town	West Bromwich A.	77	3	2	0	25	0	0	0
Keegan	JK	Kevin	14/02/51	Armthorpe		1968	1970	App.	Liverpool	124	14	3	0	17	3	1	0
Keeley	AJ	Andy	16/09/56	Basildon		1981	1982	Sheffield Utd.		77	6	4	3	1	0	0	0
Keeley	NB	Nolan	24/05/51	Barsham		1972	1979	Gt. Yarmouth	Lincoln City	259	15	20	0	37	3	4	0
Kerr	GAM	George	09/01/43	Alexandria		1967	1972	Oxford United	Lincoln C (coach)	157	10	6	0	32	4	2	0
Kilmore	K	Kevin	11/11/59	Scunthorpe		1976	1979	Jnrs.	Grimsby Town	102	3	8	0	28	0	1	0
Kirk	HJ	Harry	25/08/44	Saltcoats		1970	1972	Hartlepool Utd.	Stockport County	112	10	8	0	16	3	0	0
Kirkman	AJ	Alan	21/06/36	Bolton		1963	1964	Newcastle United	Torquay United	32	0	8	0	5	0	0	0
Kisby	CN	Chris	07/11/52	Horsforth		1970	1972	App.	Workington	39	4	0	0	2	0	0	0
Kiwomya	AD	Andy	01/10/67	Huddersfield		1994		Carlisle Utd.	Bradford City	9	0	0	0	3	0	0	0
Knight	IJ	Ian	26/10/66	Hartlepool		1989		Sheffield Wed. (loan)		2	0	0	0	0	0	0	0
Knill	AR	Alan	08/10/64	Slough		1993	1995	Bury		102	9	3	6	8	0	0	0
Krzywicki	RL	Dick	02/02/47	Penley		1972		Huddersfield T (loan)		2	0	0	0	0	0	0	0

Player			D.O.B	Place of Birth	Died	First Lge Season	Last Lge Season	Previous Club	Next Club	Appearances League	FAC	FLC	Other	Goals League	FAC	FLC	Oth.
Lamb	HT	Harry	20/04/28	Stourbridge		1954	1955	Aston Villa		36	5	0	0	0	0	0	0
Lambert	AJ	Anton	29/11/59	Nottingham		1980	1981	Long Eaton	Ilkeston Town	39	3	3	0	4	0	0	0
Lavery	J	Jim	13/12/48	Glasgow		1967	1974		Brigg Town	26	1	1	0	0	0	0	0
Lawther	WI	Ian	20/10/39	Belfast		1963	1964	Blackburn Rovers	Brentford	60	11	12	0	22	1	0	0
Lee	R	Robert	23/12/57	Newcastle		1976	1977	Doncaster Rovers	Ashby Town	19	1	0	0	0	0	0	0
Lees	T	Terry	30/06/52	Stoke-on-Trent		1984		Stafford Rangers	(Sweden)	31	3	1	1	0	0	0	0
Leman	D	Dennis	01/12/54	Newcastle		1982	1983	Sheffield Wed.	Burton Albion	38	2	2	3	3	0	0	0
Lester	MJ	Mike	04/08/54	Manchester		1982	1985	Bradford City	Stockport County	106	9	7	3	9	2	1	0
Letheran	G	Glan	01/05/56	Llanelli		1976		Leeds United (loan)		27	0	4	0	0	0	0	0
Lewis	K	Kenny	12/10/29	Bangor		1958		Worcester City	Boston United	1	0	0	0	0	0	0	0
Lillis	MA	Mark	17/01/60	Manchester		1989	1990	Aston Villa	Stockport County	68	8	1	5	24	5	1	3
Lindsey	B	Barry	17/04/44	Scunthorpe		1961	1970	App.		217	13	12	0	13	0	0	0
Lindsey	K	Keith	25/11/46	Scunthorpe		1965		App.	Doncaster Rovers	15	1	1	0	0	0	0	0
Lister	SH	Steve	18/11/61	Doncaster		1985	1991	Doncaster Rovers	Boston United	182	16	17	14	30	1	5	1
Litchfield	P	Peter	27/07/56	Manchester		1989	1990	Bradford City		25	4	3	1	0	0	0	0
Lloyd	WS	Stan	01/10/24	West Auckland		1954		Worksop Town		1	1	0	0	0	0	0	0
Lockwood	E	Edward	04/08/25	Barnburgh		1951	1952	Denaby United		9	0	0	0	4	0	0	0
Longden	DP	Paul	28/09/62	Wakefield		1983	1992	Barnsley		368	29	31	35	0	0	0	0
Luke	GB	George	20/10/32	Lanchester		1956		Sheffield Utd.	King's Lynn	18	1	0	0	6	0	0	0
Lumby	JA	Jim	02/10/54	Grimsby		1976	1977	Brigg Town	Carlisle United	55	1	4	0	29	0	1	0
Lynch	BJ	Barry	08/06/51	Birmingham		1973	1974	Grimsby Town	Portland Timbers	64	7	5	0	0	0	0	0
McCormick	JM	Joe	15/07/16	Holywell		1950		Boston United		7	1	0	0	0	0	0	0
McCullagh	PA	Paul	06/02/74	Brigg		1992		Trainee	Brigg Town	5	2	2	2	1	0	0	0
McDonald	CB	Colin	15/05/50	Norwich		1970	1972	Norwich City	Brigg Town	86	6	0	0	11	0	0	0
McDowall	JC	James	25/10/40	Glasgow		1961		Boston United		1	0	0	0	0	0	0	0
McFarlane	AA	Andy	30/11/66	Wolverhampton		1995		Swansea City		46	2	2	3	16	2	1	2
McGill	A	Andrew	11/07/24	Glasgow		1952	1956	Bradford City		183	22	0	0	15	2	0	0
McGuigan	JJ	John	29/10/32	Motherwell		1961	1962	Newcastle United	Southampton	57	2	4	0	17	1	2	0
McLaren	R	Bobby	05/08/29	Chryston		1951		Cardiff City	Barry Town	6	0	0	0	0	0	0	0
McLean	DJ	David	24/11/57	Newcastle		1986	1987	Darlington	Whitley Bay	24	2	4	4	3	0	0	0
Mahy	B	Barry	21/01/42	Doncaster		1963	1966	Jersey	New York Generals	22	2	5	0	2	1	0	0
Malan	NF	Norman	23/11/23	South Africa		1950	1955	Darlington	Bradford Park Ave.	136	18	0	0	0	0	0	0
Mann	JA	Jimmy	15/12/52	Goole		1982		Barnsley	Doncaster Rovers	2	0	0	0	0	0	0	0
Markham	P	Peter	18/03/54	Scunthorpe		1971	1976	App.		122	8	4	0	1	0	0	0
Marples	C	Chris	03/08/64	Chesterfield		1991		York City (loan)		1	0	0	0	0	0	0	0
Marriott	JL	Jack	01/04/28	Scunthorpe		1957	1963	Huddersfield T		212	11	3	0	26	0	0	0
Marshall	B	Brian	20/09/54	Bolton-on-Dearne		1974		Huddersfield T (loan)		3	0	0	0	0	0	0	0
Marshall	F	Frank	26/01/29	Sheffield		1957	1958	Rotherham Utd.	Doncaster Rovers	80	6	0	0	0	0	0	0
Marshall	G	Gary	20/04/64	Bristol		1989	1990	Carlisle Utd.	Exeter City	41	4	4	2	3	0	0	0
Marshall	PW	Peter	05/12/34	Worksop		1954	1955	Worksop Town		39	4	0	0	0	0	0	0
Martin	DS	Dean	09/09/67	Halifax		1991	1994	Halifax Town	Rochdale	106	7	8	13	7	0	1	1
Mason	CE	Cliff	27/11/29	York		1963		Leeds United	Chesterfield	12	0	0	0	1	0	0	0
Matthews	M	Mike	25/09/60	Hull		1983	1985	Wolves	N Ferriby Utd.	58	5	4	8	5	0	0	3
Matthews	N	Neil	19/09/66	Grimsby		1985		Grimsby Town (loan)		1	0	0	0	0	0	0	0
Maw	J	John	22/12/34	Scunthorpe		1957				1	0	0	0	0	0	0	0
Maxwell	J	Jason	01/09/72			1992			App. Frodingham	2	0	0	0	0	0	0	0
Middleton	H	Harry	18/03/37	Birmingham		1959	1960	Wolves	Portsmouth	29	2	2	0	11	1	0	0
Miller	I	Ian	13/05/55	Perth		1990		Port Vale	Stafford Rangers	12	4	1	1	0	0	0	0
Minton	AE	Albert	22/09/37	Walsall		1957	1958	Blackpool	Doncaster Rovers	5	0	0	0	2	0	0	0
Money	R	Richard	13/10/55	Lowestoft		1973	1977	Lowestoft Town	Fulham	279	14	21	10	4	0	0	1
						1985	1989	Portsmouth	(Youth coach)								
Mosby	H	Harold	25/06/26	Kippax		1950	1954	Rotherham Utd.	Worksop Town	149	18	0	0	21	2	0	0
Moss	PM	Paul	02/08/57	Birmingham		1981		Hull City	Worcester City	42	4	0	0	7	0	0	0
Mountford	RW	Bob	23/02/52	Stoke-on-Trent		1974		Port Vale (loan)		3	0	0	0	0	0	0	0
Mudd	PA	Paul	13/11/70	Hull		1993	1994	Scarborough	Lincoln City	68	8	4	5	4	0	0	0
Muldoon	T	Terry	10/08/51	Ashington	1971	1970		Local	App. Frodingham	1	0	0	0	0	0	0	0
Mulholland	JR	John	07/12/28	Dumbarton		1950		Grimsby Town		6	1	0	0	1	0	0	0
Mullen	A	Andy	28/07/28	Newcastle		1955	1956	South Shields	Goole Town	10	0	0	0	1	0	0	0
Murfin	AJ	Andrew				1995				1	0	0	0	0	0	0	0
Musselwhite	PS	Paul	22/12/68	Portsmouth		1988	1991	Portsmouth	Port Vale	132	7	11	13	0	0	0	0
Mynard	LD	Les	19/12/25	Bewdley		1952		Derby County	Worcester City	18	1	0	0	3	0	0	0
Naylor	G	Geoff	28/12/49	Goole		1967		App.	Alfreton Town	10	2	0	0	0	0	0	0
Neale	P	Peter	09/04/34	Chesterfield		1958	1966	Oldham Athletic	Chesterfield	226	10	9	0	7	0	1	0
Needham	A	Tony	04/01/41	Scunthorpe		1959	1964	Jnrs.	Corby Town	33	3	3	0	0	0	0	0
Neenan	JP	Joe	17/03/59	Manchester		1979	1984	York City	Burnley	191	20	12	5	0	0	0	0
Nicholson	M	Max	03/10/71	Leeds		1994	1995	Torquay United	Gainsborough Trin.	51	3	2	3	5	0	0	0
Nicol	PJ	Paul	31/10/67	Scunthorpe		1986	1989	Trainee	Kettering Town	75	3	6	10	2	0	1	0
Norris	M	Mike	27/02/57	Retford		1973	1975	App.	Scarborough	25	0	2	0	0	0	0	0
North	MV	Marc	29/05/66	Ware		1986		Luton Town (loan)		5	0	0	1	2	0	0	0
O'Berg	PJ	Paul	08/05/58	Hull		1979	1984	Bridlington Town	Wimbledon	132	16	6	4	24	2	0	0
O'Connor	D	Doug	29/04/54	Barnsley		1975	1976	Mansfield Town		31	2	3	0	9	0	1	0
O'Donnell	JD	Jon	21/03/54	Leeds		1977	1979	Hartlepool Utd.	Cambridge City	60	2	4	0	1	0	0	0
O'Halloran	KJ		10/11/75	Dublin		1995		Middlesbrough (loan)		7	0	0	0	0	0	0	0
O'Meara	AM	Alan	15/12/58	Grantham		1975	1976	App.		41	2	0	0	0	0	0	0
O'Riley	P	Paul	17/10/50	Prescot		1970		Hull City (loan)		11	0	0	0	4	0	0	0
Oates	RA	Bob	26/07/56	Leeds		1974	1982	Ashley Road	Rochdale	315	14	19	0	15	0	1	0
Ormond	W	Bill	26/08/26	Greenock		1958		Barrow	Weymouth	3	0	0	0	0	0	0	0
Ottewell	S	Syd	23/10/19	Horsley		1951	1952	Mansfield Town	Spalding Utd.	30	2	0	0	12	0	0	0

Player			D.O.B	Place of Birth	Died	First Lge Season	Last Lge Season	Previous Club	Next Club	Appearances				Goals			
										League	FAC	FLC	Other	League	FAC	FLC	Oth.
Parkinson	ND	Noel	16/11/59	Hull		1982	1983	Mansfield Town	Colchester Utd.	41	3	2	4	7	0	0	0
Parrott	JF	John	05/06/34	Scunthorpe		1955		Local		1	1	0	0	0	0	0	0
Partridge	M	Malcolm	28/08/50	Calow		1979	1981	Grimsby Town	Skegness Town	97	3	6	0	21	1	0	0
Pashley	R	Robert	09/09/37	Sheffield		1959		Gainsborough Trin.	Barrow	3	1	0	0	1	0	0	0
Passmoor	T	Tom	12/02/37	Chester-le-Street		1959	1963	South Shields	Carlisle Utd.	27	1	2	0	0	0	0	0
Paterson	JR	Jamie	26/04/73	Dumfries		1995		Falkirk		26	3	0	2	2	1	0	0
Payne	IEH	Irving 'Joe'	29/06/21	Briton Ferry		1950		Newport County	Northampton Town	40	1	0	0	2	0	0	0
Peacock	JC	John	27/03/56	Leeds		1974	1979	Jnrs.	Boston United	190	4	16	0	1	0	0	0
Pearce	DG	David	19/12/34	Scunthorpe		1958		Local		2	0	0	0	0	0	0	0
Pilling	S	Stuart	26/03/51	Sheffield		1973	1981	Hull City		262	16	14	0	26	3	2	0
Platnauer	NR	Nicky	10/06/61	Leicester		1992		Leicester City	Mansfield Town	14	0	0	0	2	0	0	0
Platts	P	Peter	14/01/28	Dinnington		1951		Local		2	0	0	0	2	0	0	0
Pointon	NG	Neil	28/11/64	Church Warsop		1981	1985	App.	Everton	159	13	9	7	2	0	1	0
Powell	G	Gary	02/04/69	Hoylake		1990		Everton (loan)		4	0	0	2	1	0	0	0
Powell	R	Ray	05/08/24	Swansea		1951		Swansea Town	Kettering Town	31	4	0	0	14	4	0	0
Pratley	RG	Dick	12/01/63	Banbury		1983		Derby County (loan)		10	0	0	2	0	0	0	0
Pugh	JG	Graham	12/02/48	Hoole		1979	1980	Barnsley	Matlock Town	55	2	2	0	0	0	0	0
Punton	WH	Bill	04/05/34	Glenkindie		1967	1968	Sheffield Utd.	Gt. Yarmouth	45	0	2	0	2	0	0	0
Ratcliffe	JB	Barrie	21/09/41	Blackburn		1964		Blackburn Rovers	Rochdale	26	0	11	0	7	0	0	0
Rees	MJF	Mal	21/04/24	Neath		1950		Barry Town	Aberystwyth T	18	1	0	0	1	0	0	0
Reeves	D	David	19/11/67	Birkenhead		1986	1987	Sheffield Wed. (loan)		10	0	0	0	6	0	0	0
Reeves	TB	Brian	18/02/39	Skelmersdale		1962	1964	Blackburn Rovers	Southport	38	1	1	0	0	0	0	0
Reid	AJ	Tony	09/05/63	Nottingham		1982		Derby County (loan)		6	0	0	0	0	0	0	0
Richardson	IP	Ian	09/05/64	Ely		1986	1988	Chester City	Staines Town	18	3	3	4	4	0	0	0
Richardson	R	Russell	21/10/64	Sheffield		1983		Trainee	Worksop Town	2	1	0	1	0	0	0	0
Roberts	DE	Dudley	16/10/45	Derby		1973	1975	Mansfield Town	Retired	59	2	3	0	17	0	0	0
Roberts	H	Harry	12/01/20	Liverpool		1953	1954	Shrewsbury Town	Gresley Rovers	17	0	0	0	1	0	0	0
Robinson	A	Alan	02/12/55	Grantham		1975		Sheffield Wed.		1	0	0	0	0	0	0	0
Rudd	JJ	Jimmy	25/10/19	Dublin	1985	1951		Rotherham Utd.	Workington	32	4	0	0	4	1	0	0
Rumble	P	Paul	14/03/69	Hemel Hempstead		1988		Watford (loan)		8	0	0	0	1	0	0	0
Rusling	G	Graham	04/04/48	Keadby		1966	1970	Local	Goole Town	81	11	1	0	17	4	0	0
Russell	WM	Billy	14/09/59	Glasgow		1985	1987	Doncaster Rovers	Rotherham Utd.	117	10	10	8	7	3	1	0
Ryan	TJ	Tim	10/12/74	Stockport		1992	1993	Trainee		2	0	0	0	0	0	0	0
Samways	M	Mark	11/11/68	Doncaster		1991	1995	Doncaster R (loan)		155	13	8	15	0	0	0	0
Sansam	C	Christian	26/12/75	Hull		1993	1995	Trainee	Halifax Town	21	3	0	5	1	0	0	0
Sargent	GS	Gary	11/09/52	Turvey		1972		Norwich City	Bedford Town	15	0	0	0	1	0	0	0
Scott	RSA	Dick	26/10/41	Thetford		1964	1965	Cardiff City	Lincoln City	47	10	1	0	8	0	0	0
Sharpe	LT	Len	29/11/32	Scunthorpe		1951	1961	Jnrs	Hull City	185	13	1	0	6	0	0	0
Shearer	DJ	David	16/10/58	Caol		1987	1988	Bournemouth	Darlington	16	0	0	3	8	0	0	0
Shutt	SJ	Steve	29/11/64	Barnsley		1984		Goole Town	Goole Town	2	0	0	0	1	0	0	0
Sidebottom	G	Geoff	29/12/36	Mapplewell		1964	1966	Aston Villa	New York Generals	59	1	2	0	0	0	0	0
Simpkin	CJ	Chris	24/04/44	Hull		1973	1974	Blackpool	Huddersfield T	61	9	4	0	2	0	0	0
Skipper	PD	Peter	11/04/58	Hull		1979		Hull City (loan)		1	0	0	0	0	0	0	0
Sloan	D	David	28/10/41	Lisburn		1963	1967	Bangor	Oxford United	136	11	14	0	42	0	0	0
Smalley	PT	Paul	17/11/66	Nottingham		1988	1990	Notts County	Leeds United	86	5	5	4	1	0	0	0
Smillie	AT	Andy	15/03/41	Minster, Sheppey		1963	1964	Crystal Palace	Southend Utd.	13	0	1	0	2	0	1	0
Smith	B	Brian	27/10/66	Sheffield		1986		Sheffield Utd. (loan)		6	0	0	0	1	0	0	0
Smith	MC	Mark	19/12/61	Sheffield		1985		Gainsborough Trin.	Kettering Town	63	7	4	6	9	0	0	0
						1993	1994	Grimsby Town									
Smith	RW	Bobby	14/03/44	Prestbury		1964	1966	Manchester Utd.	Grimsby Town	82	3	2	0	12	1	0	0
Snow	SG	Simon	03/04/66	Sheffield		1982	1983	App.	Sutton Town	2	0	0	0	0	0	0	0
Sowden	M	Maurice	21/10/54	Doncaster		1972		App.		3	1	0	0	0	0	0	0
Sproates	A	Alan	30/06/44	Hetton-le-Hole		1974		Darlington	(Australia)	24	0	1	0	0	0	0	0
Steele	SP	Simon	29/02/64	Liverpool		1983		Brighton	Worthing	5	0	0	0	0	0	0	0
Stevenson	AJ	Andy	29/09/67	Scunthorpe		1985	1992	Jnrs.	Brigg Town	103	6	11	17	4	0	1	1
Stewart	CD	Dave	20/05/58	Belfast		1979	1981	Chelsea	Goole Town	97	7	4	0	19	1	0	0
Stirland	CJ	Cec	15/07/21	Ardwick		1951		New Brighton	Retired	17	0	0	0	0	0	0	0
Stobart	SA	Sean	31/07/66	Wolverhampton		1984		Jnrs.	Dudley Town	2	0	0	0	1	0	0	0
Stokes	AW	Albert	26/01/33	Darnall		1957		Grimsby Town	Southport	5	0	0	0	2	0	0	0
Taylor	EK	Edward	17/05/56	Irvine		1974		Ipswich Town		7	0	1	0	0	0	0	0
Taylor	K	Kevin	22/01/61	Wakefield		1987	1990	Crystal Palace	Frickley Athletic	157	11	8	16	24	3	1	2
Taylor	MJ	Martin	09/12/66	Tamworth		1987		Derby County (loan)		8	0	1	0	0	0	0	0
Taylor	R	Roy	02/04/33	Hoyland		1952		Denaby United		2	0	0	0	0	0	0	0
Taylor	RE	Dick	09/04/18	Wolverhampton	1995	1950	1953	Grimsby Town	Trainer/coach	131	16	0	0	2	0	0	0
Taylor	SR	Stewart	06/04/46	Owston Ferry		1965	1968	Local	Ashby Town	67	4	0	0	0	0	0	0
Telfer	GA	George	06/07/55	Liverpool		1981	1982	San Diego Sockers	Altrincham	36	4	2	2	11	1	0	0
Thomas	BEB	Barrie	19/05/37	Measham		1959	1961	Mansfield Town	Newcastle United	143	6	4	0	93	3	0	0
						1964	1966	Newcastle United									
Thompson	D	Dennis	19/07/34	Bolsover		1955		Chesterfield		3	0	0	0	0	0	0	0
Thompson	GH	George	15/09/26	Maltby		1950	1952	Chesterfield	Preston NE	92	6	0	0	0	0	0	0
Thompson	WA	Allan	20/01/52	Liverpool		1981		Bradford City		11	0	0	0	0	0	0	0
Thompstone	IP	Ian	17/01/71	Manchester		1992	1994	Halifax Town	Rochdale	60	6	2	2	8	1	0	0
Thornber	SJ	Steve	11/10/65	Dewsbury		1993	1995	Blackpool	Halifax Town	77	5	4	5	7	0	0	0
Thorpe	AW	Arthur	31/07/39	Lucknow, India		1960	1962	Ossett Town	Bradford City	27	0	1	0	5	0	0	0
Toman	JA	Andy	07/03/62	Northallerton		1993		Darlington	Scarborough	15	2	1	1	4	1	0	0
Travis	DA	David	04/07/64	Doncaster		1985	1986	Doncaster Rovers	Chesterfield	13	1	0	1	1	0	0	0
Trebble	ND	Neil	16/02/69	Hitchin		1993		Stevenage Boro.	Preston NE	14	1	1	2	2	0	0	0
Tucker	G	Gordon	05/01/68	Manchester		1989	1990	Huddersfield T	Goole Town	15	1	2	1	1	0	0	0
Turnbull	LM	Lee	27/09/67	Stockton		1994	1995	Wycombe Wan. (loan)		33	2	2	1	6	0	0	0

Player			D.O.B	Place of Birth	Died	First Lge Season	Last Lge Season	Previous Club	Next Club	Appearances				Goals			
										League	FAC	FLC	Other	League	FAC	FLC	Oth.
Turner	J	Joseph	21/03/31	Barnsley		1960	1961	Darlington	Barnsley	22	0	1	0	0	0	0	0
Turner	PS	Phil	20/02/27	Chester		1954		Bradford	Accrington Stanley	5	0	0	0	2	0	0	0
Underwood	GR	George	06/09/25	Sheffield		1953		Sheffield Wed.	Rochdale	8	0	0	0	0	0	0	0
Varadi	I	Imre	08/07/59	Paddington		1995		Mansfield Town	Boston United	2	0	0	0	0	0	0	0
Verity	DA	David	21/09/49	Halifax		1966	1967	App.	Halifax Town	5	0	0	0	0	0	0	0
Wadsworth	M	Mick	03/11/50	Barnsley		1976		Gainsborough Trin.	Frickley Athletic	28	0	3	0	3	0	1	0
Wainwright	L	Lewis	15/12/30	Kirton-in-Lindsey		1955		Brigg Town		2	0	0	0	0	0	0	0
Waldock	R	Ronnie	06/12/32	Heanor		1956	1959	Sheffield Utd.	Plymouth Argyle	97	6	0	0	45	1	0	0
Walker	D	Dean	18/05/62	Newcastle		1981		Burnley	North Shields	1	0	0	0	0	0	0	0
Wallace	G	George	18/04/20	Aberdeen		1951	1952			33	3	0	0	8	2	0	0
Walsh	MS	Michael	05/08/77	Rotherham		1994	1995	Trainee		28	2	2	1	0	0	0	0
Walton	IJ	Ian	17/04/58	Goole		1976		Grimsby Town		1	0	0	0	0	0	0	0
Ward	JR	Richie	16/09/40	Scunthorpe		1958		Jnrs	Northampton Town	1	0	0	0	0	0	0	0
Ward	PT	Paul	15/09/63	Sedgefield		1989	1990	Leyton Orient	Lincoln City	55	5	2	4	6	1	0	0
Warnock	N	Neil	01/12/48	Sheffield		1972	1974	Hartlepool Utd.	Aldershot	72	10	5	0	7	1	0	0
Watson	JI	John	14/04/74	South Shields		1993		Newcastle United	Gateshead	5	1	2	1	0	0	0	0
Webster	AJ	Alan	03/07/48	Melton Mowbray		1966	1967	Local	Kettering Town	6	0	0	0	0	0	0	0
Webster	IA	Ian	30/12/65	Askern		1982	1985	Trainee	Goole Town	18	5	1	2	0	0	0	0
Welbourne	D	Don	12/03/49	Scunthorpe		1966	1975	App.	App. Frodingham	254	26	12	0	5	1	1	0
White	JG	Jason	19/10/71	Meriden		1991	1993	Derby County	Scarborough	68	6	2	7	16	1	0	1
White	R	Dick	18/08/31	Scunthorpe		1950	1955	Scunthorpe SC	Liverpool	133	12	0	0	7	1	0	0
Whitehead	A	Alan	20/11/56	Bury		1983	1986	Brentford	York City	108	6	8	5	8	0	1	1
Whitehead	PM	Phil	17/12/69	Halifax		1991	1992	Barnsley (loan)		16	0	2	2	0	0	0	0
Whiteside	WR	Billy	24/09/35	Belfast		1956		Exeter City	Portadown	2	0	0	0	0	0	0	0
Whitfield	J	Jimmy	18/05/19	Hull	1984	1950		Grimsby Town	Southport	120	14	0	0	31	5	0	0
						1951	1954	Southport	Boston United								
Whitnall	B	Brian	25/05/33	Doncaster		1956	1957	Hull City	Exeter City	3	0	0	0	0	0	0	0
Wigg	RG	Ron	18/05/49	Great Dunmow		1977	1978	Barnsley		50	3	2	0	7	0	0	0
Wigginton	CA	Clive	18/10/50	Sheffield		1975	1976	Grimsby Town	Lincoln City	88	2	6	0	7	0	1	0
Williams	I	Ivor	29/05/35	Scunthorpe		1959		Local		8	0	0	0	0	0	0	0
Williams	MJ	Mike	23/10/44	Hull		1970	1973	Workington	Scarborough	28	5	0	0	0	0	0	0
Wilmott	R	Richard	29/08/69			1992			Halifax Town	3	0	0	0	0	0	0	0
Wilson	A	Andy	27/09/40	Rotherham		1961	1964	Sheffield Utd.	Doncaster Rovers	112	15	12	0	14	1	1	0
Wilson	AP	Andy	13/10/47	Maltby		1968		Rotehrham Utd.	Corby Town	23	1	0	0	4	0	0	0
Wilson	DJ	Danny	01/01/60	Wigan		1983		Nottm. Forest (loan)		6	0	0	0	3	0	0	0
Wilson	PA	Paul	02/08/68	Bradford		1995		York City		40	3	2	2	1	0	0	0
Winter	J	Julian	06/09/65	Huddersfield		1988		Huddersfield T (loan)		4	0	0	0	0	0	0	0
Wood	BW	Barrie	05/12/36	Doncaster		1958		Doncaster Rovers	South Shields	3	0	0	0	1	0	0	0
Wood	HS	Hugh	16/11/60	Bellshill		1980		Grantham	Shepshed Chart.	1	0	0	0	0	0	0	0
Woods	E	Eddie	29/07/51	Pentre		1973		Bristol City (loan)		4	0	0	0	2	0	0	0
Woodward	J	John	16/01/47	Stoke-on-Trent		1975		Port Vale	Ostend	19	0	0	0	5	0	0	0
Woolmer	AJ	Tony	25/03/46	Swardeston		1970	1971	Bradford Park Ave.	King's Lynn	40	5	1	0	3	1	0	0
Young	SR	Stuart	16/12/72	Hull		1994	1995	Scarborough		28	1	2	3	3	0	0	0

Played in FA Cup and Miscellaneous Games Only

Player			D.O.B	Place of Birth	Died	First Lge Season	Last Lge Season	Previous Club	Next Club	Appearances				Goals			
Jobling	KA	Kevin	01/01/68	Sunderland		1993		Grimsby Town (loan)		0	0	0	1	0	0	0	0
Stanley	P	Paul				1984				0	2	0	0	0	0	0	0
Talbot	J	Jason	26/10/68	Gainsborough		1986				0	1	0	1	0	0	0	0
Tutty	D	David				1982				0	0	0	1	0	0	0	0